God and Human Dignity

God and Human Dignity

Edited by

R. Kendall Soulen and Linda Woodhead

WILLIAM B. EERDMANS PUBLISHING COMPANY
GRAND RAPIDS, MICHIGAN / CAMBRIDGE, U.K.

Wm. B. Eerdmans Publishing Co.
255 Jefferson Ave. S.E., Grand Rapids, Michigan 49503 /
P.O. Box 163, Cambridge CB3 9PU U.K.

Printed in the United States of America

11 10 09 08 07 06   7 6 5 4 3 2 1

Library of Congress Cataloging-in-Publication Data

God and human dignity / edited by R. Kendall Soulen and Linda Woodhead.
     p.   cm.
Includes bibliographical references and index.
ISBN-10: 0-8028-3395-0 / ISBN-13: 978-0-8028-3395-2 (pbk.: alk. paper)
     1. Dignity — Religious aspects — Christianity.   I. Soulen, R. Kendall, 1959-
II. Woodhead, Linda.

BT702.G63   2006
233 — dc22

                                                            2006011719

www.eerdmans.com

Dedicated with gratitude to
  the Center of Theological Inquiry,
    Princeton, New Jersey

Contents

CONTENTS

Creation

Redemption

Sanctification

Contents

Contributors

C. Clifton Black is Otto A. Piper Professor of Biblical Theology and Chairman of the Department of Biblical Studies at Princeton Theological Seminary. Ordained in the United Methodist Church, he is the author of numerous articles and books, including *Mark: Images of an Apostolic Interpreter, The Rhetoric of the Gospel: Theological Artistry in the Gospels and Acts, Anatomy of the New Testament: A Guide to Its Structure and Meaning* (6th ed., with Robert A. Spivey and D. Moody Smith), and *Mark,* forthcoming in the *Abingdon New Testament Commentaries.*

H. Russel Botman is professor of theology at the University of Stellenbosch, South Africa. He currently serves the university as Deputy Vice-Chancellor with a responsibility for the academic program. He is also President of the South African Council of Churches and until recently was Consultant to the World Alliance of Reformed Churches. Botman publishes regularly in the areas of missiology, social ethics, ecumenism, and church unity.

Don S. Browning is Alexander Campbell Professor of Religious Ethics and the Social Sciences, Divinity School, University of Chicago, Emeritus. He is the author of numerous books and articles, most recently *Christian Ethics and the Moral Psychologies* (forthcoming), *Religious Thought and the Modern Psychologies, From Culture Wars to Common Ground,* and *Marriage and Modernization.*

J. Kameron Carter is Assistant Professor of Theology and Black Church Studies at Duke University Divinity School. His book *Race: A Theological Account* is forthcoming from Oxford University Press. He is at work on another book-length research project, *Religion and the Black Intellectual Imagination.*

Elaine L. Graham is Samuel Ferguson Professor of Social and Pastoral Theology at the University of Manchester. Her publications include *Life-Cycles: Women and Pastoral Care* (co-edited with Margaret Halsey), *Making the Difference: Gender, Personhood and Theology, Representations of the Post/human,* and *Theological Reflections* (co-edited with Heather Walton and Frances Ward).

Robert W. Jenson, after a long career as a teacher of theology in colleges, seminaries, and universities, has for the last seven years been Senior Scholar for Research in the Center of Theological Inquiry. His most recent books are a two-volume systematic theology and a short book closely related to this one, *On Thinking the Human.* A commentary on the Song of Songs is shortly to appear.

James Luther Mays is the Cyrus McCormick Professor Emeritus of Hebrew and Old Testament at Union Theological Seminary in Virginia. He was a member of that faculty for thirty-four years and before that was minister in Presbyterian churches in Virginia and North Carolina. His previous works include *Psalms,* in *Interpretation: A Bible Commentary for Teaching and Preaching* and *The Lord Reigns: A Theological Handbook to the Psalms.*

M. Douglas Meeks is the Cal Turner Chancellor Professor of Theology and Wesleyan Studies at Vanderbilt University Divinity School and former Dean of Wesley Theological Seminary. He has authored books including *Origins of the Theology of Hope* and *God the Economist: The Doctrine of God and Political Economy* and is the editor of *Trinity, Community and Power: Mapping Trajectories in Wesleyan Theology.*

Esther Marie Menn is an Associate Professor of Old Testament at the Lutheran School of Theology at Chicago and teaches courses at the University of Chicago Divinity School. Her scholarly interests include the history of Jewish biblical interpretation, women in the Bible, and biblical narrative and poetry, especially the Psalms. She is author of *Judah and Tamar (Genesis 38) in Ancient Jewish Exegesis: Studies in Literary Form and Hermeneutics* as well as of numerous scholarly articles.

Peter Ochs is Edgar Bronfman Professor of Modern Judaic Studies at the University of Virginia. He is co-founder of the Society for Scriptural Reasoning and the Society for Textual Reasoning. Among his books are *Peirce, Pragmatism, and the Logic of Scripture; Reasoning after Revelation: Dialogues in Postmodern Jewish Philosophy* (co-authored with Steven Kepnes and Robert Gibbs); *Reviewing the Covenant;* and *Textual Reasonings: Jewish Philosophy and Text Study at the End of the Twentieth Century* (co-edited with Nancy Levene).

John Polkinghorne worked for twenty-five years in theoretical elementary particle physics, holding a chair at Cambridge University from 1968 to 1979. After ordination as a priest and five years in parish ministry, he returned to Cambridge, eventually retiring in 1996 after seven years as the President of Queens' College. He is a Fellow of the Royal Society and was knighted in 1997. The author of many books on science and religion, including *Belief in God in an Age of Science* and *Science and the Trinity,* Polkinghorne was awarded the Templeton Prize in 2002.

Hans S. Reinders is full professor of ethics at the Vrije Universiteit in Amsterdam where he also holds the Willem van den Bergh Chair for ethics and intellectual disability. Among his recent publications is *The Future of the Disabled in Liberal Society.*

Gerhard Sauter is Professor of Systematic and Ecumenical Theology (Emeritus), University of Bonn, Germany, and external member of the Faculty of Theology of the University of Oxford. He is the author of numerous books and essays, among the most recent of which are *Gateways to Dogmatics: Reasoning Theologically for the Life of the Church* and *Protestant Theology at the Crossroads: How to Face the Crucial Tasks for Theology in the Twenty-First Century.*

Christoph Schwöbel is Professor of Systematic Theology at the University of Tübingen. His publications include *Gott in Beziehung: Studien zur Dogmatik; Persons, Divine and Human: King's College Essays in Theological Anthropology* (co-edited with Colin E. Gunton); and *Trinitarian Theology Today: Essays on Divine Being and Act* (edited).

R. Kendall Soulen is Professor of Systematic Theology at Wesley Theological Seminary in Washington, D.C., and an ordained minister of the United Methodist Church. His publications include *The God of Israel and Christian Theology, Handbook of Biblical Criticism* (co-authored with Richard N. Soulen), and *Abraham's Promise: Judaism and Jewish-Christian Relations.*

Fraser Watts is Reader in Theology and Science in the University of Cambridge, a Fellow of Queens' College, and Director of the Psychology and Religion Research Programme in the Centre for Advanced Religious and Theological Studies. He is a psychologist by background and a former President of the British Psychological Society. With Sara Savage, he has recently developed the Beta course, a video-based course linking Christian faith, personal growth, and pastoral care. His recent books are *Theology and Psychology, Psychology for Christian Ministry* (with Rebecca Nye and Sara Savage), and *Forgiveness in Context* (edited with Liz Gulliford).

Michael Welker is Professor for Systematic Theology at the University of Heidelberg. He is also the director of the Internationales Wissenschaftsforum der Universität Heidelberg. His many publications include *Creation and Reality, God the Spirit,* and *What Happens in Holy Communion?*

Linda Woodhead is Head of the Department of Religious Studies and Professor of Sociology of Religion at Lancaster University. Her recent publications include *The Spiritual Revolution: Why Religion Is Giving Way to Spirituality* (with Paul Heelas), *Christianity: A Very Short Introduction,* and *Congregational Studies in the UK* (co-edited with Mathew Guest and Karin Tusting).

INTRODUCTION:
Contextualizing Human Dignity

R. KENDALL SOULEN AND LINDA WOODHEAD

The aim of these essays is to marshal the resources of theology and tradition — chiefly Protestant Christian — for the purpose of revitalizing contemporary debate about the dignity of the human being.

The need for such an enterprise is twofold. First, we believe that Christian theology has a vital role to play in diagnosing and addressing the manifold ways in which human dignity is threatened in contemporary culture and society. In assessing such threats the chapters in this book deal with topics as varied as globalization, evolutionary theory, biotechnology, representations of race and gender, death, severe handicap, and political organization. While there are already many books and articles offering theological perspectives on such topics, our aim is to bring together in a single place essays which address a wide range of contemporary challenges to human dignity, and thus to offer a book which samples their range and interconnection. Part of our intention in doing so is to suggest that one of theology's most important contributions may be its ability to situate these various threats within a common frame of reference.

The book also seeks to address a second challenge, namely, the crisis that currently surrounds the very concept of human dignity, and the pressing questions concerning its ability to serve as a meaningful point of orientation for human thought and action. At first glance talk of such a crisis may appear surprising. Since the end of the Second World War the language of human dignity and rights has become increasingly prominent within public discourse across the globe. It is cited in the founding documents of the United Nations and in the constitutions of many countries of diverse political composition, such as

Ireland, Greece, Guatemala, Turkey, and South Korea (to name but a few). Nor is this a merely secular development; the Roman Catholic Church has been notable for the way in which it has accorded the concept of human dignity a central place in its social teachings for several decades, a trend solemnized by Pope Paul VI's encyclical *Dignitatis Humanae* (1965). Moreover, the concept of human dignity shapes a range of contemporary debates on issues from war and poverty to abortion, human cloning, and euthanasia.

Yet the pervasiveness of the discourse of dignity in modern Western life masks the extent to which the meaning and substance of the term has become vague and contested. As John Witte Jr. has observed, "Today, the concept of human dignity has become ubiquitous to the point of cliché — a moral trump frayed by heavy use, a general principle harried by constant invocation."[1] The term has suffered a kind of inflation through undisciplined use to the point where its value is endangered. Even the relative strength of Roman Catholic reflection on human dignity only serves to highlight the more problematic status of the concept elsewhere, particularly among many streams of contemporary Protestantism, from which world most of the contributors to this volume come. Today Protestant Christians seem often to rely upon unexamined secularized notions of human dignity, or to reject dignity altogether as an unbiblical and therefore unhelpful concept. They are not alone in their suspicion; there has been a rising tide of criticism from other quarters as well: from feminists suspicious of a masculinist bias, from evolutionary theorists who elide the distinction between human life and other forms of life, from postcolonial theorists who regard it as the ideological accompaniment of Western imperialism, and so on (see below).

The essays collected here embody a cumulative argument that the most faithful response to the conceptual crisis of human dignity is neither further reliance on a thinned-out notion nor simple avoidance, but rather a theological *recontextualization* of the concept. The notion of human dignity is a primitive but neither self-explanatory nor self-sustaining term. Its meaningfulness is dependent on its being embedded within a broader and more comprehensive cultural, conceptual, and social framework. The contemporary crisis of human dignity results, we believe, from the fact that intersecting tendencies of modern culture and society have stripped the concept of a sustaining context, without supplying viable alternatives. This claim can be illustrated by examining in greater detail how the early Christian tradition *contextualized* the

---

1. John Witte Jr., "Between Sanctity and Depravity: Human Dignity in Protestant Perspective," in *In Defense of Human Dignity*, ed. Robert P. Kraynak and Glenn Tinder (Notre Dame, Ind.: University of Notre Dame Press, 2003), pp. 119-38, at p. 121.

concept of human dignity within a broader theological and ecclesiastical framework, and how modernity's appropriation of the term has entailed a significant *decontextualization.*

The Contextualization of Human Dignity in Early Christian Thought

"The glory of God is a human being fully alive, and the life of humanity is the vision of God."

IRENAEUS

The Christian tradition has used the term "dignity" with reference to human beings in many ways. While a complete survey of these uses is impossible in this space, we can gain a sense of some characteristic features of Christian reflection on human dignity by sampling the writings of the Church Fathers.

The Fathers did not coin the concept of human dignity, nor did they take it over directly from the language of the Scriptures, which nowhere explicitly predicate dignity of human beings (see the chapters in this volume by Mays and Black). Rather, early Christian writers borrowed the term from Greco-Roman usage (Lat.: *dignitas;* Gk.: *to axioma, he time*), even as they put it to new uses in the context of Christian belief and practice. Around the turn of the Common Era, Cicero used the term *dignitas* in two different senses, either as designating an individual's distinctive rank in society (*De Inventione* 2.166), or (following Stoic precedent) as designating humankind's distinctive place within the natural order (*De Officiis* 1.106). While Christians also used the term in both ways, they tended to give greater emphasis to the second sense in light of their faith in God's creative, redemptive, and consummating purposes for humankind. Thus, while the Fathers do speak of the special dignity of a particular person's vocation or ecclesial office (for example, martyr, virgin, or bishop), they tend to understand these in terms of a broader vision of human dignity as this appears in light of three great divine works: (1) God's work of creation and the fashioning of humankind as a whole, (2) the sphere of the church and God's work of new creation in Christ, and (3) God's consummation as the eschatological goal of creation.

The Christian apologist Lactantius (240-320) memorably addressed the dignity that comes to humans by God's work of creation when he declared that God had created humankind as a "sacred animal" *(sanctum animal)*. For this reason, he declared, God had prohibited that humans be killed, not only in those instances also recognized by public law, such as wanton murder, but in any case whatsoever, including warfare and the exposure of infants (*Divine Institutes* 6.20).[2] Giving voice to a conviction common throughout subsequent tradition, Theophilus of Antioch (late second century) holds that God "first reveals the dignity of man" in the act of creation, when God declared, "Let us make man after our image and likeness" (Gen. 1:26), and appointed him to have dominion over all earthly things (*To Autolycus* 2.18).[3] Augustine (354-430) holds that humankind is made after the image of God with respect to its rational or intellectual soul. This image is the human being's "true honor" and is not preserved whole except in relation to God, "by whom it is impressed" (*On the Trinity* 12.11).[4] Yet because the image is seated in man's very soul, certainly "it always is" even after the fall despite "the disfigurement of its dignity" (*On the Trinity* 14.4).[5] While human dignity is seated in the soul, it is also reflected in the human body, as in its upright posture;[6] indeed, Tertullian (c. 160-225) can even speak of "the dignity of the flesh" in view of its place not only in God's creation but in the final resurrection (*On the Resurrection* 5).[7]

A second context in which early Christians speak of human dignity is with respect to God's redemption in Christ and its appropriation through life in the Spirit and the practice of Christian virtue. In this connection some authors conceive of the dignity attained through redemption as something acquired gradually over time through the practice of virtue and discipleship. So Clement of Alexandria (c. 150–c. 215) holds that those who submit themselves to "the training of Christ" acquire a "moral loveliness," a "superior dignity" that is visible in "their gait in walking, their sitting at table, their food, their sleep, their going to bed, their regimen, and the rest of their mode of life" (*The Instructor* 1.12).[8] Dignity in this sense, according to Clement, is something that can be "augmented and increased" (*Stromata* 7.9).[9] In a similar

2. Alexander Roberts and James Donaldson, eds., *The Ante-Nicene Fathers* (Grand Rapids: Eerdmans, 1971), vol. 7, p. 187. Hereafter the *Ante-Nicene Fathers* are listed by the letters *ANF*.

3. Theophilus of Antioch, *Ad Autolycum*, text and trans. Robert M. Grant (Oxford: Clarendon, 1970), p. 57.

4. Augustine, *The Trinity*, trans. Stephen McKenna, C.SS.R., vol. 45 in The Fathers of the Church (Washington, D.C.: Catholic University of America, 1963), p. 358.

5. Augustine, *The Trinity*, p. 418.

6. Cf. Clement of Alexandria, *The Instructor*, bk. 3, chap. 7; Gregory of Nyssa, *On the Making of Man*, chap. 7; Basil the Great, *Hexameron* 9.2.

7. Tertullian, *Treatise on the Resurrection*, ed. and trans. Ernest Evans (London: SPCK, 1960), p. 15.

8. *ANF*, vol. 2, p. 235.

9. *ANF*, vol. 2, p. 538.

vein, Augustine holds that "Of such consequence in rational natures is the weight, so to speak, of will and of love, that though in the order of nature angels rank above men, yet, by the scale of justice, good men are of greater value than bad angels" (*City of God* 11.16).[10] In contrast, other writers in this connection seek to emphasize what they regard as the equal dignity bestowed upon all who are adopted by the Spirit into the life of Christ. So Chrysostom (c. 347-407) declares that God's calling confers "the greatest mark of dignity," whereby all who are united with Christ are made to be not merely "angels and archangels" but "sons of God" and "beloved" (*Homilies on Matthew* 12.4).[11] This great distinction comes to all equally, for "where the nobility of faith is, there is none barbarian, none Grecian, none stranger, none citizen, but all mount up to one height of dignity" (*Homilies on Romans* 2).[12] And again, he declares, "See the dignity of the Church, the angelic condition! No distinction there, 'neither male nor female.'" Nevertheless, Chrysostom also acknowledges that churches fall short of acting in accord with the reality of the church's nature: "I would that the Churches were such now!" (*Homilies on Acts* 3).[13] Yet whether the emphasis falls upon degrees of dignity according to virtue or equality of dignity, both perspectives agree that, in the words of Clement, the root of all dignity is "the greatness of the dignity of God," "[f]or the living creature which is of high value, is made sacred by that which is worth all, or rather which has no equivalent, in virtue of the exceeding sanctity of the latter" (*Stromata* 7.5).[14] And although the accent in these passages falls on the church as the locus of restored dignity, a text ascribed to Gregory the Wonderworker (c. 213–c. 270) can perceive in the divine favor shown to Mary a universal restoration of human dignity, inasmuch as "the human race receives again by thee [Mary] its pristine dignity" (*Four Homilies* 2.2).[15] Origen (c. 185–c. 254) observes that while the Scriptures speak throughout of the Divine in human terms, the incarnation brings it about that "human nature is in its turn adorned with marks that belong to the divine prerogative" (*On First Principles* 2.6).[16]

---

10. Augustine, *A Select Library of the Nicene and Post-Nicene Fathers of the Christian Church,* series 1, ed. Philip Schaff (Grand Rapids: Eerdmans, 1956), vol. 2, p. 214. Hereafter the *Nicene and Post-Nicene Nicene Fathers* are listed simply by the letters *NPNF.*

11. *NPNF,* series 1, vol. 10, p. 78.

12. *NPNF,* series 1, vol. 11, p. 347.

13. *NPNF,* series 1, vol. 11, p. 18.

14. *ANF,* vol. 2, p. 530.

15. Gregory the Wonderworker, *Four Homilies* (2.2) in *ANF,* vol. 6, p. 61.

16. *On First Principles. Being Koetschau's Text of* De Principiis, ed. and introd. G. W. Butterworth (Gloucester, Mass.: Peter Smith, 1973), p. 111.

The third context in which early Christian writers spoke of human dignity is with reference to the ultimate goal of human life. One tradition approached this by drawing a distinction between humankind as "image" and "likeness" of God. According to Origen, "man received the dignity of God's image at his first creation," which conferred on him "the possibility of attaining to perfection." But the divine likeness itself is only "reached in the end," having been "reserved for the consummation."[17] Likewise, Augustine urges his listeners to treat the present life as travelers passing on and to fix their desire on eternal blessings, which are "eternal life itself, the imperishability and immortality of the flesh and soul, the company of angels, the heavenly city, unfailing titles of nobility" (lit.: unfailing *dignitas*) (*Sermon* 80).[18]

When we consider these and similar remarks about human dignity in the early Christian tradition, several noteworthy themes stand out. A first and key point is that Christians believe that *human dignity is conferred by God*. It is not a self-grounded possession enjoyed apart from relationship to the Creator, Redeemer, and Sanctifier. As Chrysostom writes memorably in a sermon on Philippians, "Humans possess dignity of rational nature, but this comes to them as a gift, not as something they have earned. Hence there is no natural preeminence amongst us, *for no good thing is naturally our own*" (*Homilies on Philippians* 7).[19] Here Chrysostom formulates a rule that Christians apply not only to the good of creation but to that of new creation and consummation as well. This, of course, is a key theme for Augustine, who writes of the love by which the church shall at last attain the joy of eternal life: "it is not 'poured out in our hearts' by the powers of nature or the will which are found in us, but 'by the Holy Spirit who has been given to us' (Rom. 5:5)," and "who comes to the aid of our weakness and along with us restores our good health" (*On Nature and Grace* 84).[20]

Because human dignity is conferred by God, its measure and norm is to be discovered not in social convention but in God and in the pattern of God's action toward humankind in creation and redemption in Christ. Dignity consists not so much in self-possession as in dispossession, not so much in entering into oneself but in reaching out in love and care to the other. This is

17. *On First Principles*, p. 245.

18. Augustine, *Sermons III (51-94) on the New Testament*, trans. and notes by Edmund Hill, O.P, in *The Works of St. Augustine*, vol. 3/3, ed. John E. Rotelle, O.S.A (Hyde Park: New York City Press, 1997), p. 355.

19. *NPNF*, series 1, vol. 13, p. 213.

20. Augustine, *Answer to the Pelagians*, intro. and trans. Roland J. Teske, S.J., in *The Works of St. Augustine*, vol. 1/23, ed. John E. Rotelle, O.S.A (Hyde Park: New York City Press, 1997), p. 270.

a second noteworthy theme marking early Christian reflection on human dignity. Early Christian thought was distinguished not by the conviction that "God is that than which there is nothing greater or more sublime" — a belief in which Augustine says all people concur (*On Christian Doctrine* 1.7)[21] — but by the belief that God "did with such great humility so lay low the high estate of his majesty as to make it subject to death, even the death of a cross" for the sake of human salvation (*Against Marcion* 2.27).[22] Or as Augustine observes simply of Christ, "He did not esteem it beneath His dignity to wash also the feet" of his disciples, including the one who would betray him (*Tractates on John* 55.6).[23] A striking implication is that early Christians were supplied with a conception that could cast a sharply critical light on conventional conceptions of human dignity — for when Christ shrank back from being made king, "He most fully gave an example to His followers by putting into its proper place all the pomp and splendour of both dignity and power. For who should have used these rather than God's Son?" (*On Idolatry* 18).[24] In response to critics of Christianity who found it ridiculous that "poor, unskilled people should dispute about heavenly things," Minucius Felix (late second or third century) replied, "let him know that all men are begotten alike, with a capacity and ability of reasoning and feeling, without preference of age, sex, or dignity," and that unlike the rich "who gaze more upon their gold than upon heaven," "our sort of people, though poor, have both discovered wisdom, and have delivered their teaching to others" (*Octavius* 16).[25] Of course, the critical light of Christ's "transvaluation of dignity" falls not only outside but also within the church. With typical pastoral astuteness, Chrysostom asks, "Why did the disciples repel the little children?" and answers succinctly "For dignity" (*Homilies on Matthew* 62).[26] Christ's own followers no less than others must be constantly reoriented away from suspect conceptions of human worth and toward that made manifest in Christ.

A third theme that marks out the Christian view of human dignity is that its indispensable context is the church, the gathering of the faithful. Thus human dignity has an ecclesial rather than an individual horizon. Human beings

21. Augustine, *Teaching Christianity,* intro. and trans. Edmund Hill, O.P., in *The Works of St. Augustine,*vol. 1/11, ed. John E. Rotelle, O.S.A (Hyde Park: New York City Press, 1996), p. 109.

22. Tertullian, *Adversus Marcionem*, 2 vols., ed. and trans. Ernest Evans (Oxford: Clarendon, 1972), p. 161.

23. *NPNF,* series 1, vol. 7, p. 301.

24. Tertullian, *De Idololatria*, critical text, trans. and commentary by J. H. Waszink and J. C. M. Van Winden (Leiden: Brill, 1987), p. 57.

25. *ANF,* vol. 4, p. 181.

26. *NPNF,* series 1, vol. 10, p. 385.

are not whole, but part of a larger whole — the body of Christ and the communion of saints. It is in the body of Christ, according to Irenaeus, that we have access to the Holy Spirit (*Against Heresies* 5.24.1). Such access comes by way of the word and the sacraments, and such access enables us to grow into the likeness of Christ. Thus the church is a *macro-anthropos,* as Maximus puts it (*Mystagogy* 2-4) — the sphere within which divine-human union begins in this present life, a union which will be consummated in the age to come. Such union is also a union with all the faithful, for, as John of Damascus puts it, "If union is in truth with Christ and with one another, we are assuredly voluntarily united also with all those who partake [of the Eucharist] with us" (*Orthodox Faith* 4.13).[27] Human dignity is achieved in relation, not in isolation.

"For the glory of God is a human being fully alive, and the life of humanity is the vision of God" (*Against Heresies* 4.20.7).[28] Rightly understood, divine and human dignity are not contraries in Christian thought, destined to wax and wane in inverse proportion to one another. Rather, the former is the foundation of the latter, the latter the revelation of the former. "For the greatest and most regal work of God is the salvation of humanity" (*The Instructor* 1.12), says Clement of Alexandria.[29] Or again, in the admonition of St. Augustine, "The majesty of God cannot be propitiated by that which defiles the dignity of man" (*City of God* 2.29).[30]

The Decontextualization of Human Dignity in Modern Times

> *"Alas, the faith in the dignity and uniqueness of man . . . is a thing of the past — he has become an animal . . . he who was, according to his old faith, a child of God. . . . Now he is slipping faster and faster away from the center into — what? Into nothiningness?"*
>
> NIETZSCHE

The story of the emergence of distinctively modern conceptions of human dignity is too complex to recount in any detail. It is a story in which Chris-

---

27. John of Damascus, *The Exact Exposition of the Orthodox Faith* (bk. 4 chap. 13), translated by S. D. F. Salmond, in *A Select Library of the Nicene and Post-Nicene Fathers of the Christian Church,* series 2, ed. Philip Schaff (Grand Rapids: Eerdmans, 1952-1956; reprinted by Eerdmans 1969-1976), vol. 9, p. 332.

28. The translation used here is our own.

29. *ANF,* vol. 2, p. 235.

30. Compare Tertullian, "Nothing is so worthy of God as the salvation of man." *Adv. Marc.* II.27, p. 161.

tianity plays an important role, not least by grounding an account of human dignity in the creative and redemptive work of the God who takes human form — as discussed above. It is a story in which the classical tradition also has an important role to play; and Christianity was, of course, often responsible for carrying this tradition, not only by way of the Scholastic tradition but also into the creative ferment of the Renaissance. The Christian contribution is also taken forward, supplemented, and challenged by other intellectual influences, including — after the sixteenth century — perspectives shaped by the rise of the natural and then the human and social sciences. And, of course, the story of the emergence of modern conceptions of human dignity cannot be told without reference to social, political, and economic factors as well as cultural ones — including growth of property-ownership, the decline of political absolutism, the spread of democratic arrangements, the extension of the franchise, de-colonization, and globalization. War also plays an important part, with reaction against wars of religion giving new impetus to conceptions of universal humanity and human dignity after the seventeenth century, and reaction to the atrocities of World War II giving impetus to national and international declarations of human dignity and rights after 1945.[31]

Rather than recount this story in detail, we will focus in on a single aspect, namely, the modern attempt to disentangle human dignity from the theological context described above in order to make the concept — and the human being — stand on its own. Rather than seeing the meaning, value, and substance of the human as derived from the wider contexts in which it is located, the modern period sees the rise of a conception of a "substantial self," in which meaning, value, and substance are located in the self itself and, more specifically, in some aspect of subjectivity.[32] This process of "decontextualization" is the work not only of expressly secular theorists such as the French *philosophes* but also of theological writers who chose to bracket dimensions of Christian thought as irrelevant to a conception of human dignity. We will

31. The story of the emergence of modern selfhood, individualism, and a concept of dignity — and the role of Christianity — is told in a number of overlapping works. Two of the most informative are Charles Taylor's *Sources of the Self* (Harvard, Mass.: Cambridge University Press, 1989) and Nicholas Abercrombie, Stephen Hill, and Bryan S. Turner, *Sovereign Individuals of Capitalism* (London: Allen and Unwin, 1986). Steven Luke's *Individualism* (Oxford: Blackwell, 1973) is also useful, not least in offering some important conceptual clarifications.

32. This story is charted in detail in Taylor's *Sources of the Self.* Taylor differentiates between two manifestations of the substantial self: the "instrumental" self with origins in the Enlightenment, and the "expressive" self with origins in the Romantic movement. The former gives more weight to the rational and volitional aspects of subjectivity; the latter to the emotional and imaginative. Here we pay greater attention to the former than the latter.

discuss the move toward decontextualization by taking some brief soundings at various points in its unfolding.

We begin with the work of Giovanni Pico della Mirandola (1463-1494), and in particular with his *De dignitate hominis* (On the Dignity of Man), a treatise that played an important role in the emergence of modern conceptions of human dignity. *De dignitate* begins with an elaborate myth which aims to show that the excellence of the human being derives not from its central place in the hierarchy of creation but rather from its ability to choose its own place in the order of nature. Unlike other creatures, human beings can shape their own essence:

> Thou, like a judge appointed for being honorable art the molder and maker of thyself; thou mayest sculpt thyself into whatever shape thou dost prefer. Thou canst grow downward into the lower natures which are brutes. Thou canst again grow upward from thy soul's reason into the higher natures which are divine.[33]

Clearly, Pico's mythic vision echoes themes we have already encountered in Augustine and, even more expressly, in Origen and Gregory of Nyssa. But the novelty of Pico's theology is visible in what he leaves out. His myth contains no christology, no soteriology, no doctrine of grace. Its simplified vision emphasizes instead humanity's natural powers *qua* human on the one hand and humanity's radical freedom in the exercise of those powers on the other. It is in these that the dignity of the human being consists for Pico. We might say that human dignity begins to be placed on a purely *internal* basis (properties integral to "human nature") rather than on an *external* basis (the God who creates and redeems humanity). At the same time it becomes more individualistic, as humanity is seen to consist in distinct agency rather than in membership in the body of Christ.

Pico's emphasis on freedom and self-determination anticipates the thought of the man who is in many ways the paradigmatic philosopher of a decontextualized account of human dignity, Immanuel Kant (1724-1804). Blaise Pascal, who died some sixty years before Kant was born, once wrote, "The human being is obviously made for thinking; therein lies all his dignity and merit." Kant would not have agreed. Rather, the central thrust of Kant's practical philosophy is that rationality is valuable as the means to freedom or autonomy. In the *Groundwork for the Metaphysics of Morals*, Kant argues that the incomparable dignity of the human being *(Würde)* derives from the fact

33. Pico della Mirandola, *On the Dignity of Man,* trans. Charles Glenn Wallis (Indianapolis: Bobbs-Merrill Company, [1965]), p. 5.

that he alone is "free from all laws of nature, obedient only to those laws which he himself prescribes."[34] Capacity for autonomous rational agency is the root of human dignity, which in turn requires that all persons be treated and treat themselves as ends in themselves and never merely as a means to another's ends. This principle, which supplies the cornerstone of ethical reasoning in the liberal tradition, entails further requirements not to undermine the exercise of rational agency through, for example, coercion or paternalistic interference. At the end of his second *Critique,* Kant famously echoes Psalm 8 to express awe at the human being's place in the universe. Yet between the two there is a noteworthy difference: the psalmist beholds the human together with other creatures, though appointed to royal preeminence over them, whereas for Kant the individual appears alone beneath the starry heavens as the sole locus of freedom and, therefore, dignity in the world.

The theological implications of Kant's revolution are more radical still. By grounding human dignity in the capacity for autonomous rational agency, Kant attempts to vindicate a conception of dignity that stands alone, prior to, and independent of every concept of God. Once Kant believes he has achieved this, he is also prepared to reintroduce the idea of God — not as denoting a reality knowable to humankind, but as a postulate of the human mind generated for the sake of making human moral experience coherent. So conceived, of course, the relationship of God and human dignity articulated by the earlier Christian tradition is exactly reversed. The idea of God is dependent on human dignity as its source and norm, not human dignity on God.

In important ways, Kant's treatment of human dignity foreshadows the unfolding of the concept in the modern period. Three aspects seem especially prescient. First, as we have already noted, there is Kant's virtual identification of human dignity with a single preeminent faculty: (rational) freedom.[35] Second, there is Kant's elevation of human dignity to a central — indeed, foundational — normative principle for ethical reflection. Last, there is Kant's profound conceptual linkage of the concept of human dignity with corresponding and specific rights inherent in and belonging to the human person. For Kant, the key right and obligation was that of being treated as an end and not as a means only. In democratic traditions, that has been fleshed out in political terms, from Jefferson's rights "to life, liberty, and the pursuit of happiness" to Franklin Roosevelt's Four Freedoms (freedom of expression, freedom

34. Immanuel Kant, *Groundwork for the Metaphysics of Morals,* trans. Arnulf Zweig, ed. Thomas E. Hill Jr. and Arnulf Zweig (Oxford: Oxford University Press, 2002), p. 226 (4:435).

35. It is often forgotten, however, that Kant believed that freedom would often have to be restricted in practice, particularly if it threatened to bring political chaos and disorder. See Dorinda Outram, *The Enlightenment* (Cambridge: Cambridge University Press, 1995), p. 2.

of religion, freedom from want, freedom from fear). Yet what is common is the understanding of human dignity as the inner basis or foundation or source of rights that flow naturally and inevitably from it and are its inseparable expression. Compared with early Christian thought, the concept of human dignity is here pressed into a foundational role that it did not previously have to play. For Christian thought, human dignity was *derivative* of the more primitive and central notion of humans being created in the image and likeness of God, and even this last term was of course rendered intelligible by its connection to a larger framework of beliefs. For the modern tradition, human dignity becomes itself the founding concept, from which flow rights. Compared to the thickly embedded concept of the image of God, the modern concept of human dignity stands remarkably exposed — and with it the human being, whose dignity now inheres solely in his or her own possessions and achievements.

Thus the modern concept of human dignity is characterized by its fragile and contested relationship to God and the human communities which give their allegiance to him. Here too Kant is emblematic. From the nineteenth century to the present a number of critics have vigorously charged that his concept of human dignity is still too indebted to theological culture, that it attempts to keep in circulation that outmoded currency of the image of God and the community of the faithful under new coinage. Far from being emancipatory, it is charged, Kant's liberal allegiance to human dignity reiterates a heteronomous order that perpetuates the tutelage of religion under another name.

The great spokesman of this tradition is Friedrich Nietzsche (1844-1900). For Nietzsche, Kant's turn toward reason and freedom is incomplete, interrupted in mid-motion by latent theological inhibitions. Whereas dignity was once conferred on human beings by God, Kant attempts to ground such dignity in man's own capacity for rational autonomy. In doing so he lays himself open to Nietzsche's dethroning of human reason and his demonstration of the absurdity of elevating it to the status of a faculty capable of securing unproblematic access to universal truth. Nietzsche is as skeptical about the powers of scientific as of moral reasoning. For one thing, human beings cannot transcend their own particular and partial perspectives on truth; for another, reason tends to be nothing but a cover for deeper instincts, prejudices, emotions, and strategies of control. Thus for Nietzsche science is merely "an interpretation and arrangement . . . and *not* an explanation of the world," and morality is a symptom of such emotions as "hatred, envy, covetousness and lust for domination."[36]

36. Friedrich Nietzsche, *Beyond Good and Evil* (Harmondsworth: Penguin, 1979), pp. 26, 35.

Part of Nietzsche's purpose is to convince his readers that they are closer to animals than angels and to have them embrace "the joy and innocence of the animal [and] life itself." Despite his eagerness to dethrone human reason, however, he is far less willing to deny human freedom and the capacities of the autonomous human will. He brings the hammer to conventional morality in order to free his readers from the snares of a so-called "common good" and provoke them to realize their true individuality by forging unique life paths "beyond good and evil." The will to power which lies behind the propagation of "morality" to constrain people's lives should not be renounced but embraced freely, honestly, self-consciously, and without reservation — by the few who have the courage and capacity to do so. Thus Nietzsche rejects any erection of human dignity on the foundation of human rationality and goodness (let alone relationship to God), but celebrates the autonomous human will of the "superman," a will now released from bondage to any "higher authority."

There have been a number of modern philosophers who have followed Nietzsche in locating human dignity in the unfettered exercise of human freedom — of whom Sartre and other Existentialists were perhaps the most influential. More important, the "self-made man" has become a paradigmatic figure in modern Western society and self-understanding. But the more general tendency has been to reject Nietzsche's grandiose exaltation of the will while absorbing his insights about the limitations and hidden motives of human knowledge and agency. The transition from a broadly Rationalistic perspective to a broadly Romantic one has been brought about, in part, by growing awareness of the impotence of reason to restrain the crises and disasters that punctuate modern human history. The embrace of a chastened view of human ability has been reinforced by the social sciences' demonstration of the social constraints of knowledge, and the human sciences' picture of human reason as impotent to comprehend or control the deep and often unconscious drives and emotions which shape human lives and behavior.

The impact of the natural sciences on the decontextualization — and the destabilization — of human dignity is harder to assess, not least because scientific theories do not have a direct application to the issue of human dignity and have to be mediated through different frames of interpretation. Most influential, of course, has been Charles Darwin's theory of evolution, which has generally served to reinforce Nietzsche's observations about the lack of distance between humans and animals and to present a picture of a world without design. The subsequent development of the "life sciences" has helped reinforce a tendency to subsume all species within the common category of "life," and to downplay human distinctiveness (a trend taken to extremes by theorists like Peter Singer who explicitly attack the Judeo-Christian-derived conception of human dignity and distinctiveness). In recent decades, the development of new forms of medical technology that place increased responsibility for issues of "life" in human hands has also started to have a profound impact upon our understanding of human dignity, not least by blurring the boundaries of what is natural and unnatural, human and cybernetic, God-given and man-made (see the chapters in this volume by Soulen and Graham).

Finally, we must note the contribution made to the ongoing story of decontextualization and destabilization by feminism, post-colonialism, and post-stucturalism. Feminist writers have argued that "the human" is in fact another word for "the male," and that the whole humanist project managed to secure men's rights at the expense of women's reality. The claim that a woman has "human rights" is said to be a disguised and dangerous way of forcing her to align herself with male norms in order to win a modicum of respect. A related critique is offered by post-colonial theory, which, like feminism, has championed the cause of "difference" over against what it views as the dangerously homogenizing and "essentializing" tendencies of (Western) talk of "the human" and its "civilized" values. With a very different starting point in literary analysis, French poststructuralism launched a converging attack. Arguing for the constitutive role of language in the construction of "reality" — and against anything more essential that lies behind language, whether a self, consciousness, or agency — writers like Derrida and Deleuze have proclaimed the "death of the author" and of the human soul. As Foucault puts it at the end of *The Order of Things*, "Man" has been erased like "a face drawn in the sand at the edge of the sea."[37]

The Theological Recontextualization of Human Dignity

> *"In the end, it seems, the concept of human dignity is surprisingly fragile in this respect: it can be robustly maintained only within the context of a vision of reality that revolves centrally around something other than and greater than the dignity of the human being."*
>
> KENDALL SOULEN

The argument we have been developing is that once removed from theological and ecclesial context, the concept of human dignity proves remarkably fragile

37. Michel Foucault, *The Order of Things* (London: Tavistock, 1970), p. 387.

— insufficient to sustain the ethical and metaphysical weight that modern rights-talk would place upon it. There may be many good reasons why the concept of human dignity had to cut free from its theological roots, and some valuable outcomes of such decontextualization (see the chapters that follow by Watts and Welker). But the price that has been paid has been a gradual weakening of the concept, and a blunting of its power to diagnose and resist contemporary endangerments of the very dignity it strives to secure.

The essays in this volume represent a response to this crisis on the part of authors who are drawn, as noted, largely from the Protestant tradition. This orientation is significant for, as some contributors point out, the Protestant heritage displays a notable ambivalence about the notion of human dignity — an ambivalence which distinguishes it not only from secular modernity but also from the Catholic tradition. The latter draws from classical philosophy, particularly Aristotle, the notion of the "natural" goodness of human rational substance, which needs only to be "perfected" by grace. In the modern period this understanding allowed Catholic thought to develop a "personalist" position which affirmed the dignity of each and every human being *qua* human, and allowed the Catholic church to become a notable champion of freedom, democracy, and "human rights."[38] By contrast, emphasis on human sinfulness and salvation by grace alone has rendered such developments more problematic within Protestantism. Although liberal Protestantism embraced discourses of human dignity and rights in the nineteenth and early twentieth centuries — with significant sociopolitical effect — in more recent decades liberal Protestantism has found itself on the defensive, not least because of the effectiveness of Neo-orthodox criticisms of a theological orientation that has a tendency to pay more attention to the human than the divine, and to sublimate the latter to the former.[39]

As one might expect, given this background, there is no simple embrace of the notion of human dignity in the essays that follow. Nor is there agreement among their authors about the way in which the concept should be handled — just as there was no easy consensus in the discussions and debates which gave rise to these essays (hosted and sponsored by the Center of Theological Inquiry in Princeton). There is, however, general agreement (a) that

38. See Paul Heelas and Linda Woodhead, *Religion in Modern Times: An Interpretative Anthology* (Oxford: Blackwell, 2000), pp. 70-109.

39. On this anti-liberal turn in late modern Christian life and thought see Linda Woodhead, *An Introduction to Christianity* (Cambridge: Cambridge University Press, 2004). In this instance as in others, the thought of Karl Barth does not neatly fit the standard account of Neo-orthodoxy. See his discussion of the honor of the human being in *Church Dogmatics* (Edinburgh: T&T Clark, 2004), III/4, pp. 647-77.

15

there is something in the concept of human dignity worth recovering, and that such recovery must (b) not consist in a return to a modern "substantialism" with a Christian gloss, (c) entail a thoroughgoing Christian recontextualization of dignity, (d) bring the concept into faithful relation with scriptural witness and the early Christian heritage, (e) take full account of recent criticisms of the concept of human dignity, and (f) also be robust enough to be able to make a serious contribution to diagnosing and challenging practical as well as theoretical endangerments of human dignity.

What might such recontextualization look like? Here too there is diversity in the essays which follow, but here too we find common themes. Not surprisingly, given the common commitment to return the notion of human dignity to a properly theological context on the hither side of the modern project, such themes both echo and move on from the early Christian themes briefly explored in the first part of this introduction. Taken as a whole, the volume suggests that Christianity can "host" the concept of human dignity — and move it on from its modernist captivity — by bringing humanity within the context of God's *differentiated action* as Creator, Redeemer, and Sanctifier. By doing so, theology illuminates the nature and basis of human dignity and provides a robust vision of its multidimensionality.

The Program of Recontextualization

The four essays that open the volume introduce the scope of what might be involved in such recontextualization. In setting human dignity against a scriptural horizon, James Luther Mays takes his starting point not (as might be expected) from humankind as the image of God, but rather from the Psalms of Lament. It is there, Mays suggests, that the "I" of humanity comes to clearest expression in its supple multidimensionality, its neediness and worth, its physicality and sociality, and — above all — its dependence on and relatedness to God. Moreover, as Mays points out, the prominent use of the Psalms in Jewish and Christian worship has ensured that the psalmic "I" has been a primary conditioning reality of the self-consciousness of generations of Jews and Christians, shaping their experience of God, themselves, and the world. With impressive literary and theological sensitivity, Mays then traces paths outward from the lament Psalms, first to Psalm 8's starkly contrasting hymn of praise for humankind "crowned with glory and honor," then to the scriptural language of humankind and the "image of God," and finally to the broadest reaches of the canonical witness. Ultimately, Mays demonstrates how the psalmic voice within the canon serves to place contemporary threats to human wholeness within a corporate memory of and hope for God's creative, redemptive, and fulfilling purposes for humankind.

Christoph Schwöbel makes use of the methods of a scripturally informed dogmatics to make transparent how Christian views of human dignity "are rooted in a specific view of what it means to be human and how this, in turn, is grounded in a comprehensive view of reality in relation to God." Schwöbel's starting point is "relationality" and, in particular, the scriptural recognition that human existence is constituted by relation with God, oneself, neighbor, and the whole created order. Thus the ground and fulfillment of human existence lies not in the possession of certain needs or capacities but in proper relation to the God who made us. More specifically, we are related to God in three ways: as creatures made "in the image of God"; as creatures who have fallen out of relationship with God into sin and who stand in need of God's redemption; and as creatures who are restored to the image of God by the action of Christ — which (alone) sets humans in new relation to God and one another. This is not "idle theological speculation" insofar as it is reflection upon the life and vocation of the church — for "the life of the Christian church is the enactment of the relationships in which human being as relational being is constituted and reconstituted."

Expanding upon Schwöbel's ecclesiastical recontextualization of human dignity, Robert W. Jenson's essay starts with the premise that life in community is the enabling condition of human personhood, and hence also of human dignity. Threats that endanger human life in community are therefore also threats to human dignity and personhood, which can be sustained only where these threats are overcome. And if this is so, argues Jenson, then the church is in fact *the* person- and dignity-enabling community. For in its worship of the triune God, the church is constituted by address from and response to a God who has already proved victorious over humanity's most radical, community-negating powers by the resurrection of the crucified Jesus. According to Jenson, therefore, the church's defense of human dignity is enacted above all in its eucharistic practice, liturgy, proclamation, and common prayer. Other communities can and do also enable human personhood because and insofar as they are openly or secretly ecclesial in character. In sum, the church is the metaphysical condition of human community, and so of all human dignity.

The extra-ecclesial social and political relevance of a concept of human dignity conceived broadly in terms of God's creative, redemptive, and consummating activities is explored by H. Russel Botman. Writing as a long-time opponent of the apartheid regime who is now engaged in national reconstruction, Botman argues that South Africa has benefited from its ability to draw upon two distinct discourses of human dignity: those of equality and of reconciliation. These, he suggests, are related as creation is to redemption. Yet Botman argues that a third discourse and practice is needed in face of post-apartheid realities of economic globalization, one that corresponds to the Christian conception of ongoing sanctification and movement toward wholeness and fullness of life. Moreover, he suggests that the biblical concept of covenant can serve to illuminate the necessary interdependence of all three dimensions of human dignity in the political, social, and economic spheres.

Creation

The remaining essays in the volume serve to develop themes sounded in these opening, programmatic chapters, and their focus of attention falls predominately on one or another dimension of the economy of salvation.

Starting with God's work of creation, John Polkinghorne's essay addresses the question of how Christian thought about human dignity may proceed in a post-Darwinian context. He argues that, far from posing a fatal challenge to a Christian account, a proper understanding of evolution can lend fresh support to an enlarged understanding of God's creative activity and of the unique role of humanity within it. Setting human biological evolution within a broader account of human responsiveness to dimensions of reality that transcend the mere imperative of survival — such as beauty, goodness, knowledge, and fellowship with God — he concludes that "the world, and humanity within it, become fully intelligible only when they are understood as God's creation."

Echoing the belief that human dignity finds its ground in God's creative will, R. Kendall Soulen relates this belief to contemporary bioethics and, in particular, to the potentials of expanding bioethical power. Soulen uncovers the implicit anthropological assumptions of what he calls "the new eugenics," and contrasts them with the biblical witness to human solidarity (through common descent) and to God's creative/elective will. "God's election repeatedly falls not to those who by reason of natural descent occupy positions of strength and superiority, but to the unlikely, the unpromising, and, indeed, to those who could not exist at all by dint of the power of natural descent alone." Soulen argues that what is required in the face of the unprecedented power bestowed by new biotechnologies is a deeper conception of how human dignity is grounded not in a human property, power, or attribute, but rather in a divine generosity toward us.

Hans S. Reinders also criticizes an approach to human dignity which would ground it in the possession of certain faculties and powers, and demonstrates its inability to make sense of care for the profoundly disabled. Introducing us to "Kelly," a young girl who has been diagnosed as microencephalic (lacking part of the brain), Reinders asks what kind of theory is necessary to make long-term care for Kelly meaningful. Arguing that the anthropological premises of liberal society are scarcely able to provide a rationale for care for the radically disabled, Reinders asserts that receptivity rather than activity forms the foundation of human personhood. Thus, far from being an anomaly, Kelly brings to light a general and profound feature of human life *coram Deo:* being as receiving. For both Soulen and Reinders, the critical edge of Christian anthropology rests in the centrality of divine *giving* as the ground of human dignity and well-being.

Redemption

God's work of creation is not, of course, the last word on the human condition, for the image of God in humankind is tarnished by sin. Thus God's activity includes the *redemptive* work through which God reaches out to us with the promise of repairing the damage. In his exposition of the scriptural logic of redemptive action, the Jewish scholar Peter Ochs argues that logics of dignity and indignity which take a binary shape — especially characteristic of secular modernity — exclude God as necessary "third" in all human interaction, and in doing so rule out the possibility of genuine redemption. By way of close reading of a number of scriptural texts, Ochs shows that God's Redeeming Name is disclosed to us "through the way that God is with us, here, in relation to [particular] suffering." Ochs's generous participation in an avowedly Christian undertaking, as well as the group's eagerness to be challenged and enriched by it, is itself a palpable instance of the sort of scripturally enabled repair that Ochs envisions. Traditionally, Christian reflection on sin and redemption often used Jews and Judaism as a negative foil to magnify the light of Christ, while its reflection on human dignity at times focused so narrowly on Christ as the image of God as to neglect the broader witness of Israel's Scriptures. Thanks in part to Ochs's contribution, the essays in this volume steer wide of these shoals.[40]

40. Contributions toward a post-supersessionist Christian theology made by participants in this project include R. Kendall Soulen, *The God of Israel and Christian Theology* (Minneapolis: Fortress, 1996), and Robert W. Jenson, "Toward a Christian Theology of Judaism," in *Jews and Christians: People of God,* ed. Carl Braaten and Robert W. Jenson (Grand Rapids: Eerdmans, 2003).

In a close textual study of Jeremiah, Esther Marie Menn explores the importance of *land* and *exile* as central but often overlooked dimensions of the biblical vision to human integrity and sifts their significance for understanding the plight of displacement experienced by tens of millions of people around the globe today. "If," she writes, "it is true that 'land is a central, if not *the central theme* of biblical faith,' then the vital connections that peoples and individuals have with particular places, sites, and regions need to be taken seriously in order to understand what it means to be human in God's world." In particular, she explores two striking and somewhat contradictory aspects of Jeremiah's message. First, despite the rupture in Israel's occupancy of Judah by its inhabitants, Jeremiah never dismisses or qualifies the importance of this region for the people of Israel. Indeed, Jeremiah highlights the connection between land and people precisely at the moment that this connection appears to be severed. Yet second, Jeremiah does not portray the people's inhabitation as guaranteed or even indeed as possible for his own generation. Rather, the prophet surprisingly recommends that the exiled people dedicate themselves to constructive engagement in the foreign land of the Babylonian enemy, thereby holding out the possibility of human thriving in the most adverse of circumstances. By rejecting the ideal of a natural, enduring, and unchanging relation between people and land, Jeremiah makes room for human adaptation and transcendence of the particularities of locale.

In his study of three New Testament writers, C. Clifton Black reminds us of the inescapably christological horizons of theological reflection upon redemption and the human condition. He finds little about human dignity in Matthew, John, and Paul (or indeed in the Bible as a whole), but a great deal concerning "the claim that, in Jesus Christ, God has abrasively, with finality, exploded this world for its (and our) transformation" (a claim, he avers, "that sets liberal and postmodern teeth on edge"). Black evokes the way in which Christ is portrayed as at one and the same time the judge and redeemer of the human condition, and shows how both aspects of Christ's work are exercised over against the community of disciples itself, as well as humanity in general. He contrasts the modern view, in which man becomes the center of things, with the New Testament view in which Christ is at the center of an eschatological vision of a larger mystery that is being revealed to the eyes of faith.

M. Douglas Meeks unfolds the critical implications of a Christian vision of God's economy of redemption in the field of economics. Modern orthodox economic doctrine conceives of the market system not only as a peerless engine of human prosperity but as a kind of natural fact that arises from and reflects the imperatives of human nature itself. In doing so, however, mainstream economics overlooks not only the destructive effects of the market system for tens of millions of people but also the fact that a market society enshrines a highly specific and reductionistic conception of human nature — one shaped in large measure by deformed and secularized conceptions of God. At their core, Meeks argues, Israel and the church embody radically different economies that challenge the market's logic of exchange with a logic of grace and gift, economies whose mandate is to bring "the creation into household relations that serve life rather than death." In a concluding section, Meeks examines how the Christian church can extend the household of God's economy in a market society, both by advocating specific policies and by shaping shrewd players in the market who can seek for humanizing changes in the market system.

J. Kameron Carter's essay considers sin and redemption by way of close textual exegesis — not of the Bible but of Fredrick Douglass's autobiography of 1845. In one respect, Carter argues, Douglass's genius consists in his ability to reinterpret his own experience as a slave in the context of the biblical narrative of Christ's suffering and resurrection, and thereby gain a critical vantage point from which to affirm his own humanity beyond the humiliations and degradations of enslavement. Yet at the same time, Carter suggests, Douglass's redemptive narrative is an appeal to the American ideal of independent, autonomous masculinity as much as it is an appeal to the Paschal mystery of Christ. As such, Douglass's conception of victorious manhood continues to depend upon degradation of the female, dependent "other" — in this case, black women and folk culture — and therefore it continues to depend upon a compromised conception of human dignity. Carter thus points toward the need for a continuing reformation of black theology in a way that gives scriptural narratives critical power over the Christian community's uncritical embrace of American and modernist conceptions of dignity as power and independence.

Sanctification

God's sanctifying activity has tended to receive less emphasis in Protestant theology than his creative and redemptive work, and Linda Woodhead's attempt to recontextualize human dignity in the context of sanctification draws heavily on resources supplied by early Christianity and the Orthodox tradition. Woodhead draws attention to the Christian doctrine of *theosis* or "deification" and the goal of divine-human union through the work of the Holy Spirit. This extraordinary Christian hope not only raises the horizons of human dignity far beyond much secular imagining but reminds us that what it is to be truly human should be regarded as a mystery in much the same way that God is a mystery (and for closely related reasons). Attempts to delimit and define what it is to be human — whether Christian or secular — must therefore be resisted as attempts to foreclose on divine-human possibility.

Fraser Watts's essay also reminds us of the long-standing Christian emphasis on dignity as "something to be worked for, not something that can simply be assumed or something that can be demanded as a right" — and draws upon psychological insight as well as more traditional sources to make this case. Contrasting a Christian anthropology with an Enlightenment one, he points out how the latter fails to give room either to human vulnerability or to development and change. He suggests that we need not only an "absolute" quantitative concept of human dignity but a qualitative one that reflects "the extent to which the potential that comes from being made in the image of God has been realized." Watts goes on to relate the concept of human dignity to that of "gift" in order to emphasize the importance of imagination in recognition of human dignity, and to argue that it is "Christ's gift of the Spirit that makes possible the imaginative response to other people that is required if they are to be treated with proper dignity as creatures of God."

Elaine L. Graham discusses human transformation in a very different context — that of the new technologies which promise and conjure up visions of the "transhuman," of human beings taken beyond their natural limits by way of technological enhancements. Graham explores the implications of such technologies for our understanding of what it is to be human and argues that a "humane" use of technology for future transformation depends upon a proper understanding of human *creatureliness* and finitude.

The ultimate horizon of Christian hope transcends the limits of this present life, as Paul had occasion to remind his hearers (1 Cor. 15), and as some streams of contemporary Protestantism perhaps need reminding of today. In the last essay of this section, Gerhard Sauter brings the singular nature of this hope into focus through a profound meditation on facing death. Sauter takes seriously the scriptural view that death confronts us not only as a natural fact (as to be sure it does) but also as an ally of sin, as "the last enemy." For a Kantian position that identifies dignity with autonomous action, the finality of death must be received as the end of agency and therefore as destruction of human dignity: the last possible right of disposal of oneself. For the Christian, however, death with dignity consists in acceptance that one's life lies not in one's own hands but in God's, with faith in God's redemptive purpose in Christ. The crisis of death is not to be tamed either by seeking to make ourselves the masters of death or by seeking to minister to the dying by sustaining the net of social relations as long as possible. Rather, Sauter suggests,

Christians need to acknowledge once again the genuine aloneness that accompanies dying and that is the mark of each person's unsubstitutability *coram Deo.* By acknowledging this aloneness, we also yield room for speaking the gospel's promise, and so enable a living and a dying attuned to God's triumph of life over death in Christ Jesus.

The Multidimensionality of Human Dignity

The two closing essays in this volume address the *multidimensional* character of human dignity in a manner that can be said to run through all the dimensions of the economy of salvation. We noted above that early (and medieval) Christianity tended to associate humanity's creation in the image of God with possession of the faculties of reason and will, though this tendency was not quite so monolithic as is sometimes described, inasmuch as the tradition acknowledged other aspects of the image as well (for example, upright posture, bodily integrity, dominion). This collection of essays tends to place greater stress on the *multidimensional* character of human dignity. Here one may see an attempt to work against not only modern pressures to anthropological reductionism but also a one-sided emphasis within the Christian tradition itself.

Don S. Browning's essay addresses the theme of the multidimensional character of human dignity in a programmatic way. He argues that the variety of contemporary threats to human dignity have in common that they fail to respect the multidimensional character of human life. Human thought and action, including Christian thought and action, always contain narrative, ethical, premoral, contextual, and concrete practice dimensions. Reductionism is a matter of attending to one or more of these dimensions while ignoring or de-emphasizing the others. Even Christian theologies, he notes, can be reductionistic in this respect by overemphasizing an abstract narrativity without relating it carefully to these other dimensions. After faulting much contemporary Protestant theology for failing to provide a theological framework that can illuminate the importance of premoral goods — goods that are important for life but that do not in themselves make one a morally better person, such as health and knowledge — he suggests how Christian theology might begin to take this dimension of human life more seriously.

The volume is brought to a close with a concluding essay by Michael Welker which draws together many of the common threads that weave their way through the book. Rather than simply dismissing the substantial self of the Enlightenment project, he draws attention to its ability to serve as the basis of a "macro-anthropology" that is capable of hosting a whole range of "micro-anthropologies" — legal, philosophical, economic, and so on. The price, however, is high — a reductionism that brackets out much of the richness and multidimensionality of human life. Welker's proposal is for a theological anthropology that can rescue from reductionism our understanding of what it is to be human, serve as an organizing focus for micro-anthropologies, and restore our ability to appreciate the many dimensions of human dignity. Both the cosmos we inhabit and the rite of Holy Communion in which all Christians participate point us toward a God who creates, saves, and ennobles. In doing so, Welker suggests, they offer a framework in which the multidimensionality of human existence can be taken seriously, and human dignity re-established on a nonreductionist basis.

Overall then, this volume makes the case for a conception of human dignity grounded not in the "person" him- or herself, nor in any of his or her natural attributes and possessions. This is different from the Enlightenment view, which grounds dignity in the possession of reason and free will, and different in many ways from the Catholic view, which is happier to embrace a view of the person as rational substance. As this volume exemplifies, modern Protestant theology is uneasy with talk of natural and substantial "persons" and "individuals," and happier with words like "personhood" and "creatureliness," which shift the emphasis from the human self to the divine creator from whom life is derived. Close attention to Scripture, which is a feature of many of the chapters that follow, underlies this emphasis. So long as this vital theological context is preserved, the contributors to the volume believe that the notion of human dignity is one worth preserving, and one which has considerable value for moral diagnosis of our contemporary situation. But the power of that diagnosis depends, as well, on retaining emphasis on creation, redemption, and sanctification — and here too contributions to the volume suggest what different dimensions dignity assumes when recontextualized in a Christian frame. Awareness of God's action as redeemer reminds us of human sinfulness, and helps avoid sentimentalism in our diagnosis of the human condition, while also preserving against cynicism by keeping in mind God's grace and power to save. And the emphasis on sanctification reminds us that human dignity in theological context is not a static possession but an eschatological provocation and goal. In biblical language, dignity translates to "glory," to the glory of God glimpsed in his Son and offered to us through the action of God as Holy Spirit. Glory is not a natural human endowment; it is the reflection of the light of God shining in the faces of those who turn their gaze toward him.

THE SOURCE AND SCOPE
OF HUMAN DIGNITY

The Self in the Psalms and the Image of God

JAMES LUTHER MAYS

The Bible is about God and the human being. From Genesis to Revelation the subject is God and humankind. In all its books and literary genres Scripture tells about God's way with human beings and their life in the world. It can be read as a vast theological anthropology. In its theocentricity it is anthropo-centric. Any of its texts can serve as a source for reflection on the human identity and condition.

This essay is a reading of one set of interconnected texts. It begins with a cluster of texts that contain self-descriptions by endangered persons, the prayers for help in the book of Psalms. The prayers are chosen as a pivotal and organizing group of texts because the loss of what we call "human dignity" and hope of its restoration are essential features of their composition. Questions and clues emerging from the self-descriptions in the prayers lead to a hymn intercollated in them, Psalm 8. The hymn, with its description of the glory and role of the human being in the creation, calls for a consideration of the first chapters of Genesis as the prolegomena necessary to reading the Psalms. Finally, the connection between the psalmic prayers and the crucial metaphor of the image of God, on the one hand, and the portrayal of the identity and role of Jesus Christ, on the other, leads to texts in the Epistles and Gospels. The purpose of this essay is to put the subject of the worth of the human being and the hope of its realization in the perspective of this complex of texts.

The Prayers of the Book of Psalms

The Prayers for Help As Witness to the Human Condition

In the Twenty-second Psalm there is an arresting disavowal. In the course of describing his affliction the psalmist says, "I am a worm, and not human" (v. 6). This painful negation in its sharp brevity assumes a conviction about what it means to be a human being. The very experience of deprivation evokes a consciousness of what has been lost that is epitomized in the mournful cry, "not human." The description of trouble that forms the context of this negation identifies what it is that diminishes his hold on his identity as "human," and as well what its recovery requires. "Human" in the psalmist's vocabulary is not a biological classification. It is instead an existential identity that is realized and enacted in living. It is an awareness of what one is that can be lost and can be restored.

This exclamation about one's identity as "human" and its loss is a witness to what is going on in the prayers for help that compose the stock of the book of Psalms. By far the majority of the Psalms are, to use the genre customary in form criticism, Laments of an Individual.[1] They are prayers for help by a beleaguered and beset person. They record the voice of a person addressing God, describing the woes that afflict his existence, pleading for deliverance and anticipating restoration.

The psalmic prayers for help are a virtually unique access to the self-understanding of a human being in the biblical world. Nowhere else in Scripture is the first-person voice heard in such frequency and continuity as here. In the course of pleading for help an "I" speaks to a "you" about "them" and "me" and "you." If the notion of "self" can be said to represent a consciousness that can employ personal pronouns, then these prayers are poignant disclosures of "self."[2] Though the prayers employ the vocabulary and categories and relationships of their culture and its traditions, they nonetheless reveal contours of a self that transcends a particular era. They are an eloquent testimony to a view of human beings, its conditions and necessities and potentials.

It is not only their character and content that make the prayers for help

---

1. For an overview of the "Laments of an Individual" and the companion genres, see among others Claus Westermann, *Praise and Lament in the Psalms,* trans. Richard N. Soulen (Atlanta: John Knox, 1981).

2. The use of the term "self" in this way is not intended to introduce the complex discussion in psychology and philosophy about the nature and relationship of self, ego, person, and so on. See, for instance, chapters 4-6 in Wolfhart Pannenberg, *Anthropology in Theological Perspective* (Philadelphia: Westminster, 1985).

important texts for theological consideration of the human condition. The psalmic prayers have a double role in Jewish and Christian practice. They are Scripture and used for instruction about God and God's way with the world and human beings. The prayers are also liturgy, prayers and praise that are said and sung in worship and rehearsed in the exercises of contemplation. When they are used for liturgy and devotion, the self in the psalmic prayer speaks through the mind and voice of believers. The "I" of the prayer finds voice through the believer and in the process involves the user in the constitutive neediness and aspiration of the self in the prayers. Through their use, the self whose voice is there in the psalm is always potentially a conditioning reality for the self-understanding of those who hear and say the Psalms. So the way in which the Psalms view the human condition continues through their use as Scripture and liturgy to inform and guide believers to self-discovery and expression.

The Typology of the Self of the Prayers

The individual whose voice is heard in the first-person-singular psalms is not a particular person. The distinct specific experience of those for whom the prayers were composed is interpreted and described through the conventions of a mode of prayer that had been nurtured in Israel's long history with its God. The self speaks through a combination of vocabulary and literary elements that belong to the genre of individual prayers for help.[3] The selection of language and the arrangement of literary elements vary from prayer to prayer. It is this creative variation of common features that produces the particular prayers in their distinctness. But the function and language of the elements are so typical as to form a kind of template through which the self of those using the prayers is presented. The one who prays is given a self through which to be present to God. Through all the variety in the prayers there is a sense in which the self who speaks is the same self. It is the presence of this paradigmatic self in all the prayers that makes it possible to draw general observations about the representation of the self in all of them.

The typical elements of the individual prayer for help are these. The prayers usually begin with a *vocative* that names the one to whom the prayer is addressed. In a description of trouble the one praying speaks of self in terms of a neediness that is the reason for the prayer. The description typi-

---

3. For an extensive account of the typical elements that compose the prayers for help see chapter 3 of Patrick D. Miller Jr., *They Cried to the Lord* (Minneapolis: Fortress, 1994).

cally refers to a neediness in relationship to God and self and others, and follows a pattern of the three personal pronouns, "you/I/they." A petition forms the central organizing element. The petition is usually twofold, a plea to be heard and to be helped. A motive stating reasons why the prayer should be heard is frequently attached to the petition. An affirmation of trust confesses confidence in God and God's help. Usually, the prayer concludes with praise of God, either expressed or promised or anticipated.

Because these literary elements are so consistently used in the composition of the prayers and their related genres, they imply a set of attributes of the human self that is expressed in them. The profile of the self that is sketched by the prayers is, of course, conditioned by the use for which they were composed. They belong to situations in which the self is endangered or at least conscious of endangerment, but perhaps it is in times of such awareness that the contours of the self come into clearest expression. Because of this their articulation of an instance of human affliction is based on the actuality of the human and a view of its condition.[4]

The prayers, first of all, are the artifacts of a creature that can translate consciousness into communication. Of course any writing or speech or conversation is an example of the linguisticality of the human animal. But the prayers are particularly evident instances of the capacity to move what the self experiences beyond the experience itself, so that self-consciousness transcends the self. When language becomes the form that the experience of endangerment takes, something essential is disclosed about this creature. It can move physical and mental pain from the sensory and psychic sphere to the sphere of language. What is felt is brought into reach of will and thought, of memory and anticipation. Through the language the self knows that it is more than the naked experience of affliction. There is a self that can set it forth, establish even a little distance, view it, and speak about it.

Second, the prayers exhibit the self as a relational reality. The consciousness of the self in them comes to expression with the use of the personal pronouns. The style is mostly direct address; an "I" speaks to a "you" about the you and I and a "they." The prayers disclose a self whose consciousness as an I is congruent with a consciousness of others. Even when the one who prays speaks specifically of himself, the speaking is said to another. The prayers support an understanding of the human self as constituted by its relationships to other persons.

Third, the prayers portray a self that exists in three spheres: physical, so-

4. On prayers for help, see Patrick D. Miller, *They Cried to the Lord* (Minneapolis: Fortress, 1994), chap. 3.

30

cial, and theological. The threefold pattern of descriptions of trouble is based on the three spheres. The agenda of the descriptions is typically physical and mental affliction, the harmful effect of others, and the absence or wrath of God. The self is an embodied self that feels and thinks. It is a social self whose individual personhood is inextricably involved in a community of others. It is also a religious self that by individual intuition and given traditions needs and depends on a power transcendent of the human realm. In the way the prayers speak in these three constitutive contexts of the self, it is clear that they are interdependent, each conditioning the others. God, others, and the body are the skeins of which the fabric of the praying consciousness is woven.

Fourth, the prayers are the expression of an inherent neediness of the self. The petitions as the formal expression of the neediness are pleas to be heard and helped. A variety of imperatives are used, such as "heal me," "deliver me," "be gracious to me." The petitions seek relief from the troubles that are the occasions for the prayer; they seek restoration of physical well-being, protection and vindication before hostile others, reintegration into the community, acceptance by God, and freedom and cause to rejoice in praise. All these various needs are indications that the relational self is a dependent self. With dependence comes vulnerability. From time to time the psalmist offers a simple description of the self: "I am poor and needy." The assertion does not refer to economic deprivation. It is rather a confession that existence is structured by finitude and fallibility. Even where physical and social dangers are relieved, the psalmist will say of himself, "I am poor and needy."

Finally, the prayers argue that the essential neediness of the human self is for the person and presence of God. The self of the Psalms is inextricably religious in a way that includes and transcends the physical and social dimensions of its existence. The prayers are addressed to the divine You as the one who can maintain the self. They are the expression of a consciousness that includes in its nature an expectation of a transcendent being-heard. The way in which needs of the physical, psychological, and social spheres are presented shows that they involve the religious need. The pain of the various tangible problems is ultimately their effect on the consciousness of God. The urgency of the resolutions requested is their power to renew the personal knowledge of the divine. In all the prayers what the human "I" seeks is the divine "You." That God in and through and beyond all else is the need is always assumed and at times poignantly said in such confessions as, "Whom have I in heaven but Thee?/And on earth there is nothing I desire besides Thee" (73:25).

31

The Prayers As Witnesses to Human Identity and Worth

There are problems to be recognized in using the psalmic prayers as a resource in a contemporary discussion of anthropology. The prayers are the product of a specific historical culture that qualifies and limits the notions that their composers employed. In their present form they are attributed to a particular individual and related in some cases to episodes in his life. "Human" as adjective and noun in a taxonomic or moral sense is not part of their vocabulary. Nor is the worth of the individual self grounded in a natural or political status belonging to the individual as such.

In reading the prayers as documents of the self, however, it is important to remember that as a genre of human speech they are part of a larger general literature. The lament-prayer was not unique to Israel, but was composed and used across the religious cultures of the time and region of which Israel's history was a part. Many of the conventions and much of the vocabulary used to describe the troubles of the self in the Psalms appear to have been part of this ecumenical genre. This broader setting for the genre and its typical features is evidence that the self-descriptions in the Psalms participate in an "anthropology" that represents the experience of a wide and inclusive population. The self who speaks in the prayers is, of course, an Israelite self whose religious and moral consciousness is shaped by Israel's history with the God it came to know through that history. The psalmists pray as members of a selected people, and their prayers are informed by a particular knowledge and obligation that belongs to that special identity. But their prayers are a version of a general genre and a way of liturgical participation in a larger humanity that is represented by the self described in the psalms.

Another factor in the paradigmatic character of the self in the prayers is the complexity of its identity. Most of the prayers are introduced as the words of David, the prototypical messianic king whose story is told in the books of Samuel. It is evident from the redaction of the Psalms and the formation of the book that the postexilic community used the prayers as expressions of its corporate identity. It is reasonably certain the prayers were as a type originally composed and used by particular hurting Israelites. After the final formation of the book the Psalms composed in first person were read and used by individuals and the community. It is a continuation of this flexible construal that in the Christian tradition the self in the prayers has been understood as a Christian worshipper or as the corporate church or as Christ.

The Canonical Context of the Prayers

Psalm 8 and the Prayers

How these Israelite psalmists came to claim that God and a relation to God is the reality of their sense of self-worth, the prayers of lament do not explain. But there is a hymn, Psalm 8, which does. Typical of the hymns in the Psalter, the Eighth Psalm has as its subject what God is like and does. It is woven into the collection of prayers that compose Books 1 and 2 of the Psalter as if its place there were necessary. The theme stated at its beginning and end is the majesty of the name of the Lord. The theme echoes the close of Psalm 7 and the opening of Psalm 9–10 in a way that shows that they are combined into a larger literary unit. This larger whole has been edited into an interrelated context for reading.

Psalm 8 declares what the prayers assume. The glory and honor of mortals is the endowment of God. But what the hymn says about the endowment is not coherent with the identity of the self and the condition of humanity as described in the prayers.

The hymn praises God for the creation of humankind and speaks of the human being as the work of God. Humanity is described as what God made it to be. The description of God's action in making the human species is composed with the use of a metaphor. God's creative act is portrayed as the inauguration of an official in a royal administration. The Lord appears as sovereign of the universe, whose majesty pervades all the earth. The making of humankind consists of appointment to a rank, bestowal of recognition, and assignment of a role. Humans are installed at a level just below the ʾelohim, the divine members of God's court and administration.[5] The dignity and importance of the human being is marked by the bestowal of glory and honor, attributes of divine and human royalty. The assigned role is responsibility for one sector of God's creation, all other living creatures.

So the construing context for the significance and worth of humankind is "the kingdom of God." The human, corporately and individually, bears and wears the glory and honor of God in the created world. The species is portrayed as a vassal of the divine rule. What it is and does is a representation of God's reign. Its dominion is intended to correspond to the divine sovereignty and is ordained to conform to God's will and way. Thus, humankind derives its identity and destiny from its relation to God. The relationship is not formal and external. It is constitutive of what creature the human being is. Apart

---

5. See the exposition of Psalm 13 in James Luther Mays, *The Lord Reigns* (Louisville: Westminster John Knox, 1995), pp. 55ff.

from that relation the human creature has no ultimate meaning different from other living creatures.

In his reflective praise the psalmist wonders, "What is man that you are mindful of him, and the son of man that you care for him?" (v. 4). The psalmist's assertion that the human being is created for the kingdom of God in the world is the answer to the question. It is by and through the human creature that the reign of God is honored and glorified in the world. The human species, corporately and individually, is the project of God's kingdom. That is the unstated authorizing foundation of the prayers for help. God's endowment and purpose are at issue where the glory and honor of human beings are ignored and obscured.

Psalm 8 speaks about the entire human species, about "man" as everyman. The individual of the prayers speaks very much as one of these human beings, but not just as any one. The self of the prayers is a person whose sense of self is shaped by the memory of a particular people and its traditions. The "I" has a special personal relationship to God who is called "YHWH," the name of Israel's covenant deity, and who is addressed as "My God" (e.g., 3:7; 5:2; 22:1f.). The supplicant identifies himself to God as "your servant" as a way of claiming a right to be heard (e.g., 27:9; 31:16; 34:22; 35:27).

Moreover, the picture of humanity reflected in the prayers is that of a fractured and flawed race. The corporate humanity crowned with glory and honor and ordained to dominion over other creatures is distorted. The destiny of corporate dominion is being realized in the domination of some human beings by others. In the prayers framing Psalm 8, hostility, affliction, and oppression mark the human scene. Human conduct features arrogance, ruthlessness, and cunning. The predominant human corporate identities are self-seeking autonomous nations. We read of those whose actions deny the reality of God (10:3f.), of a terrorizing "man of the world" (10:18), and of petitions that humankind not succeed in domination (9:19).

The dissonance between Psalm 8's portrayal of created humankind and the testimony of the prayers of lament to historical humankind is deafening. There is a tragic incongruence between what God has created and what humans have wrought. The royalty conferred on the human being by God has become the kingdoms of this world in which it is forgotten "that they are but men" (9:20). Mortals turn the need for God into greed (10:3) and the glory given by God into pride (10:4). Reading the Eighth Psalm in the midst of the prayers evokes its eschatological tension. In its present place in the midst of the prayers it locates the human as it is created to be in the midst of humanity as it is. Historical man is between creation and realization, living an unfulfilled destiny in a flawed and perverted way.

The protological account of this dissonance is of course recorded in the sequence of chapters 1 and chapters 2–3 of Genesis. Psalm 8 is a poetic version of Genesis 1:26-28. The story of a humanity that leaves Eden (Genesis 2–4) to live the curse instead of the blessing, to murder the brother, and to fashion culture as a temple of self-assertion instead of as room for the Presence is the necessary canonical preface to the enigmatic humanity portrayed in the prayers.

The Image and Likeness of God

In Genesis 1:26-27 the nature and worth given to human beings by divine creation is designated by the term "image of God." The notion has always been the central theme of theological anthropology. From the patristic to the modern period Christian theology has connected the dignity of human nature with the theme of the image of God. The inclination has been to define the concept in terms of capacities and attributes such as reason, will, knowledge, righteousness, happiness, and so on that could be reasonably inferred from the term and other texts of Scripture. But there is broad agreement currently that the biblical text does not elaborate the term in such a way. Verses 26 and following simply use the words "image" and "likeness" to designate a relation of the human being to God in the human's created nature. The designations apply to both genders of the species and assign dominion over the other creatures as the role of the created human being.

When the usage of these defining words is examined in other texts their meaning is clear enough, and it is a reasonable assumption that Genesis 1:26-27 would be read in a way consistent with these other uses.[6] "Image" *(selem)* is used for representations of a deity (Num. 33:52; 2 Kings 11:18//2 Chron. 23:17; Ezek. 7:20; 16:17; Amos 5:26); for a likeness of mice and of tumors (1 Sam. 6:5-11) and for a likeness to men (Ezek. 23:14), all in reference to cultic settings; and once for shadows as fleeting reflections of people (Ps. 37:19). In its twenty-five occurrences "likeness" *(demut)* consistently means "similar to, but not the same as." In what the similarity consists depends on context (e.g., 2 Kings 16:10; Isa. 40:18; Ezek. 1:5; Dan. 10:16). In the repetition of Genesis 1:26 in 5:1-2 "likeness" replaces "image," and in 5:3 the order of the two terms is reversed, implying that the two are regarded by the writer as virtual synonyms. Here the terms are also used to describe the relation of Seth to his father, Adam. The meaning

---

6. On *selem* and *demut* in the Old Testament see E. Jenni and C. Westermann, eds., *Theologisches Handwörterbuch zum Alten Testament* (München: Chr. Kaiser Verlag, 1971-1976), vol. 2, cols. 556-63.

is not, however, that Seth looked like Adam, but that that which in Adam made him an image/likeness of God is passed on in the generational process. It is specific to the species, not alone to the individual first human.

The last use of "image of God" as identification of the created nature of humanity occurs in the context of God's instruction of Noah after the Flood (Gen. 9:6). The fact that humans are made in the image of God is said to be the reason why the life of each person requires ultimate respect from other men. The attribute "image of God" belongs to an individual of the species as well as to the species as a whole. It is what gives each person worth.[7] The post-diluvian setting of this text also shows that the image of God belongs to the human being beyond and through all the drastic failures of mortals recorded in Genesis 3–9.

When read in the light of Psalm 8, Genesis 1:26-28 appears to be based on the same rank-and-role pattern of identification featured in the hymn's use of a metaphor of royal ordination and installation. The rank in the psalm is "little less than *elohim*" (the divine beings?) and in Genesis it is "image of *elohim*." The role in both is dominion over the creatures. The plural style of the self-exhortation, "let us," and of "our image" almost certainly indicates that the notion of the divine royal court staffed by the *elohim* in which God exercises his sovereignty in relation with the human world is assumed by the text.[8] The specification of male and female and the use of the plural "them" to refer to "humankind" is a way of including both genders in the image-identity rather than an indication of what the image-identity is. The identification of the human being as the image of God belongs to the deep and rich tradition of thinking about God's relation to the universe as a divine sovereignty that is thematic for the breadth of Scripture. The human rank and role in the world corresponds to that of God over the world. Psalm 115:16 remarks that "the heavens are the LORD's, but the earth he has given to humankind," yet another specification of spheres of authority and responsibility as constitutive of the human.

What the "image of God" texts in Genesis and those related to them claim is that the relation of representation and resemblance to God is constitutive of human created nature. It is not separable, but part of human nature.

---

7. The human identity and destiny are given to every human irrespective of their condition and capacity. As Hans Reinders argues in his essay in this volume, "our humanity is a gift from beginning to end. . . . [D]ivine agency — not human agency — is the primary concept of theological anthropology" (p. 139).

8. The Sitz-im-Leben of the plural style is identified in Patrick D. Miller, *Genesis 1–11: Studies in Structure and Theme,* Journal for the Study of the Old Testament, Supp. Series 8 (Sheffield: University of Sheffield, 1978), pp. 9-26.

It holds for the species and individuals in it. It is central and foundational to the biblical view of God's way with the world as anthropocentric.

The Other Likeness

The texts concerning humankind as image of God all appear in Genesis 1–11, a narrative complex that has the protological formation of humankind as its subject. The complex contains a second account of creation in chapters 2–3, which with chapter 1 form a double introduction to the complex. This second account features another likeness of human beings to the *elohim* (3:5, 22). This likeness is not a representing and resembling God in the matter of God's sovereignty, but rather the opposite. It stands in tension with the created likeness. This likeness consists of "knowing good and evil."

In the story told in Genesis 2–3 the knowledge of good and evil is the fruit of the forbidden tree that stands in the center of the garden (2:9, 17), so it is a divinely prohibited possibility for human beings. It is a consummation promised and realized by the contradiction of God (3:1, 4). It is the autonomous prerogative to decide what is nourishing and beautiful and best for living life (3:6). The acquisition of this knowing evokes a self that is self-conscious before others and afraid of God (3:7, 10). It results in an experience of life where blessing is distorted by curse (3:14-19).

"Like *elohim*, knowing good and evil," means assuming divine autonomy in discerning and deciding what is beneficial to life and what is detrimental.[9] The expression does not refer to the capacity of reason and its use, but to a misuse of reason that is centered radically in the self. When the Lord God says, using the plural style of self-reference again, "Behold, the human being has become like one of us, knowing good and evil," the sovereignty of God and its mythic setting in the divine court is again alluded to (3:22; see 1:26). God is sovereign over life and living. The issue of human life and death is thematic in the story of Eden. God is source, support, and limit of human life (2:7, 9; 3:4, 14, 17, 22). That the human being should claim independent sovereignty over life puts the human in conflict with the divine (3:22). To seek in the created world apart from the creator the source that supports and enriches and directs life is the essential impulse to idolatry (Rom. 1:18-25).[10]

---

9. On the phrase "knowing/knowledge of good and evil" see Jenni and Westermann, *Theologisches Handwörterbuch zum Alten Testament*, vol. 1, cols. 687-91.

10. While the human proclivity to seek independent sovereignty over life is addressed in one way or another by most of the essays in this volume, it becomes especially thematic in the essays by Soulen and Graham.

After its twofold introduction the narrative complex of Genesis 1–11 unfolds its account of the formation of humankind. The human as protagonist of history is portrayed in stories and genealogies. The themes are relationships and alienations: between genders, siblings, occupations, parents and children, kindred, languages, nations, and throughout the narrative sequence between the human being and God. The stories are all a sequel to 3:22. They concern a corporate and individual self that has become its own center and reference in the matter of life and death. Twice in the narrative sequence there are reminders that this self is a God-imaged creature (5:1-2; 9:6). But nothing in the telling reconciles the contradiction between the two likenesses of God and humankind. The creation of the human being to represent and resemble God's sovereignty in the world seems to be a given of human identity, but a given of an essential destiny that has to be realized. The self-centered enterprise to take possession of life is a radical disconnection with the original likeness. The two identify the human creature in their contradiction, and the contrast between the two is the analog and theological preface to the disparity between the prayers for help and their explanatory hymn. If one begins with Genesis 1–11 to learn about the human condition, the disparity between Psalm 8 and its companion prayers for help is no surprise.

Representation and Likeness As Call and Promise

It is an apparent anomaly that "image of God" does not recur in the rest of the Old Testament. As crucial as it is in the account of the Beginnings, the phrase as identification of the human being disappears, leaving its one poetic echo in Psalm 8. In Genesis 12:1-3 a further identification of human beings beyond creation is inaugurated by God. It is a particular identity constituted by a command and a promise. The command is a call to a future that God will provide; the promise is a history of greatness in which God offers to all humankind the lost blessing purposed at creation. From Genesis 12 forward the biblical story will focus on particular identities of human beings created by command and promise. These further identities become the surrogate enactors of the value and significance of human beings. Corporately and individually these further identities are people of God, covenant people, servants of God. In the biblical story the rest of humanity, social groups and nations and individuals, is viewed in relation to these identities created by the command and promise of God.

While "image of God" is no longer used for the human being in the biblical story, its actuality is a structural theme of the biblical account of God and humankind. The actuality continues in the calling and destiny of human beings to represent and resemble God in the world. When this calling and destiny is given to some, it assumes and continues the purpose and possibility vested in the creation of humankind. The pivotal defining text is Exodus 19:3-6, God's inaugural words to Israel as a covenant people. Israel is given a role and destiny to represent and resemble God among the peoples of the world. Through an existence defined by the demands and promise of the covenant, Israel will have a particular and special relation to the Lord as God's priestly kingdom and holy nation who represent God's sovereignty over all the earth. The corporate people are even referred to as "Son of God" (Exod. 4:22; Hos. 11:1). Their corporate and individual life is to resemble the God whose they are. The primary divine attributes of holiness, righteousness, justice, and loving-kindness are the ethical responsibility of the people, a responsibility urged by exhortations like, "You shall be holy to me, for I the LORD am holy" (Lev. 20:7). Within the people of God the Davidic messianic king especially is given the role of representing and resembling God, first of all to his subjects but also to the nations. He is called "Son of God." He is to exemplify the attributes and do the work of the Lord. Dominion is his vocation; righteousness, justice, and peace are his tasks. All humankind in its historical identity as "the nations" is his domain (see Psalms 2, 18, 20, 21, 72, and so on).

The story of Israel as told in the Old Testament is broadly a sequel to Genesis 1–11. Israel is a part of the humanity described there and its career concerns all humankind. The Israelites' identity and destiny as the people of the Lord is a movement toward the realization of humanity's identity and destiny as image of God.

The Prayers in Context

The psalmic prayers need to be read in light of this deep background and in the context of the biblical story. They are the prayers of a creature created to be the image and likeness of God, a self that seeks life by knowing good and evil, an individual in community chosen and called to be the servant of God.

As creatures whose destiny and identity is to represent and resemble God in the matter of God's sovereignty, the psalmists bear an indissoluble relation to God. The prayers are the expression of an intimation of dependence that informs all human beings, whether denied or confessed, a longing that cannot be satisfied within and by the self alone. The prayers arise out of an inherent need for meaningfulness for existence, a compulsion of the self to find its own meaning in mastery of the world and its creatures. The psalmists pray out of an ineradicable instinct of human significance in the world. In them a self pleads for the attention that is due the one to whom the central place within creation belongs.

So the psalmic prayers are fraught with an eschatological tension. The help the psalmists seek from God is more than relief and rescue from current plights. Their petitions are the voice of an identity not yet complete and a destiny to be fulfilled. The prayers are a litany of a longing to be what the psalmists are — creatures created in the image of God.

Jesus As Call and Promise of Representation and Likeness

In the New Testament, Psalm 8 is cited, the term "image of God" reappears, and descriptions of trouble from the psalmic prayers are used to tell the story of one man's tribulation — all this concerning Jesus of Nazareth. In concert these resumptions from the Old Testament set his person in connection with the promise and predicament of the human recounted there and claim him as the realization of the identity and destiny for which humankind was created. The author of Hebrews, after quoting Psalm 8, says that the realization of humankind's destiny to represent and resemble the sovereignty of God in the world is not visible in the world. But, he adds, "We see Jesus . . . ," and he means the crucified and risen Jesus. In his suffering and death Jesus is one with humankind. Through the power of his resurrection he incorporates humankind in his realization of the identity and destiny for which they are created.

In the Gospels the accounts of the suffering and death of Jesus use elements from three of the prayers for help, Psalms 22, 31, and 69. The words and experiences of the psalmists are woven into the fabric of the passion narratives. What the self in the prayers said and suffered become the words and tribulations of Jesus. In this way the Gospels draw a connection not only between the prayers of Jesus and the Psalms, but as well between the person of Jesus and the person portrayed in the self-description of the psalm. There is a kind of recapitulation of the psalmic self in the person of Jesus. The result is a mutual twofold identification. Jesus identifies himself as one of "the poor and needy," joins himself to the company of the afflicted, and asserts a solidarity with them. The psalmic prayers, on the other hand, identify Jesus as a self like the psalmists, a mortal — vulnerable in physical, social, and religious being — who cries out for life and asks in prayer that God's will should serve his life. "In the days of his flesh, Jesus offered up prayers and supplications, with loud cries and tears, to him who was able to save him from death," observes the author of Hebrews (5:7).

He is one like the psalmists, but unlike in one radical way that is disclosed in his Gethsemane prayer: "Abba, Father, all things are possible to you; remove this cup from me, yet not what I will, but what you will" (Mark 14:36). In the matter of life, Jesus' reference to his own will is a link to the psalmic identification. But the phrase "not what I will" — an unqualified offering of the self of a human to the Thou of God — is not heard in the prayers in the Psalms. "Although he was a Son, he learned obedience through what he suffered; and being made perfect he became the source of salvation to all who obey him" (Heb. 5:8-9). This crucified risen Jesus is a perfected human self whose person opens up a possibility for other humans that the Pauline letters will call "the image of God."

In the letters attributed to Paul the concept of "image" reappears to be used to speak of the relationship between God and humankind.[11] It is used first of all to speak about who and what Jesus Christ is. Christ is "the image of the invisible God, the first born of all creation" (Col. 1:15). He renders the invisible God visible in the created world. He as image preceded the existence of all that was created, so that from the beginning he was the destiny given humankind in its creation as image of God. The gospel brings to light the glory of Christ as "image of God" as it reveals him as the manifestation and likeness of God (2 Cor. 4:4).

The second way "image" is used is to speak of the relationship between Christ and those who are being incorporated in him through faith. Christ Jesus so absolutely preempts the role of image of God that the vocation and destiny of human beings can be realized only through a transformation of their existence by his spirit (2 Cor. 3:1-8). Once in a case of misguided interpretation, Paul does call the male "the image and glory of God" (1 Cor. 11:7). So Paul thinks of humans as image of God in their created identity. But it is an identity that in human historic life has not been actualized. It is by the transformative power of the gospel that human beings are progressively conformed and transformed to the self they are created to become (Rom. 8:29; 1 Cor. 15:49-51; 2 Cor. 3:18), a transformation that is consummated eschatologically. This transformation that is a being-conformed-to-Christ is discussed in terms besides "image," such as old and new humanity (Eph. 4:22-24; Col. 3:9) and old and new creation (2 Cor. 5:17; Gal. 6:15).

The paradigmatic action that originates the transformation is the crucifixion and resurrection of Jesus (e.g., Rom. 6:5-14). Paul can say of his own self, "I have been crucified with Christ; it is no longer I who live, but Christ

---

11. On "image of God" in Pauline letters, see Udo Schnelle, *The Human Condition: Anthropology in the Teachings of Jesus, Paul and John* (Minneapolis: Fortress, 1996), pp. 98-102.

lives in me; and the life I now live in the flesh I live by faith in the Son of God, who loved me and gave himself for me" (Gal. 2:20). Through faith the love and self-giving of the representative and likeness of God begins to reconfigure the self of others in his own image.

In the Gospels, when Jesus appears proclaiming, "The kingdom of God is at hand," and calling his hearers to repentance, it is because the reign of God is present in his person and worth. His presence brings the possibility for people to undergo the transformation that relocates them in the coming kingdom of God, and so to realize the identity and destiny for which they are created. The parallel in the Gospels to Christ's taking over the self of the believer is found in Jesus' way with the disciples. He interrupts their lives with an unconditional call to follow him. His way is to be their way. Following was a giving up of self to Christ that was a form of crucifixion. They were to learn through Jesus that the effort to be the humankind of Genesis 3:2 and so to save their existence as selves is a way of losing the self (Mark 8:34-38 and par.). Along with the entire New Testament, the Gospels teach that encountering the crucified, risen Jesus inaugurates the transforming of the believer's self.

God's Anthropos Project

The psalmic prayers read in the context of the related texts that form their canonical environment support a vision of the meaning and worth of the human being. The self whose voice is heard in the prayers confesses a vulnerability and fallibility of life that belong to every mortal. That the afflictions of finitude and failure are held up to God in prayer is a disclosure of the essential neediness of the human condition. To be human is to be a creature whose nature and destiny in life is incomplete apart from God.

The presupposition and past behind the prayers is creation and covenant. Those who pray are first of all "living beings" created to glorify their creator in lives that represent and resemble God; but "all have sinned and come short of the glory of God." They are also those sinners to whom God has irrevocably committed himself in order that by call and commandment they may be drawn to a fulfillment of their created destiny in ministry to all human beings.

The prospect and promise before the prayers is Christ and consummation. Among the company of the called and commanded, one appears who bears the afflictions of mortal living in a life that perfectly represents and resembles the Creator. The Spirit of his offered and resurrected life is power to transform all and each in the whole human race into fulfillment of the destiny for which *anthropos* was created.

The human race and every individual in it are given their meaning and worth by their location within this plan, this economy of God that runs from creation to consummation.[12] The "mystery" of God and God's way with the world is disclosed in it. The story of the world is the story of God's *anthropos* project. God's *anthropos* project is the divine economy through which God is glorified. As one summary of the Christian faith says as introduction, "The chief end of man is to glorify God and enjoy him forever."[13] And Irenaeus of Lyon declares, "The glory of God is a living man and the life of man is the vision of God."[14]

---

12. See the elaboration of "The Economy of Grace" in the essay in this volume by M. Douglas Meeks.

13. This quotation comes from the *Westminster Shorter Catechism*, Question 1.

14. Irenaeus, *Against Heresies* 4.20.7.

Recovering Human Dignity

CHRISTOPH SCHWÖBEL

Human Dignity at Risk

With regard to the notion of human dignity, we are confronted in most Western societies with a deeply paradoxical situation. On the one hand, the notion of human dignity is affirmed as a foundational principle of society. In some cases, as in Germany, the principle that the dignity of the human person is inviolable is solemnly stated in the constitution. On the other hand, we encounter a profound insecurity with regard to the practical application of the principle in most spheres of social and personal life. How much freedom is demanded by the principle, how much justice? What are the implications of the principle for the political and social order of society? In what sense is the principle of human dignity to be observed in the economic realm? What does appealing to human dignity mean in a society that increasingly tends to arrange all forms of social interaction according to the market-logic of supply and demand and thereby claims the factual primacy of economic values over all other values? Furthermore, how can human dignity function as an action-directing principle in the context of modern biotechnology, where modern techniques of genetic engineering offer prospects of medical progress which seem to imply that the boundaries between genetic diagnostics, gene therapy, and genetic enhancement become increasingly blurred?

It is a crucial aspect of this situation that opposing parties in current debates can *both* appeal to the principle of human dignity. The formal universality of the principle seems to be widely accepted, but its material implications are just as widely contested. The critics of biotechnological research protest against the production of human embryos for their use in medical research by appealing to the principle of human dignity that must also be applied to the very early stages of human life, while the protagonists of genetic engineering argue for genetic research with human embryos in order to allow people whose dignity now seems to be restricted by a serious disability or illness to regain their dignity, or in order to prevent humans being born who do not seem to be able to lead a life that carries the marks of human dignity. One could easily multiply the examples. Although human dignity is formally affirmed as a universal principle, it seems to have lost its capacity of providing orientation for human practice.

One way to describe this situation is to say that the understanding of human dignity has become *decontextualized* (see the introduction to this volume). Whereas it used to be part of a Christian theological understanding of what it means to be human, this context is now ignored. Without this context it is not surprising that the ambiguities we have just indicated occur. This can be stated in the most general way: in order to discuss the material presuppositions of the concept of human dignity, the religious or ideological presuppositions on which a particular view of human dignity rests must become transparent and be made accessible in public debate. Although human dignity is an ascriptive concept, it rests on descriptive presuppositions of a religious or ideological character which are structurally metaphysical. Views on human dignity are grounded in conceptions of the human being. The normative *value* and orientational capacity of concepts of human dignity are dependent on their coherence with views of human *being*.

This is not only an abstract philosophical or theological debate. Images of what it means to be human are always socially embodied. They show themselves in the icons of humanity that we experience in our everyday lives, in relation to which we define who we are and strive to be. These images are subject to historical developments, socially and culturally conditioned, and always clothed in the rich tapestry of social fact and cultural imagination. Furthermore, they are always specific and come to expression in concrete images that shape our view of who we are and who we want to be. Yet, they are not ontologically neutral. Ontology is not only a field of abstract philosophical speculation. The different ontologies come to expression in the decisions we make, in the experiences we cherish or abhor, in the lifestyles we adopt or reject. The values that find concrete expression in the way in which we interpret and shape our *Lebenswelt* reveal our ontologies. Therefore views of what it means to be human cannot be divorced from the larger picture of our view of reality, our view of what is really real, which shapes our policies of action.

Christian theology is a good example of the connection between concepts of human dignity, beliefs about what it means to be human, and a comprehensive view of reality which sees everything grounded in, structured by, and ordered toward the relationship with the triune God. By making transparent how its views on human dignity are rooted in a specific view of what it means to be human and how this, in turn, is grounded in a comprehensive view of reality in relation to God, Christian theology makes its vision of reality publicly contestable, and thereby offers the invitation to proponents of other views of reality to make explicit the implicit assumptions on which their views rest.

If other views of reality also refer to a ground and telos of being and/or focus of meaning for the whole of reality, they are implicitly theological. The debate between different *anthropologies* is therefore a debate of different (mostly implicit) *theologies*. One could almost claim that one needs to turn Feuerbach's projectionism from its head onto its feet. Tell me what your view of humanity is and I will tell you what or who your God is! What we see as the full expression of human being, as the goal of human striving, discloses the view we have of the origin and telos of all reality. Christian theology does not enter the debate on human destiny as the only theological perspective of interpretation; it is already entangled in the battle of God and the gods that goes on behind the scenes of debates about human dignity.

This essay attempts to *recontextualize* the understanding of human dignity in the context from which it developed: the Christian understanding of reality. This attempt is motivated by the expectation that the concept of human dignity will lose much of its ambiguity once it is viewed in the context from which it derived, and that it will regain some of its capacity to provide orientation in this way.

Human Being in Relation: Some Concepts for a Christian Theological Anthropology

A Christian anthropology can be developed with the help of a few fundamental concepts that shape the framework and the structures of the exposition of a Christian anthropology. These concepts are not independent, however: they function as conceptual abbreviations for the complex narrative structures of the biblical traditions and need to be developed in dialogue with the thought of the time. They are always subject to a number of tests: their connection to the biblical narratives, their internal rationality, and their communicability outside the sphere of theology and the church. There is, of course, always the danger that the concepts of Christian dogmatics become abstracted from the rich material of biblical traditions in which they are rooted and which they try to express. This can be avoided only if they are constantly tested against the biblical traditions they try to express and if they remain open to reformulation dependent on further insight from the reading of the biblical traditions. Our attempt to recontextualize the understanding of human dignity will therefore involve paying attention to the textual worlds of meaning in which the notion of human dignity was formulated. In this sense this essay is simply a mapping exercise outlining the connection between the distinctive aspects of a Christian theological view of what it means to be human.

In the following remarks I try to point to some of the connections between the concepts of theological anthropology and the biblical narratives, especially the first three chapters of the book of Genesis. What emerges from such an attempt is a relational picture of what it means to be human. Therefore I will begin with a few remarks intended to clarify the notion of relation.

Human Being As Relational Being

In Christian theology the understanding of what it means to be human can be characterized by the fact that human being is understood as relational being. All human beings have their being in relationship to God, to themselves, and to the world, both as a world of personal and social interaction and as a material cosmos. These relations are not external relations attached to an already existing substance; they are internal relations which constitute the terms of these relations. There is never pure relationality without terms of the relations, and there are no terms of relations which can be understood apart from their relational constitution. In these relationships we find a passive and an active dimension. Human beings are indeed set within a structure of relationship which they have not constituted, but which is constitutive for their being. These relationships which are given for us comprise our relationship as creatures to God and to the whole of the nonhuman creation; they comprise our relationship to other persons and to ourselves. This structure of relatedness which is constituted for us, however, confronts us with the obligation of shaping these relationships: we are related in order to relate. The crucial question is how our active relating relates to our passive relatedness. Do we acknowledge our createdness in our relations to God the creator or do we rebel against our createdness in positing ourselves as the sovereign creators of ourselves, our world, and our God? Do we acknowledge our co-createdness with the whole created cosmos in all our relationships with all other creatures or do we deny the fundamental solidarity of all created being? Do we recognize the created sociality of all human beings or do we contradict it by constructing our individuality as the denial of all sociality?

"Relationality" has become a key word in theological parlance in recent years. It has to be kept in mind, however, that it is only a technical term for a wide variety of ways of understanding the relationships between God, human beings, and the world. The biblical traditions depict God's story with creation in many forms. Human beings are part of that story, which is vividly expressed in images from a wide variety of fields of experience and discourse. The language of relationality is an attempt to do justice to the concreteness of descriptions of the interaction between God, human beings, and the world. Therefore it does not posit an already given ontology as the background of the biblical testimonies. Rather, it attempts to construct an ontology based on the reading of the interactions of God with particular human beings in a world of particular characteristics. A relational approach takes the language of the biblical witnesses seriously in an ontological sense. Who God is, how God and what God is, becomes clear from the relationships he establishes, maintains, and restores with his creatures. And consequently, who, how, and what a human being is becomes clear from the way God relates to human beings and invites them to relate to their God, to one another, and to their world. A relational view of reality is therefore an exercise in descriptive biblical metaphysics which hopes to avoid the risks of subjecting the biblical witnesses to a prior metaphysical scheme. Thus, it has to avoid proceeding within the pre-defined framework of a metaphysics of substance or a metaphysics of subjectivity as a given starting point for anthropological considerations.

In recent discussions in theological anthropology, the relational approach has been developed as an alternative to views that define what it means to be human in terms of the capacities and incapacities of human beings or in terms of the needs that define what it means to be human. This is a crucial issue. Who is included and who is excluded if we define being human in terms of the possession of particular capacities — for example, rationality or self-consciousness? Is such an approach not liable to suggest different degrees of being human according to the degree in which we possess certain capacities, so that we could draw a line that divides a "normal" human being from a "subnormal" human being? And is a "subnormal" human being still fully human? Do we start our journey into life, when we have not yet reached our full capacities, as a fully human being, and are we still a fully human being at the end of our lives when we may have lost some or all of the capacities that define a human being in some accounts? Furthermore, are human beings first and foremost beings of needs, so that being human depends on the satisfaction of those needs? This way of interpreting human being (made popular, among other views, by Marxist anthropologies) posits the satisfaction of needs before the relationships in which humans exist. Are therefore the relationships in which we live to be judged according to the degree to which they allow us to satisfy our needs? A relational approach to the question of what it means to be human cannot ignore the question of our capacities and incapacities, nor indeed the question of our needs. It places these questions within a framework of relationships within which our capacities and incapacities and our needs and satisfactions are to be viewed, however. Capacities and needs are placed within the relational framework, but do not define it.

While most modern anthropologies locate what it means to be human in the relationship of humans to themselves (i.e., capacity for reflection, self-consciousness) or in their relationship to the world (i.e., compensation for instinctual deficiencies by means of language and culture, and so on), Christian theological anthropology locates it in God's relationship to humans. This is also the context where the concept of human dignity is to be located. Theologically, human dignity is a distinction which humans possess apart from and independent of any capacities or qualities they possess in their relationship to themselves or to the world, so that it must be acknowledged as a given which is not constituted by these acts of acknowledgement.

Being a Creature

The first concept which defines humanity in a Christian theological context is human *createdness*. Humans are creatures. Their being comes not from themselves; rather, they owe it to the will of the creator. Their ontological status is that of contingent beings. They have control over neither their beginning nor their end. They are finite, and their life requires the management of finite, exhaustible resources. On the one hand, their createdness locates human beings in the relationship to their creator, in ontological dependence (relatedness), and in their capacity to relate actively to God. On the other hand, their createdness relates them to the whole of creation in structures of interdependence that leave room for created creativity (co-createdness). This relationship to the whole created world means that humans are created of the matter of creation and bound into the regularities which shape all created matter. These regularities determine both the natural and social world and their interconnection.

According to important biblical traditions it is a crucial feature of this notion of createdness that all living creatures are dependent on the Spirit for their life. Where it is withdrawn they return to dust. The capacity for life is therefore not an inherent capacity of created matter but is rooted in its relationship to God's creative Spirit. In this relationship creation's capacity to respond to the creator is rooted as well as its directionality toward its telos. These emphases of the biblical traditions have been developed in later theological traditions in such a way that the very structure of creation bears the marks of its relationship to its triune creator in the rule-governed intelligible structure of creation (Logos) and in the dependence on an external source and telos of life which at the same time is the source of the spontaneity of created freedom (Spirit).

In the Image of God

Perhaps the most prolific notion of Christian anthropology is that of the image of God, which for most theological traditions summarizes the place of human beings in the created order. A number of elements must be noted here.

First of all, being created in the image of God means that humans are addressed by God and are given the ability to respond to the word of the creator. They are therefore responsible before God. This special distinction is given not only to some human beings (for example, as a prerogative of kings, as in Egypt), but to all human beings. Humans are called into a communion with God which is enacted as a conversation between God and humanity.

Second, being created in the image of God applies to the relational order of human life as male and female. Human relationality mirrors — albeit in the structures of created existence — the relationality which God is.

Third, the connection of the *imago Dei* with the commission to go forth and multiply implies that humanity is meant to have a future. The conversation between God and humanity is meant to have a history whose beginning and end is the divine word of address.

Fourth, the connection between *imago Dei* and the *dominium terrae* points to a divine calling for the cultivation of the earth. Human beings are meant to be cultural beings. The earth is the domain for the exercise of their created freedom, a sphere of responsible action, in response to God's commission and not in autonomous sovereignty. The human being is *imago Dei imago libertatis,* the created image of God's freedom. This created freedom is to be exercised within the realm of obedience to God's will, however. As finite freedom, humans do not possess a *liberum arbitrium* as the capacity to posit their own goals autonomously. Even in the *status integritatis* humans have a *servum arbitrium,* a will that is in need of orientation, because it cannot provide orientation for itself.

Fifth, if the *imago Dei* consists in the fact that human beings are addressed by God and called to respond to God's address, so that the image-relation is a communicative relationship, it is significant that the *dominium terrae* (if we read Genesis 2 as a "commentary" on Genesis 1) is to be exercised in naming the animals and thereby making the world habitable for humans by turning it into a cosmos ordered by signs. Human being created in the image of God is the *homo significans.*

If we apply these attempts at sketching the significance of the concept of the *imago Dei* to the question of human dignity so that human dignity can be interpreted as an implication of the fact that humans are created in the image of God, then human dignity must be understood as creatively posited by God with the fact of human existence. It is not dependent on the existence of a quality which humans possess. Rather, it is the presupposition for all qualities humans possess and the criterion of their exercise.

Sin As Dislocation

In the Genesis narrative the investment of humans with the *imago Dei* as the special position humans have in the created order is followed by the narrative of the fall, which relates how humans contradict their created status and so exercise their created freedom in rebellion against God. The notion of the *imago Dei* and the story of the fall belong together for Christian theology, and must be developed in their intrinsic connection. Paradoxically, being created in the image of God is for humans the presupposition of the fall. Only images of God can sin. Only those who have been addressed by God can contradict God. Only beings who have been called into community with God can violate this relationship. Nevertheless, the fall is not to be interpreted as a necessary stage in the process of human development. It remains a contingent fact that cannot be explained completely from its antecedent conditions. Therefore it is not an essential characteristic of human nature but its distortion.

If the understanding of humans as being created in the image of God can be developed along the lines of the five points mentioned above, it would seem that the understanding of sin can be developed in parallel.

First of all, sin is to be understood as disobedience against the divine commandment, as the ignoring of God's address to humanity. The fall occurs where humans listen to other voices questioning the address of the creator. After the fall the first humans try to escape God's address. In the situation of sin humans want God to be silent.

Second, the fall is a disruption in the relationship with God which occurs where humans attempt to take God's place in the created order. This disruption in the relationship to God spreads to all other dimensions in which humans exist. Their relationship to other people is tainted with their contradiction against God as they try to evade responsibility for their actions. Their relationship to the earth is cursed. God's gardener becomes an agricultural laborer. Sin implies the dislocation of the human person in the relational order of the created world.

Third, the temptation of sin is the promise of a different future in which humans are no longer limited by God's commandment. In spite of the fall, humans are granted a future, but this future is linked with the pain of childbirth. The future is no longer given, but must be gained.

Fourth, the temptation offered by the Serpent consists in promising a use of freedom where freedom is no longer finite, created freedom, but infinite creative freedom. In yielding to the temptation the first humans abuse their created freedom. They attempt to exercise freedom as a *liberum arbitrium* no longer bound by the relationship to God. In consequence, the limitations of human freedom are unambiguously imposed after the fall.

Fifth, the temptation consists in raising doubts about the correct interpretation of God's commandment. The Serpent promises to humans that their eyes will be opened and they will see reality as it is, that is, as God — who knows what is good or evil because he is the ultimate standard of goodness — sees it. In following the Serpent's interpretation, the first humans choose the wrong path to wisdom, the wrong interpretation of the world, including their own existence. After the fall the world becomes semiotically ambiguous for humans, in need of constant interpretation. Truth is not obvious, but must be disclosed and discovered. Humans experience a situation of semiotic (and so epistemic) fallibility. The state of fallenness does not imply that humans are consistently bound to falsehood. Rather, it is an intensified state of fallibility: unless guided by the disclosure of truth, humans will resort to self-deception in their interpretation of reality and of themselves.

Genesis 3 reads almost like a debate about how being created in the image of God is to be interpreted. What does the image-relation imply? Obedience to the divine commandment, or rebellion? The interpretation offered by the Serpent, *"Eritis sicut Deus,"* offers an interpretation of the image of God as equality with God which denies the relational character of human existence. In being like God humans will become independent of God, absolutely Godlike: that is the promise of the Serpent. If that is the case, they will define their own values, because — like God — they will have become the ultimate standard of goodness. Their status will not be a dignity conferred by God but a self-acquired dignity. The story tells us that this will lead to disaster. The denial of dependence on God in the quest for autonomous freedom will lead to the complete loss of freedom. In attempting to become more than human, humans will become less than human.

Within the framework of a relational understanding of what it means to be human, the fall is the dislocation of humans in the relational structure of creation. If sin is the disruption of the relationship to God by humans' rebellion against their created status, and so against their creator, then it seems logical that this relation cannot be restored by sinful human creatures. If creatures could reverse the effects of the fall, they would be the creators in this relationship. This is the point the doctrine of original sin makes. It is a point about the sovereignty of God's grace.

The implications of such a theological understanding of sin for the question of human dignity seem to be clear. Human dignity is threatened where it is not understood as a dignity conferred upon humans by God in a creative divine act. If the relationship to God is no longer the foundational relationship for all human life, then human dignity becomes something that is conferred or withheld by other finite entities. Human dignity becomes a social construct that is constituted in interpersonal relationships. It is no longer acknowledged and recognized as something that is already there in virtue of the fact that every human life in every stage of its development is created in the image of God, but instead becomes something actively constituted in social relationships between humans. If it is constituted in this way, however, it can also be denied and destroyed in this way. Conferring or denying human dignity becomes an act of creative human freedom. The doctrine of original sin adds an important point here. Our situation is the situation of those living east of Eden where human dignity must be recovered against its denial.

Grace As Relocation

The overcoming of sin and its consequences by God, the theme of the doctrines of redemption and reconciliation, can also be developed along the lines we have sketched with regard to the interpretation of the image of God and the character of sin. The overcoming of the human contradiction against God by God himself is the re-actualization of the image of God after the fall. It is not achieved as a return to innocence, but as the justification of the sinner. We can illustrate that again in five steps.

First of all, over against the attempt of sinners to silence God, to hide from the address of God, God addresses the fallen human creatures again. God re-establishes his conversation with humanity by maintaining and re-establishing humans' responsibility. The "history of salvation" can be construed as a "history of conversation" between God and humanity which takes up the conversation with the first humans and continues it with the fathers. Israel is established as God's covenant partner, and this covenant has its life in divine guidance through the Torah and in Israel's response. It is the conviction of Christian faith that Jesus Christ is God's ultimate word, God himself addressing humanity in human form and disclosing humanity's true response in Christ through the power of the Spirit. According to Christian faith, the relationship with his human creatures which God had established in the covenant with Israel has thereby been opened to include the nations.

Second, the re-creation of the relationship between God and humanity includes the re-creation of all created relationships that have been marred by the contradiction of sin. The covenant with Israel documents the establishment of a new relationship between God and his people which is the basis and criterion for relationships between humans. Where the relationship with God is broken, the inter-human relationships break down. The social critique of the prophets shows that the converse is also true: where social relationships deteriorate, this points to a crisis in the relationship to God, which can be overcome only by a new decisive action on the part of God. In Christ, so Christians believe, both the relationship to God and the relationship between humans receive their eschatological definition. Jesus' message of the present coming of the kingdom points to the establishment of a new universal relationship by God to humanity which includes a new universal order of relationships between humans. It includes those who by the religious and moral standard of their societies, based on the qualifications that people possess, would be excluded both from the relationship to God and from the human relationships of good society. The point that is thereby emphasized is that God's action in Christ alone is the condition for inclusion into the new relationship with God and into the community with his people. And this is precisely the element of continuity between God's action in Christ, God's action in Israel, and the relationship with his creation which God intended from the beginning of creation. Through all the discontinuities of the human responses to God, God remains faithful to his original intention to build up his community with his reconciled creation. This new relational order receives its eschatological form as a filial relationship. In the power of God's Spirit, men and women are included as God's sons and daughters in the relationship of Jesus as the Son to God the Father.

This is, third, the advent of a new future for humanity. The future that had been threatened by the self-destructive powers of sin is opened up by God. The promise of the land to God's people and the prophetic image of the pilgrimage of the nations to Zion point to a future for humanity which is not defined by the past and its history of rebellion and contradiction against God's will but by the telos that God determined for his creation from this beginning. Whereas being under the power of sin means living in bondage to the past, the justification of sinners opens up the experience of God's eschatological future in the present.

Fourth, the overcoming of sin is the reconstitution of created freedom. The loss of freedom through the alienation from God is overcome by a divine act of liberation which separates humans from their past sins, which had kept them in bondage to death, and redirects them to their future purpose. The disclosure of their true purpose to live in communion with God through Christ in the Spirit liberates humans from the false purposes which turn humans into mere means for the achievement of finite ends.

Fifth, this liberation is achieved through the disclosure of truth, which falsifies the interpretations of reality rooted in the self-deception of sin. In Christ and through the Spirit, God, whose essence is truth, discloses his grace and truth as the overcoming of all falsehood and deception. Interpreted in this sense, God's truth is the active transformation of all reality to the will and being of God, in which humans participate through the transforming certainty of faith in the triune God.

If we consider the implications of this interpretation of what it means to be human from the perspective of the Christian message of reconciliation and redemption for the understanding of human dignity, we can see that human dignity is not to be understood as a kind of Platonic ideal that is in stark contrast to the empirical reality of everyday life. The Christian understanding of human dignity can be developed only within the framework of the drama of the relationship between God and humanity in God's history with his creation. Being created in the image of God, humans contradict God's will so that their created destiny is threatened by alienation from God until God reintegrates his estranged human creatures into communion with their Creator through Christ in the Spirit. For Christian faith the image of God in humanity is disclosed in Christ, just as the glory of God is disclosed in the face of Christ. The two are connected: the glory of God in the face of Christ is the glory of the one who takes the alienation of sin upon himself and so reveals the true image of God. This, however, changes radically the way we consider the notion of human dignity. In Christ, the one who was crucified and is risen, we see God's identification with those who have lost all dignity, we see God's identification with humanity at the point where all claims to dignity seem to be utterly futile. Christ's way to the cross confronts us with images of the most radical violation of human dignity. In Christ's undignified death on the cross we see our death if Christian faith really means dying with Christ, dying the death of all dignity as defined by worldly standards. And yet it is Christ, so Christians believe, who as the first among many brothers and sisters is raised to eternal life in the communion of the triune God, raised to a dignity defined by the eternal life of God.

What does this mean for an understanding of human dignity that is informed by a Christian understanding of what it means to be human? According to the view we have attempted to develop, human dignity is creatively conferred upon humans by God through the fact that they are created in the image of God. Over against the violation of human dignity through alienation from God, the defacement of the image of God through sin, God discloses the image of God, the true ground of human dignity, in the face of Christ crucified and risen. Human dignity is therefore to be measured neither by the qualities we may possess or not possess, nor by the abilities or disabilities we may have, but by God's gracious offer of communion with those who have lost all claim to dignity. Human dignity does not rest on a quality we have in virtue of our capacities, but on being qualified by God's grace, on being dignified through God's offer of communion to justified sinners. Our entry into the drama is not at the beginning before human dignity was defaced, but at the point where human dignity is recovered and revealed in the face of Christ. In this sense Luther could claim that *hominem iustificari fide,* being justified by faith is the true definition of what it means to be human and — we may add — of what it means to have human dignity.

The Public Role of the Church in Recovering Human Dignity: Criticism and Affirmation

Most of what we have developed so far would remain more or less idle theological speculation if this understanding of what it means to be human and this notion of human dignity were not practiced in a social context where these theological ideas are embodied in a social form of life. This social context exists, however: it is the Christian church. Theology is simply an activity which, if it succeeds, is designed to help the church understand a little better what it already practices. The life of the Christian church is the enactment of the relationships in which human being as relational being is constituted and reconstituted. The proclamation of the gospel not only asserts the relationship to God as the ground, constitution, and destiny of humanity, but promises this relationship in the hope that God will enable humans to accept this promise in faith. In baptism the individual human person receives the promise of God's grace as that which constitutes an inalienable identity and an inviolable dignity that has its foundation in the relationship of God to this specific person, thereby renouncing all other relationships that could claim to be the foundation of human life. In holy communion this relationship is reconstituted through Christ in the Spirit over against the disruption of this relationship by human sin. The reconstitution of the community of the church occurs through the reconstitution of every believer's communion with God through Christ and the Spirit. The promise of the gospel in word and sacrament therefore has the structure of witness pointing away from the church's acts to God who promises to use the church's acts as God's own acts — *ubi et quando visum est Deo.* This element is absolutely central for the understanding of the church's actions. It is not that the church is the subject of the recognition of the human person so that human dignity is directly conferred by the actions of the church. The church is the medium and instrument of God's creative and re-creative action in constituting and reconstituting identity and dignity. The church's acts therefore must be sacramental in the most radical sense of becoming iconic for the action of God. Since the church's actions are based on the conviction that the view of humanity which it enacts dramatically is the true view of what it means to be human, it owes the proclamation of this truth also in all public contexts where human dignity appears to be at risk. The church is therefore obligated to enter public debate about the way the notion of human dignity is rooted in a particular understanding of humanity. The understanding of human dignity cannot be privatized, and it is the church's obligation to create the public spaces in which the foundations of the understanding of human dignity are debated. Participating in these debates is the public task of Christian theology.

But what can theology, what can the church, contribute to public debates where issues of human dignity are at stake? On the basis of our attempt to recontextualize the notion of human dignity, it is clear that the contribution of the church will have to be both critical and affirmative. It will have to criticize all views of what it means to be human — as they are expressed in the sciences, in politics, and in the economy — which define human dignity on the basis of observable attributes based on the capacities of human nature that humans may possess to a greater or lesser degree. Against all such views the church must uphold the principle that human dignity as it is grounded in God's relationship to us requires absolute respect in all stages of human existence and in all forms in which a human life is lived, and cannot be ascribed relatively in proportion to our capacities or incapacities. This critical role will be convincing only if it is enveloped by the gospel the church has to communicate. In virtue of the dignity bestowed upon them by God, all forms of human life carry the marks of creatures who are called to be images of God. What the church has to say about human dignity has the form of an unconditional promise to all humans which is unconditional because it is a promise by God, who does not make his promises dependent on conditions that humans have to fulfill.

It is, however, important to note that the church does not uphold human dignity as an ideal principle that contrasts with the stark reality of the abuse humans inflict upon their fellow creatures. A church bound by the gospel of Christ, the one who accepted the ultimate indignity of dying the death of the godforsaken sinner, of the one who is cut off from the source of all dignity, has to relate its message in those situations where human dignity is abused and violated. If the cross and resurrection of Christ point to the fact that God re-creates human dignity where it has been violated and abused, the church which claims to be the church of Christ is committed to sharing the situation of those who have lost their dignity in human eyes and to communicating to them the message that their dignity is re-created by the one who first bestowed it upon them. In communicating this promise in speech and action, the church is called to become the witness of the recovery of human dignity because humans are dignified by God.

Anima Ecclesiastica

ROBERT W. JENSON

I

In recent theology, and foundationally by Christoph Schwöbel in this volume, it is often maintained that ". . . is a person" is at least in part a relational concept; that is, the concept would not be applicable to an absolutely solitary entity — whatever, to be sure, such a thing might in general be. I am a human person, it is said, in that I am located in a network of relations to other humans, of whom of course the same must then be said. Put it so: if God were to create just one putative person, and then to refuse that creature communication with himself also, he would have failed to create a person. Thus it can equivalently be said that persons obtain only within community.

This proposition suggests but does not entail the less plausible — but nevertheless perhaps true — position that a human person, in respect of his or her humanity, just *is* the node of a set of relations, a location in a community. The more radical position accords with the logic advocated by Peter Ochs in his essay in this volume; and Hans Reinders seems committed to it as well. On alternate days, I tend to hold this stronger position, but everything that follows in this essay is, I think, compatible with both the strong and weak versions of the proposition that persons occur only in community. We need not settle the question whether the individual person or the community is ontologically prior, so long as it is agreed that the first cannot be without the second.

It is also regularly remarked that the ultimate source of insight into the relational character of personhood is Trinitarian theology. In classic Trinitarian doctrine, the Father is the Father only in that he has this Son, and only in that he is the Father is he God. The Son is the Son only in that he has this Father, and only as the Son is he God. The Spirit is the Spirit as he is the Spirit of the Father, resting on the Son, and only as Spirit is he God. And finally — still following classic doctrine — only as the Father and the Son and the Spirit are God is there the God — the one God — at all. However cautious one must be in drawing direct analogies from the Trinity to created phenomena, it is plain that this set of propositions describes the very paradigm of persons-in-community, as our discourse now tends to speak of the latter. Among theologians there is some consensus that both the notion of "personhood" and the relationality of entities characterized by the notion derive their ontological weight from the Fathers' labor to find language for the mystery of Trinity.[1]

If the less radical view is correct, that to think of a created person as a node of relations we must first think of something antecedently there to be the node, two accounts can be given of this necessity. The first depends on an old theological rule: the distinction between substances and their attributes applies to creatures but not to God; for example, a creature may be good, but God is his own goodness. Thus with God the distinction between one of the persons and his relations to the others holds only for our conceptualizing: *in re* a divine person *is* those relations; Father, Son, and Spirit subsist *only* in and by their community with one another. As a created person, on the other hand, I am not identical with what is true of me, and therefore am not identical with, among other things, my relations to other persons.

A second account — and this is usually my own view — regards the distinction in created persons between substance and actions/sufferings as a sort of inevitable obfuscation: there is no way for us to talk about ourselves without making this distinction, but nevertheless if we use it as a warrant in reasoning, we will regularly be misled. Is this obfuscation made necessary by our creatureliness or by our fallen state? For the following, that is another question to which we probably do not need an answer.

II

Along any of the possible lines traced above, human personal being is "being in community." Borrowing a famous phrase, community is a "condition of

---

1. Within ecumenical theology, John Zizioulas's remarkably influential book, *Being As Communion* (Crestwood, N.Y.: St. Vladimir's Seminary Press, 1985), is in large measure responsible for this consensus.

are no words in the church that can bear this prefix, the church has merely ceased. We can of course try to sustain the Hegelian impasse, which we secretly love: we can try to make God our slave — this is what is meant by idolatry — or we can acquiesce in slavery to God as we take him to be. But in the church, we cannot succeed in either attempt. For *what* the church's God says[15] defeats both. There is no way to use one whom we have already crucified, and who nevertheless lives to love us; and there is no way to be used by one who wills only our freedom.

Second. Persons are *embodied* for each other; a disembodied intelligence, if such a thing is indeed possible, would not be a person.[16] This is an implicate of persons' dependence on conversation with each other, but needs separate discussion. If you are to address me, you must be able to find me, there must be some way in which we can come face-to-face. Were I, in conversation with you, suddenly to be disembodied, though you could still somehow hear my voice, it would be my sudden unavailability which would quickly undo our converse. If I insulted you, in which direction would you walk to be walking out on me? Or strike out, to assail me? If you heard me say, "I love you," what portion of space would you embrace — supposing the address were welcome to you? There can be no drama without embodiment of the roles.

My body, let me suggest, is my *availability* to you and thereupon to myself, however this occurs.[17] By whatever clues you are able to locate me, able to have me as your object to be addressed or honored or assaulted, the ensemble of these is my body. In this age, human persons' bodies are organisms, but there is no reason it can only be so; Paul anticipates a body that is no longer an "organic body"[18] but is just so an *intensification* of what he means by "body" (1 Cor. 15:38-44). Thus even in God, since the Son is to be available to the Father's love he must somehow be a body for the Father.

We tend to suppose that we would be bodies with or without one another. But this is surely wrong. We can perhaps conceive of God creating a sentient and intelligent organism that stood alone; but a body, that is, the availability *of* someone, this organism would not be — which is the reason that, as earlier remarked, it would not be a person, and not only because on

---

15. In distinction, it must be said, from every other claimant.

16. Are angels persons? Not exactly. Moreover, in the sense of "body" to be developed, they also are at least *capable* of embodiment.

17. I draw this usage from Paul, whose usage after all should be determinative, since his talk about "the body of Christ" is what makes the word a theological concept in the first place. See my *Systematic Theology* (New York: Oxford University Press, 1997-1999), 1:201-96.

18. The risen body is a *soma pneumatikon* that is no longer a *soma psychikon*.

this supposition there is no one there to which to be available. For even my own identification of this thing of hands and guts and so on as a thing that *is me* depends on its prior identification *with* me by others, notoriously by the mother for the child.[19] You look in a direction determined by a certain thing in my field of consciousness and by your address let me know you are looking at me; just so I look at that same thing and recognize me. If it were my invariable experience that people looked at some other thing, perhaps six feet to my right, in order to respond to something I had said, the very measurement "six feet to *my* right" would lose its meaning.

Such mutual embodiment occurs in all communities; otherwise they would not exist. But note that the process is circular: I identify a certain thing with you as your body, and I do this also for you; and you identify a thing with me, also for me. How does this circle start to turn? Theology's answer must be that the first embodying identification is part of God's act of creation. Therefore in the cities of earth, constituted as other than the church precisely by rebellion against the Creator, mutual embodiment hangs in the air, and can fail. So, for example, during the "sexual revolution" its more thoughtful participants sometimes justified a jolly bout of multidimensional fornication by saying, "Well, it's only the body after all," as if the bodies were one thing and the persons another.

Mutual embodiment of course occurs in the church as in other communities: so, for example, the parents bring a child to the font, and they, the minister, and all who witness the act name a person and physically wash this particular organism. Just so they establish the personal identity of the child for and within this community. And now we must go on to say: in the *church* this is not liable to break down — unless, of course, the church itself breaks down, by apostasy from her Lord. For in the church, one bodily identification takes place which is simultaneously an individual identification that cannot fail, and an identification of all the church's members.

"This is my body,"[20] says the risen Christ present in the assembly, directing us to an available assembling of objects, the loaf and cup. And in the same breath he says, "You are my body."

The two remarkable and often referenced passages in 1 Corinthians

---

19. Autism seems in large part a failure of the child's intellect to grasp the associated body as its own.

20. So long as it accepted that this is an identity statement and that "body" itself is not here a trope, differences about the how of the statement's truth can be elided for the position here presented. Those who simply deny that it is an identity statement thereby espouse an ecclesiology so different from that here presumed, that little of the essay can be acceptable to them.

make a unique set of identifications (1 Cor. 10:17; 11:17-32).[21] Those who assemble for the Supper make "one body" because they eat of the one loaf. Then Paul rebukes the Corinthians for their individualism at this very rite which brings them together. In support of the rebuke, he cites his tradition's version of the dominical mandate of the Supper, which identifies the *loaf* as "my body." Then he concludes his rebuke by saying that the Corinthians' violation of their fellowship means that they fail to discern "the body" of the Lord. Which body of the Lord does he at this point mean? The loaf? Yes, because otherwise his rebuke is not grounded by the tradition he cites; moreover, he identifies failure to discern the body with profaning the body *and* blood, thus clearly referring to the eucharistic elements. The assembly? Yes, because the community is, after all, what is being sinned against.

Thus the body of Christ is at once the loaf and cup available to me, and a body which is communally my body. In the church, I can always find my body and know certainly that it is mine, by taking the bread and cup with the other members of the body. And I can always find your body and know certainly that it is yours, by the same act. When we gather around the loaf and cup, we are available to each other despite all attempts to hide and without possibility of error. Otherwise stated, the drama of the Eucharist cannot fall apart for lack of mutual availability, and participants in that drama cannot lose one another.

Third, and last for this essay — though one could probably go on with such suggestions at considerable length. A drama has a *plot*; thus a *persona* in drama has a temporal direction. To be a person is to occupy a place within a sequence of events that is not a mere succession, a "tale told by an idiot," and therefore could not be reversed: to be a person is to inhabit a world that has a telos. Now it is humankind's general conviction that the world indeed is going somewhere, a conviction not fully eradicated even by religions that seek salvation in bringing the movement to a halt. But almost as general is a sort of metaphysical anxiety, that the world might not get there; where this becomes religiously thematic it is accompanied by an accepted or even willed loss of personhood.

And indeed, what guarantee do we have that we inhabit a plotted sequence? The sciences are of two minds in the matter: modern biology is based on denial that evolution has a story, even while cosmological physics construes a universal drama, however grim.[22] The diachronic identity of a polity

21. The groundbreaking essay was Ernst Käsemann's "The Pauline Doctrine of the Lord's Supper," in *Essays on New Testament Themes* (Naperville, Ill.: Allenson, 1964), pp. 119-21.

22. Though some physicists are constrained by ideology to avoid this appearance by many-worlds theories, which — remarkably for supposed science — lack all grounds other than determination to give Christianity no comfort.

or nation can unpredictably be ruptured; what has Germany now in common with Germany before, say, 1950? My individual life can "fall apart" at any moment, that is, I can lose my grip on a dramatic connection of the events which make "my life"; and indeed, multitudes in fact live in "quiet desperation" on the assumption that Macbeth was right.

Only one thing could establish the temporal direction of our lives, and so establish that condition of our personhood: inclusion of each of our stories in what is now called a "metanarrative," a narrative that we indeed inhabit and whose universality is otherwise established than by cosmology or evolutionary narrative, both of which — at least so long as they persist in prescinding from teleology — will always be uncertain. To be sure, most of those who now speak of metanarratives do so pejoratively; liberation from inhabiting any narrative larger than the one each of us constructs is taken to be the very constitution of freedom. We need not, I think, linger long with this gospel; it is both obviously driven by ideology and in daily process of empirical refutation.

In the church, we in the plainest sense inhabit a narrative. For the church simply is the community of a specific story, the one told by the Bible. And this shows in all aspects of the church's life — at least it does when the church is vigorous. So soon as the church began to use buildings for its assembling, it made their interiors into spatial and pictorial representations of the biblical narrative, enclosing the gathering. The matter of its assemblies is recitation and varied enactments of the narrative, both on each occasion and drawn out over sequences of services. Its ethics mandate conformity to the narrative. Anyone genuinely[23] determined to defer to no metanarrative must keep far away from the church.

And this narrative — if, of course, it is true — cannot fail those who inhabit it. For it is the narrative of God himself with his people and with all his creation, where that "with" must be taken as strongly as possible. The determining dogma of Christianity, the doctrine of Trinity, is at its heart the proposition that the biblical story is not about an adaptation or condescension of God to his people, but tells God's own story in precisely the same sense in which it tells creation's story and the story of Israel and the church. Thus the direction of my life is in the church guaranteed by nothing less than the eternal coherence of God's life.

---

23. But is this possible?

IV

One matter remains to be considered. If matters stand so, how are we to account for the fact of communities other than the church, and for the fact that also in these personhood is enabled? Most of humankind has, after all, lived outside the church, and personhood has not been denied them, though as we have seen outside the church it is not reliable. The decidedly hegemonic claim to be made is that the existence of the church is *die Bedingung der Möglichkeit* of other person-enabling communities.[24]

First, this is true metaphysically. We have already noted that the network of relations that the triune God is, is the enabling archetype of created community. Now we must further note that the biblical story of Father, Son, and Spirit, as those who live the life that is God, is not an account of sheer metaphysical markers: the Son is Jesus in Israel, the Father is Father in that he has this Son, the Spirit is their Spirit and none other. No doubt this is contingently true; we must indeed say that the triune God would have been the triune God if there had been no creatures at all and so no Jesus in Israel. But with God, there is no penetrating behind contingency.

As it is — and, again, we can say nothing whatsoever about what might otherwise have been — it is the Logos who is Jesus that is the universal Logos of all things. And this Jesus is the head of the church uniquely. As it is, the Spirit which rests on Jesus and which he gives is the *spiritus creator*, the Liberator who enables all dynamisms and their spontaneity, natural or historical. And this Spirit is the communal spirit of the church community, uniquely. Were the church, as the very church it is, not existent, were the Logos not the story of the church and the Spirit not the spirit of the church, the present facts about God and his relation to created communities would not obtain. As it is, the existence of all other created communities is mediated by the fact of the church's existence.

Such metaphysical propositions, at least within theology, are meaningful only as the relations they assert can plausibly be seen also within the created narrative. Somehow, the church must enable other community also historically.

This would seem to require some sort of extension of the church beyond its own borders, some way in which communities that never heard of

---

24. The relation between the community of the church and the community of continuing Judaism is of its own sort, and cannot be treated with the general categories used here. Within this essay it must suffice to say that no "supersessionist" implications should be drawn from the generalities here propounded.

Jesus or his community are nevertheless within their historical scope. Here one must step very carefully; theological history's effort to deal with this question is littered with disasters, many in our own most recent time.

I can see two steps of such a connection. There may well be connections and mediations I do not see.

If the ontological foundation of all community in the church community, sketched above, indeed obtains, then — if there are in fact other communities than the church, which there manifestly are — all communities are called into being and given their communal shape by action beyond the church of that same Father, Son, and Spirit who call and shape the church. Thus all communities, however feebly and unreliably, must simply because they exist at all be church-like in their impact on their members. That is, there must be some sense in which the famous thesis about "anonymous Christianity" is true, *not* perhaps in an anonymously Christian character of all religions, but in an anonymously Christian character of all communities, including of course religious communities.

Now where the church is in fact present, other communities must and sometimes do perceive that she is the archetype of their own community. I realize this proposition will be received with justifiable skepticism, but would contend that the perception is often most powerful precisely where it is repressed. Why, after all, did Rome — blessed and cursed with a uniquely perceptive ruling elite — find precisely Christian groups so politically threatening? Why does post-Communist China let so many flowers bloom, except by now long indigenous Christian churches? Why, for that matter, does the American liberal establishment regard Christians in general and the Catholic Church in particular as the one religious group it is appropriate to slander?

Where the church is present she always seeks to be a public presence, and retreats into invisibility only by betraying her calling. And as a public presence she is a visible and audible promise and just so rebuke to other communities.

The church is a visible community, with her own modes of government, her own sort of patriotism, and her own inner culture, that is united around the one good which the communities of this world cannot manipulate, and moreover goes about recruiting to that loyalty. The church is gathered by a common Good that her leaders' and factions' worst efforts cannot make uncommon. The church has a hierarchy that, however unwillingly, is compelled by its own establishing documents to acknowledge that it is to serve, not dominate.

The body of Christ that *gathers* the church is the same reality as the body of mutual love the church *is* (1 Cor. 10:17-34). Thus we see that the good of a polity is not instrumental — to, for example, the national product — but is identical with the mutual service of citizens. Of course, since the good around which a community of this world gathers is not the one God, but some partial good, its mutuality will be given its actual dynamics by the character of that good, and will be infected by the *libido dominandi.*

In the church all classes and races drink from the one cup and eat the one bread, and so share equally in the good that gathers the church. The cry for "social justice" has sometimes been used as a cover for dubiously faithful purposes, but its origin is deep in the life of the church. Unless a community is fallen so deeply that its common good is in fact a poison, a chief goal of its political striving must always be equal sharing of that good.

The discourse of the Eucharist is paradigmatically common prayer. In this discourse, all speak and all are heard. No doubt merely representative democracies are relatively good polities, but one thing cannot happen within their mechanisms: I do not myself appear in the forum where decision is argued and made, so my interests cannot be transformed by the discourse there. My representative can do much for me, but he or she cannot repent for me.

So what does all this come to? That the church is the communal home of humanity, and that all other communities live by acknowledged or unacknowledged longing to be the church. Which brings us back to Luther on Genesis: had we not fallen, there would have been just the church and her members.

Covenantal Anthropology:
Integrating Three Contemporary
Discourses of Human Dignity

H. RUSSEL BOTMAN

Introduction

Human dignity has been threatened in South Africa under the auspices of the apartheid regime. Apartheid's encroachment on human dignity emerged from a complex of theological, political, and historical dimensions. In this essay I will look at post-apartheid attempts to recover and restore human dignity and I will argue that a theological understanding of human dignity has much to offer these efforts.

There are currently two distinct post-apartheid discourses of human dignity in South Africa, namely, the discourse of equality and the discourse of reconciliation. Both discourses are driven by the quest for the restoration of dignity after the oppression and repression of apartheid. These two restorative discourses are important to human dignity as well as to its political and economic underpinnings.

This essay will argue that threats to human dignity are still prevalent in the post-apartheid context, above all, in the context of economic globalization. The endangerment posed by economic globalization is different from earlier threats in its nature, dimensions, and impact on humanity. I will argue that South Africa's two contemporary discourses of human dignity (that is, of equality and of reconciliation) are not sufficient to address the contemporary endangerment of human dignity in the context of economic globalization. A third discourse of human dignity is needed in order to provide some grounding for dealing with the challenge of economic globalization. In order to accommodate and relate all three discourses of human dignity, I propose an integrative theological-anthropological metaphor, namely, "covenant."

Restorative Discourses of Human Dignity

The first discourse this section examines is equality and the second, reconciliation.

Human dignity seen through the lens of equality is a crucial dictum that generates its own discourse. South Africa's democratic constitution marked the concept of human dignity as foundational and its restoration as the country's crucial public responsibility. As such, the constitution presents itself as a driving force for practices that can overcome past injustices that have threatened humanity and caused wide-ranging distortions of human dignity. Through these consequential practices a horrific history of the threatening of human dignity must be overcome. Human dignity is benchmarked in the constitution by its commitment to the achievement of equality and the advancement of human rights and freedoms. The constitution flows out of the idea that the restoration of human dignity requires the government to accept responsibility for fulfilling and protecting the social rights of people, especially of the most vulnerable. The restoration of human dignity must be seen as more than a mere social goal. It ought to be regarded more specifically as an institutionalized practice within the public and private sector as well as in civil society.

The objective of alleviating the poverty and suffering caused by three hundred years of inhumane policies, first through colonialization and later through the devices of apartheid, requires modest state intervention. The constitution provides guidelines for such actions. Access to adequate housing, health care, food, water, and social security are defined as rights to be respected, protected, and fulfilled by the state. These rights of specifically marginalized and disadvantaged black people are enshrined in the Bill of Rights as proper entitlements. The state must be seen to "promote" and "fulfill" these rights.

Rooting these second-generation rights in the principle of human dignity requires positing equality and freedom in the realm of concrete human existence rather than in mere abstract rationality alone. The restorative root in this discourse is modeled on the idea of "empowering equality."[1] Human

---

1. Lourens du Plessis, a professor of constitutional law at the University of Stellenbosch, outlines this model in his article "South Africa's Bill of Rights: Reconciliation and a Just Soci-

dignity as equality restores dignity through the empowerment of dehumanized people.

Equality is a complex notion with different manifestations. The various manifestations of equality are the following: (1) numerical equality, that is, the equality of things such as the equilibrium of injury and indemnification when damage is recompensed; (2) geometrical equality, which provides for differential treatment postulated on personal merit or status, for example, the right to vote qualified by the age of eighteen years; (3) substantive equality, which requires that people are treated exactly the same irrespective of individual difference or merit; substantive equality is symbolized by the fact that the goddess of justice is blindfolded; (4) corrective or curative equality, which seeks to address the deficiencies of other forms of equality; corrective equality addresses historically entrenched distortions of equality through the employ of specified procedures such as affirmative action.

A second discourse looks at *human dignity through the lens of reconciliation.*[2]

Reconciliation is, as much as equality, a practice with consequences for the restoration of human dignity. South Africa has recently become known for its commitment to reconciliation after the demise of institutional apartheid. The commitment is rooted in the idea that apartheid has broken the dignity of all people, whether they were perpetrators or victims. It dehumanized black people through wide-ranging inequalities but it also distorted the human dignity of both black and white in the course of its history. South African black theologians, such as Simon Maimela, Desmond Tutu, and Allan Boesak, have argued since the 1970s that the liberation of black people would lead also to the restoration of the human dignity of whites. The freedom of blacks from suffering and oppression removes the need for the distortion of the human dignity of whites by the consequent erosion of white supremacy and white superiority. This is the full extent of the gift of reconciliation. It re-

---

ety," in *Race and Reconciliation in South Africa: A Multicultural Dialogue in Comparative Perspective,* ed. William E. van Vugt and G. Daan Cloete (Lanham, Md.: Lexington Books, 2000), pp. 141-53.

2. Cf. H. Russel Botman and Robin M. Petersen, eds., *To Remember and to Heal: Theological and Psychological Reflections on Truth and Reconciliation* (Cape Town: Human and Rousseau, 1996). See also my article "Truth and Reconciliation: The South African Case," in *Religion and Peace,* ed. Howard Coward and Gordon S. Smith (New York: State University Press, 2004), pp. 243-60. See also Roswith Gerloff, "Truth, a New Society and Reconciliation: The Truth and Reconciliation Commission in South Africa from a German Perspective," *Missionalia* 26, no. 1 (1998): 17-53; Leo J. Koffeman, "Waarheid, Verzoening en Vergeving in Zuid-Afrika," *Ruimte Voor Vergeving* (Kampen: Kok, 1998), pp. 133-46; Geiko Muller-Fahrenholz, *The Art of Forgiveness: Theological Reflections on Healing and Reconciliation* (Geneva: WCC, 1997).

stores distorted human dignity on all fronts and offers the gift of unity and humane living.

Reconciliation further became the pivotal instrument for seeking restoration of human dignity after the apartheid wars and the anti-apartheid struggle. This instrument was selected primarily because it has the power to bring embrace in a context of conflicting and irreconcilable causes. Once people find themselves defending irreconcilable causes they are tempted to dehumanize the opposing faction or to even demonize them. The dehumanization and demonization of the other prolong conflict, serve the interest of the powerful, and create optimal conditions for torture, rape, killing, maiming, and bombing. Through the practice of reconciliation, the victim and the perpetrator seek mutual embrace and freedom from conflict. A very important component of this quest for restoring dignity lies in dealing with painful memory. Remembering the past may lead to festering hatred, but within the context of reconciliation memory can be redeemed from the vicious cycle of conflict and retaliation. Redeemed memory then becomes constructive in the remaking of a community and the restoration of dignity.

Reconciliation is also, however, deeply rooted in justice. The choice of reconciliation as a root metaphor for a discourse of human dignity is not a quest for a cheap, temporary, and optimistic embrace between enemies. True reconciliation is costly, lasting, and hope-bringing. Its root in justice is of a very specific kind, namely, restorative justice. The need to overcome past distortions of human dignity has caused others to choose the option of retributive justice as their main instrumentality. The well-known Nuremberg trials represent this option.

Restorative justice is the most critical form of justice, however, especially if former opposing parties are to share a common and just future. The voice of the victim receives priority status in restorative justice. The personal, familial, and relational nature of a crime against humanity takes precedence. Lawyers replace neither perpetrator nor survivor. Both are called to express the truth in a nonthreatening context, freed from merely abiding to the rules of the professional jurist. Restorative justice seeks the meeting and embrace of hurt, degraded, and angry human beings within the framework of reconciliation. Reconciliation, for its part, provides the optimal conditions for mercy, truth, justice, and grace. Reconciliation, as a practice with consequences for the restoration of human dignity, requires its own frame of legal reference. Restorative justice is such a comparable legal framework that allows space for the victim to play a healing role rather than merely an accusing one.

Forms of justice that seek revenge or retribution, even by legal means, fail to bring about the full restoration of human dignity, even though they may leave the victim "feeling better," recompensed or authenticated in the face of the enemy or the perpetrator. Restorative justice, however, engages memory, dialogue, and embrace in its practice. It takes its point of departure from the belief that the healing of memories and the embrace of people are possible through legitimate and communal processes.

The restoration of human dignity seen through the lens of reconciliation does not seek an answer to questions related to how combatants have lived, but rather to the more complex question of how next generations are to live together in a future filled with hope. As such, restorative justice is embedded in the Christian narrative, memory, and identity. It feeds on the essence of Christianity, namely, the reconciling suffering and resurrection of Jesus Christ.

It needs to be mentioned that the South African discourse of reconciliation also relates to just and formal reparations and therefore bears a certain link with the discourse of equality. Two theologians, Tinyiko Maluleke and Molefe Tsele, have argued strongly for distributive justice as a constitutive element for peace in the future. Molefe Tsele points to a direct connection between reconciliation and the biblical notion of the jubilee (Lev. 25:9-10).[3] The process should not end with reconciliation. It should also return survivors to a better social and economic status and thus restore their human dignity. Maluleke criticizes the reparations proposals of the Truth and Reconciliation Commission (TRC). The proposals call for largely symbolic and community-based reparations. The symbols serve to commemorate victims, and the reparations focus on rebuilding local communities after the atrocities. Maluleke accuses the TRC of dealing lightly with the wounds of the people.[4] The focal point of reconciliation, they propose, is the survivor, not the nation or community structures. Maluleke and Tsele thus seek a stronger link between the discourse of reconciliation and that of equality insofar as reparations represent a form of curative or corrective equality.

I have presented the two discourses separately from each other because of their inherent differences. They do not contradict each other, but their complementary nature does permit fusing one into the other. What they do have in common, and in this Maluleke and Tsele are correct, is the quest for the restoration of human dignity. Their practices, however, are different. While one relies chiefly on the justice of law the other relies on the justice em-

---

3. Molefe Tsele, "Kairos and Jubilee," in *To Remember and to Heal*, ed. Botman and Petersen, pp. 70-78.

4. Tinyiko S. Maluleke, "Dealing Lightly with the Wounds of My People?: The TRC Process in Theological Perspective," *Missionalia* 25, no. 3 (1997): 324-43.

bodied in human beings. Both these forms of justice seek restoration and also provide for material reparation.

Globalization's Threat to Human Dignity

Contemporary South Africa has been deeply affected by globalization. And so too have contemporary discourses of human rights.

Authors from different fields perceive a certain conflict between the restoration of human dignity and the advance of economic globalization. The most recent developments in the human rights discourse — namely, respect for economic, social, and cultural rights — are often at odds with the most recent developments of the world's financial markets — namely, respect for the bottom line, respect for the value of money and trade, as well as the primacy of economic growth over social imperatives.

Among the many approaches and thought forms engaging the idea of economic globalization, a number of scholars utilize calculations of risk in their analysis. Anthony Giddens and Will Hutton,[5] Malcolm Waters,[6] Zygmunt Bauman,[7] and Ulrich Beck[8] view the reorganization of risk to humanity and to the environment as central to any understanding of economic globalization. Ulrich Beck, the German sociologist, can be regarded as the foremost exponent of this approach when he places risk at the center of his analysis of contemporary social change. Risks are constituted by the side-effects of economic globalization — for example, medical, social, and ecological side-effects that come with the increase of wealth. The side-effects constitute risks, and they are unevenly distributed in the world. It is not the hazards that are novel but their social constitution and distribution.

Ulrich Beck claims that the desire to live one's own life has become the guiding impulse for people in the Western world. This would be the answer of most people in France, Finland, Poland, Switzerland, Britain, Germany, Hungary, the United States, and Canada, although some would say that they are seeking love, God's power, or money. The ethic of individual self-interest and self-fulfillment have been given free reign in economic globalization and have become the most powerful currents affecting human beings. Paradoxically,

5. Will Hutton and Anthony Giddens, eds., *On the Edge: Living with Global Capitalism* (London: Jonathan Cape, 2000).

6. Malcolm Waters, *Globalization* (London: Routledge, 1996).

7. Zygmunt Bauman, *Globalization: The Human Consequences* (New York: Columbia University Press, 1998).

8. Ulrich Beck, *Risk Society* (London: Sage, 1992).

people are now forced to live lives constantly at risk as a result of widespread fragmentation and cultural dislocations. Simply to exist in this age is to be forced to live the life of a nomad. One is forced to live by means of a certain "polygamy of place" in the networked reality of globalization.

Like other representatives of the new analysis of risk, Beck claims that economic globalization continues to cause fragmentation to human existence, but he insists that this new and harder form of individualism may in fact strengthen the most microcosmic level of community life.

Numbered among the risk-thought scholars is Zygmunt Bauman, the political sociologist and Emeritus Professor of Sociology at the Universities of Leeds and Warsaw. He has done extensive research on the human consequences of economic globalization[9] and sees the deconstruction of politics in the context of economic globalization. He argues that economic globalization is geared toward tourists' dreams and desires rather than those of the poorest locals. A parallel reality, he argues, is that the rich, the great, and the famous people of a society no longer aspire to pastoral power — that is, they no longer see themselves as shepherds of their flocks or their people. These trends influence the way by which governments position themselves to act in the context of globalization in achieving their social responsibilities.

Bauman argues that in the classical phase of modernity, legislation was the principal tool for setting the social agenda of a nation. Legislation provided the means for restricting unbridled choice by allowing legislators to make primary decisions on behalf of the collective and in relation to the responsibilities established in the constitution. Only after legislation could individuals exercise their choices. In the interest of individuals and their social needs, the lawmakers could then reduce the range of choices open to individuals by making laws that would provide incentives for the restoration of human dignity or disincentives for actions that could hamper such development. The legislators also had a second principal tool for setting the code for decision-making. That principal tool was education. Education provided codes of conduct and also established values that guided the exercise of choosing. Education was meant to teach the distinction between the right and wrong reasons for according preference to certain actions. Further, education would form in human beings the ethical inclination to follow good impulses and resist bad ones.

---

9. Zygmunt Bauman, *Community: Seeking Safety in an Insecure World* (Oxford: Blackwell, 2001), and also his *Globalization: The Human Consequences.* Bauman's political argument is espoused in his *In Search of Politics* (California: Stanford University Press, 1999), pp. 58-108.

However, says Bauman, political institutions everywhere are currently in a process of either abandoning or trimming down their role in agenda- and code-setting. This means that these two principal functions of political institutions are now being ceded to structures and forces other than political ones. Within the framework of globalization, the insistence on curbing the states' regulatory functions gives expression to this phenomenon. Those associated with financial and commodity markets find themselves operating in a context of deregulation in which issues related to human dignity and to societal agendas and codes are effectively ignored. This leaves political institutions stripped of any effective social agency to legitimate, promote, fulfill, and serve human values. Values related to the restoration of human dignity are not exempt from the impact of globalization on the deconstruction of politics.

Given this background, Bauman develops the idea that events in the political arena, and especially their effect on human existence, are compounded by the way in which economic globalization affects human life. Economic globalization, he claims, produces two kinds of life, the tourist and the vagabond. Tourists are those human beings with the means and ability to choose to travel because they want to do so. Vagabonds are involuntary tourists forced to travel because they have no other bearable choice. The real lifeblood of the voluntary tourist is the possibility of choice. Globalization is, Bauman claims, geared toward the dreams and desires of the tourist, not those of the vagabond. In terms of the argument of this chapter, vagabonds are those who require the restoration of their dignity. They are the poor and sidelined members of the human community. They represent people living in the squatter camps of South Africa and in the ghettos of the world. The reduction of options marginalizes the vagabond from the central activity of economic globalization, namely, the unfettered right to choose. Vagabonds are seen as flawed consumers, and as such useless to the global economy. They are also unwanted. So they participate in crime as a negative expression of their desperate wish to become like the tourist. Eventually, the vagabond learns that the tourist is actually dreaming of a world without vagabonds. Tourists seek ever more secluded destinations rather than places where vagabonds wander the streets.

The vagabond is now dependent on the philanthropists of the world. The pastoral role of the philanthropist has also changed significantly. Where they earlier stood as pastors or shepherds of the flocks of vagabonds, they now simply display their lifestyles as an example to be imitated. Like people in other parts of the world, South Africans are now faced with a risk-filled existence played out on the stage of globalization. This current reality comes on top of the former apartheid situation where people were stripped of their dignity through centuries of oppression and repression.

The Discourse of *Oikos* and Human Dignity

Economic globalization necessitates an additional discourse of human dignity.[10] I have argued elsewhere that the crucial theological discourse in the context of economic globalization is that of *oikos*.[11] The term *economy* derives from the Greek terms *oikos* and *nomos* (meaning the management of the *oikos*). The Greek term *oikos* is normally translated with the English term *household* but can also mean *community*. Apartheid threatened and largely destroyed the *oikos* by taking its point of departure from the supposed irreconcilability of different peoples. South African churches and the ecumenical movement declared any theological defense of such a system heresy and idolatry. The vast relocation of black people, the pass laws, and the use of the Babel narrative of the Bible to defend apartheid were rooted in the system's anti-*oikos* nature.

Economics is essentially interest in the *nomos* (the administration) of the *oikos*. Is it perhaps possible that we are now facing a single-minded interest in the *nomos*, one that has the capacity to threaten the very well-being of the *oikos* or even, perhaps, the existence of the *oikos* as we understand it?

The term *oikos*, in any of its forms, focuses attention on the notion of the worldwide household of God. As a theological metaphor, *oikos* supersedes the narrow vision that sees history as the central category of interpretation. It reminds us that history is bound up with community, with webs of relationships, with nature, and with life together. The *oikos* is a God-given place for living.[12] It enables relationship, evokes neighborliness and living for the other rather than for mere greed and self-interest. It has an ecological structure that displays boundedness and openness, independence and relationship, the familiar and the alien, rest and movement. The Hebrew Bible is permeated by the notion of *oikos*. *Oikos* is given in creation and unfolds in Israel. God's "house rules" are given to all humanity and also, in a special way, to Israel. Their aim is to sustain relationships and true humanity within the household.

10. The essay in this volume by M. Douglas Meeks also addresses this topic at length.

11. See my paper "The Oikos in a Global Economic Era: A South African Comment," in *Sameness and Difference: Problems and Potentials in South African Civil Society*, South African Philosophical Studies, vol. 1, ed. James R. Cochrane and Bastienne Klein (Washington, D.C.: Council for Research in Values and Philosophy, 2000), pp. 269-79.

12. See also the chapter in this volume by Esther Menn, pp. 161-78.

Above all else the house rules are meant to protect the humanity and the livelihood of the weakest and poorest in the *oikos*. For this reason the concept of Sabbath becomes an important part of *oikos*. It refers to the restored order of the household of the whole creation which permits all creatures to live and dwell in peace. God covenants with Israel, thus becoming the guarantor of the ordinances and life of the household. This is the meaning of the promise that God "dwells in Israel" (cf. Exod. 25:8) and that Israel is "God's house" (Jer. 12:7; Hos. 8:1). The New Testament likewise breathes the centrality of the key word. It opens with the claim that in Jesus Christ God dwells among the people. Where the Spirit is present the group becomes a household. This key word also points to the new status of the children of God: once slaves, they are now free persons, they are sons and daughters. In the *oikos* they eat a common meal. They pray together for that common meal. The first church is depicted as a household of shared and cooperative life. Again, the weakest, the exploited, and the poorest are preciously protected within the household. They all say: Abba! Father!

The heart of the doctrine of reconciliation is the restoration of the *oikos*. The idea of "the *oikos*" is at risk in the context of the global economy as its forces of fragmentation tear at the cohesion necessary for communities and households.

The initiation of and the active quest for an *oikos*-discourse worldwide is crucial in confronting global fragmentation. The household is not relevant only to issues related to families. It has its place in discussions and actions regarding gender equality, overcoming poverty and violence, and empowering the weak and exploited people of the world. The case for an "economy of community" — one that carries universal meaning — must be made convincingly in order to counteract the forces of fragmentation affecting human dignity. In this way the wholeness of creation and the wholeness of life as a gift of grace can be argued.

Discourses in themselves are important, but they have to happen within larger theoretical frameworks if they are not to devolve into abstractions. Such frameworks, which should allow for practices consequent to creating dignity, could be political, ideological, philosophical, or even theological in nature. I have undertaken the task of identifying a proper theological framework for a contextual theological anthropology with relevance to the South African context and to developments in other parts of the world.

H. RUSSEL BOTMAN

Covenant: Divine Initiative and Dignity

The three discourses of human dignity that I have discussed can be understood to correspond to the three dimensions of the economy of salvation: creation, redemption, and consummation.[13] The discourse of equality corresponds to the work of God the Creator, the discourse of reconciliation to the work of Christ the Redeemer, and the discourse of *oikos* to the work of the Holy Spirit that brings human life to fulfillment. At this point, I wish to ask whether there is a theological point of reference that can help to integrate these three discourses of human dignity and emphasize their interdependence with the economy of salvation. In the past, Christians have spoken of covenant as a mode of God's activity that spans the economy of salvation from creation to redemption to consummation. I wish to suggest, therefore, that covenant provides a useful vantage point from which to integrate the three discourses of human dignity and the practices that they entail.

It is true that recent attempts to revitalize the notion of covenant in the context of human dignity have been abortive. The idea of "covenant" has been ill-served by the World Council of Churches' Justice, Peace, and Integrity of Creation program (JPIC) since 1991. Whilst reclaiming covenant as its theological center, JPIC subsequently failed to rise to the theological and historical challenges of its time. The reason for this was not the option for covenant, but the failure of theologians and church leaders to embrace the integrative and universal dimensions of covenant. Ecumenically the failure resulted from an inability to overcome historical posturing, doctrinal stalemate, and theo-nationalistic ideologies in the interpretations of the concept. Covenant calls for a universal interpretation of God's initiative in preserving human dignity; it also connects human beings to one another, humanity to creation, and current generations to future generations. Covenant is the most universal and proper theological category for a theological anthropology.

In many parts of the world there exists a certain stagnation regarding discussions of covenant. The South African situation displays, on the other hand, a renewed interest in the theological possibilities of covenant.[14] Re-

13. Compare Michael Welker's contribution to this volume, where he makes an analogous suggestion that the economy of salvation can help to distinguish and coordinate different dimensions of human dignity (pp. 317-30).

14. One should also hasten to add that such a trend is also prevalent in the United States. I refer to three such examples: Max Stackhouse, *Covenant and Commitments: Faith, Family, and Economic Life* (Louisville: Westminster John Knox, 1997); William Johnson Everett, *God's Federal Republic: Reconstructing Our Governing Symbol* (New York: Paulist, 1988), also his *Religion, Federalism, and the Struggle for Public Life: Cases from Germany, India and America* (New York:

cently, three South African systematic theologians — Dirkie Smit, Willie D. Jonker, and I — have revisited this theme in relation to the history of apartheid (Smit),[15] the doctrine of election (Jonker),[16] and the European discourses of the sixties (Botman).[17] The covenant (or covenantal thinking) played a constitutive role in theological anthropology for Herman Bavinck, Karl Barth, Hendrikus Berkhof, and Flesseman-Van Leer, among others. Dirkie Smit's research looked at James Michener's argument[18] that the idea of the Abrahamic covenant was the theological foundation for the justification of apartheid. He concluded that such a covenantal connection with the Afrikaner identity could not be found in the historical documents he studied. Junker warns theologians to avoid the temptation to use the notion of "covenant" as a general principle for all of theology. Covenantal thinking, however, can, he asserts, be used properly when affirming the sovereignty of God, the relationship between God and God's creation, and the freedom and responsibility of human beings.

Covenantal thinking offers an important complement to the concept of humankind as created in the "image and likeness of God," which has played a central role in Christian tradition and which has proven influential in the formation of modern conceptions of human dignity. Arguably, the affirmation that God created humankind in the image and likeness of God forms the core of the classical Western doctrine of creation. Though biblically rooted in Genesis 1:26-27, the metaphor has served to integrate the themes of creation, the fall into sin, and the re-creation of humanity. Over time, the doctrine came to be closely associated with accounts of humankind's distinctive faculties and powers, which were construed as the unique divine endowment to humanity. In this form, the doctrine also proved influential for the formation of modern conceptions of human dignity. Because God created humankind in God's own image, possessing freedom and reason, human beings possess a dignity that must be respected by others, including the state. According to this reasoning, infringements on human rights amount to violation of image and therefore also of one's likeness to God. This would contribute to the affir-

---

Oxford University Press, 1997); James M. Childs Jr., *Greed Economics and Ethics in Conflict* (Minneapolis: Fortress, 2000).

15. Dirk J. Smit, "Covenant and Ethics? Comments from a South African Perspective," *The Annual of the Society of Christian Ethics* (1996): 265-82.

16. W. D. Jonker, "Uit Vrye Guns Alleen: Oor uitverkiesing en verbond," in *Wegwysers in die Dogmatiek*, by J. J. F. Durand and W. D. Jonker (N G Kerk Boekhandel, 1989), pp. 13f.

17. H. Russel Botman, *Jesus: Nóg God, Nóg Mens? 'n Kritiese Evaluering van die Evolusionêre Verbondmatige Christologie van H, Berkhof* (1984, unpublished).

18. J. A. Michener, *The Covenant* (London: Mandarin Paperbacks, 1991).

mation of the so-called "universal" human rights regime by the Western world especially after the Second World War. Reflecting the historical tendency to interpret the image of God in ontological terms, the human rights discourse employed terms such as indivisibility, inviolability, and inalienability to describe the anthropological grounding of human rights. These concepts are prevalent in the United Nations' Declaration of Human Rights and in the constitution of South Africa.

As an African I am interested in a theological category that will not only integrate the three discourses and practices of human dignity, but also take the ideas about human dignity beyond the ontological to the relational, and specifically the relationship with the vulnerable and with future generations. Here I believe covenantal thinking can be particularly helpful. An investigation into the history of theological reflection on covenant shows that such efforts often divide into two streams, one focusing primarily on the one-sided or unilateral initiative of God toward humanity, the other based primarily on the dual-relational meaning of the notion. Both streams have valuable contributions to make. The former helps us overcome the idea of a competition between God and humanity by giving priority to God's initiative and gift, which can only be received in grace, while the latter emphasizes the co-workership between the covenantal partners. Critical engagement with the notion "covenant" as an organizing framework for the three discourses of human dignity must resist the tendency to pit these two perspectives against each other. The foundation of God's covenant with humankind is God's unilateral initiative and grace, but this initiative makes possible a history of mutuality between God and humankind, between humans and each other, and between humans and the natural world. Seen in light of God's covenant, human dignity is both an irrevocable gift and a vocation to life in community with God and others. Covenant deals with actions as well as essence. It is about act and being.

In addition, if we are to appreciate its full significance, covenantal thinking must be developed with attention not only to its biblical and systematic but also to its hermeneutical dimensions.

The Bible is especially vigilant when vulnerable life is at stake. This is the origin of the idea of God as the *God of the helpless*. This is how we came to know God as the *father of the orphans,* the *friend of the foreigner,* and *defender of the widow.* When we, therefore, speak of the notion of life in relation to global economic realities, we should be unequivocal in our focus on the status of *vulnerable* life within the system.

Covenantal thinking finds the hermeneutical key to reading the Bible in God's commitment to life and to vulnerable life above all. From a creational point of view, especially before the introduction of sin in human history, one can extrapolate all kinds of abstract and universal speculations about life. It is even possible to join such speculations to a certain kind of christology that seeks to indicate that there is no *preferential option* or *special revelation* of God in which the poor, the widow, the foreigner, the exploited, and the vulnerable have a special place. God's preferential option for the poor is rooted in the conceptual and practical meaning of covenant.

The urgency and immediacy of the relationship between God and humanity is nowhere more profoundly expressed than in the idea of covenant. Covenant is the dynamic referential category that sustains anthropology theologically throughout the Bible. In God's covenant humanity is embraced and addressed by the promises of a loving God. In the connection of covenant-creation we learn that humanity is created for this relationship with God and that every human being shares that relationship equally with other members of humankind. In the connection of covenant-redemption we learn that the destructive powers of cruelty and injustice can be overcome in ways that do not simply perpetuate the cycle of violence but create a foundation for a new and more hopeful common life. And in the connection of covenant-consummation, we are inspired to envision a world where increasing interdependence is achieved not through the maximization of profit, but through bonds of mutuality that support and enhance the power of the world's many communities to foster and enhance human life, especially among the most vulnerable. Finally, human beings now represent God in the care of creation and the economy through covenantal living. God's covenant invites all beings into a relationship in which all creation participates.

By employing the notion of "covenant," theological discussion can supersede traditional theological loci by rooting its economic and political case for human dignity in a more biblical and progressive theological hermeneutic. A major step forward in the application of covenantal thinking within the global context was achieved at the 2004 General Council of the World Alliance of Reformed Churches held in Accra, Ghana. The General Council reaffirmed the Reformed adherence to covenantal thinking and reflected on its meaning within the context of economic globalization.

Conclusion

"Covenant" remains an important theological category for re-imaging human dignity in our times. Human beings are capable of entering into covenant with each other because they are covenantal beings by nature. Their dignity resides in the fact that God unilaterally accords to every human being the status of God's own covenant partner in creation, defends that status in re-demption, and works toward its comprehensive fulfillment in the future. Covenant is an anthropological reflection not only of what humans do but also of what humans are in light of God. As such, covenant provides a suitable metaphor for integrating the discourses and practices of equality (covenant and creation), reconciliation (covenant and re-creation), and *oikos* (covenant and fullness of life).

CREATION

Anthropology in an Evolutionary Context

JOHN POLKINGHORNE

By the publication of *The Descent of Man* in 1871, Charles Darwin made explicit what had already been implicitly present in the pages of *The Origin of Species* (1859). Humankind, he concluded, was descended from "a hairy quadruped, furnished with a tail and pointed ears, probably arboreal in its habits." This caused offence to many of Darwin's contemporaries by seeming to dethrone humanity from a special place of honor and significance, and so to be endangering the concept of human dignity by a reduction to the merely animal. It also sowed doubts in Darwin's own mind about the reliability of human reason. If we are no more than a recent twig in the burgeoning bush of biological diversity, what reason is there to trust our powers of thought? Why should they be believed to extend to making sense of the world, beyond the modest extent necessary to facilitate our survival within it? In old age, Darwin wrote to a friend, "With me the horrid doubt always arises whether the convictions of man's mind, which have been developed from the mind of the lower animals, are of any value or are at all trustworthy."[1]

In order to survive, human beings certainly need to be able to realize that it would be a bad idea to step off the top of a high cliff, but does this license us to trust in the abilities of Isaac Newton and Albert Einstein to understand the nature of universal gravitation, and so to comprehend the structure of the solar system and then of the whole cosmos itself? To interpret the experience of yesterday as a guide to dealing with the dangers and challenges of to-

---

1. Quoted in Michael Ruse, *Can a Darwinian Be a Christian?: The Relationship between Science and Religion* (Cambridge: Cambridge University Press, 2001), p. 107.

day is obviously a useful power to possess, but does this really license us to trust that Darwin himself could correctly read the tale of the development of life over many millions of years in the past?

Rather similar perplexities faced Darwin's rival in the discovery of the principle of natural selection, A. R. Wallace, though he resolved them in a different way. Wallace saw that simple survival necessity did not require the sophisticated intellectual powers that had been brought to birth in human civilization. In his case, however, this did not lead him to epistemological doubt. Rather, it encouraged Wallace to think that there must have been something unique, and transcending the merely biological, in the coming to be of the human mind. It will be the purpose of this essay to seek release from neo-Darwinian captivity to a reductionist understanding of what it is to be human. That quest will require the recognition of the many-layered context within which human evolution took place and the correspondingly rich and distinctive character of the human nature that emerged. In turn this leads to the insight that the world, and humanity within it, become fully intelligible only when they are understood as God's creation.

Problems of Scientific Epistemology

The anthropological issues arising from the work of Darwin and Wallace did not go away over the succeeding years. Today, any contemporary account of human nature will certainly have to set humankind in an evolutionary context, acknowledging hominid emergence from the ranks of our ape-like ancestors, with their "arboreal habits."[2] Yet an honest account will also have to acknowledge the peculiar status of human nature. In the spectacle of Darwin using the conclusions of his rational discussion of the record of earlier forms of life on Earth to cast doubt on human powers of ratiocination, we see someone who is in danger of sawing off the very branch on which he is sitting, as he muses on his intellectual perplexities.

The situation calls for daring rather than doubt. Without abandoning ourselves to epistemological despair, we can be postmodern enough to recognize that, in the aftermath of the demise of Cartesian confidence in clear and self-evident ideas, we find ourselves in a situation in which the enterprise of rationality calls for a certain attitude of bold commitment, going farther than

2. The rejection of literalist creationism (so-called) and the acceptance of a natural origin for the genus Homo does not, of course, imply the acceptance of a social Darwinistic interpretation of society.

what could be justified beyond any possibility of logical scruple.[3] At the same time, one can see that science, with its intertwining of interpretation and experience, involves the epistemic circularity of believing in order to understand while at the same time having to understand in order to believe. The fruitfulness of human rational enquiry strongly encourages the belief that this circularity is benign and not vicious — that it constitutes what may be thought of as a self-sustaining epistemological strategy in which human knowledge pulls itself into existence by its own bootstraps. The philosophical stance taken in this essay is that of a critical realism, trusting that carefully acquired and sifted knowledge is a reliable guide to what is the case.[4]

Why this should be so is a deep question. Clearly our human epistemic ability cannot be a logical necessity. The attempt to construct a Logic of Scientific Discovery can lead only to the emptiness of a Popperian theory of the establishment of falsehood, rather than to a positive philosophy of truthful knowledge.[5] A popular tactic of late has been recourse to the notion of an evolutionary epistemology.[6] Yet the arguments already considered show that if this approach is pursued solely within the confines of a biological context, it can offer a basis only for arguing for the validity of the simplest and most banal kinds of human knowing. An evolutionary epistemology might explain our ability to do simple arithmetic and elementary Euclidean geometry, but it would leave the vast tracts of abstract mathematical thought, in topology, group theory, and much else, as a mysterious and gratuitous excess. The great extent of that excess does not encourage the view that these extra mathematical powers should be understood as happy accidents, fortuitous spin-offs from more mundane necessities. Yet Goedel's theorem, with its conclusion that mathematical systems that are of sufficient scope to include arithmetic cannot be proved to be both complete (capable of settling every question posable within them) and also consistent, adds an apophatic gloss to the account of human powers even in this most austerely rational of disciplines. Our epistemic capacities are substantial, but not unlimited.

Consideration of human abilities to make persuasive sense of cosmic or biological history, and to penetrate the counterintuitive character of the quantum world, can only add weight to the argument that humanity's know-

---

3. See Michael Polyani, *Personal Knowledge: Towards a Post-Critical Philosophy* (London: Routledge and Kegan Paul, 1958).

4. See John Polkinghorne, *Belief in God in an Age of Science* (New Haven: Yale University Press, 1998), chaps. 2 and 5.

5. Karl R. Popper, *The Logic of Scientific Discovery* (London: Hutchinson, 1959).

6. Peter Munz, *Our Knowledge of the Growth of Knowledge* (London: Routledge and Kegan Paul, 1985); J. W. van Huyssteen, *Duet or Dual?* (London: SCM, 1998).

ing is a significant phenomenon that resists reduction to something much more commonplace. Moreover, human abilities for acquiring profound mathematical and scientific knowledge are deeply intertwined, for it turns out that it is mathematics that provides the key for unlocking the secrets of the physical universe, whose fundamental equations have invariably been found to be endowed with the unmistakable character of mathematical beauty.[7]

Nevertheless, in all this discussion there is an aspect of evolutionary explanation that is indeed pointing us in the right direction in relation to epistemic questions. This factor is the focus of evolutionary explanation on the character and process of this particular world, and the refusal to attempt the grand generality of a universal philosophical argument, valid in all possible worlds. That science is a successful activity of humans, in the profound and remarkable way that has been found to be the case, is, I believe, due to the specific nature of created reality and to our character as creatures within that reality. Ultimately it is theology, rather than philosophy, that will help us understand human participation in the deep intelligibility of the universe. I believe that ultimately science is possible because the universe is a creation and we are beings made in the image of the Creator.[8]

We have acknowledged that anthropological thinking today must take place in an evolutionary context. How that context is adequately to be understood is the critical question. In turn, answering that question depends upon a metaphysical decision about the nature of reality. If, as I have been arguing, human beings display abilities that go far beyond what can be comprehended in terms of purely biological categories, that is an encouragement to seek a more adequate, multidimensional understanding of reality and of the human place within it. At the same time, this wider view will lead to the recognition of levels within human nature going beyond those amenable to discussion in purely biological terms. It is this multi-layered approach to humanity that this essay seeks to explore. In the course of pursuing the point, it will prove possible to articulate a greatly extended and refined kind of evolutionary epistemology. To do so will lead us to the development of an argument "from below" for taking with the utmost seriousness the existence of the sacred reality of God. Thus an adequate anthropology will ultimately be found to be a theological anthropology.

7. See Polkinghorne, *Belief in God,* chaps. 2-5.
8. Cf. John Polkinghorne, *Science and Christian Belief: The Faith of a Physicist* (Princeton, N.J.: Princeton University Press, 1984), chap. 2.

Psychosomatic Unity

First, however, we must acknowledge that an immediate consequence of recognizing humanity's kinship with other animals through evolutionary descent is to reinforce the case for considering men and women to be psychosomatic unities rather than dual beings composed of a spiritual soul housed within a material body. In a famous phrase, we are "animated bodies rather than incarnated souls" — a conclusion that would scarcely have surprised the writers of the Hebrew Bible. Consideration of the effects on human personality of drugs and of brain damage (the latter classically exemplified by the case of Phineas Gage, the reliable foreman turned into an unreliable wastrel in the aftermath of a severe cerebral accident) can only strengthen the conclusion.

Acknowledgement of evolutionary origin should not, however, be used as an argument in support of an unthinking reductionism. The long history of life on Earth has been characterized by a sequence of the emergence of successive kinds of radical novelty. The initiating event was the coming to be of the first living, replicating entities, arising in the context of the chemically rich but inanimate matter of early Earth. The exact pathways by which this happened are currently unknown, but there is no reason to suppose that it was not a consequence of the astonishing self-organizing properties with which matter in our universe is found to be endowed, understood theologically as the Creator's gift to creation. There seems to be no necessity for the vitalist injection of an extra "special ingredient" to make this development possible, nor should we feel that we need suppose that God did not choose to act through the powers of nature that are expressions of the divine creative will. Yet from these observations it does not follow that a bacterium is "nothing but" an immense collection of elementary particles. Later, we shall see that science is just beginning to learn something about the detailed behavior of complex systems. In the course of this developing work, it is becoming increasingly clear that wholes possess properties indiscernible simply in terms of their parts, and that information (understood as the active specification of dynamical pattern, encoded in the whole) is likely to prove as important a scientific category as the energy possessed and exchanged by the individual constituents.

The emergence of novelty characterizes cosmic process as much as it does terrestrial history. The effect of gravity on small initial fluctuations turned an originally almost smooth universe into one that became "lumpy" with stars and galaxies. Nuclear processes within those first generation stars produced the missing ninety chemical elements that had been absent from a promordial world that was made up of hydrogen and helium alone. Thus were provided the raw materials from which eventually life could come into being.

Each contingent development in this stepped process of successive emergence gave access to possibilities that were wholly new. The principal theme of this essay is that the emergence of the human mind gave novel access to dimensions of reality that had always been part of the created order but that had not previously been open to exploration by biological creatures.

Nonreductive Emergence

Some forms of emergence are relatively unproblematic in terms of lower-order explanation. H_2O molecules do not possess the property of wetness, but it is scarcely surprising that when many molecules are brought together, the resulting adjustments and exchanges of energy between them result in a surface-dependent effect related to the whole, which the physicists call surface tension and which ordinary people experience as wetness. Other emergences, however, are of wholly different character, involving the appearance of qualitatively new kinds of phenomena, as when inanimate matter gave rise to life, or life to consciousness. However sophisticated the discourses of the neuroscientists may be about patterns of neuronal firings, there seems to be a deep and unbridgeable gap between talk of this objective physical kind and the simplest subjective experiences of feeling toothache or seeing red. To assert this is not to deny that the mental has a material substrate that sustains it — a sharp tap on the head with a hammer will establish as much. Yet a crass reductionism does not follow from this linking of the mental with the material, as if it were the case that "the brain secretes thought as the liver secretes bile" (Pierre Jean Georges Cabanis, 1757-1808), or that our joys and sorrows, personal identity and free will, are "no more than the behavior of a vast assembly of nerve cells and their associated molecules" (Francis Crick, 1916-2004). Such statements are scientistically imperialist and experientially inadequate, as well as being self-destructive, since the rational processes to which they claim to appeal for their support fall under the same reductionist dismissal as everything else.

Any just account of human nature must acknowledge the equal validity of its mental and material aspects. A Procrustean attempt to reduce the one to the status of an epiphenomenon of the other (almost always involving the demotion of the mental to being a side-effect of the material) is grossly implausible. Supporters of a psychosomatic view of humanity have to strive for an understanding framed in terms of a kind of dual-aspect monism, in which the one "stuff" of the world is encountered in the complementary polarities of the mental and the material.[9] This goal is more readily stated than achieved, but it is here that a twenty-first-century anthropology will have to seek to take its stand.

Human Distinctiveness

Humanity's evolutionary origins from among the animals do not imply that human beings are not to be distinguished in several significant ways from their biological cousins. There is a particular dignity that attaches to human life. The Victorian fear that acknowledging a hairy arboreal quadruped as an ancestor would imply that men and women are no more than monkeys come down from the trees was ill-founded and illogical. It was a striking example of the genetic fallacy, of confusing how things came to be with what they now are. In fact, the evolution of hominids was an emergent event of staggering novelty in the history of terrestrial life.

We know that there must already have been conscious life on Earth in the form of our ape-ancestors and other mammals. That emergence of consciousness is, in itself, something of a puzzle from a strictly Darwinian point of view. It is clear enough that the enhancement of the power to process information being received from the environment is of value in aiding survival. But why should this process be accompanied by the additional property of awareness? Indeed, the latter's implication of a preferred focus of attention might prove disadvantageous to the extent that it could hamper the processing of information arriving from other parts of the environment outside the limits of that immediate focus.

Yet the emergence of hominids brought something strictly new into the world, for the consciousness of our animal cousins seems to be different from human self-consciousness. In their case, consciousness appears to be located in the near present, extending in the case of the primates to being able to fore-

---

9. John Polkinghorne, *Faith, Science and Understanding* (New Haven: Yale University Press, 2000), pp. 95-99. Closely related to dual aspect monism, but subtly differentiated from it, is the idea of emergent monism (see P. Clayton in T. Peters and G. Bennett, eds., *Bridging Science and Religion* [London: SCM, 2002], pp. 107-20). As Clayton says (p. 116), the latter is "temporal and hierarchical" in its character, with the mental only eventually coming to make an appearance within cosmic history, but dual aspect monism is more even-handed in its treatment of the polarities. Many of the arguments given in what follows, such as appeal to the everlasting character of mathematical truth, support an approach that does not see mental reality as simply an emergent development. What emerged were mathematicians, not mathematics itself.

see simple consequences that follow immediately on present actions (throwing the stick may dislodge the banana). This falls very far short of the remarkable human ability to look very far ahead into the future, even to the extent of foreseeing our deaths very many years before they happen. This ability to use the future tense is part of what we mean when we say that human beings are self-conscious. Here is a human characteristic of singular significance, distinguishing us from the other animals. Many contemporary biologists are strangely insistent that there is nothing very out of the ordinary about the species Homo sapiens. Yet there are many distinctive qualities of human beings that make this an unsustainable position to adopt. Abilities that may be discerned in embryonic form in some of the higher animals are found developed in humans to a degree that produces a qualitative novelty.

Another distinguishing characteristic of men and women is that we are moral beings. Humans have ethical intuitions of right and wrong and they acknowledge, however imperfectly at times, the responsibilities that follow from these insights. Animals do not appear to be moral beings in this sense. Although some wish to use the language of "animal rights" as a way of expressing the respect that is due to the animal creation, that notion would need to be balanced by a concept of "animal duties" if it were to be used as a basis for the idea of a complete equation of moral and ethical status between humanity and other sentient creatures. When we read medieval stories of animals who have injured human beings being put on trial and sentenced for their misdemeanors, they strike us as grotesque and quite inappropriate to the different character of animal life.

A significant part of the richness of human self-consciousness is enabled by our ability to use the fertile conceptual tool of language. Interesting as the experiments are in which individual chimpanzees have been taught to manipulate and combine in simple ways a limited repertoire of meaningful signs, the skills conveyed (which seem to require much effort on the part of a human teacher) have only the faintest parallel to human linguistic abilities.

The use of language is one way in which human beings exercise their considerable rational skills. One consequence of this endowment has been the scientific enterprise, leading to human understanding of the nature and processes of the world in which we live. Another consequence, related to the latter but distinct from it, is the ability to explore mathematical truth, a topic to which we shall return in due course. Some animals display modest capabilities to count small numbers and to discern very simple kinds of logical association, but once again the differences in degree when compared with human skills are so great as to amount to differences of kind.

Human scientific and mathematical abilities are particular examples of human creativity, an ability yet more strikingly displayed in the activities of art, music, and literature. A significant aspect of such creativity is that accounts of its nature often do not locate it as being entirely interior to the human person, but speak of the experience in terms of the exploration of a reality into which the human enters, and in terms of a gift that comes to the artist from without. The realm of culture, sustained by mutual exchange within society, forms a distinctive setting for the transgenerational development of human life.

Theologians will also wish to point to the presence of a degree of God-consciousness in human life, that has led to the almost universal, if bewilderingly diverse, religious expressions of human encounter with that dimension of reality that may be called the sacred. There does not appear to be a counterpart to this that can be discerned in animal life. To this must be added the belief that human standing before God is relational, involving not only our consciousness of divine reality but also the Creator's knowledge of us and care for us as individuals. Herein is located the deepest dimension of human dignity. The primary source of the unique value of a particular human individual derives from the Creator's gift of the image of God, rather than from the degree to which that person participates in the general characteristics that distinguish the genus Homo. This theological insight serves as a corrective to any merely functionalist discourse about human nature. Human beings possess many remarkable capacities, but primary human status is not dependent on the degree of that possession, as we see from the worth of the lives of those in whom disabilities may have drastically limited the exercise of some of these capacities. Hans Reinders's insightful discussion of Kelly points us to theological anthropology as the only sure ground of support for the fundamental status of human dignity (see also Fraser Watts on the qualitative and absolute senses of dignity).

A second characteristic to which theologians will also wish to draw attention is human sinfulness. There is something astray with humanity, a slantedness in human life that leads to the betrayal of ideals and the frustration of hopes. There is a ruthlessness and greed in human striving that does not seem to be reflected in anything like so widespread a way in the animal world. Many animal struggles are intense (the challenge to the α-male, for instance) but usually they are not fought literally to the death, in the way that is so often the case in human rivalries for power. The history of crusades and inquisitions shows how readily human moral perceptions can become distorted, and the arts are not only sources of delight but also, at times, agents of corruption.

This brief survey has sought to indicate a number of significant respects in which there are important differences between human beings and our animal cousins. The argument has been a denial of the biologists' assertion that there is really nothing very special about humankind. Of course, it leaves the author open to the accusation of being a "speciesist," a charge that I accept if it relates to a belief in the uniqueness of the human, but deny if it implies not assigning proper respect to the animals. It is my desire to acknowledge the worth and value of the animal creation, but that seems to me to be of a different kind from the worth and value of humanity. That is why, for example, many of us would accept the possibility of culling a herd of deer in order to preserve the type at the expense of the death of some of the tokens. The intrinsic value of human individuals would make such a policy totally morally unacceptable in the case of Homo sapiens.

These distinctions have to be discerned empathetically, and the issues cannot be settled by crude genetic calculation. It is no doubt the case that human beings share about 98.4 percent of their DNA with chimpanzees, but the observation only exhibits the fallacy of genetic reductionism. These apparently small biological differences are correlated with immense metaphysical variation. The same is clear within humanity itself. After all, Mozart and I have a very great deal indeed of DNA in common (about 99.9 percent), but that does nothing to diminish the difference between a musical genius and an off-key whistler.

The Soul

If human beings are psychosomatic unities, the human soul cannot be a detachable spiritual entity, released at death. What then could it be? In fact, its role as the carrier of human identity is almost as problematic within life as it is beyond death. What could it be that connects the adult of today with the schoolchild of yesterday? Certainly it is not mere material continuity, for the atoms that make us up are in a constant state of flux, through wear and tear, eating and drinking. The "real me" that connects together present person and past child cannot be material, but it must be the almost infinitely complex, information-bearing pattern in which the matter of the body is organized at any one time. This surely is the meaning of the soul.[10] Here is an old idea presented in a modern dress, for both Aristotle and Thomas Aquinas would have endorsed the notion that the soul is the form of the body.

10. John Polkinghorne and Michael Welker, eds., *The End of the World and the Ends of God* (Harrisburg, Pa.: Trinity Press International, 2000), pp. 38-41; John Polkinghorne, *The God of Hope and the End of the World* (New Haven: Yale University Press, 2002), chap. 9.

Three comments may be made on this proposal as it is presented in the contemporary setting. The first is that the idea is consistent with what appears to be an emerging scientific recognition of the importance of the category of information. Complex systems are found to manifest astonishing powers spontaneously to generate large-scale patterns of dynamic order. This can be seen happening physically in dissipative systems, held far from thermodynamic equilibrium by the input of energy from the environment.[11] (All living beings are systems of this kind.) It can also be seen happening in computer-generated studies of the behavior of simple logical networks, started off in a random configuration but soon settling down to cycling through a limited range of very highly ordered possibilities.[12] An understanding of these phenomena will surely call for a way of thinking in which the familiar scientific descriptions based on constituents are complemented by accounts of the self-generation of order manifested in the behavior of the whole. Of course, the systems so far studied are of a trivial degree of complexity compared with even a bacterium, let alone a human being. A concept of information-bearing pattern that might begin to be adequate for an account of the human soul would require an absolutely immense generalization beyond what is currently within our ability to grasp. Nevertheless, the concept of information seems to provide a promising and fruitful direction in which to pursue thinking about the soul.

Second, the idea of the soul here sketched differs from a purely Aristotelian concept by being both more dynamic in its character (for clearly the soul, understood in this sense, changes as new memories are acquired and as a person's character is formed) and more relational in its scope (since we must surely understand a human being as existing within a network of relationships). The dynamic character of the soul also affords the prospect of incorporating within this picture an account of the human exercise of the will, and of the distortions of pattern that result from disobedience to divine intentions and which theologically are called sin.

Third, because the soul is embodied, being carried by the material body though not constituted by it, it possesses no natural immortality. As far as science can tell the story, the pattern that is a person will dissolve with that person's death and decay. Of course, this realization does not deny to theology the possibility of telling a theistic story that goes beyond the limitations of the scientific. It is a coherent and credible hope that the faithful God will remember the pattern that is me and re-embody it in the eschatological act of resur-

11. Ilya Prigogine and Isabelle Stengers, *Order out of Chaos* (London: Heineman, 1984).
12. Stuart Kauffman, *At Home in the Universe: The Search for Laws of Self-Organization and Complexity* (Oxford: Oxford University Press, 1995), chap. 4.

rection. In making this assertion, I want to affirm the intrinsically embodied character of the human being, without supposing that the flesh and blood of this world represents the only possible form that embodiment might take.[13] (Compare this with Linda Woodhead's discussion, and also with what Paul has to say in 1 Corinthians 15:50-57.)

Clearly, the ideas presented here are a mere sketch of how one might today approach the issue of the soul. The concepts discussed certainly need considerable further enhancement and development. Yet it is to be hoped that enough has been said to indicate that this essential element in Christian anthropological thinking is not one that has to be abandoned in the light of modern scientific understanding.

An Adequate Evolutionary Context

At last, we come to the central concern of this essay. All evolutionary thinking depends for its explanatory force on an adequate understanding of the context within which the unfolding process is taking place. Classical evolutionary biology is as much concerned with questions of ecology and environment as it is with issues of genetics.[14] It was the genius of Darwin to see how the interplay of individual capacities on the one hand, and contextual demands and rewards on the other, could bring about fruitful consequences.

Neo-Darwinian orthodoxy locates the evolutionary context solely in the physico-biological world in which a competition for resources is taking place. Although this approach provides many insights into biological development, the attempt to turn it into an explanatory principle of virtually universal scope has proved unconvincing.[15] What is insightful as a perspective on aspects of human origins and human nature becomes unpersuasive when asserted to be a total view.

The sociobiological account of the nature of ethics is a case in point. No doubt there are certain instincts present in human behavior as a result of genetic imprinting. No doubt the ingenious games-theoretic calculations that optimize the mutual pay-offs attainable in certain kinds of human encounter, shed light on aspects of prudential behavior. But prudence is one thing and

13. Cf. the theme of continuity/discontinuity in Polkinghorne and Welker, *End of the World*; Polkinghorne, *God of Hope*.

14. Holmes Rolston III, *Genes, Genesis and God* (Cambridge: Cambridge University Press, 1999).

15. Daniel C. Dennett, *Darwin's Dangerous Idea: Evolution and the Meanings of Life* (New York: Simon and Schuster, 1995); E. O. Wilson, *Consilience* (New York: Alfred Knopf, 1998).

true generosity is quite another. The kind of unreckoning altruism that leads a person to risk death to save an unknown and unrelated stranger seems to remain beyond the compass of purely Darwinian understanding.

Many other human characteristics also resist a purely biological explanation of their origin. We have already commented on how vastly our scientific powers to understand the universe (from quark to cosmos) exceed anything remotely connected with fitness capacity. Equally mysterious, from a Darwinian point of view, are human mathematical abilities. Why do they go beyond simple reckoning to include the exploration of non-commutative algebras or the proof of Fermat's Last Theorem?

To pose such questions is not to reject the possibility of evolutionary insight, but to insist that if it is to be at all adequate it must have a much more profound basis than unaided Darwinism can supply. Two significant generalizations are necessary for the attainment of a credible evolutionary anthropology.

The first is the need to acknowledge the existence of a much richer, multidimensional context for the process of hominid development than that considered by biology alone. Mathematicians are convinced that their subject is concerned with discovery and not with mere playful invention.[16] They see themselves as explorers of a noetic world of mathematical entities. In their view, the Mandelbrot set did not come into existence when Benoit Mandelbrot began to think about it — on the contrary, he encountered it. If that is correct, as I believe it is, human life is conducted within a noetic dimension of the mathematical, as much as within the dimensions of space and time of familiar physico-biological thinking.

Similarly, our ethical knowledge, at its root, is neither a curiously disguised genetic survival strategy nor a tacitly agreed convention of our society (as if we just choose not to torture children), but it comes to us from our encounter with the moral dimension of the reality within which we live. Similar claims should be made for the reality of the aesthetic dimension of human experience, and for the religious dimension of encounter with the sacred. Only an account of human nature that locates us within the multidimensional reality of our actual experience can begin to describe a context adequate for anthropological enquiry (see Michael Welker's discussion of the need for the wide embrace of a macro-anthropology).

Once these dimensions of reality have been acknowledged, the unique development of humanity becomes intelligible. No longer is it necessary to strain to explain away human distinctiveness by appeal to a Procrustean reductionism. Instead, we can recognize ourselves as we really are, because we

---

16. See Polkinghorne, *Belief in God,* chap. 6.

have an ability to interact with dimensions of reality to which our animal cousins do not have access. No longer do we need to tell ourselves "Just-So" stories, alleging that human capacities are really abilities to do things that are asserted to be quite different from what in fact we know them to be. We can take our personal experiences at the face value of their richness, because the context of our lives is correspondingly pluriform and potent.

The second necessary generalization of thinking relates to the recognition that there are other forms of drive to development in addition to the Darwinian process of selective survival. In the noetic, moral, aesthetic, and sacred dimensions of reality, the key concept is not survival but satisfaction, the delight that draws on the enquirers and elicits the development of their capacities. In these dimensions of reality, transmission of experience from one generation to the next does not depend upon the slow Darwinian process of differential survival, but rather is carried out by the swift Lamarckian process of cultural exchange and preservation. Once the hominid mind had developed to the degree of complexity that afforded our ancestors novel access to the additional dimensions of reality lying beyond the immediately physical and biological, these satisfaction-driven, culturally accessed processes of development were able to begin operating. No doubt the developmental plasticity of the human brain, with the consequence that many of its complex neuronal connections are not genetically hardwired but form epigenetically in the course of responding to experience, played an important role here.

The power released through the search for satisfaction is amply illustrated by the known history of human culture and the effects of cultural memory acting within human communities.[17] The attempt of quasi-Darwinian thinking to attribute these astonishingly fruitful developments to the mutual competition of the ideological units called "memes" is singularly unpersuasive.[18] The enticing power of the exploration of newly accessible dimensions of reality, together with the deep satisfaction that results from such an exploration, seem to provide a much more adequate basis for understanding.

Theological Anthropology

An extended and enriched evolutionary account of the kind sketched above can find its appropriate place in the project of theological anthropology. Two final comments may be made.

17. See Polkinghorne and Welker, *End of the World*, pp. 284-87.
18. Richard Dawkins, *The Selfish Gene* (Oxford: Oxford University Press, 1976), chap. 11.

One is that viewing reality in the light of the existence of God considerably enhances the intelligibility of the claim of a multidimensional context for human life, for belief in the divine Creator coherently ties together the various levels of reality into an integrated whole. The physical world is rationally transparent and beautiful, and its biological life breathtakingly fruitful, because it is the creation of a God who wills it to be so, as an expression of the divine mind and purpose. Human ethical intuitions are intimations of the moral reality of the good and perfect will of the Creator. Human aesthetic experiences are a sharing in the Creator's joy in creation. Our encounters with the sacred do indeed take place in the divine presence. This integrative power of theological understanding constitutes a kind of argument from below for belief in the existence of God.

The final comment relates to the ultimate context of human life, and of all creaturely existence. We live under the shadow of the Almighty. Human life will not be seen aright until it is seen in a truly creaturely perspective. Its fundamental context is *coram deo*, in the presence of God. The nature of human beings is such that we depend upon the grace and generosity of our Creator (see the contribution of James Mays and the remarks of Fraser Watts about gifts). The essence of freedom is a true response to the nature of reality. Illusions and Procrustean reductions are sources of slavery and causes of diminishment. The recognition of human heteronomy is not at all the acceptance of a menial subservience, but it brings humanity into the presence of the One "whose service is perfect freedom." Creation is not a zero-sum game in which creatures can gain only to the extent that they assert their independence of God. It would have been a pointless divine act if this were so. Instead, the evolving history of creation is an unfolding of the consequences of divine-creaturely cooperation, resulting in the continuing enhancement of the richness of reality. "The glory of God is a human being fully alive, and the life of humanity consists in the vision of God" (Irenaeus).

Cruising toward Bethlehem:
Human Dignity and the New Eugenics

R. KENDALL SOULEN

Writing in 1979, when the revolution in biotechnology was still more prospective than real, Hans Jonas declared:

> If and when *that* revolution occurs, if technological power is really going to tinker with the elemental keys on which life will have to play its melody in generations of men to come . . . then a reflection on what is humanly desirable and what should determine the choice — a reflection, in short, on the image of man — becomes an imperative more urgent than any ever inflected on the understanding of mortal man.[1]

A quarter century later, we are on the cusp of achieving the kind of power Jonas foresaw, the power to bring vast domains of human life once subject to natural necessity or fate within the scope of human technical intervention. The time has indeed come to reflect "on what is humanly desirable." In view of our expanding biotechnical power, the questions we need to ask include these: What limits should we observe in our efforts to remove causes of suffering and improve bodily performance? What is the place of health and illness in a morally worthy life? Above all, what is the telos, aim, or goal of life in light of which we can say what ought to be valued about human life, and what the role of health, body, and medicine in it might be?[2]

---

1. Hans Jonas, "Toward a Philosophy of Technology," *Hastings Center Report* 9, no. 1 (February 1979): 34-43, p. 41.

2. I draw these questions from George P. McKenny, *To Relieve the Human Condition: Bioethics, Technology, and the Body* (New York: State University of New York, 1997), pp. 1, 7.

To answer questions such as these, Christians and others might hope for help from the burgeoning field known as bioethics. Yet, as Gerald P. McKenny observes in his significant book *To Relieve the Human Condition: Bioethics, Technology, and the Body,* much of contemporary bioethics is of surprisingly little help when it comes to precisely the kind of fundamental questions posed above. The reason for this, according to McKenny, lies in a broader "transvaluation of values" that has occurred in Western society on issues of medicine, health, and the human body. Traditionally, McKenny argues, the practice of medicine took place within a larger moral framework that served to locate bodily health, illness, and suffering — premoral goods and woes of the sort discussed by Don S. Browning in his contribution to this volume — within a broader conception of a morally worthy life. Health was regarded as a good but not as the supreme good, illness as a woe but not as the supreme woe. Accordingly, the moral worth or dignity of a human being was by no means equated with his or her health or bodily excellence. Rather, human dignity was secured by a source that transcended bodily goods alone, and was therefore shielded from the indignities of sickness, disease, and, ultimately, death.

Gradually, however, the practice of medicine has been recontextualized in an alternative moral vision that assigns a more central and regulative place to health and physical excellence. McKenny calls this alternative vision the "Baconian project," after the early modern philosopher of science Francis Bacon (1561-1626). The Baconian project seeks to expand human mastery of nature in the name of a double moral imperative: to eliminate suffering and to expand the realm of human freedom and self-determination. The limitation of standard bioethics, according to McKenny, is that it is a product of this same moral vision, and so cannot gain critical leverage against it. As ever new issues arise, the agenda of standard bioethics remains predictably limited: "to safeguard individual autonomy, calculate potential harms and risks, and determine whether or not a just distribution will follow."[3] But when ethical reflection is confined to parameters set by the Baconian project, it is largely unable to address fundamental questions about the *goal* of human life which might *guide* and *limit* the use of biotechnological power. Even the Baconian commitment to human dignity, in a sense the deepest moral intuition of the Baconian project, has scant power to make good this weakness. For in the end, it seems, the concept of human dignity is surprisingly fragile in this respect: it can be robustly maintained only within the context of a vision of reality that revolves centrally around something other than and greater than the dignity of the human being.

---

3. McKenny, *To Relieve the Human Condition,* p. 8.

A Test Case: The New Eugenics

If Christians cannot assume that contemporary conceptions of "the image of man" suffice to meet the challenges of the biotech revolution, then they must thicken and transform these conceptions by drawing on theological and scriptural accounts of the goal of human life. As a test case, I propose to examine one aspect of the biotech revolution, namely, the prospect of a "new eugenics."

Today, advances in genetic science and human embryology permit an unprecedented degree of control over the process of human reproduction. These developments hold out the prospect of genuine benefits. In some cases, genetic disposition toward devastating diseases can be diagnosed and treated at the earliest stages of human development. But with these benefits come significant dangers, too, for with greater control over human reproduction, humans also acquire *new power to determine the kinds of human persons who will exist in the future.* While the coercive eugenics movement of the late nineteenth and early twentieth century has been thoroughly discredited, a "new eugenics" is today gaining advocates, on the grounds that science now allows a healthy, non-coercive form of eugenics that is practiced by caring parents in the context of a liberal state.

In what follows, I wish to sketch some broad aspects of the biblical witness that provide a context for evaluating the new eugenics. I then turn to the new eugenics itself, and conclude by making a more detailed case for why Christians should reject the new eugenics as a profound assault on the dignity of the human being.

Scriptural Witness: Descended from Adam, Elected by God

How and to what extent should we use genetic knowledge to shape the next generation? To answer this question we must know something about how to evaluate the reality of having offspring who will participate in the finitude and vulnerability of the human condition, and the significance of such participation in light of the ultimate purpose of human life.[4] Christians naturally turn to the Scriptures to provide some illumination on these points.

Taken as a whole, the biblical writings show intense interest in two features of the human condition, and an even more intense interest in their relationship.

4. Cf. McKenny, *To Relieve the Human Condition*, p. 207.

A first feature is that the human family exists as a *single community of common descent*. The Bible portrays humanity, like other creatures, as a single extended family that exists in a sequence of generations reaching back to the first parents and forward into the future. This aspect of the human condition is an often overlooked part of what it means to speak of the human being as *finite, limited,* and *vulnerable*. Like seasons of grass, humans exist in a sequence of quickly passing generations. Our character as "begotten" creatures encompasses the fact of our conception and birth on the one hand, our possible begetting and inevitable death on the other. It determines, in part at least, our identities as this or that unique person, depending on our place in the family tree. And it determines, again at least in part, our scope of future possibility, depending on whether and to what degree we receive from our near and distant forebears a goodly inheritance. Surprisingly enough, the Bible's interest in this feature of the human condition creates a certain commonality of interest with eugenics. Both exhibit a frank acknowledgement of the importance of *inheritance* in human affairs.

Yet for all its intensity, the Bible's interest in humanity as a single family of common descent is located within a still more basic preoccupation with what we may call *the divine election*. The Bible portrays the human family as appointed to a special vocation, goal, or telos. Over the biblical history this vocation is portrayed in diverse ways, as "image and likeness of God," "covenant," "child of God," and so on. But in every case the Bible has in view a benefit that is bestowed unilaterally by God and that consists centrally in vocation to fellowship with God.

As for the *relationship* between these features of the human condition, we note the following. First, they do not belong to such radically different orders that no interaction at all exists between them, as though God's election soared high above the messy carnality of human descent. On the contrary, God's electing work deeply engages humanity as a community of descent. For example, there is a profound connection between being a descendant of the first parents and bearing "the image or likeness of God." However uncertain we may be about *what* the *imago Dei* denotes (God's viceroy in creation, being-in-fellowship, and so on), there can be no doubt about *who* bears it: everyone who is a son or daughter of Adam and Eve (cf. Gen. 5:3; 9:6). The connection appears again in God's covenant with Abraham and his chosen descendants. And we see it again in the plentiful New Testament writings that identify Jesus Christ as son of David, son of Abraham, son of Adam.

Yet this first observation is incomplete and misleading apart from a second. If God's election engages the human family as community of common descent, it is equally true that it does so in ways that upset and transform the foreseeable regularities of natural descent in unpredictable, fundamental, and lasting ways. God's election repeatedly falls not to those who by reason of natural descent occupy positions of strength and superiority, but to the unlikely, to the unpromising, and, indeed, to those who could not exist at all by dint of the power of natural descent alone. God's election singles out the younger son, the weaker combatant, the aged woman, the one without form or comeliness. Moreover, God's election bestows on them a boon, benefit, or blessing that radically surpasses the goods of natural descent, even as it may in part include them.

Consider God's election of Israel. If God wanted a nation, he had no shortage of them. There were already seventy on the map, some with great achievements to recommend them. Yet God chose to start precisely at the one point where the flourishing tree of human descent had come to disappointing end: in the childless union of Abraham and Sarai. God's election of Israel as a carnal family thus cuts athwart the natural history of the human family and provides an enduring testimony that divine love rather than fortunate birth is the foundation of divine election.

In Jesus Christ, even this surprising testimony is deepened and secured in a surprising way. Jesus recapitulates the story of God's love *for* Israel *within* Israel, seeking out the least likely, the disinherited, and the sick, and accepting them in the name of God's electing love. He pursues this path so far that he finally suffers what by every human reckoning is calamitous defeat, dying a ruined king without court or progeny. In Jesus, so it seems, even Israel's spiritual inheritance comes to naught. Only then, on the far side of defeat, is Jesus revealed as the Beloved Child of God, in whom we see the all-inclusive breadth and depth of divine love. In Jesus, God places Israel's election on an indestructible foundation, and opens its blessings to all humans of every condition.

Eugenics: Origin and Definition

The origin of modern eugenics can be traced to Francis Galton, a cousin of Charles Darwin who coined the word in 1883. Galton defined eugenics many times, but the definitions were essentially "variations on a simple theme: using our understanding of the laws of heredity to improve the stock of humankind."[5] Galton held that while "no agreement could be reached as to absolute morality," "all creatures would agree that it was better to be healthy than sick,

5. Daniel Wikler, "Can We Learn from Eugenics?" *Journal of Medical Ethics* 25, no. 2 (April 1999): 183.

vigorous than weak, well fitted than ill-fitted for their part in life." Eugenics seeks "to give the more suitable races or strains of blood a better chance of prevailing over the less suitable than they otherwise would have had."[6]

Galton's vision inspired the creation of active eugenic movements in many countries including Great Britain, the United States, and Germany. Galton emphasized a strategy known as *positive eugenics*, which seeks to increase the number of people thought to possess superior endowments. "Some day," said Theodore Roosevelt in 1910, "we will realize that the prime duty, the inescapable duty, of the good citizen of the right type is to leave his or her blood behind him in the world."[7] Others embraced *negative eugenics*, which seeks to limit reproduction by "undesirable" individuals. Thus Justice Oliver Wendell Holmes, writing to justify the sterilization of Carrie Buck and her daughter born out of wedlock, declared famously that "three generations of imbeciles is enough."

By the late 1920s, countries throughout the Western world implemented negative eugenics policies with the aim of "cleansing" the national gene pool. Only after the Second World War did public opinion turn decisively against eugenics. The Nazis forged a link in the popular imagination between eugenics and the Holocaust by amplifying to a horrifying degree the coercive and racist elements of international eugenic policy. Until recently, there has been a broad cultural consensus that eugenics was flawed in principle and that no eugenics program must ever be implemented again.

The New Eugenics

Nevertheless, we may be on the verge of entering a new eugenic era. Unlike the old eugenics, the new eugenics does not stem from the successful propagandizing of a few advocates, although it does not lack for them. Rather, it seems to be emerging almost spontaneously from existing cultural trends.

One such trend is the growth of new kinds of scientific and medical infrastructure, such as molecular genetics on the one hand and medically assisted reproduction on the other (for example, in vitro fertilization or IVF). These new capacities are not inevitably eugenic in themselves. In principle, they can be employed in ways that respect embryonic life, health, and survival

6. Francis Galton, "Eugenics: Its Definition, Scope and Aims," reprinted in Francis Galton, *Essays in Eugenics,* intro. by Roger Pearson (Washington, D.C.: Scott-Townsend, 1996), p. 36.

7. Quoted in Jeremy Rifkin, *The Biotech Century* (New York: Jeremy P. Tarcher, 1998), p. 117.

— for example, through the application of gene therapy for correcting genetic defects in the embryo. Nevertheless, these developments can provide the basis for a new eugenics that is vastly more efficient than the old. The old eugenics could not intervene directly in the reproductive process. It operated clumsily by encouraging or discouraging couples from having children. Thanks to molecular genetics and assisted reproduction, it is possible to operate much more efficiently and directly on the coming generation itself. *Whereas the old eugenics selected parents, the new eugenics will select offspring.*

Another trend is the general liberalization of laws and public attitudes toward abortion. To put it bluntly, whereas the old eugenics had little socially acceptable recourse after conception had occurred, the new eugenics will be able to discard or abort human concepts that are deemed unacceptable.

Still another trend is contemporary society's reluctance to tolerate limits to personal autonomy and self-determination. The old eugenics operated in considerable measure against the grain of modern conceptions of freedom and autonomy. Early eugenicists appealed to duty and self-sacrifice to encourage couples to marry and propagate (or not), with eugenic ends at heart. Moreover, the old eugenics used coercive state power to achieve its ends. In contrast, the new eugenics harnesses the awesome power of contemporary notions of freedom. Eugenic decisions will be exercised by parents seeking what is best for their children in the context of a liberal state and its guaranteed liberties.

Taken together, these trends suggest we may be on the verge of a new era of "laissez-faire" eugenics. It will operate not through direct state coercion but through the cumulative effect of many private decisions by parents who have access to genetic information. As Gerald McKenny observes,

> The goal of an optimally healthy and productive population no longer requires suppression of the desire of some to procreate but now operates through stimulation (by means of everything from health information to advertising) of the desire of couples to have perfect children, through myriad forms of prenatal and neonatal monitoring and screening, and through the fear of having an imperfect child in a normalizing society that values persons according to their usefulness and that constantly measures their chances of success according to societal standards of success. Power no longer requires draconian policies but operates through our choices.[8]

The plausibility of such an outcome can be seen by taking a brief look at one emerging new technology that combines molecular genetics and medically assisted reproduction, namely, pre-implantation genetic diagnosis, or PGD.

8. McKenny, *To Relieve the Human Condition*, p. 206.

Pre-Implantation Genetic Diagnosis (PGD)

Preimplantation genetic diagnosis is a method of genetic testing and selection of embyros.[9] It involves the removal of one or more cells from embryos generated by in vitro fertilization (IVF) and analysis of the DNA from those cells. Up to ten embryos may be produced in each cycle of IVF, of which only two or three, which have the desired genetic profile, are implanted in the mother, using standard IVF procedures.

David S. King points out several reasons to think that if PGD were to become widely available, it would radically exacerbate existing trends toward the emergence of a "free market" eugenic society. First of all, PGD, by its nature, obliges parents and doctors to select two or three embryos from a larger pool (usually five to ten). The inevitable consequence will be the development (or exacerbation) of a "culture of choosiness." Parents and doctors will naturally seek to select "the best" embryos that they can find, according to the genetic information available to them.

In addition, PGD tends to erase the distinction between "negative" and "positive" eugenics, between avoiding diseases and conferring advantages. Since PGD requires embryonic selection, it will seem to be common sense to not only reject embryos that carry diseases (no matter how minor), but also to select those with the most advantages, within the limits of the available embryos.

Finally, genetic testing technology is becoming ever cheaper and more powerful. Initially, PGD was used to weed out embryos genetically linked to a few severe conditions such as Huntington's disease. But since the first drafts of this essay were written, its use has expanded. In July of 2003, doctors in Australia announced that they had used PGD to deselect embryos carrying a gene mutation for deafness (though neither of the parents were themselves deaf). It is reasonable to believe ever more genes and gene combinations with relatively major effects on a wide range of genetic predispositions will eventually be found.

The end result is that as PGD becomes more widely available, "parents will adopt a far more pro-active, directing role, choosing their children in a way which is not so far removed from their experience as consumers, choosing among different products."[10] How likely is it that PGD will become widespread? At present, a major obstacle is that retrieving suitably mature eggs for fertilization is painful and potentially dangerous for the women involved. Yet

9. In what follows I draw directly on David S. King, "Preimplantation Genetic Diagnosis and the 'New Eugenics,'" *Journal of Medical Ethics* 25, no. 2 (April 1999): 176-82.
10. King, "Preimplantation Genetic Diagnosis," p. 180.

new techniques are being developed for in vitro maturation of eggs. In five or ten years, it may well be possible to remove a small slice of ovary, containing hundreds of eggs, which can be frozen and matured at will. Some have suggested it may become common for young women to undergo such a minor operation early in life, so the eggs can be stored until the woman wishes to have children.[11] If oocyte maturation succeeds, "PGD may become the technology of choice for the conscientious couple who want to make sure they give their baby the best start in life. It will be relatively easy to market PGD as a way to ensure children's genetic health, and as a guarantee of a problem-free pregnancy."[12]

Is the New Eugenics Really Eugenics?

At this point, we may wish to ask whether what I have described is really eugenics. Some hold that it is not, claiming that the new uses of genetic science are different from the old for one key reason: freedom of choice. On this view, the problem with traditional eugenics was *coercion*. The new genetics is insulated from this by the barrier of parental choice. So long as genetic decisions are in the hands of parents, and parents are free to make informed and uncoerced choices, the new regime is something qualitatively different from eugenics and therefore free of its taint.

Of course, even if this claim were true, the new genetic science might still be eugenic in practice if not in principle. Numerous social factors militate against the reality of parental "freedom of choice," and are likely to do so for the foreseeable future. As Rowan Williams, archbishop of Canterbury, observes,

> Chatter of a certain kind about freedom of choice needs chastening by reflection on who is being served by particular models of freedom, since there is no possibility of talking usefully about freedom without looking at the way power is distributed in actual societies.[13]

At present, several factors skew the practice of prenatal screening and selective abortion toward eugenic outcomes. Such factors include (1) inadequate

11. H. Newton, Y. Aubard, A. Rutherford, V. Sharma, and R. Gosden, "Low Temperature Storage and Grafting of Human Ovarian Tissue," *Human Reproduction* 11 (1996): 1487-91; cited in King, "Preimplantation Genetic Diagnosis," p. 182.

12. King, "Preimplantation Genetic Diagnosis," p. 179.

13. Rowan Williams, *Lost Icons: Reflections on Cultural Bereavement* (Edinburgh: T&T Clark, 2000), p. 8.

insurance, social services, and employment opportunities for disabled children, or even explicit threats to withdraw health coverage if at-risk fetuses are not aborted; (2) implicit "directiveness" in supposedly non-directive medical counseling; (3) failure to acquaint prospective parents of a disabled child with other adults who actually deal with children with such conditions; (4) the very fact of routinely employing medical tests to detect untreatable conditions in the unborn child, which creates an implicit presumption in favor of abortion; and so on. The power of personal choice, and cultural bias, to shape the composition of human population is already amply documented by the selective abortion of female fetuses in many Asian countries, where the number of "missing girls" in India alone is estimated to be as high as forty million or more. If genetic testing for conditions such as deafness should become routine, one may reasonably foresee similarly broad eugenic impacts over time.

In any case, even if it were possible to insulate parental choice and remove all such skewing factors, the new regime I have described would still be eugenics not merely in practice but in principle. For, as we saw, Galton's original definition of eugenics did not imply coercion or the violation of parental self-determination. Indeed, Galton himself hoped that eugenic goals would be achieved through parental choice. The essence of Galton's eugenic principle is not coercion (nor, for that matter, classism or racism) but *selection,* preferring the existence of some individuals over others on the basis of desired or undesired traits. Seen from this perspective, *the new eugenics embodies the core principle of eugenics much more successfully than did the old.* It replaces clumsy and indirect modes of selection with vastly more powerful and direct ones. In this respect, the new eugenics is eugenics *par excellence.*

Christians and the New Eugenics

But if so, the question returns: just what is wrong with eugenics? Apart from the patent evils of traditional eugenics, such as coercion and racism, is there an intrinsic evil that clings to the eugenic principle itself? Not all think so. According to Jacques Testart, the process of selecting "the best" genetically endowed embryos from a given set will be "benevolent and learned, painless and efficient."[14] As for the charge that this process leads directly to the phenomenon of "designer babies," the bioethicist John Harris replies,

14. Jacques Testart, "The New Eugenics and Medicalized Reproduction," *Cambridge Quarterly of Healthcare Ethics* 4, no. 3 (Summer 1995): 304-12, at p. 304.

The best I can do here is repeat a perhaps familiar thought, namely that although this is often taken to be a difficult question and indeed the idea of parents being able to choose such things very often causes outrage, I have found difficulty in seeing this question as problematic. It seems to me to come to this: either such traits as hair colour, eye colour, gender, and the like are important or they are not. If they are not important why not let people choose? And if they are important, can it be right to leave such important matters to chance?[15]

Christians, I believe, do have strong reasons to believe that eugenics is deeply flawed in principle. Let me explore this from four angles, each of which highlights a point at which the logic of the new eugenics is fundamentally at odds with a biblically informed understanding of the human condition understood in light of God's election of humanity in Jesus Christ.

Replacement, not Redemption

Eugenics draws its moral authority from the fact that it can pose as a doctrine of benevolence, in sync with the Baconian project of reducing suffering and increasing well-being. Yet this appearance of benevolence depends on a conceptual sleight-of-hand or optical illusion, as it were. In reality, the core doctrine of eugenics does not seek to make people better or more fortunate.[16] Rather, it seeks better or more fortunate people. Eugenics prefers healthy people over unhealthy people, smart ones to stupid ones, and so on. To the degree that eugenics can be said to confer benefits at all, it does so not by *improving* the condition of those who are needy, but rather by *selecting for existence* those for whom life can be expected to go well. Even when eugenic interventions such as PGD are successful in their own terms, they do not cure any person's disease or raise anyone's intelligence or confer longevity upon anyone. Instead, they seek to bring about a world filled with people who enjoy these advantages from their beginnings. In this crucial respect, eugenics does not really require us to have hopes for our fellow human beings, to bear their infirmities, or to labor on their behalf. Rather, it requires us to exercise a preference for the sort of fellow human beings we will have, namely, the kind who will be least likely to trouble us with their infirmities in the first place.

15. John Harris, "Rights and Reproductive Choice," in *The Future of Human Reproduction: Ethics, Choice, and Regulation,* ed. John Harris and Soren Hølm (New York: Oxford University Press, 1998), pp. 5-37, at p. 29.

16. In this section I draw on Wikler, "Can We Learn from Eugenics?" p. 187.

Advocates of genetic technologies such as PGD frequently employ a misleading language of benevolence that softens or hides the selective reality of eugenics. For example, Draper and Chadwick write that one advantage of PGD is that it "enables couples *to maximise the advantages for their future child* but within the limits of what nature provides [i.e., the number of embryos they have to choose between]."[17] In reality, couples who use PGD do not maximize a child's advantages but give preference to the child who enjoys maximum advantages. The phrase "future child" does not denote a concrete object of loyalty whose condition is to be improved, but a job-description to be filled, as it were, by the best-qualified candidate. Apart from measurable genetic advantages and disadvantages, the available embryos are in principle interchangeable, like members of a labor pool. Glayde Whitney, an unabashed advocate of eugenics, is more candid when he defends the view that prenatal testing and selective abortion is "life-enhancing and life-giving, rather than life-destroying," on the grounds that

> Instead of suffering the agony and long term problems of a defective child, the pregnancy can be terminated and *replaced* with a healthy baby.[18]

Here the essential interchangeability of persons that remains hidden in Draper and Chadwick comes openly to the fore.

Interrogation for Existence, Not "Calling into Existence the Things That Are Not"

The new eugenics not only replaces rather than redeems or heals, but in doing so it must prefer some existing human beings to others. It therefore violates any conceivable form of the ethical principle that affirms equal dignity of each human being. God's works of creation and new creation may be said to *supervene* justice in the direction of gift, excess, abundance, and inclusion, "calling into existence the things that are not" (Rom. 4:17) and justifying the needy. Eugenic selection, in contrast, must be said to *contravene* justice by treating existing human organisms unequally, confer-

---

17. H. Draper and R. Chadwick, "Beware! Preimplantation Genetic Diagnosis May Solve Some Old Problems But It Also Raises New Ones," *Journal of Medical Ethics* 25, no. 2 (April 1999): 114-20, at p. 114; emphasis added.

18. Glayde Whitney, "Reproduction Technology for a New Eugenics," *The Mankind Quarterly* 40, no. 2 (1999): 179-92, at p. 184; emphasis added.

ring common blessings (continued existence) on some while denying them to others.

The injustice of eugenic selection is heightened because it violates the principle of equal worth not just *in extremis* but in principle. Human organisms are subjected to a kind of medical interrogation that is designed to determine the relative desirability of their continued existence. At present, the scope of such interrogation is still relatively limited, but in principle it could be almost indefinitely large, as Ted Peters points out:

> As the practice of prenatal genetic testing expands . . . we can forecast that the total number of abortions will increase, perhaps even dramatically. Each pregnancy will be thought to be tentative until the fetus has taken and passed dozens, perhaps hundreds, of genetic tests. A culturally reinforced image of the desirable child — *the perfect child syndrome* — may eventually lead couples to try repeated pregnancies, terminating the undesirables, and giving birth to only the best test takers.[19]

PGD and selective abortion has the potential to interpose a thoroughgoing regime of evaluation and control at the forechambers of human life.

Clearly, the objection I am raising bears not only on eugenics per se but also on the broader question of abortion, since I assume that considerations of inherent worth and equal regard apply to human embryos and fetuses. And indeed, I do believe that the same considerations that lead Christians to affirm the intrinsic moral value of *any* human being require them to acknowledge the same value in *every* human being at whatever stage of somatic development. If every human bears the image and likeness of God, and if a human being is a living organism whose parents are human beings, then embryos and fetuses too are bearers of the image and likeness of God, as surely as any newborn babe or tottering nonagenarian. Nevertheless, I do not think that it is necessary to agree with this last point in order to agree that eugenic selection gravely injures the principle of equal regard. The injustice of eugenics, it seems to me, should be evident to all who affirm the inherent and equal dignity of human beings *at any stage of their somatic development,* even if they think a human being attains this status only at (or after) birth. The whole edifice of eugenic decision-making rests on the strong genetic and somatic continuity that exists throughout a human life from its earliest to its most developed stages. *People who make eugenic judgments do so with respect to the relative fitness or desirability of the kind of human being a*

---

19. Ted Peters, *For the Love of Children: Genetic Technology and the Future of the Family* (Louisville: John Knox, 1996), p. 92.

given embryo or fetus is likely to become. The eugenic decision deprives selected embryos or fetuses of continued existence on the supposition that they will become people of inferior value, while disregarding the fact that they will also become (supposing they are not already) people who are bearers of the image and likeness of God, endowed with a presumptive claim to intrinsic and equal worth. And an action taken against an embryo or fetus *for this reason* is inherently unjust, regardless of the moral status that one accords the embryonic human life itself.

The Last Shall Be Eliminated, Not the Last Shall Be First

Eugenic selection not only violates any conceivable notion of equal regard, but it does so to the systematic disadvantage of those deemed most wanting. Eugenic selection holds that human well-being is enhanced by preferring the strong to the weak, so that, in Galton's phrase, "the more suitable races or strains of blood [have] a better chance of prevailing over the less suitable than they otherwise would have had." Eugenic selection assumes as a matter of course that the weak have little or nothing to contribute to the well-being of the strong, but are rather a simple liability, to themselves and to others.

Nowhere is the logic of eugenic selection more palpably contrary to the logic of New Creation. The God attested by the Scriptures is a God who chooses the least likely: Moses the stutterer, or David, the youngest of eight brothers, or the Suffering Servant without form or comeliness. In God's household, it is not only the weak who are dependent on the strong. Time and again, the well-being of the strong turns out to be dependent on those who by human reckoning are least. This prominent Old Testament pattern is further magnified in the New. We need only remember Paul's admonition:

> Consider your own call, brothers and sisters: not many of you were wise by human standards, not many were powerful, not many were of noble birth. But God chose what is foolish in the world to shame the wise; God chose what is weak in the world to shame the strong; God chose what is low and despised in the world, things that are not, to reduce to nothing things that are, so that no one might boast in the presence of God. (1 Cor. 1:26-29)

Ted Peters points out that a social by-product of embracing selective abortion might be increased discrimination against people who have disabilities, with the assumption that to live with a disability is to have a life not worth living.

117

Persons with disabilities find this prospect fearsome. They fear that the medical establishment and its supportive social policies will seek to prevent "future people like me" from ever being born. This translates to "I am worth less to society." The imputation of dignity to handicapped persons may be quietly withdrawn as they are increasingly viewed as unnecessary and perhaps expensive appendages to an otherwise healthy society. . . . Given the precedent set by Jesus, who spent so much of his time with the disabled — whether born blind or having contracted diseases such as leprosy — it seems that no disciple of Jesus could lightly acquiesce to the wholesale aborting of this group of people.[20]

To be sure, as Stanley Hauerwas points out, "the most compassionate motivation" may well lie behind the decision to abort, say, a child with mental retardation. "Such policies seem good because we assume compassion requires us to try to rid the world as much as possible of unnecessary suffering. Those born retarded seem to be suffering from outrageous fortune, cruel fate, that if possible should be eliminated."[21] Thus in the name of responding to suffering, compassion literally becomes a killer.

Yet to state the basic point: Christian faith holds that a human does not lose his or her moral worth or purpose in life simply because he or she suffers genuine afflictions such as mental retardation, physical malformation, or disease. Such conditions should not be sentimentalized, but neither should they be treated as insuperable obstacles that render a person unsuited to God's electing purpose. Indeed, paradoxical and offensive though it may seem, human weakness is often the very place where God's strength is revealed. McKenny puts it this way:

As a community formed by the story of Jesus' death and resurrection, the church deals with suffering in a way that both resists and challenges the world. Its willingness to live with certain kinds of suffering, even meaningless suffering, reveals the moral vacuity and even cruelty of a world that would eliminate suffering in part through the office of medicine.[22]

20. Peters, *For the Love of Children*, p. 93.
21. Stanley Hauerwas, *Dispatches from the Front: Theological Engagements with the Secular* (Durham, N.C.: Duke University Press, 1994), pp. 164-65.
22. McKenny, *To Relieve the Human Condition*, p. 167. Some proponents of PGD argue that the procedure is ethically warranted so long as its application is confined to screening embryos for such serious conditions as, for example, Huntington's disease or muscular dystrophy. In response, however, one must observe that while such diseases are indeed potentially devastating to those who suffer from them and to their families, they are not incompatible with meaningful, happy, and productive lives. Surely, a decent society's primary obligation in dealing with

Counting Traits, Not Beholding Name and Face

Eugenic screening and selection is obviously fatal to the deselected. But it also leaves its imprint on the selected. For the selected person now owes his or her existence to the possession of desired traits or propensities. However beneficial in themselves, these come at a high cost: the gifted nature of one's personal identity as a whole is mortgaged to them. The selected human being exists thanks to the calculation that the propensities he or she possesses will make his or her life worthwhile, for him- or herself and for others.

Eugenic selection fundamentally alters the character of the parent-child relationship. Children whose parents selected them for existence because of traits they are likely to exhibit can expect to undergo heightened parental scrutiny with respect to those traits (superior intelligence, health, athletic ability, and so on). Such children are more apt to wonder if their existence is welcomed unconditionally as an occasion of gratitude and joy, simply because they are, or if it will be assessed according to success in conforming to parental expectations. We are already familiar with adoptive parents who have sued adoptive agencies for placing children with unknown or undisclosed medical problems. Eugenic selection opens up the real prospect that similar lawsuits might be brought when pregnancies result in biological children whose selected traits and propensities fail to meet expectations.[23]

Moreover, if, as eugenics holds, it is permissible and even desirable to eliminate those who will eventually suffer from certain undesirable conditions, then it becomes hard to understand why actually existing persons (those selected for existence) should rationally wish to go on living in the event that they are overtaken by those same diseases or conditions. For it seems inevitable that the logic that applies to embryos in view of their anticipated future lives would apply to the lives themselves as they actually unfold.

---

such devastating illnesses is to assist those who suffer from them by seeking treatments and cures, thereby honoring the intrinsic good of such lives. By contrast, a society that embraces PGD and selective abortion as morally acceptable "treatments" for these conditions effectively declares its belief that the burden imposed by the disease outweighs the good of the lives of those who suffer from them. In such a society, it is reasonable to fear, the will to invest the resources necessary to find cures for persons living with such diseases would be undermined.

23. In March 2006 the Ohio Supreme Court heard the case of a couple who brought suit because they were mistakenly informed by their doctor that their unborn child did not have a genetic condition the mother carried, on the grounds that they would have aborted had they known. On the virtues of parenting and the use of reproductive technology and genetic intervention, see especially the insightful work of Sondra E. Wheeler, "Contingency, Tragedy, and the Virtues of Parenting," in *Beyond Cloning,* ed. Ronald Cole-Turner (Harrisburg, Pa.: Trinity International, 2001), pp. 111-23.

If, however, it is correct to protest that a person's dignity persists despite being overtaken by disease or accident, then these protestations apply equally to those not yet born.[24]

By weighing traits rather than beholding name and face, eugenics embodies a crude utilitarian reversal of the form of prophetic call story. In the prophetic call, God transcends the limitations of *what kind* of person one is ("only a child," poor speaker, and so on) by knowing and calling a person *by name* (Jer. 1). The prophet's *what* is beheld in light of the prophet's *who,* and the prophet's *who* is beheld in light of God's call. In contrast, in the eugenic "call story," a person's *who* is subordinated from the earliest beginnings of existence to the person's *what.* Of course, the Scriptures too frequently depict humans in terms of their different kinds: male, female, Jew, Gentile, old (i.e., frail and dependent), young (i.e., vigorous and healthy), and so on. Moreover, the advent of the New Creation in Christ and the Spirit does not simply do away with humans in their kinds. Yet in light of the New Creation it appears that persons *of every kind* are acceptable before God, and that what was formerly true of the prophet is true of everyone in Christ. God beholds *what* we are in light of *who* he calls us to be in Jesus Christ.

There is nothing inevitable about the new eugenics. Even at the height of its popularity in the 1920s, the old eugenics failed to win official endorsement in some countries such as Poland and Czechoslovakia, "largely because of the influence of the Catholic Church. The church opposed eugenics in principle (and was virtually the only institution to do so)."[25] And ultimately, of course, all other Western countries also repudiated eugenics with deep revulsion. Today, too, there are signs that some countries are thinking seriously about how to embrace the promise of genetics and fertility science without opening the door to a new eugenics.[26] Christians will not be the only people who oppose a new eugenic chapter of human history, but they have special reason to be among those who do.

---

24. For an illuminating sifting of these issues with respect to end-of-life debates, see Timothy P. Jackson's helpful essay "A House Divided, Again: Sanctity vs. Dignity in the Induced Death Debates," in *In Defense of Human Dignity,* ed. Robert P. Kraynak and Glenn Tinder (Notre Dame, Ind.: Notre Dame University Press, 2003), pp. 139-64.

25. Wikler, "Can We Learn from Eugenics?" p. 185.

26. In March 2004, Italy enacted legislation designed to ensure that IVF techniques are used in ways that balance parental desire for children with respect for all embryonic human life. Among other provisions, it prohibits the genetic screening of embryos for purposes of selection, limits to three the number of eggs that doctors may gather and fertilize, and requires that all three be implanted in the prospective mother's womb.

Human Dignity in the Absence of Agency

HANS S. REINDERS

Introduction

Let me introduce you to Kelly, a young girl whom I encountered a number of years ago in an institution for people with mental disabilities. Kelly is endowed with very little mental capacity to live her life as a human being. At birth she was diagnosed as micro-encephalic, meaning that a significant part of the normal brain was missing. Kelly is what some people prefer to call a "vegetable."

The first time I visited the group where Kelly lives, I found a twelve-year-old-girl with beautiful red hair and big brown eyes, sitting in a wheel-chair, "staring without seeing," as was my first reaction. I asked the staff a few things about her and was invited to stay for the afternoon in order to get an impression of how she lived. So I stayed. I noticed that the nurses around her never spoke of Kelly as if she were a "vegetable." For them Kelly was simply Kelly, who could be just as "happy" or "sad" as any other human being. The view that leads others to speak of human beings in her condition as "vegetables" was not completely alien to the institution where she lives, however. This I inferred from what the director of this institution told me about her condition when she was a little baby:

> When Kelly was still a baby, the only thing she seemed capable of doing was taking a deep breath now and then. In her case we did not think of "sighing" as if she were lamenting her condition, but assumed her taking a deep breath was only a respiratory reflex. We thought this until somebody

noticed that it depended on who spoke to her. When she was spoken to by particular voices, the changing respiration pattern stopped. Once the voice stopped, she started again. Thank heavens! At last she could do something, even if it was only "sighing." Our Kelly turned out to be human.

The guiding idea in assessing Kelly's condition was, presumably, that in order to be truly human one has to be capable of at least *doing* something, even if it is only as little as responding to a voice by taking a deep breath. The relief that the director testified in this connection is very significant, I think, because it indicates a sense of awkwardness. It is the sense of awkwardness that reflective people in our society feel in thinking about human beings such as Kelly. Suppose that Kelly had not been capable of something as minimal as "sighing," how could she then be called "human" other than in a vegetative sense?

Given the sensibilities of our secular moral culture, the question of what it means to be human raises all kinds of vexing questions in the face of profoundly disabled people like Kelly. This is especially true when the disabling condition is such that we doubt to ascribe "being a self" to the person. If we follow the moral presuppositions of our culture, the notion of a person does not even seem to apply. That notion presupposes the capacity of being aware of ourselves, even if only in a limited sense. Human lives, in our culture, are lives of subjects with a potential for being meaningful to them. Human lives are lived "from the inside."

These reflections suggest that, given the presuppositions of our moral culture, only lives that meet the conditions of self-referentiality and subjectivity can be properly called "human."[1] Within this culture, the point of being a subject is that one has at least a conception of what it is to be "oneself." That conception being absent, one's humanity is questionable — not in the biological sense, of course, but in the moral sense. Once one's *humanity* is questionable in the moral sense, however, so is one's dignity, because dignity is ascribed to human persons, not merely to human beings.

This essay addresses the question how to think theologically about human beings like Kelly. If human beings like her are to be dignified, then the ground of this dignity cannot be found in human agency, unless one wants to accept a "different" kind of human dignity for a "different" kind of human being. The theological task, then, is to think about human dignity in the face of people like Kelly in a way that avoids the implication of an anthropological

1. See Hans S. Reinders, "Mental Retardation and the Quest for Meaning: Philosophical Remarks on 'The Meaning of Life' in Modern Society," in *Meaningful Care: A Multidisciplinary Approach to the Meaning of Care for People with Mental Retardation,* ed. Joop Stolk, Theo A. Boer, and R. Seldenrijk (Dordrecht: Kluwer, 2000), pp. 65-84.

"minor league." This requires that the presuppositions of our moral culture are overturned to the extent that they deny Kelly a share in our humanity. From a Christian point of view this denial cannot but mean that she is denied as a creature of God. While for many Christians the denial will be intuitively objectionable, as it should be, it is by no means clear what to say positively about Kelly's humanity.

A Theological Approach to the Question

How do we speak theologically about human dignity with regard to someone like Kelly? The question forces us to think about the characteristically human that is implied in that notion. For whatever human dignity may mean, it must have something to do with what we consider to be special about humans. So what is it?

Initially the answer to that question may appear to be quite simple. "Being human" is defined by the fact that one is born out of human beings, as the Roman Catholic Church teaches. To define the characteristically human solely in terms of biological origin, however, is not sufficient for a theological anthropology. This requires a more demanding answer, one that includes not only the origin but also the destiny of human beings. After all, Christians do not simply believe in God; they believe in God the Father, and the Son, and the Holy Spirit. The Trinitarian understanding of God entails both the beginning and the end, Alpha and Omega, protology and eschatology. To speak of the former is to speak of the latter. To be a creature is to be created, and to be created is to be created with a purpose. That is why our destiny as humans is not a *donum superadditum* — something that is added to a subsistent being.[2] This implies that theological anthropology cannot explain what it is that dignifies human beings without referring to both their origin and their destiny. What the Christian faith tells us about our final destiny, that we will be resurrected with Christ, is intended in the beginning. And what it tells us about our origin, that we are created in the image of God, is consummated in the end.[3] All of which is to say that theological anthropology as it is understood here, must be grounded in the Christian narrative as it is found in Scripture.

2. Cf. Martien E. Brinkman, *The Tragedy of Human Freedom: The Failure and Promise of the Christian Concept of Freedom in Western Culture* (Amsterdam: Rodopi, 2003), p. 32.

3. Here I am referring implicitly to Karl Barth's famous dictum of how the covenant between God and man is the inner ground of creation, whereas creation is the external ground of the covenant. Karl Barth, *The Doctrine of Creation*, vol. 3 of *Church Dogmatics*, trans. G. Bromiley (Edinburgh: T&T Clark, 1958), part 1, § 41.

But even on its own account the biological answer is not sufficient to answer our question. This is clear when we ask what it is that makes human beings special. From classical antiquity the biological answer to that question has been that the human being is a "rational animal." As a matter of fact it is quite obvious that from the point of view of biology human beings such as Kelly cannot but be characterized as "defective" because they do not fit the description of the Homo sapiens. Whatever one may want to say about Kelly, she is not a "rational animal."

Can a theological account succeed in avoiding such qualifications? It occurs to me that in order to succeed, theological explanation cannot proceed from the presuppositions of our contemporary moral culture. It cannot proceed, that is to say, from a description of the necessary conditions of what distinguishes human beings from other beings in order to declare these conditions to be the ground for human dignity.

A theological anthropology that is grounded in Scripture should follow none of these steps. Giving the preferred set of necessary conditions for being "human" espoused by our moral culture — the conditions that constitute moral selves — that culture has no grounds left to reject the view that people who fail to be "moral selves" can be considered human only in a marginal sense. The problem is revealed by its spatial metaphor of "marginal cases," which implies that some human beings are more human than others, and some may even be considered not human at all. Since this strategy dominates most of modern moral philosophy, it will have a hard time recognizing the humanity of people such as Kelly.

Theological anthropology, in my view, does not proceed this way because it has a different point of reference. Its point of reference is the belief that we are God's children because he is our loving Father. From the point of view of Christianity — a viewpoint shared with Judaism and Islam — our humanity is given, not in the sense of *data* but as *donum*.

Nor is there any need for theological anthropology to proceed in this way, we should add. Theologically speaking, our humanity is received as a gift before it is anything else, which is something human beings like Kelly share with the rest of us. This is what theology has to explain, which it cannot do if it also starts with defining the human by means of biological, psychological, or philosophical description. Christians believe — again, together with Jews and Muslims — that all human beings are created in the divine image. They do not believe that God created only some human beings in his image. To put it briefly, but not inaccurately, Christians claim that in the loving eyes of God the Father there are no marginal cases of being "human."

But theology, as I understand it, does not need to refute philosophical understanding. It has its own logic, depending on the story of the God of Israel who came to be acclaimed by Jesus as his Father. Theological understanding is couched in narrative, not in philosophical conceptualization or classification.

Defending a distinctive theological approach to the question of what it means to be human, however, one must expect an objection, namely, that the truth about human nature cannot be claimed for a particular religious tradition. What is true about human nature should at least be accessible to all human beings. That rules out any reference to particular sources of knowledge to understand the meaning of "being human."

I am not inclined to take this objection very seriously. First of all, answering the question of what constitutes our human dignity from the perspective of biblical faith in no way rules out that what is claimed holds true for all human beings. It does rule out, however, the possibility of establishing this truth independently from that faith. Second, the fact that many people do not believe the basic tenets of the Christian religion to be true does not imply that they cannot be adequately explained to them. There is a distinction between explanation and justification. People may see what you mean without accepting that what you mean is true. Third, this epistemic condition holds for any other approach to our question as well. To answer the question about human nature from the perspective of, say, evolutionary biology in no way rules out that what is claimed in that regard holds true for all human beings. It also does not rule out that its tenets can be adequately explained to those who doubt the truth of evolutionary biology. But it does rule out that this truth can be established independently from the philosophical presuppositions of evolutionary biology.

The Image of God in the History of Western Theology

Keeping these preliminary thoughts in mind, where to start? The answer to this question is fairly obvious. If there is a single notion in Christian theology that resists deferring particular human beings to an anthropological "minor league," it surely must be the notion that all human beings are created in the image of God. As the history of this doctrine shows, however, theological reflection has always been tempted to explain the divine image in terms of individual human capacities and faculties.[4] Unsurprisingly, the powers of reason

---

4. Berkhof claims that the tradition has by and large explained the image in terms of a "static-idealistic-individualistic conception of man." Hendrikus Berkhof, *Christian Faith: An Introduction to the Study of the Faith,* trans. Sierd Woudstra (Grand Rapids: Eerdmans, 1979), p. 180.

and the will have frequently served as the prime candidates for the "seat" of the image.[5] It is not at all clear, therefore, that the theological tradition on the meaning of *imago Dei* is helpful with regard to our question.

Contrary to what some might expect, this verdict holds true also for the Protestant tradition, despite the fact that it is known for its insistence on a "relational" rather than a "substantial" view of the image. The issue between Protestantism and Roman Catholicism has been, of course, the question of how "nature" relates to "grace." One way to pose that question is this: are our human capacities to be valued because they allow us to receive the gift of grace, or does the gift of grace expose the esteem for our human capacities as the source of our sinfulness? On this issue the Roman Catholic tradition defined its position by saying that grace does not eliminate human nature but makes it more perfect: *gratia non tollit naturam sed perficit*. Human capacities obviously deserve to be kept in high esteem, a view that returns in Roman Catholic thought in the knowledge of God as the ultimate end of human beings.[6]

In contrast, the Protestant tradition has by and large always understood the question of "nature" and "grace" in terms of opposition rather than continuity. There is nothing in fallen human beings that qualifies them for receiving the grace of God, because only God overcomes human sinfulness. Consequently, our human capacities cannot be the mark of our worth before God. As it is often put: the coordinates of Protestant theology are "sin" and "grace" rather than "nature" and "grace."

Outside the context of human salvation, however, matters often appeared to be different. Regarding the powers of reason and the will, classical Protestant sources spoke of *reliquiae*, "remnants" or "vestiges," particularly with regard to morality.[7] In spite of the claim that, soteriologically speaking, the elevation of human capacities was the mark of sinfulness, these capacities often reappeared on the stage in a more positive tone as soon as the possibil-

5. Fletcher, for example, understood the divine image to refer to the capacities for "intelligent causal action." See Joseph Fletcher, *Morals and Medicine* (Boston: Beacon, 1954), p. 218. That Fletcher stood in a long tradition in this respect is shown in D. J. Hall, *Imaging God: Dominion As Stewardship* (Grand Rapids: Eerdmans, 1986), pp. 89-98.

6. For a recent specimen of this thought see Josef Pieper, *Happiness and Contemplation*, introduction by Ralph McInerny (South Bend, Ind.: St. Augustine's Press, 1998).

7. See Gerrit C. Berkouwer, *Man: The Image of God* (Grand Rapids: Eerdmans, 1962), pp. 117-47. Berkouwer shows how the Protestant confessions maintained the notion of "remnants" in relation to the knowledge of good and evil in civil life. See also E. Brunner, *Der Mensch im Widerspruch* (Zürich: Zwingli Verlag, 1937), pp. 94-98, 154. According to Brunner, not only Luther himself but also Melanchthon and Calvin spoke of *reliquiae* in connection with the *lex naturalis*. Further, see Hall, *Imaging God*, p. 222, fn. 34.

ity of ethics was considered.[8] While the doctrine of salvation invoked the possibility that the divine image had been lost in the fall, that very possibility was regarded as implausible with regard to the moral life. Accordingly, the notion of "remnants" provided the ground for distancing anthropology and ethics from soteriology. The argument was that the fall had robbed human beings of their relation with God but had not eliminated their humanity. After the fall, the capacity for taking moral responsibility remains intact.[9]

Whatever the correct explanation of this theological state of affairs may be, the point to be kept in mind here is simply that with regard to theological anthropology the Christian tradition has by and large adhered to an anthropology of individual capacities and faculties.[10] Since that anthropology does not have much to say for those human beings who are lacking in individual capacities and faculties, the question is how this tradition can repair its own inadequacy at this point.[11]

That it needs to be repaired can hardly be a matter of dispute, in my view. Given the presuppositions of our moral culture, many of our contem-

---

8. The exception to this rule is Karl Barth, who developed his conception of Christian ethics as obedience to God's word ("das Gebot der Stunde"), which presupposes an actual relationship with him. Barth's conception never gained much support in Protestant ethics. The same is true for Barth's interpretation of the *locus classicus* for the divine image — Genesis 1:26-27 — in terms of an analogy of the relation between God and man on the one hand and the relation between men and women on the other. See Hans S. Reinders, "Imago Dei As a Basic Concept in Christian Ethics," in *Holy Scriptures in Judaism, Christianity and Islam: Hermeneutics, Values and Society,* ed. Hendrik M. Vroom and Jerald D. Gort (Grand Rapids: Eerdmans, 1995), pp. 187-204.

9. Hall, *Imaging God,* p. 100 (especially fns. 33 and 34). The notion of *vestigia* in fact continued the theological tradition that since Irenaeus of Lyon had distinguished between "similitudo" and "imago" — the Latin translation of the Hebrew phrase *tselem wa demut* of Genesis 1:26-27 — saying that in the fall we lost the former but not the latter. In this way the Western tradition created anthropological space to talk about human nature independently from the work of Christ.

10. Cf. Hall, *Imaging God,* p. 89, where he writes: "A long and influential tradition of Christian thought looks upon the *imago dei* as referring to something inherent in *homo sapiens.* Humankind in God's image, according to this view, means that as it is created by God, the human species possesses certain characteristics or qualities that render it similar to the divine being." The underlying concept was that of human nature as a particular kind of substance. Hence the notion of a "substantialistic concept of *imago Dei*" (p. 89).

11. Cf. Brinkman, *The Tragedy of Human Freedom,* p. 31, who brings out the implication: "Thus both the Protestant and the Roman Catholic tradition recognize a central continuity with respect to fallen human beings remaining human. The fallen human person has not become an animal." From the perspective of the *animal rationale,* Kelly is merely an animal. This conclusion is inevitable when the individual capacities of reason and freedom are identified as the *continuum* of the human.

poraries doubt the humanity of human beings like Kelly. But for Christians, I take it, the decisive question is how we are seen in the loving eyes of God, regardless of what our moral culture tells us about ourselves. Consequently, any view implying that only some but not all human beings have been created in God's image must for that very reason rest on a theological mistake. To accept any such view would be to accept that the existence of mentally disabled human beings is a creational error. To my knowledge the Christian tradition has never endorsed this possibility, which means that there is reason to look for a theological conception that neither entails nor allows it.[12]

The possibility of repair will be explored by looking at recent accounts of Trinitarian theology that rethink the classical doctrine not as a piece of theological metaphysics but as part of the biblical narrative. The outstanding feature of these attempts is that they ground the Christian understanding of personhood in the story of the Father, Son, and Holy Spirit. I will explore what this development in Trinitarian thought implies for our understanding of human dignity.[13]

The Turn to Inwardness[14]

The elevation of the powers of reason and the will as the characteristically human has been the hallmark of Western thought since its inception in ancient Greece. But there is a peculiar twist to this tradition that identified the powers of reason and the will as constituting the individual self. Consequently, the tradition of the West embarked on a course that located the characteristically human in an inner space. This development was inspired by Augustine's psy-

12. In this connection Martin Luther is frequently mentioned as the proverbial exception to this rule, because he once suggested to the prince of Sachsen Anhalt that an apparently mentally disabled youngster be drowned because he was nothing more than a *massa carnis* — a heap of flesh — without a soul. Martin Luther, *Tischreden* (Stuttgart: Reclam, 1987).

13. This exploration will take us far away from Kelly and the people in her group home, but it is their existence that we will have in mind all the way. A theological account of their existence has to take the burden of asking what its own history contributed to the cultural marginalization of these people's lives. Looking at that history will make us realize that the task ahead is quite formidable indeed.

14. The theological move that follows is dependent upon recent developments in Trinitarian theology in which "relationality" is a key concept. My approach to the discussion owes a great deal to Catherine Mowry LaCugna, *God for Us: The Trinity and Christian Life* ([San Francisco]: HarperSanFrancisco, 1991). For a brief overview covering much of the literature, see David S. Cunningham, *These Three Are One: The Practice of Trinitarian Theology* (Malden, Mass.: Blackwell, 1998).

chological doctrine of the Trinity. In Augustine's view, divine personhood was understood in terms of relation, but the distinguishing feature of Augustinian persons turned out to be that they have a relationship *with themselves.*

Augustine's mature view on anthropology is found in his treatise on the Trinity. There he reasons that if human beings are created in the image of God, and if this God is a triune God, then the Christian doctrine of man must somehow reflect the Trinity. Hence the fact that Augustine's psychological doctrine of the Trinity is mirrored in a psychological doctrine of man. The crucial step in this connection has been what Charles Taylor has coined as Augustine's turn to radical reflexivity.[15] "Radical reflexivity" in Augustinian sense means that the understanding of the subject as itself is a reflective act. The "I" as the source of its own existence is a model that Augustine draws from his understanding of God as "Being itself." For the theologian in the fourth century that he was, this implied the understanding of the relations between God as the Father, Son, and Holy Spirit. According to Augustine, the relationships between the three could not be relations of difference. They had to be relations of identity. Accordingly, he argued that divine personhood was predicated of the Father with respect to the Father himself. God the Father is called a person not in relation to the Son or the Spirit, but in respect to himself, just as he is called "good," "great," or "just" in respect to himself.[16] Thus "Father" refers to God's being, "not insofar as He is Father," as Augustine puts it, "but insofar as He is."[17] In conceptual terms, the three are God because they equally possess the divine *ousia* but not because of the differentiating relations between them.

Augustinian explanation of divine personhood has stirred much debate in recent times because it fails to recognize the crucial importance of relationships for Christian theology. Accordingly, Robert W. Jenson has commented that in Augustine's view the differentiating relations between the three are irrelevant to their being God.[18] For a *relational* understanding of

---

15. See Charles Taylor's *Sources of the Self: The Making of Modern Identity* (Cambridge: Cambridge University Press, 1989), pp. 127-42.

16. Augustine, *De Trinitate,* VII.6.11: Quocirca ut substantia patris ipse pater est, non quo pater est sed quo est; ita est persona patris non aliud quam ipse pater est. Ad se quippe dicitur persona, non ad filium vel spiritum sanctum; sicut ad se dicitur deus et magnus et bonus et iustus et si quid aliud huiusmodi.

17. Augustine, *De Trinitate,* VII.6.11.

18. Robert W. Jenson, *Systematic Theology,* 2 vols. (New York: Oxford University Press, 1997-1999), vol. 1, p. 112. The conclusion seems correct in that Augustine explains "person" as equivalent of "great," "good," and "just," each of which cannot be relative terms with regard to God. The deity is not both God and great, because God *is* greatness in the absolute sense.

personhood, Augustine's conclusions are fatal, because when he says that "person" does not refer to a relation between the Father and the Son, but to the Father *with respect to himself,* he in fact inaugurates the concept of a self-enclosed relationality.[19]

Grounded in this model of Trinitarian thought, the Western conception of human personhood in terms of a relational interiority emerged. Just as Augustine's conception refers to God the Father in respect of himself, so the Western conception of human personhood refers to the human individual in respect of itself.[20]

The seeds of the latter conception are already apparent in Augustine's *De Trinitate.* There he argues that the "trinity in man" cannot be found in love, because this involves a three-term relationship: the one who loves, that which is loved, and the love that brings them together *(amans, amatum,* and *amor).*[21] Since this three-term relation locates one of its terms outside man — the object of his love — it does not satisfy the condition of being like the Trinity in God, because that Trinity is a relation of three equal hypostases *within* one being or essence. Consequently, not love but self-love provides the solution. Self-love allows for the conceptual possibility of a relation within

19. Schmaus concludes from this argument that "Ist 'Person' kein relativer Begriff dann ist er ein absoluter. Der Schriftsteller [sc. Augustine] betont die vollständige Identität von Wesen und Person. . . . Person sein, gut sein, gross sein, und Wesen liegen alle auf der gleichen Linie. Wohl behauptet Augustinus so die Substanzialität der Personen, spannt aber zugleich die Identität von Person und Substanz so hoch, dass die Relativität der Person verloren geht und auch fur subsistente Relationen kein Platz mehr bleibt." Michael Schmaus, *Die psychologische Trinitätslehre des Heiligen Augustinus* (Münster, Westf.: Aschendorf, 1967), p. 149. See for a similar conclusion LaCugna, *God for Us,* p. 103.

20. This is not to suggest, of course, that Augustine shared the modern conception of the individual, but it is to suggest that in Augustine's *De Trinitate* there is a clear correspondence between the "inner life" of God and the inner life of man. Cunningham (*These Three Are One,* pp. 229-30) has defended Augustine against criticisms that make him responsible for the development of "modern forms of individualism," by arguing that Augustine's was a "communal," not an individual, understanding of the human faculties. His argument fails to address the point at stake, however, which is not whether in Augustine's view the faculties of the mind were "communally shaped," but whether the relations of the self are constituted by interiority. See also David S. Cunningham, "Trinitarian Theology Since 1900," *Reviews in Religion and Theology* (1995): 4, 8-16, where the author makes the same point: "Augustine was well aware that an *individual* cannot reflect the inner life of God, because it is not an *individual* who is created in the image of God." But, as we will see shortly, Augustine in *De Trinitate* says that the *vestigia trinitatis* in man cannot be located in an exterior relation between one human being and another. He explicitly denies that the concept of love can provide us with a proper understanding of the Trinity in man.

21. Augustine, *De Trinitate,* IX.2.

the soul between the self as both the one loving and the one loved, and the love of self as the middle term between these two. In this manner "we discern a trinity, not yet indeed God, but now at least an image of God."[22]

I want to suggest that the notion of the human person grounded in this psychological introspection has deeply influenced Western anthropology and ethics. Augustine can be held only partially responsible for this development because for him the inward road is the road to God.[23] The step that severed this connection was made by Descartes. It is a huge leap from Augustine to the seventeenth century, of course, but even then it does not seem to be inappropriate for Charles Taylor to speak about Augustine as a "Proto-Cartesian."[24] Without ignoring that Augustine's view was radically distinct from what Descartes believed, the conclusion must be that relational personhood in *De Trinitate* is located in the domain of interiority.[25] In other words, the concept of personhood as a relation of the self with the self was not what Augustine intended, but he opened up a possibility that eventually would lead to the elevation of interiority and self-referentiality as the defining characteristics of the human.

Interlude: A Moral Point about Language

The analysis of Augustinian theology shows how the possibility of an anthropological "minor league" is opened up by the turn to inwardness. Without a relationship "within," no inner life; without an inner life, no "self"; and with-

22. Augustine, *De Trinitate*, XIV.8.

23. Moltmann states that Augustine's view contains the first theological traces of the notion of the "absolute personhood" of God. He explains: "Every human being finds in himself the mirror in which he can perceive God. The knowledge of God in his image is surer that the knowledge of God from his works. So the foundation of true self-knowledge is to be found in God." Jürgen Moltmann, *The Trinity and the Kingdom* (Minneapolis: Fortress, 1993), pp. 14-16.

24. Taylor, *Sources of the Self*, pp. 132-33. Taylor points out the difference between Augustine and Descartes by saying that in Augustinian introspection the soul discovers its ultimate ground in God, who is closer to the self "than my own eye," while Cartesian introspection results in the sure inference by my own intellectual powers. Whereas Augustine is in search of an encounter with God "within," in Descartes the soul finds itself.

25. *Pace* Cunningham I do not see that Augustine's *De Trinitate* can be regarded a key source of Trinitarian thinking against "the modern cult of the individual" (see Cunningham, *These Three Are One*, pp. 229-30). Brian L. Horne has argued that in the *Confessions* Augustine develops a quite different and much more convincing view on personhood. Brian L. Horne, "Person As Confession: Augustine of Hippo," in *Persons, Divine and Human*, ed. Christoph Schwöbel and Colin E. Gunton (Edinburgh: T&T Clark, 1991), pp. 65-73.

out a self, no person in the modern sense. Doubts about people's selfhood must lead to doubts about their dignity as humans. It is only with regard to human beings lacking a self in this sense that people may venture to argue that in taking their lives we cannot take anything that is valuable to them.[26]

At this point, I want to go back to Kelly, the severely disabled girl introduced in the opening section of this essay. The afternoon when I first visited the place where she lives, I noticed a nurse coming in for the late afternoon shift. Having entered the room she approached Kelly with a spontaneous, "you are looking cheerful today." On subsequent visits to Kelly's home, I noticed that such ascriptions of mental states were frequently made. It might be that somebody said that she looked sad, or that she loved to be bathed. Apparently Kelly was included in the language we use to speak to and about one another.

I realized that from the perspective of individual selfhood this language raises serious questions when used to refer to people like Kelly. Each of the phrases in question — "looking cheerful," "being sad," "love to be bathed" — imply intentionality on her part. They presuppose a capability of having mental states and of engaging the world in certain ways. Since this is highly questionable with regard to Kelly, we are forced to conclude that the things said about Kelly are in fact said metaphorically. To use intentional language in her case is to turn that language into metaphor. People speak to and about Kelly *as if* she were happy, or *as if* she were sad.

The problem arising from these considerations, it occurred to me, is that from the perspective of individual selfhood one cannot in good faith talk about Kelly as a human being. That is to say, one cannot talk that way when one knows that the language that implicates her as a human being is used metaphorically. In other words, people speak about Kelly *as if* she were a human being. If correct, what to say then to the skeptic who argues that using this language with regard to Kelly is a form of self-delusion?[27]

Pondering these thoughts made me very uneasy. Suppose that the people who work with Kelly and her friends[28] also believe that having the mental

---

26. Cf. Peter Singer and Helga Kuhse, *Should the Baby Live?* (Oxford: Oxford University Press, 1985).

27. I vividly remember a scene when the director of an institution introduced me in a group home similar to Kelly's. We watched a nurse who said she was playing a game with a severely disabled man. Upon leaving the scene, the director apologized to me for the nurse: "Of course the man has no clue what is going on, but I greatly admire these nurses. I could not do it." That remark indicated a skeptical mind.

28. Note how skeptical doubts about the language immediately start to multiply: can one work "with" someone like Kelly? Can she have "friends"?

states of inwardness is what makes us human. Suppose they then realize that they cannot in good faith speak to and about Kelly as a human being without fooling themselves. What would be the effect of that belief on their practice of caring? To take the possibility seriously is in fact quite chilling. What is the point of treating something as if she were a human being when one knows for a fact that she is not a human being? The question is inevitable, it occurred to me, once one has accepted the perspective of selfhood as the originating source of our humanity. From that perspective, it is difficult to see how one could regard Kelly otherwise than as a "vegetable," which is, indeed, to regard her as a "something."

I then asked myself what the staff in Kelly's group home would say to all this. Supposedly many of them *do* believe something like modernity's claim that being human is being in the possession of a self. But somehow it does not seem to hold them back from engaging themselves in the practice of caring for Kelly and her friends. For them Kelly is just Kelly, as I said before. They include Kelly in the language that constitutes and shapes the meaning of what is going on in her home. To give an account of that language, I take it, they have no use for the philosophical beliefs of modernity, regardless of whether these beliefs may in fact coincide with their own. This does not mean, of course, that they don't have the responsibility to think critically about what they are doing within their practice of caring. But it does mean that their critical reflection will not proceed from presuppositions that invite them to question Kelly's humanity.

The point of these reflections is to open our eyes to what the preoccupation with selfhood in our contemporary moral culture may do to our understanding of the practice of caring for dependent human beings such as the severely disabled. The language of that culture cannot but make the practice appear as an oddity remaining from a religious past that is in rapid decline. This does not necessarily mean that the practice of caring for the disabled is as such in danger, but it does mean that the moral grounds that once served to support and inspire it are exposed to cultural erosion. Among the more important of these grounds was the view that they too are children of God. Now that our society has the technological means to enhance selective procreation, many of our contemporaries have ceased to look upon their children in this light. Instead they believe that it is our duty to make "responsible reproductive decisions."

Notwithstanding the fact that many of our contemporaries hold this view, the task for Christian theology, I want to suggest, is to sustain the practices of caring for disabled human beings such as Kelly and her friends. This is not to say that, subjectively, these practices are dependent upon a theological meta-discourse. That is obviously not the case. Usually the professionals involved in it do not have much use for meta-discourse of any kind because they are too busy running the place. I do mean to say, however, that *objectively* the practices of caring for the mentally disabled — in particular the severely disabled — cannot be accounted for from the perspective of modernity and its beliefs about selfhood as the originating source of our human dignity.

"Ecstatic Personhood": The Greek Orthodox Alternative

Therefore, a theological alternative to the moral discourse of modernity is called for. Given the problem resulting from the turn to inwardness, the question before us is how to think about the human in a way that is not premised by a psychology of the human faculties. Regarding this question I believe Augustine was right in thinking that theology's conception of humanity is grounded in its understanding of God. But unlike the tradition following Augustinian inwardness, I think that the relations constituting divine and human beings are relations *between* persons, rather than *within* an absolute personhood.

Recent Trinitarian accounts to support this claim have been developed in close conversation with the Greek Orthodox tradition. It is well known that compared with the West, the tradition of Greek Orthodoxy has approached the doctrine of the Trinity in a distinctively different key.[29] By and large the West has followed Augustine's neo-Platonism by emphasizing God's simplicity. "Being itself" — *Ipsum esse* — is considered the first ontological principle. In contrast, Greek orthodoxy, particularly in the Cappadocian Fathers, proceeded from the "monarchy" of the Father. In their view God's fatherhood is ontologically prior.

The Greek Orthodox theologian who has defended this tradition consistently is John D. Zizioulas.[30] His work in this connection has been recognized as an influential contribution to contemporary Trinitarian thought.[31] As Zizioulas shows, the Cappadocians replaced the neo-Platonic "Being" as

29. See Walter Kasper, *Der Gott Jesu Christi* (Mainz: Matthias Grünewald, 1982), p. 361, who argues that "the Greeks" proceeded from the three persons to establish the unity, whereas "the Latins" proceeded the other way around. See also Jenson, *Systematic Theology*, vol. 1, pp. 115-16.

30. See in particular John D. Zizioulas, *Being As Communion: Studies in Personhood and the Church* (Crestwood, N.Y.: St. Vladimir's Seminary Press, 1985).

31. See Jenson, *Systematic Theology*, vol. 1, p. 116. See also Miroslav Volf, *After Our Likeness: The Church As the Image of the Trinity* (Grand Rapids: Eerdmans, 1998).

the ultimate principle of reality by God the Father from whom everything else proceeds.[32] This procession is not a matter of ontological necessity. Instead, Zizioulas argues, the procession is an act of communion by which the Father brings forth the Son and the Spirit. The act of communion that constitutes the Holy Trinity is a free act of love. Accordingly, Greek Orthodoxy regards divine personhood as constituted by an *ecstatic* act of communion. It is ecstatic in the sense that God's very being is identified in an act of communion. That is how God exists.[33]

What follows, according to Zizioulas, is that human personhood necessarily depends on divine personhood. The reason is that the main characteristic of personhood is freedom. Personhood breaks the chain of ontological necessity. This is what the phrase "being as communion" is intended to convey. To be free as a person is to be free for another in an ecstatic movement. Now the question arises how humans can be free from the necessity of their temporal being. We find ourselves inevitably determined by all sorts of conditions that make us the concrete beings we are. Zizioulas responds that the movement of "ecstatic being" can never be complete in the case of natural beings. The only person who can absolutely affirm its own existence as *freedom* is God the Father. Only his is true freedom because freedom cannot plausibly be derived from necessity.

According to Zizioulas, this means that as a "biological hypostasis" man is intrinsically a tragic figure. Unlike the persons of the Trinity that exist as communion, human persons are characterized by the *separateness* of their being in the natural world. Humans cannot per se exist freely on the ontological level. Therefore, Zizioulas argues, the possibility of ontological freedom is only realized in our union with God that is realized in Christ. Hence the "locus" of true human freedom is the ecclesial community where we anticipate what we will be in the "final outcome of our existence." This eschatological reality is mediated, according to Zizioulas, by the sacraments and the liturgy

---

32. Zizioulas, *Being as Communion*, pp. 36-37, 40f.

33. See Jenson, *Systematic Theology*, vol. 1, p. 103. Jenson argues along similar lines that engaging himself in relation with the Son, and, thereby, with human history, is how God exists: against the timeless and immutable deity of the surrounding Hellenistic culture that saved human beings from the contingencies of their existence, "the gospel proclaims a God who is not in fact distant, whose deity is identified with a person of our history; antiquity's struggle to overcome a supposed gulf between deity and time is discovered to be moot in light of the gospel." In Jenson's thought "overcoming a supposed gulf between deity and time" is exactly why the relation that identifies the Father with the Son is crucial in the biblical narrative. Consequently, God "himself" cannot be abstracted from this person, nor from his death, nor from his career, nor from anything else that characterizes the Son's mission into the world.

of the church. Only it can defeat the separation between individuals caused by natural necessity.

Going back to the question that we are pursuing in this essay — the question about the dignity of those that have no conception of themselves as humans — it is clear that the notion of ecstatic personhood looks like a promising move in Trinitarian thinking. It does not presuppose any notion of the human person as an individually subsistent being. Participation in ecclesial personhood is not premised by what we as individuals can or cannot do, but in what God does for us. It is grounded in God's act of communion that is mediated in the Eucharist.

Here the question arises of whether God's act of communion is connected to human acts of communion. The question arises because Zizioulas does not seem to have any use for other acts of communion in his account. As acts of natural beings, such acts cannot be truly free, which presumably means that they cannot be true acts of communion either. The reason is that on the ontological level natural human beings cannot exist as persons. The fallenness of human beings means that *we are* indeed separated individuals. This points to the conclusion that Zizioulas inadvertently reinforces the traditional Western view of the individual as a self-enclosed being. In his view, openness for the other is realized in the Eucharist as the act of God's love that draws us into the triune existence. But somehow this act, as Zizioulas explains it, does not inform our understanding of how we in reality exist as human beings.

Robert Jenson's Account of Personhood

It is with regard to this question that I finally turn to Robert Jenson's account of Trinitarian personhood. Jenson shares much of the criticism I directed against Augustine, most notably the fact that Augustine regards Trinitarian personhood as predication of God's being. This results in the view that when the triune God acts he acts singly, which eliminates the differentiation between the agency of the Father, the Son, and the Spirit that is attested by the biblical narrative. Notwithstanding the objections to Augustine's Trinitarian theology, however, Jenson also wants to criticize the one-sidedness of the Cappadocian view, which he sees as precisely located in their limited account of the ontology of Trinitarian personhood.

Jenson points to the fact that the Cappadocians recognized three ontological questions — "Is it?" "What is it?" and "How is it?" — and taught that only the third question applies to the Trinitarian *hypostasis*. Their explanation of the divine persons was about their "way of having being," not about the two other questions. What they wanted to say is that only the question "How is it?" differentiates the persons, not "Is it?" or "What is it?" Consequently, what kind of being the *hypostasis* were implied to be remained obscure.

For this reason, Jenson argues for an ontological definition of the concept of the person as a relation in the mode of substance. The divine person is a relation that itself subsists and is not merely a connection between subsistent entities. This definition gives the concept of personhood a clearly distinctive ontological status. It states that the Trinitarian persons are, in Jenson's language, "relational identities." He credits Tertullian for having seen — long before the Eastern tradition — that *persona* signifies a subsistent social relation. With his understanding, Tertullian specified an identity "that is constituted in a particular set of social relations of address and response." Moreover, this view enabled Tertullian to remain faithful to the mutual exchanges in the biblical dramatic narrative in which the Father, the Son, and the Spirit have different agencies that shape their different parts as *dramatis Dei personae.* Consequently, Tertullian ruled out the view that regarded "Being" as somehow the "real" God of which the three persons were the concrete manifestations. The triune God *is* no other than the Father who exists in relation to the Son from which relation proceeds the Spirit.[34]

The conceptual space created by the notion of personhood as relational identity is further developed when Jenson makes his second move, which is to consider the possibility of different ways of "being personal."[35] It is customary in the Western tradition to think of a person as the focus of consciousness, that is, as an "I" which is the originating source of its own self. From the act of identifying the transcendental "I" with the self springs the possibility of freedom. But this freedom must then be "a relation internal to a fundamentally closed single entity," which results in the view of selfhood as self-enclosure. Jenson wants to break away from this "conceptual straightjacket" by considering the possibility that personality and identity are not necessarily correlated one-to-one: "There may be *more than one way to be personal,* even to be 'a' person, so that indeed, . . . I may in one way be one person with Adam and Christ and in another way distinct from them not only by identity but also personally."[36] Accordingly, there can be more identities related within

---

34. Augustine explicitly denied the explanation of the relational being if that implied that "neither is the Father God without the Son nor the Son without the Father, but only both mutually are God." See Jenson, *Systematic Theology,* vol. 1, p. 112.

35. The problem Jenson addresses in this connection is that of interpreting the Trinity itself as personal without introducing a fourth person in it. This problem will not be my concern, but only its anthropological implication for understanding human personhood.

36. Jenson, *Systematic Theology,* vol. 1, p. 120; emphasis added.

one person, as when we speak of a corporate person, which is said of Israel standing before God and addressed as one person, but also of the human race as Adam's descendants, or of the Christian community that is one person with Christ. The person as a subsistent social relation is not necessarily limited to the relatedness of one being to another, but it is conceivable as the complex relatedness of beings with different identities in communion. This, I think, is in fact what Zizioulas's notion of "being as communion" is intended to express. The freedom that for Zizoulas and Jenson is the hallmark of personhood is not necessarily a "relation internal to a single entity" as modernity believes it to be. Instead it is a relation grounded in an act of communion between beings with different identities. In this sense it can be said, as does Zizioulas, that to be free as a person is to be free for another in an ecstatic movement. Our freedom is received from God the Father who created us with and for another in the name of the Son and the Spirit.

Conclusion: Kelly's Dignity

If the theological tour de force undertaken here is to be helpful with regard to our initial question, it must give substance to the phrase written above this final section. Given what I explained about Kelly's existence, what does it mean to speak of her dignity? First of all, the notion of dignity cannot refer to any subjective condition as it is implied in the notion of the person as a self-reflective agent. Human dignity does not have individual action as its originating source. But then, this is no shortcoming, because the argument in its entirety was conceived precisely to avoid grounding dignity on such notions. Kelly's dignity does not depend on what she is or is not capable of doing. It is a dignity she possesses as a human person with a relational identity. It is a dignity that is communicated to her in the acts of people caring about her and about her well-being. If the chaotic force of her natural condition would have had its way, Kelly would have been dead years ago. Her dignity is that she has been accepted as God's creature, which is what she shares with all of us. For others to accept her and include her in their relationships *is* a genuine act of communion.

The theological warrant for this view is that human beings are dignified, regardless of their state or condition, by a divine act of communion. In the resurrection of Christ, God the Father draws human beings into his own relationship with the Son and the Spirit and saves them from the bonds of natural necessity. This does not mean, as Zizioulas seems to imply, that personhood is the prerogative of ecclesial beings participating in the sacramental life of the church. But it does mean that in participating in that sacramental life, we learn to see what and how God intended us to be from the beginning. We learn to see that including Kelly in our relationships is a genuine act of communion that glorifies God the Father.

Having explained our dignity as originating from the act of communion by which God has first created us, and then has re-created us, we have shown that our humanity is a gift from the beginning to the end. We have received it, before we did anything, and we are promised the fullness of this gift in the end. This indicates why divine agency — not human agency — is the primary concept of theological anthropology. Because of what God does, we can see Kelly as a child of God who is lovable in his eyes just like any other of his children. When seen in that light, Kelly fits Jenson's description of personal being, according to which "a person is one whom other persons may address in hope of response."[37] The hope of response in her case must be eschatological hope, the hope for what she and we will be in the final state of our existence, as Zizioulas did put it. Given that Christian hope, we may regard the acts of communion that include her in personal being as acts that prefigure the future of God.

37. Jenson, *Systematic Theology,* vol. 1, p. 121.

REDEMPTION

The Logic of Indignity and the Logic of Redemption

PETER OCHS

To cause indignity is to tarnish the *imago Dei;* to suffer indignity is to suffer the tarnishing of the *imago.* There is no direct way to depict or even represent what we mean by the *imago,* but we can identify what fails to represent the *imago,* what tarnishes it, what helps remove that tarnish, and what it means to polish the image of God. The goal of this essay is to identify what I will call the "logic of indignity" — or the logic of either tarnishing the image or suffering its tarnishing — and what I will call the "logic of redemption" — or the logic of interrupting and removing that tarnishing. By "logic," I mean a visible mapping of patterns of activity in this world that would otherwise be merely implicit in our activities and, in that sense, invisible. What we *can* map in this way is bounded, on one side, by what modern philosophers call "logic": humanly constructed diagrams of the rules of human reasoning. It is bounded, on the other, by what Philo of Alexandria called "the Logos": the Word that issues forth from God to humanity. For the Church Fathers, this is the begotten Word that God sent into the world; for the rabbinic sages, it is the Torah that God spoke to the people Israel (God's spoken-word, or *dibbur*). In this essay, we apply the term "logic," strictly inside these bounds, to refer to a third something: an activity of reading Scripture for the sake of repairing humanly constructed logics.

Modern philosophers and modern theologians alike will find this an odd way to talk about logic. Both seem to agree that logic is a discipline of human reason, while Scripture is either more than human or less than rational. For the theological orientation represented in this essay, this agreement is precisely the problem, a mark of modern civilization's tendency to imagine that the world is divided into separate spheres of "religious" and "secular-rational" life, with no apparent mediator between them. For what I will call "postliberal" theologians, however, Scripture is itself a witness against such a division, since it displays a Word that is not of this world but yet walks among us in this world so that we, who live in the world, can also learn to walk in ways that are not dictated by the world. For those — Jews and Christians alike — who acknowledge this witness, our powers of reasoning are no more resistant to this learning than our powers of eating or of making a fist or of speaking words. *All* these powers are marked by the inveterate human tendency to sin and thereby tarnish the *imago*. But *all* these powers are marked, as well, by the innate human capacity to receive instruction from the redeeming Word, which means to imitate the ways it walks in this world. The tendency to sin is the tendency to tarnish the *imago;* the capacity to walk after the Word is the capacity to share in the work of removing that tarnish. According to this reading of the scriptural witness, the modern tendency to divide spheres of religion and secularity is itself a mark of sin, but of a particular kind.

Two Kinds of Sin, One Source of Redemption

Our reading of logic and Scripture draws on a single set of assumptions about the two natures of Adam, to which correspond two orders of sin and one order of redemption. The first assumption is that, while created as an abode of the *imago* — "And God created Adam/Humanity in His image" (Gen. 1:27) — human beings fail, nonetheless, to overrule covetousness. Incurably desiring what is not theirs, Adam/Eve desire the apple, Cain desires the favor bestowed upon Abel, and the consequence is violence.

> YHWH paid heed to Abel and his offering. Cain was much distressed and his face fell. And YHWH said to Cain, "Why are you distressed . . . ? Surely if you do right, there is uplift; but if you do not do right, sin crouches at the door; its urge is toward you, yet you can be its master." Cain said to his brother Abel, "Let us go out into the field." . . . Cain set upon his brother Abel and killed him. (Gen. 4:4-8)[1]

The second assumption is that violence is not intrinsic to human nature, but arises only as a consequence of humanity's inability to control its covetousness. Of this too, we can "be its master," but we perennially fail, as a

---

1. Translations in this essay are my own.

consequence of which "The earth became corrupt before God; the earth was filled with violence" (Gen. 6:11).

Our third assumption is that God recognizes both the capacity of his creatures to honor the *imago and* their inveterate failings to fulfill their capacity: "Never again will I doom the earth because of Adam/humanity, since the devisings of Adam's/humanity's mind are evil from youth" (Gen. 8:21).

Our fourth assumption is that, dealing mercifully with his creatures' inveterate failings, God chose to start again with us, not by literally wiping the slate clean and re-creating us (the flood will not suffice), but by sending out his Word again, this time not to create the world, but to redeem the sin humanity releases into it.

Our fifth assumption is that this Word is sent and resent in many forms. There is the Word to all Noah's children: protect the *imago!* ("Whoever sheds human blood, his blood shall be shed by humans. For God made humanity in his Image" [Gen 9:6].) The Word to Abraham: Go forth and form a people whose habits will be reshaped by my direct commands (Gen. 12). The Word to Israel, by way of Moses: know that I am the Lord your God and walk after me by following these commandments (Exod. 20). The Word Christians identify as the Son of God.

Our sixth assumption is that there is nothing more humanity has to do but learn from this Word how to replace its covetousness with faith in God, its desires with love of God, and its impatience with hope in God. The end of violence will come only as a consequence of this learning:

> And God created Adam/Humanity in His image. . . . On the seventh day God finished the work that He had been doing. . . . God blessed the Sabbath day and declared it holy. (Gen. 1:27; 2:2-3)

The peace of *shabbat* — God's indwelling presence *(shekhinah)* in this spatio-temporal world — is the end of a "week of work" that provides the *imago* an earthly abode.

Our seventh assumption is the topic of this section as a whole: that humanity sins, however, a second time over — not through mere creaturely covetousness, but by neglect of the Word sent to redeem this impulse. Despite the presence of the Word, Noah's children desire a tower to make a name for themselves, Abraham's grandchildren covet Joseph's coat, the children of Israel desire a golden calf, and, in the Gospel record, even Peter betrays the Word, and the people of Jesus' flesh fail to acknowledge the presence of the Word among them. These are the second-order sins of turning away from the redeeming Word through neglect/forgetfulness or through rebellion/pride.

For the sake of terminological clarity, I will label these second-order sins "heresies," and say that heresies are either misguided efforts, or failures, to reform first-order sins. While heresies do not necessarily express primary impulses to evil, such as covetousness, they indirectly strengthen such impulses by weakening the power of the Word to redeem them.

The Reformatory Work of Postliberal Theology

Our reading of logic and Scripture does not begin nakedly, therefore, but already clothed in seven assumptions, which are themselves not mere givens but the working assumptions of contemporary societies of postliberal Jewish and Christian theologians. Most simply put, we may identify these "postliberals" simply as Scripture-based theologians who work out of assumptions like these. More specifically, we may say that their primary work is, in service to the seventh assumption, to criticize and reform tendencies among modern and contemporary Jews and Christians either to ignore the redeeming Word (as if humanity were not particularly in need of redeeming) or to challenge it (as if humanity could repair its own sins without divine help). Christian theologians who exemplify the postliberal approach tend to practice theology as a means of helping the church identify and reform the tendencies to disunity that characterize its life in each given generation. They argue that, in the present age, the greatest source of ecclesial disunity is neglect of the scriptural word itself as agent of ecclesial reform. They tend, in this way, to reaffirm the primary doctrines of the Reformation, such as *sola scriptura*, but they also come to reform them. Reformation theologians have tended, at times, not only to affirm the authority of Scripture but also to segregate it from the complementary authorities of doctrinal tradition and of the Holy Spirit at work among the contemporary community of interpreters. These postliberal theologians reaffirm all three modes of authority, citing the efforts of both Barth (in redirecting the church to its scriptural grounding) and Thomas and the Cappadocian Fathers (in resituating Scripture in the church's ongoing traditions of doctrinal deliberation).

Jewish postliberals pursue analogous concerns. They are students, ultimately, of the ancient rabbinic practice of reading Scripture as Torah and, thus, as their means of entering into intimate relation with the Word that creates the world, that guides right conduct in the world, and that will redeem it fully in the end of days. Students, more proximately, of thinkers like Franz Rosenzweig and Emmanuel Lévinas, they criticize modern Jewish thinkers who neglect the practice of scriptural and rabbinic text study as the context for encountering Jewish "beliefs and ideas." At the same time, they criticize rabbinic text scholars who segregate Talmudic and related scriptural studies from the Jewish community's ongoing practices of political and religious reasoning. As reformers, the Jewish postliberals call for the reintegration of Jewish philosophy into the living contexts of rabbinic text study, and of academic theorizing into the living contexts of Jewish social life. They name their integration of sacred text study and worldly reasoning "textual reasoning."[2]

Extending this name to a wider context, a society of postliberal Jewish and Christian theologians[3] has adopted the term "scriptural reasoning"[4] to refer to their overlapping practices of reintegrating sacred text study and worldly reasoning. The Jewish and Christian postliberals practice theology as a source of reformatory responses to crises in the life of the church or of the people Israel. For both of them, the greatest crisis of the present day is disunity within each religious community, the greatest source of which is the separation of reformatory work from traditional and contemporary practices of reading Scripture. They claim that the greatest responsibility of theology today is to identify and reform the source of this separation, and they identify this source with a tendency, introduced by modern philosophers and philosophic theologians, to replace the practice of reading Scripture with practices of examining concepts. There are many differences between the two kinds of practice. The scriptural practice is, ultimately, communal and dialogic; the

2. For these Jewish theologians, "sacred text study" includes the study of both base texts (Tanakh or Bible) and interpretive texts (from rabbinic, post-rabbinic, and contemporary eras); "worldly reasoning" may include philosophical, practical (ethical, behavioral, legal, and thus societal), empirical, literary, and hermeneutical modes of reflection.

3. This is the Society for Scriptural Reasoning (SSR), formed in 1995 by Daniel Hardy, David Ford, and Peter Ochs, and soon joined by such thinkers as Steven Kepnes, Robert Gibbs, Laurie Zoloth, Oliver Davies, Nick Adams, Ben Quash, James Fodor, Basit Koshul, Tim Winters, and Muhammad Suheyl Umar. By 2004, SSR included six participating sub-societies, among them the Scriptural Reasoning Theory Group at Cambridge University, the Scriptural Reasoning Research Consultation of the Center of Theological Inquiry at Princeton, and the Children of Abraham Institute, with projects in nine different nations. The SSR publishes *The Journal of Scriptural Reasoning* (http://etext.lib.virginia.edu/journals/ssr/). The SSR would also identify the practices of most "postliberal" theologians as exhibiting or as comparable to what it calls scriptural reasoning: for example, the theological practices of Stanley Hauerwas, Robert Jenson, and so on.

4. For theologians in SSR, the word "textual" in the term "textual reasoning" is used to refer to any tradition of secondary literature through which Scripture is interpreted as the sacred source of specific guidelines and wisdoms for life in the world. "Textual reasoning" refers to the interpretive activity that animates any *particular* tradition of this kind, such as the rabbinic tradition of reading and reasoning according to Torah, the patristic tradition of reading and reasoning according to the gospel or the Bible, a Sunni tradition of reading and reasoning according to the Qur'an, or, more specifically, a twentieth-century "Reform" tradition of rabbinic reasoning and practice or Methodist tradition of Christian reasoning and practice.

conceptual practice is best performed by superb, individual thinkers. The scriptural practice reads complex and, ultimately, mysterious narratives as disclosing different dimensions of meaning with respect to different contexts of religious and communal life; any reading can potentially be challenged by the Word itself, the way "YHWH replied to Job out of the tempest and said, 'Who is this who darkens counsel, speaking without knowledge?'" (Job 38:1-2). The conceptual practice, on the other hand, discerns clear and distinct values and universal principles that may be applied to all contexts of human life. It tends either to replace scriptural tropes with philosophic/ethical ones, or to claim (as, for example, in Hegel) that the Word has fully embodied itself in forms of human discourse that no longer require being marked with a distinctly scriptural pedigree.

For postliberal reformers, the greatest challenge is that, when the conceptual practice is imported into the scriptural practice, it is difficult to show when and how the former supersedes the latter, that is, when we have cases of merely implicit or covert heresy. In these cases, postliberal reformers must be able to show, on the one hand, *that certain patterns of theological reasoning betray neglect of Scripture even when their authors claim to be scripturally grounded,* and, on the other hand, *that certain patterns of reasoning display a scriptural grounding, even when their authors are engaged in apparently extrascriptural inquiries.* The general thesis of this essay is that there is, indeed, a *logic of Scripture,* the study of which should provide postliberal theologians criteria for discerning both sets of patterns. The availability of such a logic challenges the modern presumption that we can discern the logic only of "human reasoning" and, even then, only when this is a reasoning that humanity itself constructs. It also challenges the postmodern assumption that, for this very reason, "logics" must be strictly local — that we can discern the logic only of what literally *we* construct, as members of some concrete community, so that "logic" in this sense means nothing more than the "grammar" or "contingent order" of our local practices. Articulated according to assumptions that are not addressed in either the modern or postmodern projects, a postliberal logic of Scripture is "logic" of a different sort and with a different etiology. It displays, for example, aspects of the "localism" demanded by postmodernists as well as of the "universalism" presumed by modernists, but understood in new ways. It arises out of some reading of Scripture that is occasioned in some moment by some immediate concern, but that also generates patterns of reason and of action that appear, after the fact, to be analogous to patterns generated in an indefinite series of previous moments like this one. These are the patterns of what we have called "scriptural reasoning." As we will suggest below, these patterns involve some relationship between conditions of indignity and of redemption. But there is little more that we can say until after an illustrative reading.

Exodus 3 As Prototype for the Overall Practice of Scriptural Logic

Consider the Exodus account of Israelite suffering as an introductory lesson in how the logic of Scripture first manifests itself. "The Israelites groaned under the bondage and cried out, and their cry for help under the bondage rose up to God. God heard their moaning, and God remembered his Covenant with Abraham, Isaac, and Jacob" (Exod. 2:23-24). The defining relationship here is between the Israelites' cry and God's hearing. The stimulus for scriptural logic, as we will see, is human suffering but, in particular, suffering that God "hears." One factor in the "hearing" is the character of the suffering itself: it is a sign of the kind of oppression that tarnishes the *imago*. A second factor is the character of the hearing: God responds with respect to a covenantal relationship. "God looked upon the Israelites and God took notice of them. . . . An angel of the Lord appeared to [Moses] in a blazing fire out of a bush. . . . The Lord said, '. . . I have come down to rescue them. . . . Come, therefore, I will send you to Pharaoh and you shall free My people'" (Exod. 2:25-3:10). The defining relationship in these verses is between God's noticing the suffering Israelites and God's sending a Messenger to redeem them. Once having "heard" a case of human suffering, God redeems by way of the action of human agents, and God directs that action by way of his speech to them. As the rest of the Exodus narrative shows, this speech nurtures leaders and institutions of leadership within the community of those who were oppressed. God directs them to organize themselves into a community of action, to confront the individuals and the systems that oppress them, and thereby to return to the relationship to God that they once enjoyed and that they may enjoy once again, albeit in surprisingly new and unexpected ways.

In narrative form, we have just overviewed the two elemental features of a scriptural logic. One is what we will call the "logic of indignity," or the type of relation that connects human suffering to divine hearing. The other is what we will call the "logic of redemption," or the type of relation that connects divine hearing to acts of redemption.

The logic of indignity concerns what we will call the "dyadic" or two-part relation between suffering and hearing: one either hears suffering or one does not. The issue is not the suffering by itself, but the hearing. As I will argue, this is a crucial distinction, for only a logic of hearing offers us a useable

criterion for evaluating what constitutes the suffering that stimulates redemptive action and what does not. Without reference to the hearing, debates
about the meaning of suffering are interminable. As François Lyotard has
dramatized in his image of the plaintiff who is "divested of the means to argue and becomes for that reason a victim," it is not always self-evident when
and how a given social system is oppressive.[5] According to our reading, Scripture discloses the only reliable criterion we have for judging what is oppressive, what causes indignity, and what repairs or redeems it. The term we use to
refer to this criterion is the *imago Dei*. What is at issue here is not simply a label, but what form of understanding and recognition is signified by that label,
and what forms of *Bildung*, community formation, and individual spiritual
formation are necessary for nurturing human beings who will share in this
understanding and recognition.

The logic of redemption concerns what we will call the "triadic" or
three-part relation among the hearing, the redeeming Word, and the condition of oppression. My primary argument will be that redemption displays a
third something — a Word — that is absent in conditions of oppression, so
that, according to this logic, *hearing* oppression is not a sufficient basis for redeeming it. This observation is crucial, because it implies that, in formal
terms, the logic of simply hearing oppression retains the dyadic form of the
oppression itself. In other words, without the redeeming Word as a third
party, responses to oppression may also prove to be oppressive. This observation also implies that *each* action of redemption must retain the triadic form
of the first act of God's sending of his Word. So, for example, "Moses said to
God, 'Who am I that I should go to Pharaoh and free the Israelites?'" (Exod.
3:11). Moses' response to God also displays the triadic form, interrelating
(1) God's speaking to (2) Moses' hearing to (3) the condition of the Israelites.
This leads us back to the subject of this section of our essay: *the triadic form of
scriptural logic itself, as well as of this effort to introduce it.*

The signal difference between a logic of Scripture and modern logic is
the existential meaning of the difference between two and three. In scriptural
logic, the logician is him- or herself implicated in a three-part relation among
what we will call (1) the material signs of the logic (as marked, for example, by
some claims written on a page like this one), (2) the attributed "author" of the
logic (or its authority: Scripture or the divine Word), and (3) the context of
its actual composition (which implicates the logician). According to this
logic, the latter context must bear some relation to the kind of oppression

---

5. Jean-François Lyotard, *The Différend: Phrases in Dispute,* trans. Georges van den
Abeele (Minneapolis: University of Minnesota Press, 1988), p. 9.

that God "might hear." It may seem embarrassingly dramatic to speak of "oppression" as the context of an academic essay, but this embarrassment may itself be a mark of the oppression: something in the context of academic writing leads us to fear public disapproval if we speak this way. Since we are clearly in the context of second-order behaviors — reflective responses rather than such primary behaviors as "covetousness," "violence," and so on — this logic suggests that, if this "something" is indeed problematic, then it may concern heresies rather than what we called first-order sins. As noted earlier, heresies may be merely "implicit" or "covert" within our practices of conceptual or scriptural inquiry. In this case, we cannot claim to *see* the heresy, but only to see certain patterns of relation that lead us to *hypothesize* that heresy may be at work and, then, to offer ways of testing our hypotheses. In a brief essay, I cannot conduct such tests, but I can at least offer the reader proofs that my hypotheses are at least *reasonable*. Here, then, is one illustrative hypothesis and one illustrative proof.

My hypothesis is that, however dramatic it may sound, the Exodus narrative also provides a prototype for the context of writing a postliberal logic of Scripture. More precisely, (1) my writing to you about the logic of Scripture may also represent (2) a response to the scriptural Word as it (3) responds to some situation of oppression or indignity. According to the logic of Scripture, this situation must display a dyadic form, which suggests that it may be a mark (a) of schisms in the church or within the people Israel today; and (b) of academic and ecclesial institutions that reproduce those schisms by propagating dyadic models of second-order conduct. According to postliberal theory, these may be models for repairing conditions of human indignity or oppression *without recourse* to the scriptural word. In other words, postliberal theologians may experience ("hear") the academy as a potential source of indignity and oppression to the degree that its dominantly modern and postmodern models of academic inquiry *suppress or displace* scripturally grounded inquiry into the sources of indignity and oppression. This "hearing" may stimulate postliberal theologians to appeal, afresh, to the scriptural Word as the source of their own responses to the modern/postmodern condition of the academy. And these responses may include the work of scriptural logic, itself, as an effort to distinguish the distinctively triadic form of their responses from the ultimately dyadic form of conceptualist (modern/postmodern) responses to conditions of indignity and oppression. The purpose of this logic is to identify otherwise covert marks of the difference between dyadic (modern/postmodern) and triadic (postliberal) responses.

My proof of the reasonableness of this hypothesis is, simply, that a recognizable movement of respected academics engages now in postliberal theology. The logic of their work merits testing just as much as the work of any other sizable community of scientists or scholars.

Illustrations of Scripture As Instruction in the Logic of Indignity and the Logic of Redemption

For the rest of the essay, my task is to display more details of this hypothesis by illustrating more specifically how a postliberal reading of Scripture can demonstrate the crucial differences between a logic of indignity and a logic of redemption. Grounded in both traditional and historical-critical studies of the scriptural sources, our postliberal readings are guided by a logic derived from the prototype of Exodus 3: that we read scriptural passages in order to uncover means of responding to some perceived condition of indignity or oppression or to some perceived heresy. In this case, it is the heresy of modern/postmodern efforts to separate reparative inquiries from their scriptural guidelines.

Scriptural Models of the Logic of Indignity

Case 1: Causing and Suffering Indignity: The Logic of Oppressive Behavior

Our first set of readings suggest that "oppressive behavior" — which I will define as activity that causes indignity — is informed by a strictly dyadic logic of action. This is logic that requires only two elemental terms, so that every action or judgment made according to the logic either affirms one term or the other, and the affirmation of one term means to deny the other.

The Example of Cain and Abel

YHWH paid heed to Abel and his offering. Cain was much distressed and his face fell. YHWH said to Cain, "Why are you distressed . . . ? Surely if you do right, there is uplift; but if you do not do right, Sin crouches at the door; its urge is toward you, yet you can be its master." Cain said to his brother Abel, "Let us go out into the field." . . . Cain set upon his brother Abel and killed him. (Gen 4:4-8)

We can map Cain's actions through a series of dyadic statements: Cain gives an offering. God favors Abel's offering. God does not favor Cain's. Cain is angry. God says, "Do not be angry. You can control anger." Cain remains angry. Cain kills Abel. With one exception, no action toward an object is mediated by a third-something. The exception is that God offers guidance that could interrupt the two part relation between Cain and his anger: if Cain had accepted the guidance, then we would have an action that could be mapped only through a triadic statement: (1) God's Word (2) led Cain (3) away from his anger. Abel's fate can be mapped by the same logic: Abel's offering is favored. Abel is hated by Cain. Abel is killed by Cain.

The Example of Sarah and Hagar

Sarai said to Abram, "YHWH has kept me from bearing. Consort with my maid, perhaps I shall have a son through her." . . . Sarai said to Abram, "The wrong done to me is your fault! I myself put my maid in your bosom; now that she sees that she is pregnant, I am lowered in her esteem." . . . Then Sarai treated her harshly, and she ran away from her. (Gen. 16:2-6).

Once again, we can map the oppressive behavior through a series of dyadic statements: Sarai wants a child. She has no child. Sarai asks for help. Sarai resents the help. Sarai hates Hagar. Sarai acts against Hagar. And we can map Hagar's being oppressed through a comparable series, ending with: Hagar is mistreated by Sarai.

Case 2: The Logic of Seeing the Oppressor and Hearing the Oppressed

Our second set of readings offer a transitional moment between oppression and redemption. Here, the logic of attending to someone's oppression contains a moment that can be identified only through dyadic statements, but it opens as well to the possibility of three-part relations.

The Example of Cain and Abel

He said, "What have you done? Hark, your brother's blood cries out to Me from the ground! Therefore, you shall be more cursed than the ground." . . . Cain said to YHWH, "My punishment is too great to bear! . . ." YHWH said to him, "I promise, if anyone kills Cain, sevenfold vengeance shall be taken on him." And YHWH put a mark on Cain. . . . (Gen 4:10-15)

Reading this text leads us to re-read the first one. God's warning to Cain appeared as if dyadic: Do this or that will follow. But the warning is more than dyadic, since Cain lives on, bearing a mark that redirects this warning, outward, to any who would want to kill Cain. The warning thus becomes a third-something: (1) a sign of (2) Cain's ongoing relations, at once, (3a) to God and (3b) to any other human he may meet. But, just as the warning *to Cain* converts into a protective mark *to others,* so too do we learn that the act of "seeing the oppressor" is coterminous with the act of "hearing the cry of the oppressed." In each case, seeing and hearing are two-part relations (one either sees/hears or does not), but they open out to the possibility of three-part relations. If one oppresses Cain, then God will act against the oppressor: the act against Cain will also be a mark of the divine-action-that-will-come. If one *sees* Cain oppressed, therefore, one can also anticipate that the oppression one sees is at the same time a sign of divine-action-that-will-come. In this way, the life of Cain also introduces a general possibility into the world: that any act of oppression/being-oppressed is a sign that God *could* respond to that act (although we do not know if God will respond). The mark of Cain is thus a potentially triadic sign, linking oppressed and oppressor to divine action and linking the act of oppression to consequent actions in the future. At the same time, the mark is only potentially triadic: Cain lives on with his mark, but, reading ahead, we know that his descendents will display more of his earlier tendencies than of his later actions: "The earth became corrupt before God; the earth was filled with violence" (Gen. 6:11).

The Example of Sarah and Hagar

YHWH took note of Sarah as He had promised. . . . Sarah conceived and bore a son to Abraham in his old age. . . . Early the next morning Abraham took some bread and a skin of water, and gave them to Hagar. He placed them over her shoulder, together with the child, and sent her away. . . . God heard the cry of the boy, and an angel of God called to Hagar from heaven and said to her, ". . . Fear not, for God has heeded the cry of the boy where he is. . . . I will make a great nation of him." (Gen. 21:1-2, 14-18)

Read in light of Genesis 16, this narrative is complex all the way through. Here we begin to see that acts of indignity *seem* to introduce binary oppositions between oppressor and oppressed, but that, in fact, these oppositions are binary *only* in the eyes of the oppressor and the victim *qua* victim. God does not act on this presumption, so that God is with-Sarah in criticism, just as God is with-Hagar in her suffering. The fact that both are with-God in this way alludes to the redemptive possibility when both will be with each other in the future. For now, they are joined only by sharing in the narrative (where they are in the Word) and, within that narrative, by sharing in the relation of being-with God. The ambiguous form of the narrative thus says something beyond its story line. When Sarai reads her condition in dyadic terms, then she becomes oppressor. When Hagar reads her condition in dyadic terms, then she is victim, alone, without hope. When we read the scriptural narrative in dyadic terms, then it is a story only of oppressor and oppressed. But *if* Sarah could read her condition in relation to God (and perhaps she never does), then her apparent barrenness is a sign of potential miracle, rather than a condition for covetousness. When Hagar hears that, as victim, she is also with-God, *then* "God opened her eyes and she saw a well of water" (Gen. 21:19). Redemption *begins* with the "mere" presence of God's Word with the sufferer; this is the beginning of the transformation of the dyadic pair (Sarah vs. Hagar, Hagar-in-pain) into a triadic relation (Sarah-with-God-with-Hagar, Hagar-in-distress-but-with-God). When we read the scriptural narrative in triadic terms, then it is a story about the potential transformation of oppression into redemption. But this is not merely the transformation of an oppressed character in the story into a redeemed character. It is also the transformation of our dyadic relation to the scriptural text (as mere subject of our reading) into a triadic relation, which, by the example of Sarah and Hagar, must mean a relation that joins text and us *with God*. But what does it mean to read with God?

Scriptural Models of the Logic of Redemption

For rabbinic Judaism, Exodus remains the prototype of God's capacity to transform suffering into redemption. So, we return for our models to the prototypical narrative of Exodus 3. This time, we will focus on how Moses' interrogation of God uncovers several names of the redeeming Word.

> An angel of YHWH appeared to [Moses] in a blazing fire out of a bush. . . . He said, "I am the God of your father, the God of Abraham, the God of Isaac, and the God of Jacob. . . . Now the cry of the Israelites has reached Me; I have seen how the Egyptians oppress them. Come, therefore, I will send you to Pharaoh and you shall free My people. . . ." But Moses said to God, "Who am I that I should go . . . ?" And He said, *ehyeh imach,* "I will be with you; that shall be your sign that it was I who sent you. . . ." Moses said, "When [the Israelites] . . . ask 'What is His name,' what shall I say to them?" God said to Moses, *ehyeh asher ehyeh,* "I will be what I will be. . . . Tell the Israelites, *ehyeh,* 'I will be' sent me to you." Then

God said further to Moses, "Thus shall you speak to the Israelites: 'YHWH, the God of your fathers . . . has sent me to you.' This shall be My name forever, this My appellation for all eternity." (Exod. 3:2-15)

Case 1: You Already Knew Me: Redeemer and Redeemed Already Knew One Another

Before Moses asks his name, YHWH introduces himself to Moses as "the God of your father, the God of Abraham, the God of Isaac, and the God of Jacob." In rabbinic tradition, it is common to interpret this repetition of the patriarchal epithets as demonstration that God is God in relation to each one who calls upon him. Another rabbinic tradition identifies the generic epithet of "God," *elohim*, as naming, in particular, God's attribute of justice, as distinguished from his attribute of mercy displayed in the proper name YHWH. God is *elohim*, in other words, independent of specific covenantal relations, unless these relations are specified. In the context of Exodus 3, God's self-introduction suggests, for one, an act of reassurance: that this is indeed the God whom your ancestors knew. It suggests, furthermore, that the redemptive acts that follow make sense only in the context of an already established and ongoing relationship among the people who cry out and the God who hears them. Redemption is a relational affair, and relations have histories. God's self-introduction also indicates the remarkable role of human leadership in the logic of redemption. God's Word redeems by way of human agents whom God selects for service and whom God honors with the intimacy of direct dialogue. But the self-introduction also suggests that there may be more yet to come. God's name does not yet bear any other particularizing relation to the people Israel as God now finds them: generations removed from Jacob, now in a strange land, suffering terribly, and leaderless.

Case 2: But Who Shall I Say You Are? Something New Has Entered the Relationship

"Who am I?" asks Moses, "And who shall I say You are?" Moses' queries introduce several new elements into our unfolding logic of redemption. First, *the redeeming Word does not operate on its own, as it were, but through its triadic relation to the oppressed community* as well as through some, as yet unclarified, relation to the oppressor community. Second, the community receives the redeeming Word both through the agency of its leader(s) and directly (all Israel was "present at Sinai"). Third, these leaders do not necessarily represent the community's traditional leadership before or during the time of oppression, but may, as in Moses' case, represent the Word as it has not previously fully been received by the community. *Redemption also brings change.* Fourth, the redeeming Word reconnects the community to its primordial sources and its antecedent traditions, while also introducing the new forms those traditions may now assume. Fifth, the leader(s) who serves as agent of redemption is not a passive recipient of the redeeming Word, but establishes an active and dialogic, albeit respectful, relation with the God who delivers it as well as a complementary relationship with his or her community. Finally, Moses' questions of God suggest that the leader's goal is, in part, to uncover something close to what we call the logic of redemption. By asking God's name, Moses is, in part, seeking ways of justifying his authority on behalf of the community, but the traditional commentaries on Exodus suggest that he is also seeking to understand what he can about the character of the Word that leads him.

Case 3: These Are My Names: The Logic of Redemption Unfolds

"Who shall I say You are?" God's response introduces a progressive series of divine namings that introduces the essential elements of redemptive logic.

Case 3a: ehyeh imach, *"I Will Be with You"*

The Name is disclosed in response to a human question: Who is the one who redeems us? It is one "who will be with you." Since our postliberal reading arises to *repair* conceptualist modes of inquiry, this is not the occasion to be led by Aristotelian commentators, like Maimonides, who identify this name with the "self-revelation" of God's essence as "Being." We are drawn, instead, to commentators like the medieval mystic and philosopher Nahmanides, who, against Maimonides, argues that the meaning of this name must fit its narrative context. The God of Israel says something here with specific relation to the community who awaits his help: do not fear, but know that I am with you in your suffering and I will be with you whenever you suffer. Nahmanides' reading captures this elemental rule of the redeeming Name: that "being-with" is all it takes to introduce the mediating Word into the dyadic relation of oppressor/oppressed. This marks the beginning of redemption, since "I will be with you" means that you are no longer alone. If you are the oppressor, you know that there is someone else who measures your actions and before whom you may have a reckoning; if you are the oppressed, you know that another way of life is really possible and you may begin to act in anticipation of it.

We therefore lack any knowledge of God's redeeming Name other than what is disclosed through the way that God is with us, here, in relation to this suffering. We do not know this Name *for others. This is how God both attends to and redeems the binary logic of our suffering.* Through an act of divine *tsimtsum,* or *kenosis,* God limits his redeeming divinity to the particular conditions of our suffering, thereby taking on the binary character of this suffering — that it is this and not that. In that same act, we are drawn up into the divine presence, which we know only through this redeeming Name that also bears in it our own name, but through which we come to know the God who would redeem us and all sufferers and all humankind. But this God, the Redeemer of all sufferers, is *not* one whom we know by his Redeemer Name. To claim to know this name is precisely what, in the logic of redemption, we must call the error of reducing divinity to the limitations of human concepts — indeed, of our own conceptual constructions. This becomes the heresy, moreover, of seeking to separate our part in the work of redemption from the work of scriptural inquiry, for the conceptions we derive from our experience of suffering are not themselves adequate to the scriptural Word. *Ehyeh imach* is God's word to Israel there in that suffering — the name of our Redeemer only in so far as we are "in" that Israel on that occasion.

Case 3b: ehyeh asher ehyeh, *"I Will Be What I Will Be"*

For Nahmanides, the God of Israel asks, "Am I not known by My acts (alone)?" God's redemptive relation to us will be there where it will be, and it is not for us to say *now* that it *will be* either this or that — either having a certain character (we cannot say a certain character will appear universally) or not having it (we also cannot say that it will *not* appear this way universally). The text offers explicit instruction *that* the Name will appear to us in our suffering, but it does not deliver to us the foreknowledge to say when, what, and how the Name will appear. While the humanly constructed concepts of strict "particularity" and strict "universality" cannot be predicated of the Name, the Name may indeed predicate itself or predicate any or all instances of our suffering. This means that the constructed concepts of particular and universal are not just done away with, as if their construction was not in response to a legitimate, religious need. They are *replaced* by correlates that belong appropriately to divine self-disclosure rather than to expressions of human desire and will.

The concept of "universal" is replaced by the Name *ehyeh asher ehyeh,* not merely as it is written here, but as it reappears, performatively, in the reappearance of the redemptive Name throughout salvation history, past and future. *That reappearance is the activity whose absence leaves humans anxious and hungering for what they call "universality." But to seek "universals" is a symptom of frustrated desire for the divine presence.* The Redeemer God "is" the soteriological universal in human life: the scriptural text instructs *that* this is so, but how and when and in what name it is so is not something we can be told a priori. Universalistic discourse, and the binary logic that accompanies it, are therefore symptoms, at best, of God's felt absence from human life (our yearning for the presence); at worst, they are symptoms of idolatrous conduct (our presuming the generality of our own reception of God's care). Receiving the Name *ehyeh asher ehyeh* is thus one cure for the heresy of conceptualism, for it reminds us that we seek the purported universality of concepts when we fear the absence of God's own redeeming presence. But, provided you have entered into a covenanted community and tradition, that presence "will be there [with you] wherever it will be," and the "wherever" has no limits.

The concept of "particular" is replaced by the Name *ehyeh asher ehyeh* as it *appears* in a given time on a given occasion: *this ehyeh* as it will be *ehyeh* each time it appears. No appearance of the Name is merely here-and-now; it is always here-and-also-then, meeting us here and leading us out from here to then. The Redeemer God "is" the one, alone, who accompanies us here in the present of our suffering when we are otherwise wholly alone. Individualistic discourse, along with the binary logic that accompanies it, are symptoms, at best, of God's felt absence from human life; at worst, they are symptoms of self-isolation from God. Receiving this Name is thus also a cure for the "separatism" espoused by some anti-conceptualists (or anti-modernists); in Amos's words, the God of Israel is also the God of Moab.

Case 3c: YHWH

In Jewish tradition, this is the proper Name of God: *hashem,* "the Name," as Jews say, to avoid pronouncing either the Name (which, since the fall of the temple, no one can pronounce) or the name that substitutes for it in second-person address, *adonai,* "My Lord." The Jewish mystical tradition, or *Kabbalah,* has much to say about the meaning of this name as the Name of Names and the instruction of instructions in the logic of redemption. We will, however, remain mute on the subject in this essay, since any reception of this Name belongs to the intimacy of relation between God and Israel. In the same way, we may also say that, for Christians, any reception of "Jesus Christ" as the Redeemer Name belongs to the intimacy of relation between God and the church.

Conclusion

For postliberal theology, Scripture is a book of logic as well of faith. As displayed in the prototypical narrative of Exodus 3, this book offers instruction in the logics of both indignity and redemption, where "indignity" means tarnishing the image of God in humanity and "redemption" means removing that tarnish. According to the logic of Scripture, indignity may be characterized as a dyadic relation between oppressor and oppressed, and the act of taking notice of indignity may be characterized as a dyadic relation between observer and observed. The act of redeeming indignity, however, can be characterized only as a triadic relation among the agent of redemption, the condition of indignity, and God's redeeming Word. This means that the capacity to "take notice of indignity" is not itself the capacity to redeem it. According to the logic of Scripture, philosophic and theological programs for repairing human indignity will therefore fall short of their goals if these programs are reducible to a logic of dyadic relations. This is the case, for example, when the "redeeming Word" is identified with a method of reasoning, with universal principles, or with wholly nongeneralizable events or situations. In these cases, the Word is ultimately assimilated to the agent of repair. Postliberal theologians observe that, when they assimilate this Word to any extra-scriptural practice, modern and postmodern theologians tend to offer dyadic, and therefore failed, programs for redeeming human indignity. To repair these programs is to reintroduce them into the triadic relations of the logic of redemption.

Land, Displacement, and Hope in Jeremiah and in Today's World

ESTHER MARIE MENN

If it is true that "land is a central, if not *the central theme* of biblical faith,"[1] then the vital connections that peoples and individuals have with particular places, sites, and regions need to be taken seriously in order to understand what it means to be human in God's world. Never has the urgency of the geographical dimension of human existence been greater. At the end of 2000, more than 34 million persons, the majority of them women and children, found themselves uprooted from familiar and habitable places and surviving in physical, social, and cultural limbo, and during 2001 an estimated 5.5 million more, at the rate of 15,000 a day, fled their homes to live in camps and other marginal areas.[2] The refugee crisis is larger now than at any other time in human history, and it encompasses the globe. The situation is particularly grave in the Middle East, Africa, and South and Central America, but it also affects Europe, the Pacific, and North America, so that nearly one-half of the world's 191 countries are affected.[3] The crisis challenges Christians every-

1. Walter Brueggemann, *The Land*, vol. 1 of Overture to Biblical Theology (Philadelphia: Fortress, 1977), p. 3. The emphasis is Brueggemann's.

2. For current statistics on refugees in all parts of the world, see www.refugees.org. See also André Jacques, *The Stranger within Your Gates: Uprooted People in the World Today* (Geneva: World Council of Churches, 1986); Carole Kismaric, *Forced Out: The Agony of the Refugee in Our Time* (New York: Random House, 1989); Judy A. Mayotte, *Disposable People? The Plight of Refugees* (Maryknoll, N.Y.: Orbis, 1992); and Elizabeth G. Ferris, *Beyond Borders: Refugees, Migrants, and Human Rights in the Post–Cold War Era* (Geneva: WCC Publications, 1993).

3. The plight of the refugee may be seen as paradigmatic of the situation of many other

where to reflect theologically and practically about how our understanding of humanity as the image of God, who has been extended the promise of life abundant, might apply to masses of displaced persons existing in degraded and seemingly hopeless conditions.

Addressing this crisis is a daunting task, especially in tragically complex cases such as the ever-escalating Israeli-Palestinian conflict. The emergence of the state of Israel in 1948 helped ameliorate the situation of hundreds of thousands of Jewish refugees following World War II, but it simultaneously created another displacement crisis of unprecedented dimensions. Although the exact count depends on how a variety of factors are considered, the largest single group of refugees in the world today consists of millions of Palestinians, including those displaced during the wars of 1948-1949 and 1967 and up to four generations of their descendants, a substantial percentage of whom live in camps administered first under Egyptian and Jordanian and now under Israeli jurisdiction. Compounding the ethnic and national aspects of the conflict are interfaith dimensions involving competing Jewish, Christian, and Muslim claims.

In this and other modern predicaments involving refugees, the ancient Scriptures that the church shares with the synagogue emerge as a rich resource for theological reflection. In particular, the Hebrew Bible, with its long historical perspective, vividly expresses the vital attachment to particular lands enjoyed by individuals, families, and the people of Israel, as well as the tragic reality of displacement, wandering, and exile — all of which are experienced within an enduring relationship with the one creator God.

Of special relevance are the prophet Jeremiah's paradoxical perspectives on the significance of Jerusalem and the land of Judah for the people of Israel and for their God. Jeremiah was familiar with the reality of human displacement. Living in Jerusalem in the sixth century BCE, he was an eyewitness to the Babylonian army's destruction of the city and surrounding areas and to the forcible relocation of a significant portion of the population, including much of its leadership (2 Kings 24–25; Jer. 39:1-10; 52:1-34). Late in his own life, he was taken against his will by fellow Judeans to Egypt (Jer. 43:5-7), where he apparently died. Jeremiah's theological perspectives on land loss and resettlement provide a lens through which to sharpen our view of the analogous situation of millions in the present age. Even the problematic as-

---

categories of displaced persons that do not fit the definition of the "refugee" as it has evolved over the last half-century through the work of the United Nations High Commissioner for Refugees and other international and nongovernmental agencies. For the evolution of the definition of "refugee," see www.refugees.org.

pects of Jeremiah's anthropology that evoke our critical response can prod us to new insight and engagement.

Two striking and somewhat contradictory aspects of Jeremiah's message for his beleaguered contemporaries deserve emphasis. First, despite the rupture in the occupancy of Jerusalem and Judah by its inhabitants, Jeremiah never dismisses or qualifies the importance of this region for the people of Israel. In fact, he develops the connection between place and population extensively and dramatically, through employment of his dominant metaphor of the land as the ancestral inheritance of the God YHWH, who brings Israel to dwell with him there as bride or heir or who, alternately, plants the people in the land as a gardener would root a choice vine in the soil. Jeremiah's expressions of anguish and mourning at the separation of land and people attest to the depth of the bond between the two, as do his visions of Israel's restoration, which always include a landed dimension. Jeremiah highlights the connection between land and people precisely at the moment that this connection appears to be severed.

Second, Jeremiah's claim concerning the enduring connection between land, people, and God does not portray the inhabitation of the land by the people as automatic, guaranteed, or even possible for his own generation. Rather, life in the land for Jeremiah is always conditional on the people's religious, social, and political behavior, as an expression of their loyalty and obedience to their God. We may recoil from Jeremiah's assertion that Israel's landlessness is divinely mandated as a punishment for the people's sin, because it appears to blame the victims of military disaster for their own suffering. Yet the prophet's surprising recommendation that the exiled people of Jerusalem and Judah settle down and dedicate themselves to constructive engagement in the foreign land of the Babylonian enemy holds out the possibility of human thriving in the most adverse of circumstances. Even with the eventual return to their own land, Jeremiah imagines no easy resumption of the former status quo but something radically new. Jeremiah's description of Israel's restoration remains evocative rather than definitive, leaving open the emergence of a more authentic enactment of the relationship between people, land, and God in the future. Jeremiah's rejection of the ideal of a natural, enduring, and unchanging relation between people and land leaves room for human adaptation and transcendence of the particularities of locale.

Jeremiah challenges our common Christian assumption that issues of land and place are of little consequence for human life. This assumption may seem to be well-founded, for Jesus himself says in the Gospel of John, "My kingdom is not of this world." And Christian scholars of the Old Testament have contrasted the fertility cults of the nations surrounding Israel with the superior worship of YHWH, in which divine revelation came through events in the history of a particular people, not in the repetitive cycles of nature upon which ordinary life in the land depended.

The assumption that land is not important in Christianity has been influential, but it is also simplistic, because events and history always happen in particular places and never exclusively in time. To ignore or deny that human existence is grounded in the particular places that support our physical, social, and cultural existence is an abstraction of our human condition beyond recognition.[4] It continues a false dichotomy that portrays Judaism as the superseded carnal religion of the earth and a particular land, and Christianity as the superior spiritual religion of the universal kingdom of heaven. It ignores the whole creation groaning awaiting the redemption of our bodies, as Paul expresses it — bodies which, according to the ancient creation narratives of Genesis, came from the ground, are sustained by work in the land, and return to the dust of the earth. It minimizes the impact of the Christian understanding of the incarnation of God in a historical person from a particular small town in Galilee, who, although he claimed to have no place to rest his head, yet lived his life, taught and healed the sick, befriended many, died a humiliating death, and appeared resurrected to his followers, all within the intimate landscape of Galilee and Jerusalem. The materiality of our existence is also embodied in the materiality of the sacraments, which employ elements taken from the earth: the primal element of water and the cultural elements of bread and wine, manufactured from the produce of the land that supports all human life.

Jeremiah's perspective challenges another assumption held by certain Christians across the centuries, that the most militant biblical land traditions, including the conquest narratives in Joshua and the apocalyptic visions of return found in some of the prophets and in John's Revelation, should be read literally as mandates for violent dispossession of lands occupied by other peoples. Such interpretations have been used to legitimize European colonial movements in the Americas, Africa, and the Middle East and to justify wars, forced removal of peoples, even genocide.[5] Also problematic are hyper-literal readings of the Bible by Christian Zionists, in which the only really significant land is that of biblical (and contemporary) Israel, since Jewish return and possession of this land has a cosmic, apocalyptic significance as a prelude to

---

4. Liberation theologians of recent decades have begun to assert the importance of land for human life, because salvation includes not only a heavenly reward but also temporal dimensions, including health, social and economic fairness, and peace on earth.

5. Michael Prior, *The Bible and Colonialism: A Moral Critique*, Biblical Seminar 48 (Sheffield: Sheffield Academic, 1997).

the second coming of Christ. This understanding of history as contemporary apocalypse ignores Palestinian connections to cities and towns, family fields, and other places of tenancy in the same land, and colludes with disastrous policies that fail to address human displacement.[6] Some biblical perspectives on land have clearly proven to be disruptive and harmful for human life and well-being. Alternative positions within the Bible, including some of those presented in the book of Jeremiah, can challenge Christians to develop a more inclusive theological anthropology that values God's gifts of land and community for all humanity.

A Broken Anthropology of People, Land, and God

One starting point for Jeremiah's anthropology appears to be an ancient myth of origins that defines human identity in terms of membership among a particular people who live upon a certain land specially apportioned by the high god and who worship the local deity immanent in that land. A version of this myth lies behind a passage in the Song of Moses in Deuteronomy: "When Elyon [the Most High] apportioned the nations, when he divided humankind, he fixed the boundaries of the peoples according to the number of the gods; YHWH's [the LORD's] own portion was his people, Jacob his inheritance" (Deut. 32:8-9).[7] In this passage the emphasis shifts from an etiological explanation of the origins of national territories and religious practices to the special relationship between the deity YHWH and the people Jacob (Israel). Geographical language persists, however, in the description of the "boundaries" between peoples and in the metaphorical designation of Jacob as YHWH's regional "portion" and ancestral "inheritance." Jeremiah further qualifies the original narrative when he acknowledges YHWH as not only Israel's national god but also creator of heaven and earth (10:12; 31:35; cf. 23:23-24) and when he claims that YHWH himself directs the destiny of all nations (1:10; 18:7-10; 25:15-27). Still, what Jeremiah develops most extensively is the relation between YHWH, the land of Canaan, and the people Israel (3:19; 12:14-17).

A luminous feature of Jeremiah's description of this close connection between deity, land, and people entails his various ways of employing the concept of the "inheritance" (Hebrew, *nahalah*) of ancestral property passed

---

6. For an overview and critique of this phenomenon, see Barbara Rossing, *The Rapture Exposed: The Message of Hope in the Book of Revelation* (Boulder, Colo.: Westview, 2004).

7. Biblical quotes are taken from the NRSV, with modifications to bring out my understanding of the Hebrew.

down with inalienable tenure from generation to generation. As in Deuteronomy 32:9, Jeremiah portrays the people of Israel as the deity's family real estate, as YHWH's "inheritance," suggesting that the people themselves are the place where YHWH dwells. YHWH is portrayed in related terms, as the territorial "portion" of Jacob, so that what emerges is a mutual dwelling of deity and people each within the other (Jer. 10:16; cf. 51:19). In a more physical extension of the metaphor of agricultural property, Jeremiah elsewhere portrays the whole people of Israel as occupying their national territory as their ancestral "inheritance" (3:18; 17:4). In his most extensively developed usage of the concept of "inheritance," Jeremiah envisions the actual region where Israel dwells as YHWH's own "inheritance" (2:7).[8] This anthropomorphic depiction of the deity as a traditional landowner, with his great pride in what he considers the best and most beautiful of all agricultural properties (2:7; 3:19; 12:10), reveals Jeremiah's understanding of the significance of land for human life. Jeremiah's varied employment of this concept of the inalienable "inheritance" weaves YHWH, land, and people into a single fabric.

In Jeremiah's prophecies that develop the metaphor of YHWH as owner of agricultural property, YHWH's history with Israel moves directly from the exodus from Egypt, through the wilderness, and onto his own "inheritance" (2:6-7; cf. Exod. 15:17). In this version of the story, the land is not already occupied by native peoples but remains unspoiled, fruitful, and ready for occupation. There is no conquest of Canaan in Jeremiah's account, so he does not depict the divinity as a mighty warrior driving out enemies who have polluted the land and must be expelled prior to Israel's settlement (Lev. 18:24-30).[9] Rather, Jeremiah employs familial and agricultural images corresponding with the dominant metaphor of YHWH's inheritance. YHWH brings Israel to live with him on his ancestral property as a bride (2:2; 31:4) or child (3:19), not as a servant or slave (2:14). His intention is to dwell in the land with the people (7:7) and to pass it on to them as their own inheritance (3:18; 17:4). Things do not work out as intended, however. It is striking how consistently Jeremiah uses familial imagery not to legitimate and idealize Israel's possession of a certain region but to stress the people's rejection of YHWH, as an unfaithful wife leaves her husband (2:32; 3:20) or a rebellious child his father

8. See 1 Kings 21:3. Norman Habel discusses Jeremiah's understanding of the land as YHWH's inheritance as one of the six biblical land ideologies in *The Land Is Mine: Six Biblical Land Ideologies* (Minneapolis: Fortress, 1995).

9. While this omission avoids the depiction of the genocide of native populations, it even more completely eradicates the existence of these populations by eliminating even their memory and positing the myth of an "empty land" that has been influential until this day. Norman Habel, "The Myth of the Empty Land," *Semeia* 59 (1992): 79-93.

(3:19-22). Jeremiah portrays a family in crisis, at the point of dissolution and painful abandonment of the farmland that supports them and serves as their source of delight, cohesion, and identity.

Jeremiah also uses the metaphor of viniculture, in which YHWH plants Israel as choice vine stock on his inheritance (2:21; 5:10; 31:27-28; cf. Exod. 15:17). This imagery stresses the divinity's initiative and investment in establishing Israel in the land as well as the people's deep roots in its soil. It also suggests YHWH's expectation of some yield from his select planting ("first fruits," Jer. 2:3). Jeremiah's unexpected labeling of those taken into exile in Babylon as "good figs" (24:5-6), harvested even as Israel is plucked up from the land, draws on a similar agricultural metaphor.[10] As in the case of the familial images of Israel as wife and child, the choice-vine image is not primarily employed by Jeremiah to claim a natural or eternal tenure in the land, even though it accentuates the organic connection between people and land. Jeremiah's focus is rather on the disappointment of the divine horticulturalist in his vineyard (2:21; 5:10). The people have not recognized that it is YHWH, and not the local deity Baal, who provides the fertility of the land upon which their flourishing depends (2:8, 23; 3:3; 5:24; 14:22).

Jeremiah's blame of his contemporaries for their own expulsion from the land becomes especially problematic when we consider how his prophecies might inform our perspectives on the refugees of our own day. Still, the role of human sin and its consequences in Jeremiah's theological interpretation of human history must be considered in order to fairly represent his views. Jeremiah identifies idolatry, particularly worship of Baal with its promises of blessing for the land and of assistance in a time of political instability (2:8; 9:13), as one of three sins through which Israel defiles YHWH's precious inheritance (2:7, 11, 23). Jeremiah graphically imagines Israel's idolatry in terms of adultery, divorce, and invalid return to the first marriage (3:1-10), bringing guilt upon the land (cf. Deut. 24:4). Similarly graphic is Jeremiah's portrayal of the blood of the innocent poor that defiles Israel's skirts (2:34). Social injustice, the second of Israel's sins, harms the land by depriving it of its divinely bestowed fertility. Exploitation of the needy by scoundrels, and the failure of the courts to protect vulnerable members of society, including the foreigner, widow, orphan, and poor, also bring war upon the land (5:24-29; 7:6).[11] The third of Israel's sins consists of political alliances with the powerful empires of Egypt or Assyria,

---

10. By contrast, Jeremiah regards the people left in the land as "bad figs," whose utter destruction will leave the land empty and ready for a new beginning (24:8-10).

11. Compare Amos 8:4-6; 5:11; 7:11, 17, where the exploitation of tenant farmers by the wealthy landowners results in the parceling out of their property by lot to others.

even apart from worship of their gods, since these overtures are viewed as a rejection of YHWH's leadership and protection (2:17-19). Rather than prosperity and safety, these alliances will bring shame for the people and destruction of the land by invading armies (2:15, 36-37; 30:14).

Jeremiah's descriptions of the consequences of Israel's sins make clear that the behavior of the people, and particularly of their leaders (kings, priests, and prophets), severely affects the land. Polluted with Israel's idols and abominations (16:18) and laid waste because of Israel's lack of obedience and loyalty (9:12-14), the land suffers because of its interdependency with its culpable human inhabitants (12:1-13; 14:1-6).

In turn, YHWH suffers from the ruin of the land by Israel and its leaders. The deity protests: "They have made my pleasant portion a desolate wilderness. They have made it a desolation; desolate, it mourns to me. The whole land is made desolate, but no one lays it to heart" (12:10-11). The people mistakenly think that YHWH does not care about what has happened to his inheritance (5:12; 7:9; 12:4), but the harm that they inflict on the land raises divine indignation and judgment.

According to Jeremiah, all of these factors — the need of the land for reprieve from its defiling inhabitants, the cumulative effect of human idolatry and sin, and the disappointment and anger of a passionate God — work together to turn the fertile inheritance into a wilderness empty of all inhabitants, even of birds and animals (4:5-8; 6:8; 7:34; 9:10-11; 12:1-4; 36:29). The severity of the transformation is expressed in Jeremiah's portrayal of a return to primordial chaos, as God's word of judgment reverses the creative word in the beginning, rendering the land once again "formless and void" (4:23-28).[12]

Far more than the expulsion of the land's inhabitants, what Jeremiah describes is the dissolution of the triad of land, people, and God considered essential for human life. Jeremiah articulates the fracturing of this dynamic unity in his prophecy of the destruction of the most tangible symbol of the divinity's presence among the people, the Jerusalem temple. Yet, even within Jeremiah's message of judgment, the prophet holds forth the ideal of Israel dwelling with their divinity in the ancestral land:

> Amend your ways and your doings, and let me dwell with you in this place. Do not trust in these deceptive words: "This is the temple of YHWH, the temple of YHWH, the temple of YHWH." For if you truly amend your ways and your doings, if you truly act justly one with an-

---

12. Emptying a land of all its inhabitants, both human and animal, is portrayed as God's method of punishing other nations, including Babylon (Jer. 51:62; cf. 50:3, 13, 39-40; 51:2, 6, 29, 37).

other, if you do not oppress the alien, the orphan, and the widow, or shed innocent blood in this place, and if you do not go after other gods to your own hurt, then I will dwell with you in this place, in the land that I gave of old to your ancestors forever and ever. (Jer. 7:3-7)

As in many other passages in Jeremiah, God's dwelling with Israel in the ancestral territory is contingent upon the people's adherence to justice and true worship, not upon the deity's eternal attachment to any particular place, even to the land elsewhere described as the deity's own "inheritance." Jeremiah warns that Jerusalem is no different than Shiloh, the site of the ruined Israelite temple where the prophet's own ancestors served as priests, and where in former times YHWH was immanently present among the people of Israel. Jeremiah's hope for Jerusalem even on the brink of destruction, as the place of YHWH's dwelling with the people, is negated in his portrayal of the divinity's vacating his own home and ancestral property: "I have forsaken my house, I have abandoned my inheritance" (12:7). In what had once been the most familiar and beloved of all places, the deity becomes a transient, wandering through the terrain "like a stranger in the land, like a traveler turning aside for the night" (14:8). Similarly, the people cannot remain in Jerusalem and Judah. Jeremiah depicts YHWH asking, "What right has my beloved in my house, when she has done vile deeds? Can vows and sacrificial flesh avert your doom?" (11:15). YHWH scatters the people "among nations that neither they nor their ancestors have known" (9:16; cf. 34:1-3). Jeremiah describes the severing of the dynamic connection as a time of dislocation and crisis for the understanding of what it means to be human.

Voicing Displacement

Jeremiah's vivid expressions of the grief brought about by the devastation and depopulation of the land ("terror on every side," 6:25; 20:10) help us to feel something of the suffering of Jerusalem and Judah over two and a half millennia ago and to imagine as well the pain of today's displaced persons. Jeremiah laments his humiliating and almost unbearable role as spokesperson for the age: "Whenever I speak, I must cry out. I must shout, 'Violence and destruction!'" (20:8). Abhorrent as the prophet found his calling, Jeremiah's passionate articulation of the emotional dimensions of the loss of life in a beloved place provides a point of entry into a tragic yet persistent reality, conveying the agony of displacement across the distance left by cold facts and statistics about refugees.

The pathos is nowhere more clearly expressed than in Jeremiah 4:19-20: "My anguish, my anguish! I writhe in pain! Oh, the walls of my heart! My heart is beating wildly; I cannot keep silent; for I hear the sound of the trumpet, the alarm of war. Disaster overtakes disaster, the whole land is laid waste. Suddenly my tents are destroyed, my curtains in a moment!" Assuming the perspective of an eyewitness to battle, Jeremiah describes the sheer physicality of the terror felt by himself and by all of the inhabitants of Judah and Jerusalem, including convulsions of the body, palpitations of the heart, and involuntary screams that echo the blasts of war trumpets.

Yet, as "disaster overtakes disaster," it becomes less clear exactly whose anguish is so vividly described. Especially striking are the reference to the heart's "walls," pulsating with the frenzied movement and alarming din characteristic of an enemy's breach of a city's defenses, and the expression of dismay over the sudden destruction of fragile dwellings described as "my tents" and "my curtains." These details suggest that the speaker may be the land itself, with its "heart" located in Jerusalem as the center of human habitation (4:18). An additional level of meaning is implied by "tents" and "curtains," traditionally associated with God's dwelling with Israel in a tabernacle from the earliest days in the wilderness. This passage can therefore be read as a divine reaction to the destruction of the temple in Jerusalem, the overwhelmed "heart" of his own inheritance. It was there in Zion that, according to popular understanding, God dwelt as the people's king (8:19).

The responses of the prophet (or some other stylized citizen of Jerusalem), of the land, and of God are blurred together in this first-person expression of panic, distress, and sorrow. This ambiguity of speaker is not accidental but highly significant. It heightens the tragedy of the transformation of habitable land into desolate wilderness and of the destruction of human and divine dwellings in the heart of God and Israel's ancestral territory. One naturally expects that humans will suffer from the destruction of their homes and way of life, but in this passage there are cosmic and theological dimensions to the loss as well. God, people, and land are essentially connected through their mourning with a single, undifferentiated voice (cf. 8:18–9:1).

In other passages, Jeremiah deals more specifically with the people's departure from their customary living spaces. The devastation of battle results in panicked flight from settled areas into the wilderness: "At the noise of horseman and archer every town takes to flight; they enter thickets; they climb among rocks; all the towns are forsaken, and no one lives in them" (4:29). This spontaneous migration of the population from the path of war soon yields to a more organized displacement, as the Babylonians forcibly take into captivity the leaders of the country along with a sizeable population, first in 597 BCE and again in 586 BCE. When describing the removal of King Jehoiachin and other members of the court from Jerusalem to Babylon in 597, the prophet employs strong, metaphorical verbs to suggest the violence of the action. The king and his unfortunate offspring are "hurled out and cast away in a land that they do not know" (22:28).

Exile is even worse than death (Jer. 8:3). Speaking still of the deported King Jehoiachin, Jeremiah advises, "Do not weep for him who is dead, nor bemoan him; weep rather for him who goes away [into exile], for he shall return no more to see his native land" (22:10).[13] As Jerusalem's inhabitants are expelled from their beloved city, there are cries of humiliation and keening:

> Consider, and call for the mourning women to come; send for the skilled women to come; let them quickly raise a dirge over us, so that our eyes may run down with tears, and our eyelids flow with water. For a sound of wailing is heard from Zion: "How we are ruined! We are utterly shamed, because we have left the land, because they have cast down our dwellings." (Jer. 9:17-20)

Because the basic definition of being human includes being part of a people dwelling in a particular land and worshiping the resident god, life outside is almost unthinkable. Worse than death, it is merely a shadow existence. The people, the land itself, and YHWH all suffer. Jeremiah's vivid portrayal of the pain of deportation allows us to vicariously experience the loss of land as a tragedy that confounds and threatens human life.

Welfare of the Land: Human Transcendence and Immanence

Two aspects of Jeremiah's message are especially amazing, though repugnant to his own beleaguered generation and perhaps to our own sensibilities. First, he advocates no resistance to either the presence or the policies of the Babylonians, including their forcible removal of the elite members of the community from Jerusalem and its environs. Jeremiah's unpopular stance earns him a reputation as a traitor against Judah and as a pro-Babylonian agitator (38:4; 40:4), but he regards Nebuchadrezzar's victory as part of God's plan for the people's future (34:1-3, 19-22) and advocates complete compliance with the invaders (38:17-23; 42:10-12). The second surprise, given the importance of the land in Jeremiah's theological anthropology, is that after the Babylonian deportation

---

13. This verse contrasts the fate of Josiah, who died in battle, and Jehoiachin, who was taken to Babylon.

he puts no stock in the popular hope for a speedy return to Jerusalem. Instead, he castigates the prophets among the exiles in Babylon who give false assurances of an imminent return (29:8-9).

Jeremiah offers a paradoxical stance that has been extremely influential in Jewish history to the present day and that may be helpful in reflecting on the situation of other displaced peoples, although such analogies should be drawn with extreme caution. Jeremiah never denies or minimizes the importance of a particular geographical region, in this case on the eastern Levant, for the people of Israel. Indeed, with his development of the metaphor of the land as YHWH's own special inheritance, Jeremiah strongly emphasizes the connection between land and people. At the same time, once the people have been violently removed from the land, the prophet does not consider its occupancy a necessary condition for human life or even well-being. He even advocates an extended period of landlessness lasting seventy years (25:11; 27:7; 29:10), during which the people should actively engage themselves in the place where they have been forcibly relocated. Jeremiah thus proposes a complex portrait of human transcendence of any particular land, even of that very geography that retains an orienting and community-defining force, combined with an imperative of provisional immanence, consisting of constructive engagement in the locale where one finds oneself.

Jeremiah's position is articulated in his letter to the members of the Jerusalem community in Babylon, in which he conveys an unexpected message from YHWH of Hosts, the God of Israel:

> Build houses and live in them; plant gardens and eat what they produce. Take wives and have sons and daughters; take wives for your sons, and give your daughters in marriage, that they may bear sons and daughters; multiply there, and do not decrease. But seek the welfare of the city [or land, in the Septuagint] where I have sent you into exile, and pray to YHWH on its behalf, for in its welfare you will find your welfare. (Jer. 29:5-7)

Three aspects of this passage deserve comment, including the imagery of building and planting, the instructions for marriage and multiplication, and the welfare of the foreign city (or land) and the people.

The verbs "building" and "planting" that open this passage, and that are repeated in the short summary of Jeremiah's message to the exiles in Jeremiah 29:28, stress the physical and concrete nature of the involvement required in Babylonian territory. These verbs are highly significant, in that they are the last pair of words contained in Jeremiah's commission as a prophet over nations and kingdoms: "to pluck up and to pull down, to destroy and to overthrow, to build and to plant" (1:10). The destructive actions in the first part of this list appear to have been accomplished through the military campaign against Jerusalem and Judah. Unexpectedly, the building and planting that Jeremiah is to oversee will not immediately take place in the devastated land but rather in the country of the enemy destroyer. The provisional nature of the people's creative involvement in the foreign land is heightened because it is temporally bracketed by similar actions in the past and in the future by YHWH within his own special inheritance. Long ago, when YHWH brought Israel into the land designated for them, he "planted" them there as a choice vine (2:21). In the future restoration, the deity promises to bring them back to the land: "I will build them up, and not tear them down; I will plant them, and not pluck them up" (24:6; cf. 31:27-28; 45:4). In Jeremiah, the confidence and hope that make human exertions for life in a foreign land possible are grounded in the larger vision of corresponding divine exertions on behalf of the people in their own land.

Jeremiah's letter concerning marriage, family, and descendants strongly contends that the future of the exiles is not gradual assimilation into the dominant culture or disappearance through attrition with the death of the deported generation. It is not even survival as a small, threatened group. It is the flourishing of a distinctive multigenerational community upon foreign soil. These instructions contrast markedly with Jeremiah's own biography, since he was prevented from taking a wife and having children as a prophetic sign of the severe conditions in the land (16:1-4). In Jeremiah's day, YHWH banished from the land "the voice of mirth and the voice of gladness, the voice of the bridegroom and the voice of the bride" (16:9), until these might be heard again when YHWH restored the fortunes of the land as at first (33:10-11). In the meantime, Jeremiah envisions the joys of marriage, family, and children robustly enacted outside of the land.

Seeking the welfare of the foreign city and praying to YHWH on its behalf is presented as the way for the people to secure their own welfare in exile. In the Septuagint reading, the word "land" appears rather than "city" ("seek the welfare of the *land* where I have sent you"), making clear that what has transpired is the temporary substitution of a foreign land for the native. Even more central to the paradoxical impact of this injunction is the semantic range of the Hebrew word translated as "welfare" *(shalom)*, which can also mean "health," "wholeness," and "peace." The word's sense of "peace" creates a profound irony, in that the exiled community is asked to work for the peace of the very country that had brought brutal warfare within its own borders and effectively prevented a resumption of peaceful life in Jerusalem and Judah. Every bit as remarkable is Jeremiah's imperative to pray, not for the restoration and welfare of the distant land of origins, the ancestral inheritance of both this deity and his people, but rather on behalf of the enemy territory in which the community resides as unwilling guests.

Jeremiah asks a great deal from the exiles in Babylonia. To follow the prophet's advice they would surely have to overcome strong negative feelings toward their captors and hosts. They also would have to set aside their hopes for a rapid return to their native land and begin earnestly to resume the ordinary things that make for life — building homes, planting gardens, raising families. Astoundingly, Jeremiah also urges them to refuse the temptation to attend only to the well-being of their own displaced community and to begin to see themselves as contributors to the well-being of their host country. Only someone like Jeremiah, who experienced the horrors of military defeat along with the rest of his people and who truly seeks their welfare as the prophet of YHWH, could dare ask the nearly impossible.

While Jeremiah counsels full investment in Babylon, his understanding of life outside of the land as "exile" assumes a continuing orientation toward the former place of residence, memory, and belonging. The seventy-year period of landlessness means that more than a generation of individuals will experience no actual connection with the land of their forebears. Yet, they live with the promise that YHWH has given for their welfare and for a future in the land (29:10-11). So important is the return to the land that Jeremiah envisions a redefinition of the pivotal episode of Israel's history:

> Therefore, the days are surely coming, says YHWH, when it shall no longer be said, "As YHWH lives who brought the people of Israel up out of the land of Egypt," but "As YHWH lives who brought the people of Israel up out of the land of the north and out of all the lands where he had driven them." For I will bring them back to their own land that I gave to their ancestors. (Jer. 16:14-15; cf. 23:7-8)

Jeremiah signifies the people's persistent connection to the land when he purchases ancestral property in Anathoth from his cousin Hanamel to keep it in the family, even as the country is being overrun by the invading army (32:6-15). His action symbolizes, indeed enacts, God's promise that "houses and fields and vineyards shall again be bought in this land" (32:15), though Jeremiah himself is forcibly taken to Egypt (43:6) and never sees the return of his people.

While Jeremiah is certain that the future of the people includes their eventual restoration in the land, his vision concerning the shape and form of that restoration is evocative rather than practical. Whatever else it might include, the return to the land will not be a return to the former status quo. Human life in the redeemed land includes new social and theological realities, indicated by Jeremiah's concepts of the new heart, the new covenant, and universal knowledge of YHWH (9:2, 5; 31:31-34). With this transformation of humanity, no false teachings of priests and prophets and no destructive policies of kings will mislead the people and cause their scattering. YHWH himself will gather the remnant of his flock out of all the lands where he has driven them and will raise good shepherds for them so that they may be fruitful and multiply and live without fear (23:3-4). The righteous branch raised up for David will execute justice and righteousness in the land (23:5), protecting the oppressed, alien, orphan, widow, and innocent (22:3-5).

Jeremiah's understanding of the future in the land includes a reversal of the defiling injustice and lack of loyalty to YHWH that led to the people's expulsion. In the prophet's vision, human wisdom, power, and wealth are of little import compared to intimate knowledge of YHWH. Jeremiah provides only intimations concerning the future dwelling in the land, including visions of God's new planting (32:36-40; cf. 31:27-28, 31) and of the people's rejoicing in the divinely bestowed bounty of grain, wine, and oil, and of flock and herd (31:10-14). Yet Jeremiah insists that the future includes a land of fertility and prosperity, and of justice and righteousness. As for the actual course of history, only a minority of the descendants of those taken to Babylon ever returned, leaving larger and wealthier communities outside of the land, in Mesopotamia and later in other parts of the world such as Alexandria.

Toward Conclusions

Jeremiah's influential vision of a place for those who had been displaced asserts that being human includes participation in a community with an enduring connection to a particular land and that this connection has theological dimensions, imperatives, and promises. He sustains an emphasis on these vital connections even during a period when a decisive fracture is suffered. His perspectives can prod today's Christians, especially those of us who are relatively secure in our places and communities, to reconsider the importance of land for theological anthropology. We may take our own rootedness for granted and even enjoy exercising opportunities for mobility, not recognizing that these opportunities are based on our security within structures that have regional dimensions. Jeremiah's description of the horrors of expulsion and the corresponding loss of traditional ways of life and worship can sensitize contemporary readers to the extreme and vulnerable situation of those who have been displaced, whether in the Babylonian period or in our own time. While Jeremiah speaks primarily of his own community's experience during the sixth century BCE, his witness resonates with the experience of modern refugees from all nations, races, and regions, who are too easily ignored.[14]

Understanding the anguish of the refugee through the words of eyewitnesses, poets, and prophetic figures such as Jeremiah must be only the first step toward more intentional action to prevent, ameliorate, and resolve a major human crisis. Of primary importance is how we shape the international policies of our governments so that they do not cause or exacerbate the flight or removal of peoples from their lands and communities. For existing conditions, adequate resources need to be allocated to support national and international, religious and other nongovernmental programs designed to improve temporary conditions and to negotiate more permanent solutions, including return to the place of origin, permanent settlement in the host country, or secondary relocation in a third country.

Although secondary relocation is by far the least frequent form of resolution for displaced persons, most readers of this essay will directly encounter refugees as new residents in their own neighborhoods, towns, and cities. Involved sponsorship by churches and other organizations continues to be a positive way to create welcoming communities in a foreign land, in which refugees can build and plant, marry and have families, and not only seek their own survival but also engage in activities that further the common welfare.

Consideration is needed for the vulnerabilities of particular displaced populations that resettle in new lands. This can be illustrated by reference to two issues germane to the situation in the Middle East that are of special concern for Christians. First, the history of anti-Judaism and anti-Semitism in the Christian West that culminated in the Shoah, or calamitous destruction of one-third of all of world Jewry in the last century, calls for persistent vigilance. Christians need to dedicate themselves to fostering positive and respectful relations with their Jewish neighbors so that never again will the choice be death or flight from "terror all around." Second, in the case of Palestinians relocating in Western countries, and especially in the United States after 9/11, special efforts are needed to prevent anti-Muslim and anti-Arab prej-

---

14. Jeremiah does not portray loss of land and return as uniquely Israelite experiences. In his oracles against the nations, he views other peoples who dwell in particular regions with their own gods, and who because of their sin also come under judgment and undergo the punishment of captivity. In several of his oracles, these other displaced peoples will ultimately also be restored to their own lands (46:26; 48:47; 49:6; 49:39).

udices and hostilities. American Christians, who worship the same God as Christian and Muslim Palestinians do, can take the lead in establishing our communities as safe havens. Palestinians living in the United States, which heavily supports the state of Israel, face exactly the paradoxical situation that Jeremiah advocated, of settling into what might well be considered enemy territory. Christians have a responsibility to push for national policies that might effect a fair resolution in the region.

These general recommendations may appear obvious on a simple humanitarian basis, without drawing substantively upon the perspectives of Jeremiah. Further engagement of Jeremiah's message, beginning with a critique of his most objectionable claim, can contribute to a theological analysis of the human crisis in our time. Jeremiah understood forcible displacement as YHWH's punishment for Israel's sin. To infer from this that the world's refugees of today are to blame for causing their own suffering, as if landlessness were a clear sign of moral degeneracy and failure, is simply pernicious. Jeremiah struggled with his own concepts of collective guilt and punishment through deportation, moving toward a more nuanced position (31:29-30). Human sin is no doubt involved wherever whole communities are expelled from their homes, but this sin can more easily be seen in the brutality and violence of aggressors causing displacement and in the apathy and negligence of those who fail to respond to the injustice.

The magnitude and persistence of displacement today suggests that, at least at some unconscious level, refugees continue to be ignored as less than human. Whatever else may be said about Jeremiah's understanding of the exile, he regards the humanity of deportees with utmost seriousness. Jeremiah not only holds out hope for their eventual restoration but also assumes that they retain an intrinsic dignity and potential in the interim to forge a new life, even in a hostile land. Jeremiah's prophecies of restoration to land, community, and right relationship with the divinity stress that God will not leave humanity marginal and diminished.

Viewed in light of Jeremiah's theological anthropology, God has an unfinished agenda — work on behalf of the displaced. Refugees cannot be ignored, because God will not ignore them. Among Jeremiah's many portraits of divine suffering over the separation of people and land, his fleeting depiction of YHWH as a homeless wanderer, seeking nothing more than a place to rest for the night (14:8), lingers in memory. God does not ignore the refugee but joins their ranks by becoming one. Jeremiah's haunting vision of God as a displaced person in turn highlights the divine image in every refugee. If we ignore the humanity of the refugee, we ignore the God who joins them in their homelessness and promises them restoration.

In his letter to the community from Judah and Jerusalem in Babylon, Jeremiah identifies Israel's God as the one who returns refugees to their land, and who gives them homes and gardens and families even in exile. To be out of place, to be dislocated, to be without a home cannot be the end of humanity, since we have God's promise: "For surely I know the plans I have for you, says YHWH, plans for your welfare and not for harm, to give you a future with hope" (Jer. 29:11).

God's Promise for Humanity in the New Testament

C. CLIFTON BLACK

The Bible As Broom

Scripture can be adopted for many purposes. For much of Christian history, it has been raised as "a lamp unto my feet, and a light unto my path" (Ps. 119:105 KJV). Lamentably, still too many Christians seize it as a claymore for laying waste to their antagonists. A gentler and important use is that of a broom, which sweeps away the mind's cobwebs. Scripture performs that necessary function when the contemporary church considers what it means to be human. Thus, one learns that "human dignity," strictly speaking, is not a biblical topic.[1] With James Luther Mays[2] I concur that the nearest biblical parallel to such a claim may be the psalmist's wonderment that our Lord has made mortals "little less than the angels" and "adorned [them] with glory and majesty" by reason of the sacred trust over God's creatures that is placed into human hands (Ps. 8:5-9).[3] Notwithstanding its importance in subsequent theological anthropology, humankind's creation "in the image" *(selem)* and "likeness" *(demut)* of God is, in the biblical tradition, a claim that is comparatively rare (found only in Genesis 1:26-27; 5:1-3; 9:6) and conceptually obscure. Such ambiguity surprises when Genesis is read against the backdrop of

1. For an alternative view, which may exaggerate Christianity's hierarchical character, see Robert P. Kraynak, "'Made in the Image of God': The Christian View of Human Dignity and the Political Order," in *In Defense of Human Dignity: Essays for Our Times,* ed. Robert P. Kraynak and Glenn Tinder (Notre Dame, Ind.: University of Notre Dame Press, 2003), pp. 81-118.

2. See, in this volume, "The Self in the Psalms and the Image of God."

3. Translations in this chapter are my own, unless otherwise noted.

ancient Chinese, Egyptian, and Mesopotamian creation myths, where creation of humanity in God's image is frequently narrated and remarkably graphic.[4] Given the Bible's reticence to address anthropological questions in terms to which its twenty-first-century readers may gravitate, Edward Curtis aptly observes, "the interpretation of the image of God has often reflected the *Zeitgeist* and has followed whatever emphasis happened to be current in psychology, or philosophy, or sociology, or theology"[5] — to which one is tempted to add the biological sciences.

The first thing to be said, therefore, is that throughout Scripture humanity's worth is not intrinsic but, instead, derivative of creation *after God's likeness.* In the Bible, human dignity depends entirely on humanity's possession by God and on God's decision to esteem and redeem it.[6] To grasp that point is critically important. Immediately, it challenges the language of "human dignity" in a postmodern situation, which is occasionally mesmerized by soft respect for a variable "Other"[7] and a not infrequent, anthropocentric pursuit of self-esteem. To speak with candor about the promise of God and God's perdurable achievements throws down a challenge to Western societies that are functionally if not avowedly atheistic.

A second point needs registering. Christian Scripture bespeaks numerous antinomies in its varied interpretations of humanity, its predicament and promise. At first glance, that may appear cause for disappointment, if not complaint. On reflection, however, one may celebrate the Bible's internal tensions as a precious gift. From the start, Christian visions of the human being have been as multidimensional, to borrow Don Browning's characterization in his essay, as human creatures themselves. My task in this chapter is to invite its reader to begin coming to terms with this aspect of the New Testament's multidimensionality. I aim to map and to correlate three discrete, significant streams within the New Testament that take seriously what it means to be human, in the sight of God in whose image we are created. Of necessity, such an

4. See Claus Westermann, *Genesis: An Introduction* (Minneapolis: Fortress, 1992), pp. 36-38.

5. E. M. Curtis, "Image of God (OT)," *The Anchor Bible Dictionary* 3 (1992): 389-91 (quotation, pp. 389-90).

6. For a systematic examination of this claim, see Christoph Schwöbel's contribution to the present volume.

7. For Emmanuel Lévinas, the "other" refers primarily to another human self, to whose integrity attention should be paid at the point of one's encounter with it (*Ethics and Infinity* [Pittsburgh: Duquesne University Press, 1985]). Although subsequent deconstructionist theory has sometimes celebrated "difference" *tout court,* Gillian Rose replies, "'The Other' is misrepresented as sheer alterity" (*Judaism and Modernity: Philosophical Essays* [Oxford: Blackwell, 1993], p. 8).

essay must be selective, representative, and suggestive. Even so, it should suffice to allow Matthew, John, and Paul each to have his say, while demonstrating large areas — eschatological, christological, and theological — where their different voices overlap.

The Matthean Vision

No other Gospel addresses more studiously than Matthew the vocation and destiny of those subject to "the kingdom of heaven" (see, e.g., 5:1–7:29; 13:1-52). So extensive is this consideration that Matthew has long been regarded, with good reason, as a manual of discipline for that *ekklesia* ("church") built by Jesus (Matt. 16:18). The First Gospel is not, however, simply a compendium of regulations. In form, of course, it is a story of Jesus; as the Evangelist tells it, that story illuminates in the first instance Jesus' own character and conduct, then by implication that of his disciples and of the world they are commissioned to evangelize (28:16-20). That story's presiding theme is righteousness *(he dikaiosyne):* pure and perfect obedience to God's will that marries thought, deed, and word in the manner evinced by Jesus, "God-With-Us" (1:23; 5:48). A basic premise of Matthew's theological approach is that God's Torah, or instruction, is the healthy ordering principle for human, not merely Christian, life. Because Jesus' life was in deepest accordance with that teaching, perfectly rectified to its shape and substance, Christ is Torah's *norma normans* (5:17-20). In castigating Israel's leaders for their failure to uphold the law, Jesus stands in the venerable line of prophetic critique exemplified by such figures as Jeremiah (5:1–9:26) and Ezekiel (12:21–14:23). It is thus fundamental that Jesus characterizes the moral ecology of God's kingdom neither as the highest good nor as the realm in which human virtue is validated, but as righteousness. Leander Keck aptly paraphrases Matthew's metaphor: "Where God's kingship is fully effective, there all things are right . . . and rightly related to everything else."[8] In other words, created humanity's *summum bonum* is an obedience rectified to the Creator's sovereign will, proleptically active in Jesus.

The fundamental threat to humanity, to which Jesus himself was exposed yet did not succumb, is the fragmentation of righteousness into a diabolical disintegrity (Matt. 4:1-11): the severance of deed from word, the divorce of inner intention from outward appearance, the masking of interior

---

8. Leander E. Keck, "Ethics in the Gospel according to Matthew," *Iliff Review* (Winter 1984): 39-56. The quoted clauses are reversed in the original (pp. 47-48).

corruption by a pious veneer (cf. 6:14-24). Matthew's customary term for this internal division is "hypocrisy" (23:28), about which at least three things should be registered. First, the First Gospel's "typical hypocrites" are those scribes and Pharisees (23:18, 23) whose emergent leadership in the Evangelist's own day threatened the self-identity and existence of his fledgling, Christian Jewish-Gentile community (23:1-2).[9] Second, hypocrisy for Matthew seems not merely a matter of pretense but, rather and more fundamentally, the condition of those who are radically self-deceived, both about their inner selves and about humanity's relationship to God and the world (23:25-28).[10] Such persons delude themselves by acting as though ostentatious religiosity could secure God's approval, or human approbation were the proper end of life (6:2, 5, 16; 23:5-7). Third, hypocrisy in the First Gospel afflicts not only the adversaries of Jesus and his disciples but also the church itself. Were that not so, Jesus in Matthew would have no reason to lament the inadequacies of Pharisaic Judaism before the crowds and his disciples (23:1-39), to castigate a brother who is deluded in his judgments (7:1-5), or to warn followers that their entry into the heavenly kingdom could be forever barred (5:17-20). As John Meier has noted, "The cleavage between good and bad thus runs through the whole of humanity; it does not run neatly between the church and unbelievers."[11] Matthew's Gospel describes the quest for integrity among disciples in the Matthean church, metaphorically captured in Jesus' aphorism, "The body's lamp is the eye: If your eye be clear-sighted, whole and luminescent will your body be" (6:22).[12]

The linchpin in Matthew's theology is christological: All lines converge upon Jesus, his identity, conduct, and significance. Jesus is more than a mere herald of the kingdom's dawning (4:17); the sum of his life, from birth to death and resurrection, "fills to the full" the law and the prophets (among others, 1:22-23; 2:15, 17-18) by recapitulating the story of Israel, this time obediently plotted to the arc of God's will (3:13-17). To Jesus may be correctly applied every christological title: teacher (8:19), healer (8:1–9:38), Son of God

---

9. Thus, among others, Graham Stanton, *A Gospel for a New People: Studies in Matthew* (Edinburgh: T&T Clark, 1992), pp. 113-68.

10. Dan O. Via Jr. *Self-Deception and Wholeness in Paul and Matthew* (Minneapolis: Fortress, 1990), pp. 92-98.

11. John P. Meier, *The Vision of Matthew: Christ, Church and Morality in the First Gospel* (New York: Paulist, 1979), p. 177.

12. Compare Abba Bessarion's miniature midrash on this text: "The monk ought to be as the Cherubim and the Seraphim: all eye" (Benedicta Ward, ed., *The Sayings of the Desert Fathers: The Alphabetical Collection*, rev. ed., Cistercian Studies 59 [Kalamazoo, Mich.: Cistercian Publications, 1984], p. 42).

(8:29), Son of David (9:27), Son of man (8:20), Lord (14:28, 30), Wisdom incarnate (11:19). It is hard to discern any of these titles as central; Matthew interweaves them all into his Gospel's tapestry. To mix the metaphor, Jesus in Matthew is truly "the man who fits no formula"[13] but, rather, gathers up all formulations — anthropological and ecclesiological — then explodes them. Moreover, in the First Gospel, Jesus cannot be understood in isolation from either everyday society or eschatological commonwealth. In Jesus God's kingdom and community meet:

> Now when John while in prison heard about the works of the Christ, he sent word by way of his disciples and said to him, "Are you the one who is coming or are we to expect another?" And Jesus answered them, "Go, announce to John what you hear and see: the blind see anew and the lame walk, lepers are cleansed and the deaf hear, and the dead are raised up and the poor are evangelized. And blessed is the one who does not stumble because of me." (Matt. 11:2-6)

In no sense is Christ extrinsic to the morality he teaches. Mature obedience is not simply commanded (5:48); it inheres in Jesus himself, who models its realization.

This invites some nettlesome exegetical questions. Does Matthew regard the human self *in se* as fractured, or only human deeds as needing correction? Put differently, is the anthropological problem one of essence or of action, a flaw in the doer or in the deed; and what difference does Christ's intervention make in resolving that problem? The answers are not blindingly obvious. Matthew is not clear; his theological tendency is to blend a variety of views at the expense of systematic coherence. From cursory inspection of this Gospel, one could leave it convinced that the self is quite competent to do what is expected of it — as dilated in the Sermon on the Mount — and that, if only Moses had said it more adequately (5:21-48), Jesus needn't have bothered. John's query is not stupid: "Are you the one who is to come or are we to expect another?"

Jesus' ultimate reply, however, suggests that matters may not be so simple: "Blessed is the one who does not stumble because of me." In fact, the First Gospel is littered with those who stumble over Jesus, often with murderous effect (2:13-17; 21:33-44). Seventy-five percent of those who hear word of the kingdom are unable to grasp it (13:18-22); weeds and wheat are intermixed, because both the sower and his enemy are at work (13:24-30). Something

---

13. Eduard Schweizer, *Jesus* (London: SCM, 1971), pp. 13-51.

within the tenant farmers is so wretched that they would kill for an inheritance not theirs (21:33-41); Rachel's grief is inconsolable, for her infants are no more (2:18). Even at their best — as parents who know how to give their children good gifts — human beings are evil (7:9-11). The context of these passages is unmistakably eschatological, suggesting that the righteous and wicked things we do occur on a cosmic battlefield bigger than the individual conscience (*nota bene* 13:37-38). In that regard, the wording of Jesus' spontaneous thanksgiving to God in Matthew 11:25-27 is crucial, for it makes clear (first) that receipt of "all things" from the Lord of heaven and earth depends entirely upon revelation to nursing infants, not upon ratiocinations by "the wise and discerning," and (second) that such revelation comes only through the Father's Son, to whom "all things have been delivered." The last clause, echoed in the Great Commission of the risen Christ at the Gospel's end (28:18), suggests, without fully articulating, that Jesus for Matthew is more than the moral exemplar *par excellence,* the pattern for what those who can do should do. It is because the Christ of the church is "God-With-Us" (1:23), right now (18:20) and unto the consummation of the age (28:20), that his disciples can do what he commands of them. In Matthew, christology effectively absorbs pneumatology: in place of the Spirit's empowering presence is Immanuel, who has eschatologically burst into human history and promises never to abandon his church.

The Johannine Vision

John's view of humanity before God is harsher than Matthew's, in part because it stems from a more vitriolic separation of Christians from Jews near the end of the first century.[14] While the matter remains vigorously debated, Matthew, the most overtly Jewish of all the Gospels, seems to me reflective of a community in transition: firmly embedded in Judaism, the First Gospel appears to be peeling away from an increasingly dominant Pharisaism toward a Christian sect still recognizably Jewish (e.g., Matt. 23:1-3). In the Fourth Gospel, however, the divorce between Jews and Christians appears complete, and almost completely ugly: "For already the Jews had decided that if anyone confessed [Jesus] as Christ, such a one was to be expelled from the synagogue" (John 9:22; see also 12:42; 16:2). "The Jews" — at times identified with the

14. The now classic articulation of this proposal is J. Louis Martyn, *History and Theology in the Fourth Gospel,* third ed., New Testament Library (Louisville: Westminster John Knox, 2003).

Pharisees, though not consistently so (7:1–8:59; 9:13-41; 18:33-38) — are rendered as antagonists almost to the point of anachronism: one could read John and nearly forget that Jesus and his disciples were Jewish, as Matthew and the other Synoptics take for granted and as John himself does not deny (4:22). In Matthew, Jesus' controversy with his co-religionists more obviously pivots upon Torah and its proper interpretation: "For I tell you that unless your righteousness far surpasses that of the scribes and Pharisees, by no means can you enter the kingdom of heaven" (Matt. 5:20). In John, the sticking point has more obviously become the Messiah himself, the claims made for Jesus' dignity and divinity: "The Jews answered [Jesus], 'Not for a noble work do we intend to stone you, but for blasphemy — for you, though a human, make yourself out to be God'" (10:33; see also 5:16-18, 30-47; 7:14-44; 8:21-59). No wonder they think so. Jesus of the Fourth Gospel is more than merely Israel's Messiah (1:43-51). He is, as C. H. Dodd put it, "the final concentration of the whole creative and revealing thought of God, which is also the meaning of the universe, in an *individual* who is what humanity was designed to be in the divine purpose."[15] It is as though John has carried Matthew's christological premise of Christ as Immanuel to its radical conclusion: Jesus more than simply testifies to God's glory; he actually radiates it (1:14; 17:22, 24).

Although John does not use the terms as exact synonyms (see, e.g., 14:19, 27, 30), "the Jews" of the Fourth Gospel to some degree represent "the world," this Evangelist's multivalent shorthand for the human condition. John 1:10 conveniently bundles this term's various connotations: the true light was in the world (a neutral comment about the created order), "and the world came to be through him" (a positive affirmation, restated in 3:16-17; 12:46), "yet the world knew him not" (a negative assertion of religious humanity's general rejection of God's self-revelation in Jesus). The negative view of the world assumes precedence in John, defining the pole of all things antithetical to God: sin (15:22, 24), lies (8:44), enslavement (8:34-36), death (5:24), and especially darkness (1:5). Jesus' coming into the world exposes its perversity: "This is the judgment, that the light has come into the world, and people loved darkness rather than light, for their deeds were wicked" (3:19). Accordingly, in Jesus' declaration to the crowd, John comments with deceptive simplicity on the parlous condition of humanity without faith in Jesus:

> "Now is the judgment of this world, now will the ruler of this world be cast out: . . . Yet for a short time the light is among you. Walk while you

---

15. C. H. Dodd, *The Interpretation of the Fourth Gospel* (Cambridge: Cambridge University Press, 1953), p. 282 (emphasis added).

have the light, that the darkness may not overtake you; for the one who walks in darkness does not know where he is going. While you have the light, entrust yourself to the light, that you may be sons of light." These things Jesus said, and, having gone away, he hid himself from them; for though he had done so many signs before them, they did not trust in him. (12:31, 35-37)

Apart from believing in and confessing Jesus as the Son of man in whom God is decisively glorified, humanity is "in the dark." For those like Nicodemus, "a ruler of the Jews [who] came to him by night" (3:1-2), attracted to Jesus yet unable to make a commitment to him, darkness registers as befuddlement, a comical misunderstanding of what Jesus is driving at (3:3-15). For other religious authorities, stumbling in the dark turns murderous: "They will excommunicate you from the synagogues; indeed, the hour is coming when all who kill you will think they are offering sacrifice to God" (16:2).

By contrast, "doing the truth" means entering the light (3:21), which for John is tantamount to believing in God = believing in Jesus = accepting by faith that Jesus uniquely reveals God (1:18; 12:44; 14:10-11; 17:8). Those who believe in Jesus are drawn into a new and indestructible sphere of life (3:14-16; 5:24; 6:40, 47), characterized by public testimony to Christ in the teeth of persecution (15:18-27), assurance in the face of mortal danger (10:1-18), joy and peace amidst the world's tribulations (16:21-33), and — most emphatically — obedience to Jesus' commands, epitomized as self-giving love for one another (13:34-35; 15:12-17). Here the Fourth Evangelist's point of contact with the First is at once both obvious and obscure. In John's Gospel there is none of the exquisitely detailed moral instruction that Matthew unrolls by the yard. Nevertheless, the love-command in John arguably distills Matthew's mass of paraenesis, much as Jesus himself in Matthew identifies unreserved love for God and love of neighbor as one loves self as the two commandments from which depend the law and the prophets in their entirety (Matt. 22:37-40). Matthew is more explicit than John that one's enemies are to be loved (Matt. 5:44), but John does not contradict that injunction. Indeed, by refusing to endorse violence or reciprocity of that hatred to which Jesus' disciples are inevitably subjected (John 15:18-25; 17:14), the teaching of Jesus in John resonates with that of the Matthean Jesus, who insists that loving as God loves is utterly gratuitous, never a matter of tit for tat (Matt. 5:43-48).

John's moral discourse matches Matthew's in at least four other respects. First, in both cases self-renunciation for others' benefit is a moral norm (John 12:25; Matt. 5:38-42). Second, the commandment is not restricted to members of the community; its scope is universal (Matt. 28:19-20; John

12:32-33). Third, love is learned within the context of the church, which subverts this world's political and cultural mores (John 10:31; Matt. 12:34-39). Fourth, love expresses the disciple's obedience to Jesus, which cannot be reduced to mere confession, however orthodox (Matt. 7:21-23; John 13:34-35).[16]

If, for all their points of contact, Matthew is richer than John in moral teaching, John is more direct than Matthew in articulating the decisively new situation into which Jesus' incarnation, crucifixion, and glorification has thrust human life, as well as the means by which Christ's continuing presence is realized among the company of disciples. Release from the world's darkness and delusion is ultimately God's doing: in Johannine terms, one is "begotten of God" (John 1:13), "begotten from above," or "begotten of the Spirit" (3:3, 8). Because the Son does nothing of his own accord but only what he sees done by the Father who sent him (5:19-24), then it is equally true to say that Christ is the proximate cause of human liberation: "If you abide in my word, truly you are my disciples; and you will know the truth, and the truth will set you free" (8:31-32). That is the real reason behind John's seemingly odd insistence that Jesus is "not of this world" (8:23; 17:14; 18:36-37). Only one whose origin is from God and whose activity transcends this world's blighted warrants can liberate the human self for God's radical reconstitution.[17] Likewise, the Holy Spirit, characterized as "another advocate" (14:16), is sent from beyond this world by the Father, to abide with Jesus' disciples, to remind them of all that he has said, and to judge this world's sin (14:17; 15:25-26; 16:7-11). The baptismal formula in Matthew's Great Commission ("in the name of the Father and of the Son and of the Holy Ghost," 28:19) may be proto-Trinitarian in form, but John actually nudges us in the direction of what later Christian theology unfolded as the economic Trinity.[18]

Finally, however, Matthew concurs with John that the believing self can take no credit for its faith but has only God to thank for its election. While neither Evangelist offers a reasoned account for unbelief, both of them point to the same human culpability — the desire to be recognized and praised by other mortals, rather than by God (Matt. 6:1-4; John 12:42-43) — and both interpret resistance to Jesus by appealing to Isaiah's oracle of Israel's blinding by

16. In this paragraph's formulation, I have been aided by D. Moody Smith, "Ethics and the Interpretation of the Fourth Gospel," in *Word, Theology, and Community in John*, ed. John Painter, R. Alan Culpepper, and Fernando Segovia (St. Louis: Chalice, 2002), pp. 109-22.

17. See Leander E. Keck, "Derivation As Destiny: 'Of-Ness' in Johannine Christology, Anthropology, and Soteriology," in *Exploring the Gospel of John in Honor of D. Moody Smith*, ed. R. Alan Culpepper and C. Clifton Black (Louisville: Westminster John Knox, 1996), pp. 274-88.

18. See, for instance, Claude Welch, *In This Name: The Doctrine of the Trinity in Contemporary Theology* (New York: Charles Scribner's Sons, 1952), pp. 293-94.

God (Isa. 6:9-10; Matt. 13:14-15; John 12:40). Contrary to later gnostic schemes, the self does not awaken to knowledge of its "incomparable self" and god-like nature.[19] To the contrary, "You did not choose me, but I chose you" (John 15:16); "No one can come to me unless drawn by the Father who sent me" (6:44; cf. Matt. 16:17, which ascribes Peter's confession to divine revelation, not to flesh and blood). Both Matthew and John construe as a supernatural event, not as a mortal achievement, Christian faith that Jesus is definitively the Christ, "the Son of the living God" (Matt. 16:16), who by his crucifixion reveals, while radically redefining, God's essential glory (John 7:39; 13:31; 17:5).

The Pauline Vision

Paul's view of the human condition and its divine redemption bears some resemblance to John's. In both cases, our predicament is one of radical bondage to the tyranny of sin, from which Christ liberates those who entrust themselves to him and transfers them into a new relationship with him and with God (thus, among others, John 8:31-36; Rom. 6:17-23; Gal. 4:4-7). Alongside Romans 7:7-25, Romans 1:18–3:20 is Paul's key statement of religious humanity's plight viewed with hindsight, from the vantage point of the cross; in that sense, we may observe Paul's soteriology unfolding in reverse, from solution to plight. In John, Jesus explicates that retrospectively Christian point of view: "If I had not come and had spoken to them, they would not have sin; but now they have no pretext for their sin" (John 15:22).

The differences in Paul's formulation are of both degree and kind. Nowhere in John or Matthew is the pathology of sin probed with the intensity of Romans 1:18–3:20. In John, sin is characteristic of "the world" that refuses to believe in Jesus, choosing instead to hate him and those who confess him (15:18–16:11). For Matthew, sin is less christologically focused, bearing instead the conventionally Jewish connotations of "missing the mark" (18:15, 21), failure (3:6), or guilt (12:31; 27:4). While such nuances are certainly present in his letters (e.g., Rom. 2:12; 1 Cor. 8:12; Gal. 1:4), Paul markedly personifies sin as a tyrant, a domain of enslaving force, to which humanity — even religious humanity at its best — is inexorably subjected unless liberated by a superior power: "For we have already accused all, both Jews and Greeks, as being under

19. "God created men, and men created God. . . . It would be fitting that the gods should worship men" (*Gospel of Philip* [Nag Hammadi Codex II.3.71-72]). Consult Kurt Rudolph, *Gnosis: The Nature and History of Gnosticism* (San Francisco: Harper and Row, 1987), pp. 88-113.

the power of sin" (Rom. 3:9b). Within this context, we may distinguish Paul's radical consideration of the law. Beyond the Fourth Gospel, which in a general way regards Scripture as bearing witness to Christ (John 5:39-40; cf. 1 Cor. 15:3-4), and contrary to Matthew, who describes righteousness as fulfillment of Torah's every jot and tittle (Matt. 5:17-20), Paul denies that humans, by dint of satisfying the law, can be rectified with God (Rom. 3:20; Gal. 2:16).

Paul's reasons for this denial are many and not systematically coordinated, but at least two may be mentioned here. First, while the law subordinately points to Christ (Rom. 3:21, 31; Gal. 3:1-29), it cannot supplant Christ's lordship: "For if justification [*he dikaiosyne*] is by legal means, then Christ died for nothing" (Gal. 2:21). That is to say, in cases where Torah is regarded as a rival to Christ for human salvation, legal righteousness must yield to "the word of the cross" (1 Cor. 1:18; so also Matt. 12:1-14). Second, while the law exposes sin (Rom. 7:7, 13) and serves a temporarily custodial function (Gal. 3:23-26), the law itself has been commandeered by sin's power; consequently, justification by Torah is constitutive of that deathward, *ancien régime* from which Christians, by faith, are set free (Rom. 7:1–8:8). Sin has twisted God's own commandment, which is "holy and just and good" (Rom. 7:12), eliciting the very opposite of that for which the religious self aspires: the service of sin precisely in the service of God.[20] Here, Paul offers a theological reason for Matthew's compatible though unexplained claim: even in nurturing parenthood, the very point where humanity functions at its selfless best, humans remain evil (Matt. 7:11). Paul also explores in greater detail the circumstances by which God makes possible genuine integrity. Those who have been baptized into Christ Jesus, buried with him by baptism into his death (Rom. 6:1-23; see also Gal. 2:20), are transferred from wretchedness into a fundamentally new creation that partakes of a new life restructured by the Spirit (Rom. 8:1-39), reconciliation with God (2 Cor. 5:16-21), and conduct controlled by Christ's love (Rom. 12:1–13:10). As in John and Matthew, Paul is explicit that the signature of life in the Spirit is self-renunciation inspired by Christ's own *kenosis*: "And for all Christ died, that those who live may live no longer for themselves but for him who for them died and was raised" (2 Cor. 5:15). The moral implications derive from a deeper theological shift: "It is only under the lordship of Christ that the devout man ceases to make his worship a means of self-justification and self-praise."[21]

---

20. For acute analysis of this aspect of Pauline thought, see Paul W. Meyer, "The Worm at the Core of the Apple: Exegetical Reflections on Romans 7," in *The Word in This World: Essays in New Testament Exegesis and Theology*, ed. John T. Carroll, New Testament Library (Louisville: Westminster John Knox, 2004), pp. 57-77.

21. Ernst Käsemann, "On Paul's Anthropology," *Perspectives on Paul* (London: SCM,

Even a cursory treatment of Pauline anthropology and soteriology must reckon with "Adam, a type of the one to come" (Rom. 5:14). Here the exegetical waters are deep and treacherous, though a few points may be registered with some confidence. To begin at the least controversial place: By drawing the contrast between Adam and Christ in both Romans 5:12-21 and 1 Corinthians 15:20-28, Paul is making an *eschatological* statement about the complete break from humanity as it has labored under sin, disobedience, and death, and the radically new creation bound up in Christ's obedience on the cross and its vindication by God's having raised him from the dead. Paul is reasonably clear about this. For him, Christ does not represent, as Irenaeus seems to suggest (*Against Heresies* 4.38.1), the pinnacle of humankind, advancing from childish immaturity to a consummation of latent potential. Contrary to Irenaeus (3.18.1; 4.38.1-3; 5.19-21), Ambrose (*Exposition of Luke* 7.142), Augustine (e.g., *City of God* 14.10-11, 26), and a host of interpreters afterward, it is not indisputably evident that Paul presupposes a theological scheme that progresses from original blessedness, through a fall from righteousness, to the restoration of humanity's fractured image of God. Paul, in fact, never discusses humanity's "original state." Notwithstanding a subtle reference to lost glory in 1:23, Paul's real focus in Romans 1–3 is on the plight of humanity as it is: thoroughly estranged from God. Paul speaks, not of the restoration of Adam's lost blessedness, but of Christ as humanity created eschatologically afresh, alive in the Spirit and apart from the dust of the old (1 Cor. 15:20-50). To understand human beings as Paul does, one does not start with Adam, whose creation in "the image and glory of God" Paul of course knows from Genesis (certainly, 1 Cor. 11:7; Rom. 1:23, possibly) but never develops soteriologically. Instead, one begins with Christ's crucifixion and resurrection. From that vantage point, one may look backward, upon our shared mortality with Adam, as well as forward to humanity's conformation *in Christ,* who is the image of God (Rom. 8:29; 1 Cor. 15:49). Similarly, "our hope of sharing God's glory" lies exclusively "through our Lord Jesus Christ" (Rom. 5:1-2; Phil. 4:19). Significantly, Paul does not refer to a restoration in us of the glory Adam knew. Rather, "glory [is] of the Lord, [and we] are being changed into his likeness from one degree of glory to another; for this comes from the Lord who is the Spirit" (2 Cor. 3:18 [RSV]).[22]

Closely related with this Adamic imagery are Paul's references to humanity's restoration in accordance with the divine image *(he eikon).* While

---

1971), p. 16; see also Victor Paul Furnish, *Theology and Ethics in Paul* (Nashville: Abingdon, 1968), pp. 162-206, 224-27.

22. In thinking through the issues in this paragraph, I have been helped by John A. Ziesler, "Anthropology of Hope," *The Expository Times* 90 (1979): 104-9, and John Muddiman, "'Adam, the Type of the One to Come,'" *Theology* 87 (1984): 101-10.

Paul does not synthesize his comments in this matter, his extant letters give us enough clues to discern a rough shape for his thought. An *eikon* was a representation of something or someone: a portrait or likeness, such as the image on a coin (Matt. 22:19-20 and parallels) or embossed medallions *(signa)* of the emperor's head on military banners (Josephus, *Jewish War* 2.169; *Jewish Antiquities* 18.55).[23] Paul applies the language of "image" in two directions, to the redeemer and to the redeemed. In 2 Corinthians 4:4, Christ is the *eikon* of God: If one could hold a mirror to the invisible God, the reflection would be that of Christ. While Paul assumes the claim, in Genesis 1:26-28, that creation in God's image is a property of man (and woman: 1 Cor. 11:7),[24] as living beings humans have worn "the image of [Adam,] the dusty one" (1 Cor. 15:49). In a different context, Paul speaks of primordial sin as idolatry, humanity's foolish exchange of the incorruptible God's glory for derivative images of corruptible creatures (Rom. 1:23). In effect, Christ's coming reverses that polarity: Those whom God has called are predestined to conformity with the Son's image (8:29). Those who have worn the image of the earthly one will wear the image of the heavenly one (1 Cor. 15:49). Those who behold in Christ God's radiance are undergoing metamorphosis, from splendor to splendor, into God's own image, which Christ reflects (2 Cor. 3:18). In ways that have cast doubt on its Pauline authorship, the Epistle to the Colossians develops such claims, with respect both to the redeemer and to the redeemed. More explicitly than in 1 Corinthians 1:18–2:16 or Philippians 2:5-11, Colossians "christologizes" Hellenistic Judaism's view of primordial Wisdom as God's agent in creation and redemption (Sir. 24; cf. Prov. 8:22-31), reassigning those majestic achievements to the crucified and exalted Christ (Col. 1:15-20). While Colossians 3:3-4 maintains Paul's restraint in speaking of the eschatological consummation as lying in the future (Rom. 6:4-5; 1 Cor. 15:42-57), at other points Colossians speaks of believers' resurrection as an accomplished fact (2:12-13; 3:1). Nevertheless, individual and corporate morality is the product of a divinely driven human destiny, "ongo-

---

23. Irenaeus's differentiation of "image" from "likeness" — Jesus being the *imago Dei,* humans created "after" his likeness (*Against Heresies* 5.16.2) — subsequently developed in medieval theology, presses a distinction that cannot be scripturally sustained.

24. Paul's allusion, in 1 Corinthians 11:2-16, to the creation accounts of Genesis occurs within his convoluted argument about appropriate attire for men and women at worship — an exegetical knot that cannot and need not be unraveled here. For our purposes, we need only observe that, in 11:7, the narratives in Genesis 1 (the Priestly account) and 2 (the Yahwist legend) have been harmonized, allowing Paul to assume simultaneously human creation in the image of God (Gen. 1:27) and woman's fabrication out of man (Gen. 2:21-23). Such an assumption permits Paul in this case to reason out a sequence of reflected glory (woman mirrors man's glory, which mirrors God's) while preventing him from claiming that woman is the image of man. By implication, in 1 Corinthians 11:7, both woman and man are *God's* image.

ing renewal in [obedient] knowledge, in the likeness of its creator" (3:10; cf. Gen. 1:27; Rom. 12:2). Like Romans (6:1-14), Colossians (2:11-12; 3:5-17) ties God's burial of the old person and resurrection of the new with baptism into Christ and life within Christ's body.[25]

The Visions Converge

It is time to summarize our Cook's tour of anthropological views within the New Testament. I have expended enough effort in distinguishing the approaches adopted by Paul, John, and Matthew that sharpening our focus on their areas of agreement seems a fit conclusion.

First, *each of these views is radically eschatological.* In the New Testament, humanity's glory lies not in the best calibrated balance of aspirations against achievements — personal *vis-à-vis* corporate, enlightened or otherwise — but only through the invasive disclosure of God's integrity through Jesus Christ incarnate, crucified, and raised from death. "From that time Jesus began to proclaim, saying, 'Repent — for the kingdom of heaven has drawn near'" (Matt. 4:17). "For God's righteousness is being unveiled in [the gospel] through faith for faith, as it is written: 'The righteous will live by faith'" (Rom. 1:17; cf. Hab. 2:4). "This is the judgment: The light has come into the world, and people loved the darkness more than the light, for their deeds were evil" (John 3:19). For these witnesses, human destiny is one piece of a larger mystery being revealed to the eyes of faith (Matt. 13:11; 1 Cor. 2:1, 7; John 9:35-41). Humanity's encounter with God — and thus with itself — through Jesus Christ is, in Joachim Jeremias's felicitous expression, "an eschatology in process of realization" *(sich realisierende Eschatologie).*[26] In the New Testament world, at least among some Hellenistic Jews, the eschatological dimension of this claim was probably not as disturbing as the predicate of its unfolding in Jesus of Nazareth. In our own world, the problem is more often the reverse. We can tolerate various affirmations of a progressive revelation into which Jesus can be incorporated. It's the claim that, in Jesus Christ, God has abrasively, with finality, exploded this world for its (and our) transformation that sets liberal and postmodern teeth on edge.

---

25. A similar conclusion, eucharistically framed, is drawn in Robert Jenson's *"Anima Ecclesiastica"* in this volume.

26. Joachim Jeremias, *The Parables of Jesus,* second rev. ed. (London: SCM, 1972), p. 230. Jeremias credits Ernst Haenchen with this phrase. Linda Woodhead's chapter in this volume gazes without flinching at the anthropological implications of God's mystery, into which humans are being drawn.

That assertion leads directly to the second area of appreciable overlap among the anthropological claims of Paul, Matthew, and John: *their christological concentration.* As recent excursions into the renewed "quest for the Jesus of history" have amply demonstrated, the ghost of the liberal Jesus — the sage raconteur of proto-Kantian ideals — stubbornly resists exorcism. For contemporary sensibilities, one of the most baffling features of Jesus Christ, as presented in the New Testament, is a scandalous particularity that in no way compromises his critical, universal personhood. Put bluntly, in the Fourth Gospel and in Paul's letters — even in Matthew, to a surprising degree (see 11:25-30) — Jesus is not important because he is a wise teacher. He *is* God's Wisdom, and therein lies his importance. To draw from a different metaphorical range, Jesus is not Everyman but, rather, the Son of man — the apocalyptic measure against which human fidelity to God's will is or shall be measured (e.g., Matt. 24:26-44; John 1:43–5:29; 1 Thess. 5:1-11). Christ is not the purveyor of tips for social amelioration or better self-adjustment; he is Adam's antitype, the corporate person into whom believers are consolidated, nothing less than God's new initiative for a creation reconciled to himself (Rom. 5:12-21; 2 Cor. 5:16-19). Whatever their modes of expression, these representative views concur in regarding Jesus Christ as intrinsic to God's renewal of the human being, along with everything else.[27]

Thus we come to a final point of commonality: *Like the New Testament generally, Paul, Matthew, and John regard the human being as inextricably related to God.* As the doctrine of the incarnation assumes and maximizes, the God of Scripture is inherently relational: God-With-Us, with Israel and the nations, from ages unto ages (Matt. 1:23; 28:18-20). In essence, the human plight is the refusal of that relationship: the overweening decision to go it alone, the inflating of our precariously contingent claims to an ultimate importance they cannot bear, our regarding God — if at all — as a convenient ally of our dependent self instead of as Creator, Judge, and Redeemer.[28] The only dignity the New Testament envisions for human beings is their Christ-

---

27. A profound outworking of this insight is expressed by Maximus the Confessor (c. 580-662): "[Christ's] relationship with man . . . is something much wider than redemption; it coincides with deification. The real anthropological meaning of deification is Christification" (quoted by Panayiotis Nellas, *Deification in Christ: Orthodox Perspectives on the Nature of the Human Person* [Crestwood, N.Y.: St. Vladimir's Seminary Press, 1987], p. 39). In another chapter of the present volume, J. Kameron Carter offers a bracing critique of modern theological attempts to construe human dignity apart from renewal by "the mind of Christ" (1 Cor. 2:16b).

28. This book's contributions by Elaine Graham and Douglas Meeks demonstrate the devastating consequences of this mistake with reference, respectively, to contemporary technology and the market system.

driven realignment with God (Matt. 5:48; John 1:12-13), their liberating transformation into that splendor God has always intended for them (John 17:20-
26; 2 Cor. 3:12–4:6; Phil. 3:20-21).

Of all pills this may seem the nastiest to swallow, for the simple reason
that Western secularism since the Enlightenment usually operates with something more akin to Hellenistic Stoicism than classical Christianity. Cicero put
this point of view concisely:

> There is, I assure you, a medical art for the soul. It is philosophy, whose
> aid need not be sought, as in bodily diseases, from outside ourselves. We
> must endeavor with all our resources and all our strength to become ca-
> pable of doctoring ourselves. (*Tusculan Disputations* 3.6)

Doctoring ourselves — whether by philosophy, business, politics, science, or even theology — seems the standing order of our day. And so we
recklessly demean those like Kelly, whom Hans Reinders introduces to this
volume's readers, who cannot act as their own physicians (cf. Matt. 9:12-13).
For the Stoics, one *can* be one's own physician, because humans are essentially reasonable creatures; one *must* be one's own physician, because human
dignity is realized by becoming precisely as self-sufficient and indifferent to
human turmoil as the gods are believed to be. Just there is Martha Nussbaum,
by her own declaration sympathetic to Stoicism's particular "therapy of desire," brought up short by the limits of its treatment:

> [The Stoic] is to trust nothing and nobody but herself. But how deeply,
> then, can she trust and care for others? . . . She is to value her own reason
> as *the* source of her humanity and her integrity, the one thing of real in-
> trinsic worth in her life. So long as that is with her, she can go through life
> fulfilled. So long as that is free, she has her dignity, whatever the world
> may do to her. But what, then, can she consistently think of her deepest
> ties to other people? Of the prospect of losing them or being betrayed by
> them? . . . Can one live in reason's kingdom, understood in the way the
> Stoics understand it, and still be a creature of wonder, grief, and love?[29]

In the last analysis, by rejecting what Nussbaum calls "reason's zealous
hegemony" as adamantly as it embraces God's passionate involvement with

---

29. Martha C. Nussbaum, *The Therapy of Desire: Theory and Practice in Hellenistic Ethics*
(Princeton, N.J.: Princeton University Press, 1994), p. 358. To Nussbaum I am obliged for the
quotation from Cicero, immediately preceding (*Therapy of Desire*, p. 316). For a perceptive analysis of "Nussbaum's enriched liberalism," consult Eric O. Springsted, *The Act of Faith: Christian
Faith and the Moral Self* (Grand Rapids: Eerdmans, 2002), pp. 193-214.

the world and its creatures, the New Testament remains one of our culture's most annoying gadflies. Permeating its various views, the central theological issue in human dignity is the merciful sovereignty of God.[30]

30. This essay's indebtedness to my fellow contributors is plain. I thank also Dale C. Allison Jr., Beverly R. Gaventa, and Marianne Meye Thompson for their gracious critiques of an earlier draft.

The Economy of Grace:
Human Dignity in the Market System

M. DOUGLAS MEEKS

"I hunger." So cry all human beings.[1] From the beginning human beings have organized themselves in response to this ubiquitous visceral cry in order to assure survival. This performance is the oldest significance of the word *oikonomia,* whose driving question is, "Will everyone in the household get what it takes to survive the day?" The role of the *oikonomos,* the economist in the ancient sense, is to respond to the prayer, "Give us this day our daily bread." "Economy," no matter how much this elemental meaning is eclipsed by the sophistication of the modern economic sciences associated with it, is about human surviving and thriving.

If *oikonomia,* in its original sense, had to do with establishing the conditions of home, it also acknowledged the fact that human beings are shaped according to the economy or household in which they live.[2] To be homeless is

---

1. The practice of economy, however, often fails to discern that the cry of starving children with distended stomachs is different from the hunger pangs of regularly surfeited people.

2. Adam Smith and Karl Marx were not the first to make this claim; it was held by Amos and Jeremiah, Plato and Aristotle, St. Paul, the Christian Fathers, and the whole Christian tradition until the seventeenth century. Both Plato and Aristotle extol the virtues of *oikonomia* and derogate the shaping of life according to commerce *(chrematistics).* They argue that the different modes of subsistence and of acquiring property produce "different ways of life" or different associations of human beings. Human beings are constituted by their associations and the goods their associations serve. Until the end of the seventeenth century the church and its theology followed Aristotle's arguments that human community and the polis/state must regulate property, and regularly argued, as part and parcel of its anthropology, for fair price, just wage, complex space in which there was place free from commodity exchange, and the wisdom of sumptuary laws. They also condemned usury as the unnatural assumption that an inanimate thing, money, can work.

to be subject to death. That is what makes us creatures of economy. Though many humane economists intend that economics serve human life, modern orthodox economic theory does not include human livelihood or the life of nature in its logic.[3] So these questions come to the fore: To what extent do some economic theories and the global market system endanger human dignity? Is the global market system a home in which human beings and nature can survive? To grapple with these questions we will contrast two economies and their bearing on anthropology: the *market system* and the *oikonomia tou theou* (the "economy of God").

The Market System

The market system, the principal way in which the developed world coordinates human activity, is best conceived as a set of relationships or performances. This is the reason that when we think of the market system, we should think society, not narrowly conceived economics.[4] The market system cannot be reduced to the space of marketplace, workplace, or stock exchange. Rather, the market system tends to make all space homogenous by making the market logic the dominant, if not exclusive, rule in all dimensions of society. As modernity moved inexorably from a market economy to a market society, the tendency was to think of everything as if it were in the market. When everything is in principle for sale, the market system in its most extreme self-conception assumes that the market has the right and competence to govern in human matters.

The modern market system undoubtedly should be extolled as the most successful human instrument in modernity. Even beyond its effect in the astonishing growth in living standards, its most winsome and weighty claim is that it coordinates and governs masses of human beings peacefully, without command or coercion.[5] This lends credence to its claim to be the only agent capable of fulfilling the Enlightenment dream of eternal peace and freedom. The majority of people in the developed world tend to take for

3. Karl Polanyi, *The Livelihood of Man,* ed. Harry W. Pearson (New York: Academic, 1977).

4. The market system is "the most embracing and precise system of enormously large-scale coordination that humankind has ever invented or stumbled into." Charles E. Lindblom, *The Market System* (New Haven: Yale University Press, 2001).

5. Adam Smith's *Wealth of Nations* begins with an effusive description of how enormous masses of human beings are related to each other in the differentiated functions of producing everyday goods.

granted this ultimate justification of the market society. That the nature of the human being should conform to the "incorrigible" assumptions of the market is seldom doubted where it is thought that the market system can perform optimally.

The logic of the market system's rule, *quid pro quo*, however, threatens the human being by challenging the viability of society and human community.[6] This most important glue of modern society is at once also one of its significant threats. If it is the case, as seems undeniable, that the market system over time destroys human community, then what human beings construct for their own security turns out to be a possible source of their insecurity. It is urgent, then, for Christian anthropology to question the view of the human being at work in the market system.

The market system's claim to produce harmony without power is premature, and, in fact, the power of the market system is often hidden by its own self-presentation. Since Adam Smith's "invisible hand," the market has demonstrated a remarkable explanatory power as regards human transactions, but it has harbored its own mystification. As I have previously argued, the market system often plies its self-justification by employing deformed concepts of God.[7] The market system touts its own self-regulating laws, but, in fact, it cannot function without power external to itself and it does not reveal the potentially inhumane power on which it often depends. For example, the theory of the market system pretends to require very little from the state, but, in fact, extreme forms of laissez-faire market systems have actually existed only when the state has been strong enough radically to change the rules and structures of the market and civil society.[8] In our epoch, for the second time in modernity, laissez-faire theory has resulted in globalization and is freshly accompanied by theories of empire.[9]

---

6. See Karl Polanyi's classic narration of the rise of the modern market and its impact on human communities, *The Great Transformation* (Boston: Beacon, 1957).

7. M. Douglas Meeks, *God the Economist: The Doctrine of God and Political Economy* (Minneapolis: Fortress, 1989).

8. See John Gray, *False Dawn: The Delusion of Global Capitalism* (New York: New Press, 1998).

9. See, for example, two works by Niall Ferguson: *The Cash Nexus: Money and Power in the Modern World* (New York: Basic, 2001), and *Empire: The Rise and Demise of the British World Order and the Lessons for Global Power* (New York: Basic, 2003). Cf. Michael Hardt and Antonio Negri, *Empire* (Cambridge: Harvard University Press, 2000).

The Market System Extended

Globalization can be understood principally as the spread of the market system's domain or the ideology of free markets writ large. Orthodox global market ideology maintains a simple equation: privatization plus deregulation plus globalization equals global integration by the market system equals prosperity.[10] The economic integration of the world promises lasting affluence and peace.[11]

But the results of the current globalization, not unlike the first modern globalization (ca. 1870-1929), do not support this fundamentalist utopianism. Everywhere it reaches, intense globalization generates massive wealth. The new wealth stems primarily from the resources that are set loose by the destruction of inefficient practices through competition and that are then lodged in the financial markets. Firms and entire industries that were previously state-owned, subsidized, or protected by regulations and tariffs have been particularly targeted. Also destroyed, of course, are the secure jobs of their former employees. While millions lose their livelihoods, the architects and beneficiaries of global change are enriched at a rate and scale never before seen. Economic efficiency increases but so do societal inefficiencies. The global market system endangers human dignity by putting all localities and communities in jeopardy and thus preventing for great numbers of people the communal belonging necessary to human dignity.

For millions of people globalization has not meant the enhancement of life; it does not work for most of the world's abject poor and working poor. For them life has worsened as they have seen their jobs destroyed and their lives become more insecure. They have felt increasingly subject to forces beyond their control. They stand by as their democracies are undermined, their cultures eroded, and their natural environments degraded. "Globalization, as it has been advocated, often seems to replace the old dictatorships of national elites with new dictatorships of international finance."[12] Growing income inequality and chronic high levels of unemployment lead to a decline of family

10. For the following, see Edward Luttwak, *Turbo-Capitalism: Winners and Losers in the Global Economy* (New York: HarperCollins, 1999), pp. 25-44.

11. "Evidence that contradicts those beliefs is summarily dismissed. For the believers in free and unfettered markets, capital market liberalization was *obviously* desirable; one didn't need evidence that it promoted growth. Evidence that it caused instability would be dismissed as merely one of the adjustment costs, part of the pain that had to be accepted in the transition to a market economy." Joseph E. Stiglitz, *Globalization and Its Discontents* (New York: W. W. Norton, 2002), p. 7.

12. Stiglitz, *Globalization and Its Discontents*, p. 247.

and communal life. A seething anger leads to despair, and despair becomes the fodder for social pathologies and terrorism. If there is a kind of inevitability to globalization, especially because of the technologies of communication and transportation, Christian anthropology has to press the question whether globalization can be guided in ways that humanize. What view of the human being and what polity would this require?

The Economy of Grace

By "economy of God" we mean (1) the way the triune God calls into being and redeems the creation, and (2) the peculiar communities of the household of Israel and the household of Jesus Christ that God brings into being to serve God's creation of the conditions of home for all of God's creatures. These economies form the "system" through which God's people are human *coram Deo* and all things are held together ("systematized," Col. 1:17) in the crucified risen Jesus, the Son of Israel's God, and in the embodiment of the "economy of grace." The human being as created in the *imago trinitatis* is meant to live in an economy of common loves upheld by trust in God's promise and praise for God's faithfulness aimed at a new *polis*. In this *oikonomia* God offers Godself in a risky form of vulnerable humanity, and correspondingly the church seeks to overcome the unilateral and invulnerable power of the world that God renounces in the history of Israel and Jesus. The practices shaped by Word and sacraments are the means by which God creates homemakers, that is, "economists" or "disciples." The mandate of this economy is to bring the creation into household relations that serve life rather than death.[13] As the narratives of Israel and Jesus Christ show, the *oikonomia tou theou* must accordingly be thought initially in the most concrete terms of life imaginable: hunger in relation to table and bread.

Forming Economy at Table

The biblical narratives through which Israel and the church construe the relationship of God and human being begin at table: the Seder Meal and the Eucharist. In this respect the economies of the households of Israel and Jesus are formally not different from other human economies and institutions. Every

---

13. The question of how and where the ecclesia can exist in the market system is a test case for the possibility of humanization at all in our time.

economy is shaped around a table (or the cultural analogues) through narration of the stories that constitute its identity; the failure of such practices usually signals the breakdown of the economy. The crucial events of life largely transpire around tables: the operating table, the board of directors table, the war room table, the computer table, the negotiating table, the calculating table, the kindergarten table, the gaming table, the banquet table, the seminar table, the kitchen table. Its life at table shapes the larger life of the household. Life at table leads to dispositions, habits, ways of relating to one another, in short, to *table manners* that constitute the ways in which the household members are to relate to each other and the world, so that merely sitting at this or that table comprises a whole world complex of relationships. The character of an economy (including a corporation) may be discerned in the answer to these questions: (1) who is included around the table and how are they to relate to each other, (2) what is on it, (3) what is the object of the discourse at table, and (4) what are the ensuing table manners? Not surprisingly, these are the questions Paul asks regarding the means of constituting the church through the Eucharist.

This is the reason that parents the world over teach their children table manners, for their children's lives depend on their knowing the manners of a host's table where what is necessary for life is shared.[14] Likewise, all economies teach table manners and judge their participants according to conformity to them. Being able to sit at table, having access to a household in which the social goods necessary for life are distributed, is thus the most important blessing or right or achievement of any human being. Belonging to an economy or having place at a table is tantamount to access to the conditions of life. Should we not find a table open to us to stave off our hunger and slake our thirst, to give us name and recognition, confidence in ourselves, embrace by those who forgive us, and hope for our future, we will not long survive.

The drama of the biblical narratives begins in Deuteronomy 5–7 with this table narrative: "Remember that you were a slave in the land of Egypt, and the LORD your God brought you out from there with a mighty hand and an outstretched arm" (Deut. 5:15). We began as slaves and first came to know who God is while we were yet in "the house [economy] of slavery" (Deut. 5:6). For Christians, this story culminates in the astounding claim that in order to redeem us from the economy of slavery, the Son of God becomes a slave, an economist in the ancient sense (Phil. 2:7ff.). Biblical anthropology is above all concerned with which economy and which household relations can prevent our falling into slavery again. All questions of slavery, including the ultimate

14. Margaret Visser, *The Rituals of Dinner* (New York: Grove Weidenfeld, 1991).

slavery to the "law of sin and death," are referred to the economy of grace at the Lord's table. God redeems the creation by spreading a table of grace.

The Mystery of Bread

In order to say who God is and who we are before God, these narratives tell the story of bread.[15] The households (economies) of Israel and of Jesus Christ narrate their origins and upbuilding by treating very mundane questions: How did bread, the staff of life, the symbol of all social goods that are necessary for life, arrive? How is it produced, exchanged, and consumed? Are there any rules that should govern these relationships and processes? Our relation to God, others, and nature is epitomized in our relation to bread — for example, our hunger for what is not bread, for that which will not satisfy (Isa. 55); our holding back bread from the hungry poor; and our obedience to the "Bread of Life" who satisfies every hunger in the strange way of intensifying the hunger for righteousness.

The later Genesis cycles narrate how we got into the economy of slavery and the answer revolves around *bread*, Pharaoh's storehouse bread. At the bidding of brother Joseph, author of a *Wirtschaftswunder* and now the economist of Pharaoh, we exchange first our money for bread, then our livestock, then our land, and, finally, our bodies, ourselves. Then comes the ominous sentence, "As for the people, he made slaves of them from one end of Egypt to the other" (Gen. 47:21). Bread as storehouse commodity becomes the instrument of our going into slavery. Bread discloses the mystery of Pharaoh's power to possess, withhold, and dispose all land and people. The power to exclude others from what is necessary for life becomes the sign of power opposed to Israel's God.

The new economy of grace begins with a new bread called "manna," which is exactly opposite of Pharaoh's storehouse commodity bread (Exod. 16). It cannot be stored up. It cannot be accumulated for hoarding. It cannot be priced. It cannot be exchanged for value received. The reason is simple: it is

---

15. Adam Smith and Karl Marx thought that if you narrated the history of a commodity, such as a pin or a peasant's coat, you would sooner or later discover all the micro and macro economic relations that went into its production, selling, purchasing, and owning. This narration would expand to include all the relations of a society and could provide insight into the ills, dysfunctions, and cooperative possibilities of a society. Adam Smith, *The Wealth of Nations* (Chicago: University of Chicago Press, 1976), pp. 7-16; Karl Marx, *Capital*, trans. Ben Fowkes (New York: Vintage, 1977), pp. 125-77. Something like this is already a literary-theological device of the scriptural narratives.

a gift, the embodiment of God's grace. And because it is gift, it must be distributed according to a different logic, the logic of grace. Those "who gathered much had nothing over, and those who gathered little had no shortage" (Exod. 16:18). They gathered according to what was needed for life. They gathered according to the giftedness of bread.[16]

The fact that all human beings experience hunger has made bread, or its cultural equivalent, the primary sign of the conditions of life, and hunger the exemplary sign of human desire. Bread has remained the most comprehensive symbol of all social goods necessary to life and life abundant. A serviceable memory in this economy evokes two kinds of bread: on the one hand, the bread of slavery, the bread of misery, the bread of tears, and, on the other, the bread of freedom, the bread of joy, and the Bread of Life. Obviously, bread can become a commodity, but if it is exhaustively a commodity, many will starve or become slaves and those who eat their bread in isolation from the hungry will discover the hell of an empty life. The quality of human life is defined by how bread is brought into being, the shared communal meaning of bread, and the way bread is distributed, and these, in turn, are mutually affected by life at table.[17]

From life in the desert, the narrative carries us to Sinai where we receive from God the Torah household rules of the economy of grace that have been at the heart of the tradition of *oikonomia* through the prophets, the teachings of Jesus, the Church Fathers (East and West), and the medieval and Reformation churches: (1) Do not charge interest to the poor; (2) when you harvest your field, do not harvest it all the way to the edge, but leave gleanings for the poor; (3) practice hospitality; (4) practice the tithe; and (5) practice the Sabbath.[18] They are constitutive of the ecclesial understanding of the human being we are developing. It is nigh impossible to overemphasize the importance of these economy laws for the social, legal, and political *theoria* of the West until John Locke's argument for the labor theory of property in the *Two Treatises* of 1690 initiated their societal dissolution.

---

16. But compare the "graves of craving" of those whose desire is not disciplined for life (Num. 11:32-34; cf. Ps. 78:20-31; 106:13-15).

17. "Take, eat" (Matt. 26:26); "Feed my sheep" (John 21). With these commands Jesus gives shape to the community of disciples, who as they accompany Jesus on the way to God's eternal banquet, gather around their Lord's table to be fed, to discern who they are, where they are going, and by what manner they are to feed those whom Jesus seeks beyond the table. The church, the Household of Jesus Christ, is thus inescapably an economy existing for God's economy of the redemption of the world.

18. For a discussion of these economy rules see Meeks, *God the Economist,* pp. 75-97.

Eucharistic Humanity in the Triune God

For Christian anthropology the story of God and bread culminates in the eucharistic elevation and breaking of the bread that is the body and future of the crucified risen Jesus. In communion with the triune God the human being receives the grace that is the being of the human.

The Trinity as a hermeneutic of God's gracious giving opens up the possibility not only of thinking of God's being through the hyperbolic logic of giving, but also of thinking of the human being and human giving as God's gift. The Father, the Son, and the Holy Spirit constitute God by their mutual self-giving to each other and for the world's redemption. Redemption is participation in this community of giving. As the communion of perfect self-donation, the Trinity is the community of extravagant, overflowing, and self-diffusive goodness. The gratuity of God's giving is the mystery of God's being.[19] The persons of the Trinity give themselves unstintingly to each other and thus constitute each other as distinct persons and as perfect communion.

We cannot be this perfect communion of giving, for we live under the conditions of sin, evil, and death. Yet, as creatures of God's acts of love participating by God's grace in this communion of giving, we are to be and to give like God. God's being as love seeks affiliation, a society of persons who are both free and connected through acts of excessive and mutual giving. God aims at a community that responds to giving with further giving, creating relationships of mutuality and responsibility.[20] Thus Paul views the creation and new creation of human beings in the "system" of grace as they cohere around the Lord's table, receive and give thanks for the *charis* of God, and share God's grace with the world. The logic and nature of the economy of Jesus Christ are signed in table performances. It is the liturgy, the gracing of God and our sharing of God's grace, that makes us who we are.

Christian Perspectives on Being Human in the Global Market System

A juxtaposition of elements that belong to the market system at its core with perspectives of the *oikonomia* that emerge from the narratives of the Christian tradition no doubt surfaces formal similarities but also significant disso-

---

19. John D. Zizioulas, *Being As Communion* (Crestwood, N.Y.: St. Vladimir's Seminary Press, 1993). Jean-Luc Marion, *God without Being,* trans. Thomas A. Carlson (Chicago: University of Chicago Press, 1991), has taken this direction in a very creative but in the end too extreme way.

20. Meeks, *God the Economist,* pp. 114-20.

nances. Christian anthropology contends with core components of the market system insofar as they become exhaustive definitions of the human; it resists the perspectival reductionism described elsewhere in this volume by Don Browning.[21]

Neoclassical economists generally consider several components as *conditio sine qua non* to the market system: liberty, exclusive private property, the logic of commodity exchange, competition and comparative advantage, money as commodity, complex social relations organized by transactions in homogenized space, corporations, and entrepreneurs.[22] I cannot deal with all of these elements or any in detail but rather am interested in the practices and gestalts that shape human life as human beings live in these dimensions of the market system. These practices of the market system can be set in relation to what I take to be the primary performances of the economy of God that shape human life: giving, forgiving, welcoming, and sending.

Desire, Artificial Scarcity, and Debt

Christian anthropology imagines the end of the human being as praise of God; the market system views the end of the human being as maximized utility. Both market and Christian anthropology, however, view the human being as a creature of desire. The problem of being human is how desire is to be directed and disciplined.

Market anthropology describes human behavior according to a formal account of insatiable desire. It maintains that desire finds its end in the satisfaction of pleasure and the avoidance of pain. Economics, the self-proclaimed "hard" science, falls back on human desire as the prime mover of the market. The introductory chapter of most neo-classical economics textbooks contains an argument that runs like this: No matter how much we ever produce, there will never be enough to go around. The reason is that the human being is an infinite desirer, an infinite acquisitor, an unlimited consumer.

Christian anthropology, on the other hand, describes human beings and human actions from the desire accounted in the contingent history of Israel and Jesus Christ. Desire finds its end in the praise of God's glory and in participation in the abundance of God's communion through God's grace. All human life is aimed at friendship with God and participation in the es-

---

21. See pp. 305-9 of Don Browning's essay in this volume.

22. For the most part I follow Lindblom's discernment of the market system's "bones beneath the flesh," *The Market System*, pp. 52-60 and passim.

chatological banquet at which God's reconciled creatures will feast in the plenitude of God's love. We are created with the capacity to love the infinite God infinitely. We fall into sin by desiring infinitely what is not God, the creature rather than the creator. Our idolatry, that is, the infinite love of what we have made with our own hands, thought with our own minds, and achieved with our own efforts, refuses our being as God's grace. Loving the finite infinitely creates artificial scarcity, the pervasive sense that reality itself is governed by the lack of the conditions for life.

The modern market view of the human being trades on this assumption about the human being and puts *artificial* scarcity incorrigibly at the heart of human existence.[23] This presupposition is not so much about shortages as a metaphysical lack that pervades life.[24] Accepting this tragic lack as the way things are leads to agonistic existence. Human beings become convinced that a noncompetitive life cannot survive in a competitive world. Competition over scarce resources (increasingly, knowledge) remains the officially unquestionable signal of what it takes to survive and flourish.

Artificial scarcity leads to another matter that appears prominently in both anthropologies: debt. The market system depends upon debt as the structure that holds all things together. Human beings engage in debt as a way of dealing with scarcity. The sense that one lacks what it takes makes one susceptible to the market's commodified offer of security, future, and happiness and to the compulsion to purchase them on credit. The market view of the human being asserts its vaunted realism by assuming that debt is inevitable if scarcity is a permanent fixture of reality. Thus if debt is the structure of human decisions and actions, and even if it is sin that drives debt, then why not let the pricing of all goods manage lack and debt? Debt becomes the primary rationale of obligated human relations. Debt management can take the place of human moral judgment. But the warnings of the Torah remain urgent for persons, communities, and nations: debt leads inexorably to slavery or to exclusion from community, which is death before death.[25]

---

23. Meeks, *God the Economist*, pp. 17-19.

24. Cf. Steve Long, *Divine Economy: Theology and the Market* (New York: Routledge, 2000), pp. 242-45 and passim.

25. The Torah places severe restrictions on interest and debt because they lead to slavery. Interest may not be charged to the poor and nothing may be taken as collateral which a person needs for life (Exod. 22:25-27; Deut. 23:19-20; 24:6, 10-13). A kind of debt multiplying without end presents itself as a way of ensuring indebted relations. Infinite, unpayable debt could mean the possibility of infinite command and unbending domination.

Commodity Exchange and Gift

The market system depends on the logic of exchange, *quid pro quo*. Excluding the right to own slaves or physically to coerce others and recognizing the merely intermittent success of persuading others to barter, the remaining possibility to meet my need is a contingent offer of a benefit to others in exchange for their fulfilling my need.[26] Money as such a universal benefit makes the exchange relationship universally available.[27] No one can doubt the great benefit of exchange relationships in allocating goods and services. But modern market anthropology tends toward the exclusion of gift in the picture of the human being, harboring the ancient prejudices against gifting and dreaming up additional ones. Market human beings are suspicious of gifting because it entails ambiguity fed by the faint sense of debt, competition, and domination.

The response of the Christian view of the human being to artificial scarcity, debt, and commodity exchange is grace. A Christian anthropology focused on gift-giving as grace rather than on commodity exchange points to the triune community's freeing of human giving from the reality of debt. This is apparent first in the way God gives in creating. God gives without the guarantee of return.[28] This is so because God gives everything that we are, and thus there is nothing in us that could establish an obligation toward God. "What do you have that you did not receive? And if you received it, why do you boast as if it were not a gift?" (1 Cor. 4:7). Furthermore, God gives us Christ and in him union with the Triune Community and in this all things (Rom. 8:32), simply because of our need, not because we are deserving. God's *pleroma* lacks nothing we could pay back. We have nothing more to return than what God has already given us. God's gifts to us are not loans, nor does God stop giving when we squander or misuse the gifts. Even when we fail to give, God is willing to give more. Our failure to give removes the blessing of giving that God intends for us, but it does not cause God's giving to cease. Everything about our lives should be a reflection of this gift.

God's gift in the cross further blocks "commerce with God," a Roman definition of religion. The gift of the cross does not produce an infinite debt that is in principle unpayable. It is not that in the cross God has somehow rec-

26. Lindblom, *Market System*, pp. 53-54.

27. Karl Polanyi, *The Great Transformation*. Both barter and money economies are taken to be great advances over gift economies, since, as Lindblom observes, "gifts obligate the recipient to make a reciprocal gift" (*Market System*, p. 54).

28. For the following, cf. Kathryn Tanner, *Jesus, Humanity and the Trinity: A Brief Systematic Theology* (Minneapolis: Fortress, 2001), pp. 82-95.

ompensed our debts or tendered the obedience we could not render. Rather, God cancels the possibility of debt itself and therefore debt economy as the source of obligation and security.[29] But, according to Paul, the decisive point is that in giving us an unreturnable gift, God forgives our debt. If God accounts us as having no debt, the possibility of our being restored to God's economy of graceful giving is opened up. In this sense God's redeeming work transforms the economy of debt into the economy of grace. The appropriate prayer to be prayed in the economy of grace is, "Forgive us our debts as we forgive our debtors." To be the *homo economicus* in God's economy of grace means that we are shaped by God's giving rather than by maximizing utility.

If God gives to the creation in a way that undermines debt economy, we are left with the question *how* we should give. God's excessive giving creates space and time for human reciprocity. "Owe no one anything but love." Our obedience in giving is not a matter of clearing our debt to God, and yet God does give to us with the expectation that this giving will be reflected in our covenanted giving. Christian anthropology understands the life-serving shape of human life to be the eucharistic existence gifted at the spreading of the Lord's table. Our obligation is to give as God gives to meet the needs of the creatures for whom Jesus Christ has died.

Whereas commodity exchanges are anonymous, the emphasis in giving as God gives is on the persons brought into relationship, not on the objects that are exchanged and therefore taken out of circulation. Gift-giving creates communal relationships of interdependence. The giver accompanies the gift. A commodity transaction ends the relationship as soon as goods are exchanged so that one is free immediately to enter into another transaction. This may serve a kind of equilibrium but not reconciliation and mutual life with the different other. Furthermore, commodity transactions cannot proffer the most important right to life resulting from God's claim on every human being, that is, the right to be included at table, the right to belong to a primary community in which the conditions of life are mediated. If all goods of life become commodities, however, such mediation cannot take place.

Society is saturated with arguments that things human beings used to think could in no sense be commodities should now be properly commodified: blood, organs, fetuses, personal genomic information, children, and air. What should not be a commodity? What is necessary for life

29. "We are ransomed on the cross from the suffering and oppression in which a debt economy has thrown us; taken from the cross we are returned to our original owner God, to God's kingdom of unconditional giving, snatched out of the world of deprivation and injustice from which we suffer because of our poverty, our inability to pay what others demand of us." Tanner, *Jesus, Humanity and the Trinity*, p. 88.

should not be a commodity or exhaustively a commodity. Only the shared life of a community can decide what is a commodity and what is not;[30] failing such a community, the market decides what counts as a commodity.

A community that through shared understanding could designate a good or service as a gift rather than a commodity requires face-to-face communicative life and sustained association, communal qualities that are themselves increasingly threatened by the spreading commodification of life. The humanization of economy thus demands that we once again recognize that economy is embedded in community and exists for the sake of the enhancement of community. The viability of human community is a greater value than free trade and the increase of wealth through financial markets.

Liberty, Property, and Hospitality

Many proponents of the market system would say that *liberty* is its most essential component. There must be in place custom and law that secure the ability of human beings to use and control their bodies and energies and to move and enter into transactions as they will. The market view of the human being requires the assumption that I have a property in myself, that I own or possess myself. No one has any claim on me or any right to my person.[31]

But is this really freedom, or is it a kind of subjugation to a system that may offer freedom from restraint or freedom of choice[32] but not the freedom for the engagement with others for life that is ultimately the only real freedom? For Christian anthropology, whatever freedom can mean exists under the belief that we do not possess ourselves (Isa. 43:1; cf. 1 Cor. 6:20; 7:23). A humane economy requires that human beings not be determined by a narrow view of freedom as the ability to choose among commodity and service options. Human beings become genuinely free through their calling by God for a life with and for others.

The modern history of property beginning with Locke's labor theory of property seeks to justify exclusive private property as a *conditio sine qua non* of the market system. Christian anthropology, on the other hand, stresses a universally recognized *inclusive* property right in what it takes to be human.

---

30. Michael Walzer, *Spheres of Justice* (New York: Basic, 1983).

31. C. B. Macpherson, *The Political Theory of Possessive Individualism: Hobbes to Locke* (Oxford: Clarendon, 1962).

32. For the denial of freedom in the "freedom of choice" see Barry Schwartz, *The Paradox of Choice: Why More Is Less* (New York: HarperCollins, 2004); Gregg Easterbrook, *The Progress Paradox: How Life Gets Better While People Feel Worse* (New York: Random House, 2003).

What belongs to each, what is due each, cannot be decided simply by modern theories of exclusive property irrespective of God's creation and redemption of each human being. Rather, all human beings have a property in or claim on (1) what is necessary for life against death, and (2) what is appropriate to fulfilling one's humanity (as *imago Dei*) by serving God and neighbor. For Jews and Christians human hospitality (giving the other the goods and space for life) is the other side of God's goodness extended to all of God's creation. God excludes no one from life, and neither may we.

I have argued that the conditions of home are constitutive of human dignity and that human beings are shaped according to the economy/home to which they belong. In this ecclesial understanding of the human being, God's grace is the being of the human; the human is the gift of God. Human beings know redemption as participation in the divine community of giving. Human life is constituted and redeemed in ecclesial-like relations of accountability, mutual giving, and redistribution. The triune God will redeem the creation by bringing all creatures into household relations that serve life rather than death. It is this eschatological bearing that distinguishes the economy of grace from all other economies. And yet the economy of grace seeks to qualify all other economies as humane.

Public Practice of the Economy of Grace

What would it mean concretely to practice the economy of grace publicly? In what ways can the church as imperfect economy of grace intervene, interrupt, intercept, and intercede in the public economy that takes the form of the market system? What are ways in which the church as the household of God's economy might serve the extension of human dignity? Mainline Protestant and Catholic churches have great difficulties in thinking through these questions. The spectrum of responses extends from doubt about the church being involved in political economy at all to a confidence that Christian conceptions are already implicit and operative in the structures of the market system.[33] When the church simply assumes that the market system is autopoetic and buys into its seemingly fated views of the human being, its actual historical impact on public economy is minimal. If the economy of grace is meant

---

33. The state of the debate can be seen in the exchange of Jeffrey Stout, *Democracy and Tradition* (Princeton, N.J.: Princeton University Press, 2004), and Stanley Hauerwas, "Postscript: A Response to Jeff Stout's *Democracy and Tradition*," in *Performing the Faith* (Grand Rapids: Brazos, 2004), pp. 215-41.

for the world's redemption, the narrative at tables in the market system and in civil society has to be changed in order for the assumptions of the market system to be changed. The market system can work with different, more humane assumptions about the being of the human. Further, the market system will thrive better and more justly if it is not narrated merely as redemption through material progress but rather as a system for realizing an economy of mutual benefit of all human beings and of nature, which is their home.

Effective witness of the economy of grace in the world would require a new theology of mission and a new practice of *oikoumene*.[34] The loss of mission and *oikoumene* in the first world church simply left the field clear for un-impeded imperial-like incursions of globalization. The congregation un-avoidably has an interest in the global because the *oikoumene* is present at the Lord's table; those who are graced with the table manners of the Lord must work for the transformation of the world's economy.

The church engages in public witness by seeking correspondences, rough analogies of the economy of grace, in the public household. The strange table manners and distribution of the Bread of Life at the Lord's table can have corre-spondences in the public production and distribution of goods for life. The concrete practice of the economy of grace in the congregation can form beliefs, dispositions, virtues, and habits of persons who can change the public narra-tive. This is true also for entrepreneurs, corporation executives, and financiers who are shaped by an ecclesial economy that does not function on the principle of *quid pro quo* but is a space and time in which the logic or law of grace can govern. The economic and monetary parables of Jesus have been interpreted according to the virtues of modern commerce for such a long time that we have lost their intention and ability to set the gospel of grace in the midst of the hard-est practices of the market. For example, the so-called "dishonest manager" (Luke 16:1-13) should be better translated as the "one who handles unjust things." He is a handler of unjust things before he could be called virtuous or not, honest or not. So are Christians in the congregation. The church's failure of nerve is its failure to bring the economy of grace into the market system. The manager of Jesus' parable is shrewd; the master says so and approves such shrewdness in giving, even though this upsets the normal debt system. The church should look to such shrewd players in the market, converted by the economy of grace, for humanizing changes in the market system.[35]

34. Lamin Sanneh argues that recent critics of mission, far from being on the progressive cutting edge, are reflecting a colonial consciousness. *Whose Religion Is Christianity? The Gospel Beyond the West* (Grand Rapids: Eerdmans, 2004).

35. See the several essays in *Theology Today* 60 (2003) for ways in which this is beginning to happen.

The public practice of the economy of grace recognizes the limits of the market system, but it is not aimed simply at stop-gap measures but rather at changing the assumptions about the human being and the rules of the market. The polity that the economy of God works for publicly will include nonmarket means of humanizing the market.

The Economy of Giving

Beginning with the passing strange story of the didrachma coin in the mouth of the fish (Matt. 17:24ff.), the narrative of Jesus' entrance into the reigning political economy of Jerusalem traces his increasing awareness that he is facing the regime of money. The only lasting strategy against the regime of money and its pricing of all goods is *giving*. The market system works against public giving; the church and other institutions of civil society have maintained that the market and all other economic systems depend on some real systems of giving.[36] There can be no human dignity without giving, also in the public relations of human beings. In the system in which it is assumed that everything can be priced,[37] the economy of grace works to open up spheres that are beyond pricing and therefore can be shaped by gifts which are not returnable.

In our society this means not allowing welfare to be demolished, but instead protecting the public gift to the needy, without the expectation of return, simply because of their need. This assumes the ancient Jewish and Christian law that welfare is based on the right of the needy rather than the largesse of the affluent as well as the undermining of the distinction between the deserving and undeserving poor in deciding provision. To be sure, however, the economy of grace works for a welfare system in which the unreturnable gift is meant for further giving; that is, the reason for giving to the needy is their participation in community, not making strangers between donors and recipients. Public giving is aimed at sustenance but also at the recipients' thriving through the generation of the generations, raising children well, education in an information and high-tech economy, and other factors that relate to their dignity as full participants in the community. The economy of grace seeks laws that recognize that the sustainable engine of humane growth is not the lowering of labor costs but the enhancing of the contribution of all to the economy.

36. This is the primary argument of Karl Polanyi, *The Great Transformation*.
37. The extent to which this assumption can be applied even in the realm of the family can be seen in the work of Gary Becker.

The Economy of Inclusion

In the global market system, however, profit is generated by relative exclusion. In underdeveloped countries and the rural and urban areas of the developed countries, people are absorbed in the "golden straitjacket" of the global system, but their own thriving is not served by the system. Techniques of increasing profit work off of "comparative advantage" or inequality of circumstance. Those who are obligated to the economy of grace will work for international measures to prevent the competitive advantage of developed nations from becoming permanent. We are faced with either a transformed function of international regulatory bodies (like the Bretton Woods agencies: the International Monetary Fund, the World Bank, the World Trade Organization) or the creation of new bodies to interrupt the consequences of views of competition that allow so many win-loss situations.

The win-loss catastrophes for large numbers of people in the global market system cannot be long sustained. In the developing world forced austerity, corruption, discrepancy in wealth and income, and the perception of unfair trade stoke violence and terrorism. Even large-scale markets in the developed world are experiencing backlash to the strategy for oversupply, that is, the seemingly unending increase in artificial needs for products that do not meet basic human needs. The economy of grace raises the question whether the market can actually work on competition alone — even on its own basic assumptions. Competition disintegrates without some degree of equilibrium. If you destroy all competitors, you destroy a competitive market. The circulation on which a rough equilibrium depends is eliminated. A viable global system would have to make available what is necessary to assure functioning competitors. On the local and international scene this means the legal protection of *inclusive* property as well as exclusive property. This also means, of course, that the economy of grace publicly seeks a meaning of freedom beyond the lack of restraint in expressing preferences. Freedom is not fundamentally a choice, "I choose, therefore I am." Freedom is life with the other. The practice of the economy of grace therefore focuses on the creation of the commonweal that mutually assures dignity for all.

Some would say that such an economy of livelihood and public common good is simply impossible. But because Christian anthropology looks for God's consummation of creation in which this world and its economy will be redeemed, Christian hope proffers the energy to work for the reality of an economy of grace now. The divine act of new creation is not completed until the redemptive work of God embraces the totality of humanity and the creation. And thus Christian anthropology begins and ends with the communal and cosmic symbol of God's reign of righteousness in the eschatological banquet at which "the more than enough" of God's grace embraces all of God's creatures.

Repetition, or the Theological Failures of Modern Dignity Discourse: The Case of Frederick Douglass's 1845 *Narrative*

J. KAMERON CARTER

Every autobiography, after all, is a figure of a figure, the repetition in language of a human figure.

Henry Louis Gates Jr.[1]

I

This essay probes the ethics of dignity and why such discourse often fails us. Immanuel Kant's second formulation of the universal categorical imperative, a *locus classicus* of such discourse, in its own way, encapsulates the problem. It is, thus, worthwhile recalling briefly his formulation. "Autonomy," he says, "is the ground of the dignity *[Würde]* of human nature and of every rational nature," the ground, that is, of its "unconditional and incomparable worth."[2] From this precept Kant advances his second formulation of the imperative: "Act in regard to every rational being (yourself and others) that he may at the same time count in your maxim as an end in himself."[3] The dignity of human beings, whose nature is rational, consists, as Kant would have it, precisely in this. In that the rational creature "exists above all the mere things of nature," its worth consists in its self-legislative capabilities, by which the human being

1. Henry Louis Gates Jr., *Figures in Black: Words, Signs, and the "Racial" Self* (New York: Oxford University Press, 1987), pp. 116-17.

2. Immanuel Kant, "Grounding for the Metaphysics of Morals," in *Classics of Western Philosophy*, ed. Steven M. Cahn (Indianapolis: Hackett, 1977), p. 1040.

3. Kant, "Grounding for the Metaphysics of Morals," p. 1042.

is an end in itself rather than the means to an end. By living into and thus re-alizing its 'ends' status, the self is both morally affirmed and enacted. It fol-lows from this account of dignity that the dignified, rational creature, in con-trast, for example, to the slave, is autonomously 'self-made' (to employ an Emersonian and thus late-nineteenth-century North American grammar) rather than heteronomously related to a master. So understood the self is it-self precisely through its own internal legislative capacities, rather than through its relationship to an external legislator. The task of civil society, then, is to enact that "possible . . . world of rational beings," that community of dignified persons, who in themselves are "a kingdom of ends," a kingdom, that is, in which "[self-]legislation [belongs] to all persons as members." In such a society of the dignified and kingdom of the self-made, "every rational being must so act as if he were through his maxim always a legislating mem-ber in the universal kingdom of ends."[4]

It is this and related accounts of dignity, accounts that lay unique claim upon the modern imagination, about which I am suspicious. This essay ex-plains why. It does so, however, not by analytically appraising the details of 'Kantian' accounts of human dignity. Rather, it does so by considering what happens when those on dignity's underside nevertheless take up its discourse, but for emancipatory purposes. I want to consider why this quite often fails, why it often re-produces an ambiguous self and tenuous dignity. That is, I want to consider why it is that this type of resistance discourse often echoes what is most troublesome in modern accounts of dignity, thus producing "a figure of a figure," a tragic repetition of the form of the self that needs overcoming. A con-sideration of Frederick Douglass's 1845 Narrative will help me do this.[5]

The Narrative tells the story of Douglass's movement from bondage to freedom, from property to prophet, from chattel to abolitionist spokesman. It tells the story of how Douglass re-made himself beyond the constricting con-fines of modern racial reasoning. In order to do this Douglass engages in a kind of 'racial writing'[6] that has as its goal repeating or 're-presenting' him-

---

4. Kant, "Grounding for the Metaphysics of Morals," p. 1042. For more on Kant's formu-lation of the dignity of persons see Roger J. Sullivan, *Immanuel Kant's Moral Theory* (Cam-bridge: Cambridge University Press, 1989), pp. 193-211.

5. Frederick Douglass, "Narrative of the Life of Frederick Douglass, an American Slave," in *Autobiographies: Frederick Douglass,* ed. Henry Louis Gates Jr. (New York: Library of Amer-ica, Penguin, 1994). Subsequently referred to internally.

6. Wilson J. Moses, "Writing Freely? Frederick Douglass and the Constraints of Racialized Writing," in *Frederick Douglass: New Literary and Historical Essays,* ed. Eric J. Sundquist, Cambridge Studies in American Literature and Culture (Cambridge: Cambridge University Press, 1990).

self, but in a different light, one that positions him as liberated and dignified. I want to draw attention to how the *Narrative,* in portraying Douglass within dignity's light, revaluates the meaning of dignity, and, in fact, re-performs it. The revaluation takes place by criticizing the place religion and theology had come to occupy in the 'production' of (in-)dignity — the dignity, that is, of whiteness and the indignity of blackness — in America's political economy of slavery and in the myth of American peoplehood and national identity that sustains it.[7] Douglass isolates the work that the Christian Easter story is made to do in all of this, and then attempts to reinterpret its significance so that Easter works sociopolitically on his behalf, namely, the work of upholding his dignity and freedom. With the Easter story reinterpreted, and thus with dignity and national identity (the two are bound together) revaluated, Douglass represents himself as an end in himself, rather than as the means to white America's ends. As master of his fate and no longer white America's slave, he portrays himself as the representative black *man* and as the quintessential American.

It is precisely here, however, that an ambiguous self and a tenuous dignity reassert themselves, for if Douglass rescues racial dignity, he does so by propagating gendered indignity. That is, his worth as a black *man,* and so as an American, comes at the cost of representing the feminine, particularly the black woman, as the repository of indignity. She becomes the means by which he can be an American, an abolitionist intellectual, and the representative black man, who is an end in himself. In this way Douglass repeats the form of the self that must be overcome, and he does so, I begin arguing here and more fully develop elsewhere,[8] because he insufficiently overturns the religious dimensions of the ends-means binary logic that is embedded in how dignity is often thought.[9] Religion, Douglass's critique of it notwithstanding, continues to be nothing more than that cultural phenomenon through which power is

---

7. My use of myth is informed by the definition provided in the introduction to Craig R. Prentiss, ed., *Religion and the Creation of Race and Ethnicity: An Introduction* (New York: New York University Press, 2003). See also the fine essay by Eddie J. Glaude Jr., "Myth and African American Self-Identity," in the same volume. My use of the term "political economy" is informed by the account given in Jeffrey Sklansky, *The Soul's Economy: Market Society and Self-hood in American Thought, 1820-1920* (Chapel Hill, N.C.: University of North Carolina Press, 2002). In speaking of the "political economy of slavery," I mean to indicate the ways in which slavery regulated the sociopolitical order and informed national self-understanding.

8. See my article "Race, Religion, and the Contradictions of Identity: A Theological Engagement with Douglass's 1845 *Narrative*" (*Modern Theology,* January 2005). I also address this problem in *Race: A Theological Account* (Oxford University Press, forthcoming).

9. For a sustained analysis of logic and human dignity, see the essay in this volume by Peter Ochs, pp. 143-60.

expressed, the power by which certain persons are ends in and for themselves, while other persons are simply the means to their ends.[10] Insofar as this is so, Douglass may have inverted the logic of dignity so that it now comports to his flourishing as a black man, but he has not escaped it — and this, precisely, is the problem. He remains embedded within (in-)dignity's network of production and reproduction, of iteration and reiteration, in short, of repetition and re-duplication.

I want to catalogue this complex set of affairs. I do so by paying particular attention to two scenes in the *Narrative:* chapter one's record of the beating of Aunt Esther and chapter ten's account of Douglass's adolescent altercation with the reputed slave-breaker Edward Covey. All of the things mentioned above — race, gender, and the failures of religion and theology — dramatically converge as Douglass attempts to bring dignity out of these episodes of indignity when he was a slave.

II

Let me begin unraveling this problem by turning to the subtly complex scene of the beating of Aunt Esther, which is recorded in the *Narrative's* opening chapter. "Mr. Plummer," the overseer who worked for Douglass's childhood master Aaron Anthony, is its protagonist, the one who moves the scene's action. Yet as the quotation below reveals, the real object of concern in the scene is less Mr. Plummer than Aunt Esther. It is through Douglass's representation of Esther that he is able to cast the scene as one of indignity, indeed, as metaphoric of the indignity of black life as a whole in slaveholding America. Thus she, being a metonym of black indignity in this scene's representation of things, is the scene's primary subject, while Plummer is its secondary one. About the latter, Douglass has this to say:

> [he] was a miserable drunkard, a profane swearer, and a savage monster. He always went armed with a cowskin and a heavy cudgel. I have known him to cut and slash the women's heads so horribly. . . . He was a cruel man, hardened by a long life of slaveholding. He would at times seem to take great pleasure in whipping a slave.

---

10. For more on the problems involved in modern uses of the category of religion, see Talal Asad, *Genealogies of Religion: Discipline and Reasons of Power in Christianity and Islam* (Baltimore: Johns Hopkins University Press, 1993), particularly chap. 1; Richard King, *Orientalism and Religion: Postcolonial Theory, India and 'the Mystic East'* (London: Routledge, 1999).

And then, as if Plummer's function is to be but a literary prop (though he certainly is more than this, as will become evident shortly), one whose function is simply to set up what follows, the scene's center of gravity decidedly shifts — to Aunt Esther. "I have often been awakened at the dawn of day," Douglass says,

> by the most heart-rending shrieks of an own aunt of mine, whom he used to tie up to a joist, and whip upon her naked back til she was literally covered with blood. No words, no tears, no prayers, from his gory victim, seemed to move his iron heart from its bloody purpose. The louder she screamed the harder he whipped; and where the blood ran fastest, there he whipped longest. He would whip her to make her scream, and whip her to make her hush; and not until overcome by fatigue, would he cease to swing the blood-clotted cowskin. (p. 18)

From this quotation — and from the scene's subsequent unfolding — Douglass shows how violence mediates both white dignity and black indignity alike. Both, that is, are brokered through Plummer's "cowskin and a heavy cudgel" and sealed in fast-flowing "blood." The result of Plummer's "bloody purpose" is to render his white life articulate. Yet the articulation of white dignity is possible only by subjecting black life to a violent "hush" and distorting its speech into that of a harsh 'scream.' I will have more to say momentarily about the nature of the violence portrayed in this scene. For now, however, it is enough to note an important implication of this scene as it bears on my present endeavor, which is to probe why modern dignity discourse often fails us. The implication is that violence is the deep structure, one might say, of the logic and practice of (in-)dignity in modernity.

But more must be said precisely on this point, for Douglass in this scene is not content simply to register the fact that violence mediates (in-)dignity. Rather, he sets out to show that the violence at issue is of a specifically religious and sacred nature, one that grounds the mythos of American exceptionalism and peoplehood and the vision of the aims and ends of humanity nestled within it. The result is that the scene brings violence and the sacred into close proximity.[11] Brokering that nearness is a particular use of Scripture. That is, Old and New Testament Scripture is the contested ground of (in-)dignity, the contested ground of the meaning of human life. Given this, the scene is crucial to Douglass's broader strategy in the *Narrative:* to do autobiography as exegesis — moreover, as counter-exegesis — and exegesis as

---

11. For a literary and philosophical engagement with this issue see René Girard, *Violence and the Sacred* (Baltimore: Johns Hopkins University Press, 1977).

autobiography. Autobiography is thus being done in such a way as to challenge the hermeneutical and theological basis of America's self-understanding and its vision of the human and to struggle for an alternative.

As a first step toward establishing this claim consider how the scene plays on Old Testament imagery. In speaking of Plummer's "bloody purpose," Douglass seems to align the overseer Plummer with the biblical figure Cain. His suggestion is that as Cain was bent on drawing his brother's blood (cf. Gen. 4), so white brutality, in the person of Plummer, remained determined in its "bloody purpose." That purpose was not just physically to incarcerate the black 'body in pain,'[12] but also to render it mute and utterly inarticulate. In this way the white man Anthony and his overseer, Plummer, rather than blacks (in the person of Douglass), are shown to be the savages; indeed, Plummer is "a savage monster." This is shown to be the case because of the speechlessness, inarticulacy, and illiteracy Plummer foists upon Aunt Esther and even upon Douglass himself, who says that he labored, because of the psychological effects of this incident, through his own inarticulacy, as it were, to "commit to paper the feelings with which [he] beheld [the ghastly scene]" (p. 18). Thus, the scene reveals that speechlessness, inarticulacy, and illiteracy are the unique markers, the signs, of indignity and bondage. By contrast, speech, articulacy, and literacy: these are the markers of dignity, freedom, and autonomous agency, markers that Douglass as self-made man and abolitionist intellectual represents himself as now embodying.

The Old Testament dimensions of the scene receive further amplification when they are read as aligning Esther with the scriptural figure Abel. The crucial link is that for both their inarticulacy and indignity is the condition of possibility for the articulacy and dignity of their antagonists. Indeed, both Abel and Esther are articulate only in a nonconventional way: Abel, through his blood crying out from the ground; and Esther, through her "heart-rending shrieks," "screams," and the "hush" — all punctuated with the presence of fast-flowing blood. And then in both stories there is the third *dramatis persona:* God. In the fratricidal story of Scripture, God is the one to whom Abel's blood cries out demanding, in some sense, that God justify himself by vindicating the slaughtered victim. In the case of the scene of the whipping of Esther it is again before God, the one who is seen as ostensibly underwriting the social arrangement of white dignity over black indignity in America, that prayerful tears are shed, crying out for the vindication of the victim Esther. In having the beating of Esther resonate in this way against the backdrop of the

---

12. See Elaine Scarry, *The Body in Pain: The Making and Unmaking of the World* (New York: Oxford University Press, 1985).

story of Abel and Cain, Douglass is able to make a claim to the effect that the 'genesis' of black indignity lay in the moral failures of slaveholding Christianity. But more starkly put, its genesis, the scene in fact suggests, lay in God's failure, if not outright culpability for black indignity. God, and how the idea of God sociopolitically functions in America's political economy, is culpable in that Esther's screams, which plead for a rectifying response, go unanswered. The situation thus appears analogous to that of Abel's cry to God — a cry, mind you, that is unconventionally uttered (his 'blood' utters it and then only by way of the voice of the Mosaic author) — and the circumstances surrounding this cry (cf. Gen. 4:10).

This reading is only deepened once one takes into account how the dramatic persons in the scene of the whipping of Esther are further figured through New Testament allusions. Here Douglass, as is the case in much of the Christian tradition's reading of the Abel figure, subtly aligns Esther, an Abel figure herself, with Christ. In reading Esther christologically Douglass deepens his subtle attack on American religion's complicity in black indignity and in the logical and practical failures of modern dignity discourse. Troped through Christ's Easter dereliction, Douglass's aunt, he says, could utter "no words, no tears, no prayers" that could effectively intervene in her plight. Thus, in one fell swoop Douglass is able to dramatize how the black body is configured as the papyrus onto which religious letters are violently emblazoned in justification of the primacy of whiteness in American peoplehood and in theological 'justification' of the political economy of slavery. In linking the Old and the New Testament together in this way he suggests that black existence is forced into a scriptural economy, an economy that in fact ventriloquizes, its religious language notwithstanding, the political economy of slavery. Its ventriloquism of the political economy of slavery is at its most intense and most subtly masked in how the Christian Easter story is made to function in the American sacred mythos. It is here, I want to argue, that Douglass's religious critique of the American performance of modern dignity discourse cuts deepest, for arguably he wants to disclose the work the story of the Pasch sociopolitically accomplishes in its way of grounding the American order of things and the meaning of human life for both blacks and whites in that order. Douglass represents this by framing the episode of the whipping of Esther in paschal terms, for Esther becomes a figure of the crucified Christ. In so doing, he takes his scriptural criticism and (counter-)exegesis to its most trenchant level, the level of theology itself — the theology of the passion or of suffering. It is here as well, however, that the promise of and problems with Douglass's strategy crystallize. The promise concerns the creative way in which Douglass uncovers how the Easter story is made to ground white dignity. The problems concern the way gender functions in his own redeployment of that story.

To get at what I mean by this I want to consider more closely how Douglass frames the beating of Esther through the Easter story. Subsequent to detailing the 'facts' surrounding Esther's beating — facts framed, as just argued, through allusions to Old and New Testament Scripture — Douglass immediately registers the psychic effects the beating had on him as a child. He says:

> I remember the first time I ever witnessed this horrible exhibition. I was quite a child, but I well remember it. I never shall forget it whilst I remember any thing. It was the first of a long series of such outrages, of which I was doomed to be *a witness and a participant*. It was the blood-stained gate, the entrance to the hell of slavery, through which I was about to pass. It was a most terrible spectacle. I wish I could commit to paper the feelings with which I beheld it. (p. 18; italics mine)

Literary scholar Jenny Franchot has powerfully argued regarding this scene that Esther's suffering enables "[Douglass's] acquisition of 'manhood'" and in this way of autonomy. She further observes, commenting on this scene as Douglass later tweaked it in *My Bondage and My Freedom* (his second autobiography), that "the whipping provokes [Douglass's] eventually emancipatory inquiry into the 'nature and history of slavery.'"[13] The scene, in other words, allows Douglass to dramatize an ontology of slavery and the ethical structure of white articulacy and black inarticulacy. That ontology is one in which black identity has as its precondition a rupturing of the placid state of 'childhood' innocence. The complementary aspect of this rupture is a recognition of one's state of inarticulacy and a concomitant desire to change that condition, that is, to bring articulacy out of inarticulacy. Such is the struggle for liberation. In the concrete terms of this scene, the young Douglass, by virtue of being "a witness and a participant" to the whipping of Esther, is 'ontologized' into the cavernous and dark inner recesses of the indignity of slavery. He is brought into the *logos* or inner (ir-)rationality of modern racial reasoning, and into the struggle for freedom, for a different mode of consciousness, that comes with having been awakened. In Douglass's case, it is the black intellectual *qua* abolitionist orator and 'representative man' who uniquely realizes this different, liberated mode of consciousness. What is distinctive about this

13. Jenny Franchot, "The Punishment of Esther: Frederick Douglass and the Construction of the Feminine," in *Frederick Douglass: New Literary and Historical Essays*, ed. Eric J. Sundquist, p. 143.

new mode of consciousness and of the agency it makes available is its insight into the uses and meanings of religion for, in Douglass's specific case, overcoming the indignity of inarticulacy.

What is disconcerting in this, however, concerns the gender conventions at play in how Douglass has even represented the problem of black indignity; for indignity and the feminine, particularly the black feminine, are made virtually equivalent. What this means, consequently, is that manhood, positioned in opposition to the feminine, is the place of redemption and therefore of dignity. And again, how Douglass represents the Easter story is central to how these gender protocols work. Franchot has uncovered an important aspect of the problem about which I am speaking. Thus, it would be worthwhile in moving my argument forward to engage her important research. She has observed that the whipping of Esther had "the force of 'revelation'" for the child Douglass. That is, the event, through its "diabolic imitation of Christ's manifestation of the concealed divinity," disclosed for him "the hitherto disguised interior of slavery."[14] Franchot does not quite put it this way, but it is fair to say that that disguised interior is framed as metaphorically 'christological' but only by being at the same time somatically feminine. Thus, the problem of black indignity is, in fact, the problem of religion; but the problem of religion proves to be the problem of the black feminine, the figure of black weakness. Douglass, thus, brings the problematics of religion, race, and gender into close proximity. At their intersection, he registers both the meaning of his aunt's beating and the psychological effect it had on him. This may be why "the awful force" of slavery "struck" him at that precise moment. Having been a voyeur of sorts to the beating, which is staged as a kind of rape in which he was made, as he says, to participate, the child Douglass can no longer see the world as pure and virginal. Again, the epochal status of the beating reveals itself, as it will be the first of many beatings to which he will be privy. He realizes that the modern construction of race, which rationalizes black indignity, is a violent affair. But, as his language suggests, the world is now also seen as complexly gendered in its violent configuring of race and disfiguring of persons. The beating inducts him into a vision of reality that, in short, is gendered and engendering. His employment of phallic imagery to portray the beating confirms as much, as he re-presents himself as about to pass through the hymenal veil, as it were, and so enter into "the blood-stained gate." Theological language, at this point, language by which Douglass deepens his imagistic use of New Testament Scripture, is the husk that facilitates his portrayal of

14. Franchot, "Punishment of Esther," p. 141.

what he takes to be really going on behind the religious discourse that is America — for "the blood-stained gate" through which he "was about to pass" from innocence and to consciousness was in fact his "entrance to the hell of slavery."

But what is this bloodstained gate, this descent into the 'unholy' Saturday of slavery, the veritable sojourn through Hades, if not the brutal beating of Esther? And Douglass participates in this beating, he himself confesses, as a witness. He participates by virtue of his identity with her insofar as he too was a slave. Her abuse, in other words, is vicariously his abuse; her inarticulacy is again vicariously his inarticulacy, an inarticulacy that he "wish[ed] [he] could commit to paper"; and the indignity of her femininity, which showed itself on her bruised body, is in fact his acquiescing 'femininity' in the face of the dignified masculinity, freedom, and articulacy of the brutal father-figure Plummer/Anthony. The important point in all of this is that the black female body made figural in his aunt's body becomes the *summum in nuce* of the indignity of chattel existence; woman or the feminine as acquiescent passivity effectively comes to represent what it means to be a slave, while the symbolism of the Easter Pasch serves to facilitate that representation. It follows from this that freedom, which entails the struggle for release from the condition of racial indignity, is for Douglass a struggle against the loss of masculinity. Hence, freedom as the movement toward dignity comes to be represented as resistance to the feminine, to enslaved unconsciousness, as part and parcel of the quest to seize the consciousness of manhood and thereby the self-consciousness of self-reliance, articulacy, and hence manhood.

III

The reading just given of the beating of Esther, which is recorded in chapter one of the *Narrative*, showed how the symbolism of the Easter Pasch facilitated Douglass's representation of the meaning of slavery. That is, the Easter story was drawn into Douglass's dramatic portrayal of slavery's ontology through his alignment of Esther with Christ in his passion. In this gesture, it should be noted, Christ too is feminized. By the time, however, one gets to Douglass's account of his adolescent altercation with Covey in chapter ten of the *Narrative* there is a shift in how he deploys the image of Christ's passion. Douglass now uses it as a way to represent his seizure of dignified manhood and ultimate overcoming of the feminine. The Easter story, thus, becomes a masculine saga. I want to consider how the scene does this.

Chapter ten of the *Narrative* unfolds as a series of 'smaller' altercations.

Douglass says that these altercations had as their goal beating him into sub-mission and breaking his will for freedom. Eventually buckling under the weight of the brutality — for "[during] the first six months, of that year," he says, "scarce a week passed without his whipping me. I was seldom free from a sore back" (p. 56) — Douglass records that his passion for freedom was erod-ing. And so, fairly quickly he is reduced to saying, "I was somewhat unman-ageable when I first went there, but a few months of this discipline tamed me"; and, "Mr. Covey succeeded in breaking me. I was broken in body, soul, and spirit. My natural elasticity was crushed, my intellect languished, the dis-position to read departed, the cheerful spark that lingered about my eye died; the dark night of slavery closed in upon me; and behold a man transformed into a brute!" (p. 58). In due course, Douglass reached his nadir in the great altercation of the chapter and of the *Narrative*. The account builds to this confrontation, the point where he reverses his "[transformation] into a brute," undoing "how a *man* became a slave" (italics mine). Thus, as literary scholar Richard Yarborough has said about the *Narrative*, "'manhood' . . . is the crucial spiritual commodity that one must maintain in the face of oppres-sion."[15] But how does Douglass represent this "spiritual commodity," and, furthermore, how does he "maintain [it] in the face of oppression"? On both scores Douglass once again resorts to the Easter story, portraying it as the im-material 'superstructure' that structures his materially dramatic fight with Covey and hence his resistance to oppression.

As portrayed in the scene, Douglass one day takes ill with "extreme diz-ziness" to the point that he "trembled in every limb," and at "about three o'clock of that day [he] broke down; [his] strength failed [him] . . . [he] could stand no longer, [he] fell . . ." (p. 60). Covey nevertheless immediately demanded that Douglass return to work. "Exceedingly feeble," though, he does not comply. This merited Douglass a number of swift kicks and, finally, "a heavy blow upon the head, making" — like the crown of thorns forced upon Christ's brow — "a large wound." The result: "the blood ran freely" (p. 61). Bleeding, Douglass remained on the ground, probably only semi-conscious, and Covey, seeing him in this quasi-dead state, "left [him] to [his] fate."

With momentary relief, Douglass decides to abscond from Covey's plan-tation and to return to the town of St. Michael's for the intervention of Mr. Thomas, the master who sent him away to Covey, the "nigger-breaker," in the

---

15. Richard Yarborough, "Race, Violence, and Manhood: The Masculine Ideal in Freder-ick Douglass's 'the Heroic Slave,'" in *Frederick Douglass: New Literary and Historical Essays*, ed. Eric J. Sundquist, p. 167.

first place. While on route, however, Douglass loses consciousness again from his wounds: "I fell down, and lay for a considerable time. . . . For a time I thought I should bleed to death," he says (p. 61). He lies there, as if dead; but with strength quickly found, he journeys on, arriving that night at Master Thomas's residence only to encounter his refusal to assist him and his subsequent insistence that Douglass return to Covey's plantation in the morning. As Douglass went out of his way to note the three o'clock hour of his beating the previous day, so now he goes out of his way to further establish the timeline: "I remained all night," he says, "and, according to [Master Thomas's] orders, I started off to Covey's in the morning, (Saturday morning,) wearied in body and broken in spirit" (p. 62; parenthesis original). This will prove most important for the symbolism of Douglass's account of his acquisition of dignity. Seeing Covey coming toward him at about "nine o'clock" Saturday morning "with his cowskin to give me another whipping" (p. 62) and therefore fearing for his life, Douglass, with success, retreats into a field to elude him. All of this occurred on Saturday, while on the previous day (Friday afternoon), Douglass was left as if dead, metaphorically crucified, with death symbolically descending upon him at the three o'clock hour (cf. Luke 23:44).

In all of this Douglass is continuing to wage the subtly antagonistic war against scriptural enslavement begun in chapter one of the *Narrative*. This scene continues his counter-exegesis of Scripture and of the self by claiming Jesus' three o'clock hour of dereliction for himself. With this move Douglass seeks to alter the very structure of Christian consciousness and slaveholding religion by carving out space for the dignity of black life within America's mythological use of Christianity. Stated differently, in bringing attention to the time of his own quasi-death as occurring at three o'clock, Douglass unites his death with the death of Jesus on Good Friday and ultimately with the inner meaning of slavery in the nation.

But there is more to Douglass's use of Easter symbolism in his remapping of black identity and dignity. Consider his portrayal of his dealings with "an old advisor," a slave acquaintance, Sandy Jenkins, from whom he sought "advice as to what course [of action] it was best for [him now] to pursue." Sandy's counsel was for Douglass to

> go back to Covey; but that before I went, I must go with him into another part of the woods, where there was a certain *root*, which, if I would take some of it with me, carrying it *always on my right side*, would render it impossible for Mr. Covey, or any other white man, to whip me. . . . I at first rejected the idea, that the simple carrying of a root in my pocket would have any such effect as he had said, and was not disposed to take it;

but Sandy impressed the necessity with much earnestness. . . . To please him, I at length took the root, and, according to his direction, carried it upon my right side. This was Sunday morning. (p. 63; emphasis original)

This scene introduces ambiguity into Douglass's Easter portrayal of events, and as such it introduces ambiguity into his efforts to articulate a liberated and dignified self. The ambiguity has to do with the scene's questioning of whether it is Christianity, even if it be a distinctively black Christianity, or the "root," which is emblematic of black folk ways, customs, and culture, that will mediate his deliverance from Covey. How Douglass literarily represents Sunday's and Monday's events — for Douglass's dealings with Sandy occur on Saturday — shows his dissatisfaction with both options. The first option would ground his dignity as a black man on the black feminine (and her supposedly acquiescent religiosity), while the second would ground it in black folk life and culture. In the *Narrative's* representation of things, however, these two ways of conceiving and rescuing black dignity are not far apart. Indeed, it would appear that the *Narrative's* judgment against the black feminine entails as well a judgment against black folk life, for black folk life is itself represented as feminine.[16] Hence, both must be sublated — almost in Hegelian fashion *(Aufhebung)* — into his consciousness as abolitionist intellectual. The scene's subsequent unfolding portrays just this. This goes far in explaining why the rest of the altercation scene unfolds as it does. That is, Douglass portrays the retrieval of his dignity as a simultaneous overcoming of the feminine and the folk. They must be overcome principally because of their quiescent religiosity, which tends toward a nonradical politics. The rest of the scene is Douglass's attempt in the *Narrative* to enact an emancipatory politics of dignity precisely by enacting a liberating and thus dignified politics of black religion.

Hence, with the root at his side, Douglass returns to Covey's plantation. Importantly, his return is made against the backdrop of the symbolism of the three holy days of Easter. Because he was not fully persuaded of the power of Sandy's root, Douglass actually expected a confrontation with Covey. There was, however, no fight. Rather, on 'Easter' Sunday morning "out came Mr. Covey on his way to [church] meeting." Douglass continues by observing that "[Covey] spoke to me very kindly, bade me drive the pigs from a lot near by, and passed on towards the church. Now, this singular conduct of Mr. Covey really made me to begin to think that there was something in the *root* which

---

16. In my essay, "Race, Religion, and the Contradictions of Identity: A Theological Engagement with Douglass's 1845 *Narrative*" (*Modern Theology,* January 2005), I develop the argument that in the 1845 *Narrative* black folk life is feminized.

Sandy had given me." And so Douglass became "half inclined to think the root to be something more than I at first had taken it to be" (p. 63), that there actually might be something positive about black folk culture.

Douglass, however, is quickly awakened from his slumbers: "All went well till Monday morning. On this morning, the virtue of the *root* was fully tested" (pp. 63-64). As it turned out, the root's virtue consisted only in delaying the inevitable, for on Monday morning Covey commenced whipping Douglass for the weekend's indiscretions. Douglass, however, fully resists him, meeting violence with violence and, in the end, relies neither on black folk religion nor on American Christianity, but rather on himself to bring about his own 'resurrection.' With this move Douglass seizes manhood and thus overcomes the black feminine even as he overcomes Sandy or the limitations of black folk culture for the realization of dignity.

In order to see more clearly how Douglass's victory over Covey is a masculine triumph of self-reliance and begin to conclude the essay, it is worth providing a few more important details of the altercation. "Long before daylight," Douglass says,

> I was called to go and rub, curry, and feed, the horses. I obeyed, and was glad to obey. But whilst thus engaged, whilst in the act of throwing down some blades from the loft, Mr. Covey entered the stable with a long rope; and just as I was half out of the loft, he caught hold of my legs, and was about tying me. As soon as I found what he was up to, I gave a sudden spring, and as I did so, he holding to my legs, I was brought sprawling on the stable floor. (p. 64)

Covey's attempt to tie Douglass "with a long rope" as from a joist in the stable invokes the beating of Esther, which he witnessed when just a child. Recall that Mr. Plummer, the cruel overseer, "used to tie [Esther] up to a joist, and whip upon her naked back" (p. 18). Douglass, by eluding Covey's efforts to do the same to him, portrays himself as resisting Covey's efforts to femininize him through beating him. He seizes masculine dignity, and thus freedom, by refusing to submit: "Mr. Covey seemed now to think he had me, and could do what he pleased; but at this moment — from whence came the spirit I don't know — I resolved to fight; and suiting my action to the resolution, I seized Covey hard by the throat; and as I did so, I rose" (p. 64).

Interestingly, Douglass's resolve to fight Covey and so deny white male dominance is a complicated Christian moment that is refracted through the Easter mystery and its language of the resurrection: "I rose." Douglass here claims New Testament authority to challenge scriptural enslavement. But what is also apparent here is Douglass's reversal of his negative portrayal of Christianity's Easter story as tending toward feminine docility and submissiveness. In laying claim to the Pasch for himself, his own freedom and dignity are now made coterminous with his being literally made 'christoform' or paschally shaped. The Easter story has now been recast as the story not of femininity but of recuperation of masculinity. Such is his recovery — as he put it in the *Narrative's* important appendix — of "the impartial Christianity of Christ," a recovery that has embedded within it a problematic gendering of Christianity and of Christ. From this one sees in a most poignant way how Douglass has repeated the problematically oppositional, means-ends logic of modern dignity discourse. The difference now, however, is that his problematic repetition of the logic of the cross, a logic that itself mimes the logic of the cross at work in American slaveholding religion, has brought the vexed relationship between race and gender (and indirectly, even class) to light.

Douglass's subsequent comments on his struggle with Covey make the gendered aspects of the fight strikingly apparent. Having encountered Douglass's resistance, Covey is described as being "taken all aback" and as "trembl[ing] like a leaf." At this Douglass was buoyed, "[holding] him uneasy, causing the blood to run where I touched him with the ends of my fingers" (p. 64). Interestingly, here near the end of the altercation episode the imagery of blood resurfaces — but with a difference. For now it is Covey who is bleeding, and it is Douglass who brandishes the symbolic lash, as his fingers become instruments of the very violence he once received. Having inverted the structures of power and authority, Douglass can now battle Covey for some two hours until Covey concedes defeat, that is, until Covey is made to acquiesce, as it were, to feminization. For, "[the] truth [was]," Douglass says, "he had not whipped me at all" (p. 65), since at no point "had [Covey] drawn . . . blood from me, but I had from him." From this quote we see that the presence of blood has throughout the *Narrative* been the sign of the feminine. But finally, that this was for the Douglass of the 1845 *Narrative* all along not just a racial fight, but also a gendered one, Douglass himself admits, for the altercation, he says, "revived within me a sense of my own manhood" (p. 65).

IV

What is to be made of Douglass's repetition of dignity's failings, of his newly acquired, virile humanity, and, importantly, of the religious and theological claims bound up in all of this? To be sure, another essay would be needed to give this question the attention it deserves. Short of this, however, I can offer here only this rather terse 'concluding unscientific postscript.'

What I have been laboring to show is that the dignity Douglass seizes is a failed dignity, a dignity whose il-logic is at root religious and is parasitic on a Christian narrative. In an important sense, Douglass grasps this. Thus his attempt to recontextualize dignity by restoring lost dimensions of the theology of the cross and thereby circumvent dignity's failings is a constructively powerful one. Yet, in another sense, Douglass has not reckoned with the degree of theological recontextualization his profound insight requires. He has not come to terms with what I should like to call the Trinitarian structure of dignity, which the cross christologically enacts and which the resurrection pentecostally draws the world into.[17] Instead, Douglass, writing within the constraints of racial grammar and all that goes with those constraints, still reads religion and, more specifically, Christian theology's reflections on the death and resurrection of Jesus of Nazareth as a cultural reflex and as a story of national identity. Thus, he repeats the failures associated with such an approach to dignity. What should the way forward entail? Minimally, it will require doing what Douglass never really did: engaging how Easter, in its sacramental fullness from Good Friday through to the Pentecostal sending of God's Spirit, re-performs dignity and identity as gift, developing inter-humanity within these terms.

---

17. In the essay mentioned in n. 16 above, I begin filling out this highly compressed claim.

SANCTIFICATION

Apophatic Anthropology

LINDA WOODHEAD

God became human so that we might become God.

Athanasius, *De Incarnatione* 54.3

This chapter makes a simple suggestion: that one of theology's most important contributions to the anthropological enterprise is to undermine it. This is not to say that theology has nothing to say about the human and human dignity — as the chapters in this volume indicate so well. The point is rather that there is inbuilt theological resistance to the task of defining the human, and even more so to defining the human by reference to humanity alone. Instead, theology brings the human into the sphere of the divine, and in doing so alters the terms of reference of the anthropological enterprise. Above all, it will be argued, it reminds us that since human nature is fulfilled through participation in God, it shares in the *mystery* of God — and can never be pinned down.

In what follows, this suggestion is developed in dialogue with that strand of theological reflection which places as much emphasis on divine-human union as on divine-human distinction, and which often makes use of the language of deification, divinization, or *theosis*. This tradition has biblical and Patristic roots and, although more closely associated with the Eastern than the Western tradition, is far from unknown in the West.[1] As

1. See, for example, A. N. Williams, *The Ground of Union: Deification in Aquinas and Palamas* (New York and Oxford: Oxford University Press, 1999), which demonstrates the funda-

well as drawing attention to the anthropological implications of this tradition, my aim in what follows is to demonstrate its bearing on the debate about human nature and dignity. The final part of the chapter brings this tradition into dialogue with a contemporary area of debate about human flourishing in order to demonstrate its continuing relevance and critical bite.

In the Image of God

Then God said, "Let us make humankind in our image, according to our likeness."

GENESIS 1:26

The centrality of this verse for much theological reflection on the human condition serves as an important indication of an unusual and iconoclastic approach to anthropology. Immediately it is apparent that reflection on the nature of humanity and of God will not be pulled apart, since the human is to be understood by reference to the divine. Before long something else will also become clear — that this important text does more to open up the question of human nature than to close it down.

The difficulty in pinning down the meaning of Genesis 1:26 is apparent in the long, varied, and inconclusive tradition of interpretation that surrounds it. Sometimes the divine image in humanity is identified with the "dominion" that God grants in the second part of the verse. Augustine prefers to delve into his own subjectivity in order to discover analogies by which we might understand the divine life, using the Trinity as his starting point in the search for similitudes. Other Patristic writers identify the divine image with what they regard as the highest faculty of man — with soul, mind *(nous)*, or reason *(logos)*. Such accounts are challenged by Irenaeus, Gregory of Nyssa, and Gregory Palamas, all of whom believe that both the immaterial and material aspects of human beings — body as well as soul — have been created in the image of God. Others, reflecting on the story of Adam and Eve that follows this verse, identify the *imago* with human freedom and the faculty of inner determination.

The persistent and extensive nature of this interpretative dispute may

mental agreement between Aquinas and Palamas. It has even been suggested that deification is prominent in the works of Luther: see Tuomo Mannermaa, "Theosis As a Subject of Finnish Luther Research," *Pro Ecclesia* 4 (1995): 257-79.

have theological significance in its own right. If the divine essence *(ousia)* cannot be grasped, then surely the same is true of the human — if the human is indeed made in the image of God. If God and humanity are as closely related as Genesis suggests, then the impossibility of understanding or speaking of the divine nature also applies to human nature. In other words, we are pointed toward the necessity of an apophatic approach in anthropology as well as in theology.

Apophaticism insists that the divine lies beyond words, concepts, and understanding. Despite its importance in the Christian tradition, the apophatic imperative is constantly transgressed. Such transgression can occur even when apophaticism is explicitly affirmed. Origen, for example, insists repeatedly on divine unknowability but still defines God as "Monad *(monas)* and Unity *(enas)* . . . the source and origin of all intellectual and spiritual nature."[2] Likewise, Aquinas affirms the apophatic imperative, but perhaps comes close to making negative theology a handmaid of affirmative ("cataphatic") theology when, in his discussion of analogical signification, he insists that we can attribute human perfections to God so long as we deny our human understanding of these perfections.[3]

A more serious and straightforward transgression occurs where Christians imagine that God *really is* a Father seated on a throne, bearing the marks of earthly authority — crown, scepter, robes, beard. Despite theological denials, the church has often been happy to endorse such representation. By the medieval period it had also become common to assimilate the image of God to that of priest and pope. Later on, when both Catholic and Protestant churches became more anxious to sanctify the family unit, images of "the holy family" became popular. Today, as feminist agendas push their way into the theological citadel, God becomes "God/ess," Sophia, Wisdom. Such examples are easy to criticize, because the image of God is so obviously employed in order to legitimate the claims of a particular social group seeking — or seeking to maintain — power. To speak of God as Life, Spirit, Being, and so on may have less temptation surrounding it. But *any* image of God is misleading if it is identified with the reality of God.

The underlying insight of the apophatic approach is that God's essence is — of its essence — beyond all knowing. God's substance is inaccessible, unknowable, and incommunicable. The Eastern tradition expresses this by saying that what can be known about God is not the divine nature but the divine "energies," "powers," "operations" *(energia, dunameis)*. These are "forces

---

2. Origen, *On First Principles*, P.G. XI, 125 A.
3. Aquinas, *Summa Theologiae* 1.1

proper to and inseparable from God's essence, in which He goes forth from Himself, manifests, communicates, and gives Himself."[4]

Since Christian talk of God is talk of Trinity, even the description of the Son as a "revelation" of the Father can easily be misconstrued, for it can be taken to mean that the Son is an energy or outpouring of God (the Father) who makes God known to us. This suggests not only that the Son is subordinate to the Father, but also that by knowing the Son we know the Father. Neither is true, for the Son is consubstantial with the Father (of the same essence), and his nature is therefore as unknowable as that of the Father. The idea that we can somehow grasp the essence of Jesus, and in so doing lay hold of the nature of God, is yet another evasion of a genuine apophaticism.

The same can, of course, be said of the Holy Spirit, the third *hypostasis* (instantiation) of the one divine *ousia* (essence). Interestingly, however, it needs to be said less often, for Christians are less prone to try to capture and contain the Spirit in words and images. The Spirit has no face, so we find it less tempting to clothe "him" in the garb of human power (or weakness). The Spirit has no body, so we find it less tempting to think of "him" in exclusively male or female terms (both are used in the tradition). The Spirit "blows where it wills," so we are less likely to try to contain the Spirit in temples made with human hands. Similarly, the Spirit is harder to spatialize, since it acts both from "inside" humans and the whole created order and from "outside." Of course, attempts to control the Spirit *are* made, as by limiting its sphere of operation to the church and its sacraments (more tempting for Catholics) or to the interpretation of the Word (more tempting for Protestants) — or, more radically, by subordinating the Spirit to Father and Son (as in some interpretations of the Filioque). Nevertheless, the fact that the Spirit is less easily captured in categories of human understanding gives it particular importance in the formulation of apophatic anthropology.

Divinization

That you may . . . become participants in divine nature.

2 PETER 1:4

By resisting the temptation to define and capture the essence of God we hold open the possibility of a genuinely apophatic anthropology. Human beings,

---

4. Vladimir Lossky, *The Mystical Theology of the Eastern Church* (Cambridge: James Clarke, 1991), p. 70.

made in the image of God, do not contain their essence in themselves but in the God into whose image they are to grow. They become human by becoming divine — which means growing into something we do not know or control rather than something we already possess.

Though central to Patristic thought, and important in the Bible, the theme of divinization has often been overwhelmed in the West by an Augustinian emphasis on human sinfulness.[5] For Augustine, Luther, Calvin, and others, human nature is so utterly corrupted that it can do nothing on its own but contribute to its own downfall. Even the choice to run to God and receive his forgiveness can be made only by an invasion of grace that completely overwhelms and overrides the sinful human will. Salvation is a more prominent theme than divinization, for the best that the human can hope for is to be saved from his or her wretched condition by God's infinite love and mercy. It is not that he or she escapes from this condition, but rather that human sinfulness is forensically reckoned as righteousness in spite of itself. Humans are saved not because they become divine, but because God chooses to gaze on them as found in Christ rather than as they are in their own wretchedness. The human must decrease so that he may increase. It was left to more radical strands within Protestantism to revive the theme of divinization by way of the doctrine of sanctification.

The scholastic humanism of Aquinas offers a more positive view of a human nature that is not wholly corrupted and may be perfected by grace. Aquinas agrees with much of the Patristic tradition, and with Eastern thinkers like Gregory Palamas, in presenting the goal of human life as union with God. Human beings are *made* in the image of God, as well as having to *grow into* that image. That does not mean that they are created already possessing some divine spark that is already whole and entire and has only to free itself from whatever holds it down in order to float free and be reunited with its divine source — as if a fragment of divinity were trapped in a human body (a view more common among some Platonists). It means that human beings are created possessing the capacity to be deified — a capacity that some of the Fathers identified with freedom to cooperate with God's will. This capacity belongs to the whole person, body and soul, and it is the whole person who is also to be deified — in this life as well as the next. In the East, where the Augustinian reading of Genesis 3 never took hold, Adam and Eve's actions were not thought to have erased the image of God in human beings, nor the capacity to choose between good and evil. What Adam and Eve failed to do was to

---

5. Chief amongst the biblical sources cited by the Fathers are 2 Peter 1:4, Psalm 82:6 and John 10:34, Romans 8:11, 1 Corinthians 15:49, and 2 Corinthians 8:9.

realize the divine image within them, and thus to attain to the immortality that God had intended for them. Their action has not corrupted the will of their descendents, but has made them mortal — and mortality provides a motive and an occasion for sin.

That does not mean that human beings become God in the way that the Father is God, the Son is God, and the Spirit is God, for human beings are not *hypostases* of God: they are not of the nature of God by nature. They are created, not uncreated, and are created *ex nihilo* — out of nothing. Genesis expresses this by saying that God creates Adam "out of the dust of the earth" and breathes life into humanity. Humanity is shaped by grace from the point of creation, but the image of God exists as a potential to be realized. Irenaeus expressed this by drawing a distinction between the "image" in which we already find ourselves and the "likeness" into which we are to grow. Though the image cannot be erased, it might not be fulfilled — and it can be fulfilled only by human incorporation into God rather than vice versa. Whereas in Christ the divine becomes human, in human beings the human must become divine. In participating in the divine nature the human not only realizes the perfection for which it was created — a perfection seen in Christ — but in doing so comes to possess the unknowable character of the divine being. This is why it is impossible to define what constitutes the divine image in man and woman.

Spiritual Bodies

> *It is sown a physical body* [soma psychikon], *it is raised a spiritual body* [soma pneumatikon].
>
> 1 CORINTHIANS 15:44

In speaking about the nature of divinization many of the Fathers are keen to insist that it is the whole human person that is called to become divine, both body and soul. It is not a part of human nature that is to be divinized, but the whole human being. As Gregory of Nyssa puts it, "Thus man is made in the image of God, that is to say the whole human nature; it is that which bears the divine likeness."[6] This is a theme which can be traced back to one of the most fascinating aspects of Paul's reflections on (perfected) humanity.

Paul's reflections occur in the context of a discussion of resurrection, where he introduces the idea of a "spiritual body." He explains that

---

6. Quoted by Lossky, *Mystical Theology of the Eastern Church*, p. 120.

There are celestial bodies and there are terrestrial bodies; but the glory of the celestial is one, and the glory of the terrestrial is another. There is one glory of the sun, and another glory of the moon, and another glory of the stars; for star differs from star in glory.

So it is with the resurrection of the dead. What is sown is perishable, what is raised is imperishable. . . . It is sown a physical body *[soma psychikon]*, it is raised a spiritual body *[soma pneumatikon]*. If there is a physical body, there is also a spiritual body. (1 Cor. 15:40-44)

To a contemporary audience, whether Jewish or Greco-Roman, the idea of a spiritual body would probably have been as confusing as it is to post-Cartesian moderns, for it disrupted established categories of understanding and expectation. It was not that late antiquity was not otherworldly (or, as Peter Brown prefers to put it, "upperworldly").[7] In the Hellenistic imagination, the world above was both more real and more perfect than this world. It was the world of the celestial bodies, of which we can catch a glimpse from this lower world. The sight of the heavens — silent, stable, perfect, unchanging — instilled in earth-bound mortals a longing to be rid of the material bodies that weighed them down, and to release their souls to soar upward to a more appropriate home. While the contemplative life might raise the virtuous soul toward the heavens, it was only death that would finally release it "passing to the sky, as quick and dry as a lightning flash leaving the lowering, damp cloud of the flesh."[8]

Paul was well aware of this upperworldly imaginary. To some extent, he inhabited it. That is why, when he tries to explain resurrection, he begins with familiar contemporary talk about celestial bodies and the glory of the sun, the moon, and the stars. But then he moves on to something much less familiar: the idea that a physical body could share in heavenly glory. To most Hellenistic minds, this was a simple category mistake. The material and spiritual were separated by as significant a fault line as the heavens and the earth. What Paul does is to smudge this line. In doing so, he is merging Jewish ideas of physical resurrection with Hellenistic ideas of the glory of the immortal soul.[9] His thought is led not by an attempt at clever intellectual synthesis, but by the task of representing what has happened in the resurrection of Jesus. For Paul this is no second-hand event but one which he has personally

---

7. Peter Brown, *The Cult of the Saints: Its Rise and Function in Latin Christianity* (London: SCM, 1983), p. 2.

8. Brown, *The Cult of the Saints*, p. 2.

9. On Paul's understanding of the spirit and the flesh see Daniel Boyarin, *A Radical Jew: Paul and the Politics of Identity* (Berkeley: University of California Press, 1997), pp. 57-85.

experienced, since the risen Christ had appeared not only to the disciples, brethren, and apostles, but "last of all, as to one untimely born," to him (1 Cor. 15:3-11). And the risen Christ disrupts the normal categories of body and spirit.

Paul witnesses to this disruption when he tries to describe his own encounter with the risen Christ. Using a Hellenistic turn of phrase he speaks of his having been "caught up to the third heaven," but adds an important qualification: "whether in the body or out of the body, I do not know, God knows" (2 Cor. 12:2). The Gospel accounts are similarly unclear about whether the risen Jesus is "in the body" or "out of the body." In some respects he seems pure spirit: he refuses to let Mary touch him, he appears and disappears like a ghost, he can glide through walls. In others, he seems pure body: Thomas thrusts his hand into his side and his fingers into his wounds, Jesus breaks bread and cooks his disciples a fish breakfast. The overall impression that he is both and neither is reinforced by the confusion about whether or not this is the fleshly Jesus of Nazareth. Mary mistakes him for the gardener, the disciples do not realize who he is until Peter walks across the water to meet the risen Lord, and the disciples on the road to Emmaus recognize him only in the breaking of bread. And it is not only after death that Christ disrupts the normal categories of spirit and body, earth and heaven, human and divine. During his lifetime he is also a "spiritual body," as is revealed to his disciples on Mount Tabor. It is not that Jesus changes, but that they suddenly see him for what he is — a dazzling body. Similarly, Paul affirms that the resurrection life is a life that those who have been baptized into the life of Christ can begin to live here and now, even before death.

It was this same belief, and this desire to be transformed into a spiritual body even in this life, that shaped the spiritual striving of many early Christians. Some, we know, ventured into the desert in order to pursue their spiritual aim without distraction. Their goal was to attain the state of perfected humanity that had been ordained for Adam but achieved by Jesus.[10] Possessing the image of God, they would grow into God's likeness through cooperation with his Spirit. In order to achieve this they did not necessarily require Scriptures or sacraments — some of the *Sayings of the Desert Fathers* seem to indicate an active hostility to such externals of the religious life. Instead, these early Christian ascetics sought to destroy the passions and desires that tied them to "the world" narrowly conceived (that which can be "possessed" and become part of a "me" and "mine," which can be confused with

---

10. See Peter Brown, *The Body and Society: Men, Women and Sexual Renunciation in Early Christianity* (New York: Columbia University Press, 1988), pp. 213-40.

my true nature). By the exercise of love and humility, they also sought to overcome attachment to another false self that can also be confused with the true self-in-God (the "me" that achieves things, including its own spiritual perfection). By such means they sought to be transformed by the dazzling uncreated light of God that would shine from body and soul:

> There came to the abba Joseph the abba Lot, and said to him, "Father, according to my strength I keep a modest rule of prayer and fasting and meditation and quiet, and according to my strength I purge my imagination: what more must I do?" The old man, rising, held up his hands against the sky, and his fingers were fringed with fire, and he said, "Why not be changed wholly into flame?"[11]

It is this same tradition of spirituality that feeds into the Eastern tradition of monasticism and mystical theology. The theology of deification is related to spiritual practices kept alive in some of the monasteries and hermitages of the Byzantine empire and, after the ninth century, of Bulgaria, Romania, Serbia, and Russia. In the latter, for example, the tradition of the individual holy man living in seclusion until he achieves deification, then opening his doors in order to give spiritual direction to others, survived right through to the modern period — to influence Tolstoy and Dostoevsky, among others. And the theme of the spiritual body, transformed by the uncreated energies of God, recurs in a form that seems to bring the deserts of Egypt, Syria, and Palestine into direct connection with the frozen lands of the north. The following conversation between Seraphim of Sarov and a disciple from the early nineteenth century echoes those recorded in the *Sayings of the Desert Fathers* well over a thousand years before:

> "I don't understand how one can be certain of being in the spirit of God. How should I be able to recognize for certain this manifestation in myself?"
>
> "I've already told you," said Father Seraphim, "that it's very simple. I've talked at length about the state of those who are in the Spirit of God; I've also explained to you how we can recognize this presence in ourselves. . . . What more is necessary my friend?"
>
> "I must understand better everything that you have said to me."
>
> "My friend, we are both at this moment in the Spirit of God. . . . Why won't you look at me?"

---

11. *Sayings of the Desert Fathers* 12.8. The translation is my own, based on *The Desert Fathers: Translations from the Latin*, intro. by Helen Waddell (New York: Vintage, 1998), p. 117.

"I can't look at you, Father," I replied, "your eyes shine like lightning; your face has become more dazzling than the sun, and it hurts my eyes to look at you."

"Don't be afraid," he said, "at this very moment you've become as bright as I have. You also are present in the fullness of the Spirit of God; otherwise, you wouldn't be able to see me as you do see me."[12]

As in Paul, the Spirit transfigures both body and soul. Both alike, filled with the power of God, become part of God. "Shall I take the members of Christ and make them members of a prostitute?" Paul asks rhetorically as he condemns fornication (1 Cor. 6:15), for the Spirit of Christ is present in body as well as soul. The spiritual perfection that can be accomplished through Christ consists not in leaving behind some aspect of the human being but in entering more deeply into the reality of one's life — a life which is physical as well as spiritual. This is not a monistic anthropology in which the stream of self runs into the ocean of the One and dissolves into it, but an anthropology in which the divine energy enters into human life to transform it. The Holy Spirit enters into the person not in order to obliterate human nature but in order to perfect it. This is one reason, we may speculate, why the Holy Spirit does not show its face other than in the faces of those whom it inspires.

A Contemporary Application

The anthropology that is implied by talk of divinization and "spiritual bodies" is not holistic in the modern sense, for it does not view a person as a psychosomatic whole in which *psyche* and *soma* are equal partners. Rather, it pictures a hierarchy of body, mind/soul, and spirit in which spirit is the higher part that should rule and inspire the rest. Thus it is not for the body to control our life, but for the mind/soul inspired and led on by the (Holy) Spirit. However unpalatable this may be to a modern sensibility, an apophatic anthropology considers biological nature — and biological ties — less significant than spiritual ones. In doing so it can claim the authority of Jesus, who disparaged biological ties compared to the spiritual ties that bind the community he has come to establish on earth ("if anyone comes to me and does not hate his own father and mother and wife and children and brothers and sisters . . .") and who refused to let people's bodily ailments, diseases, and differences dictate the shape of their lives and the measure of their spiritual

12. Quoted by Lossky, *Mystical Theology of the Eastern Church*, pp. 227-28.

worth (if we understand his healing not in the sense of restoring to normality, but of welcoming into the fullness of the kingdom of God).[13]

It is because it sees human nature as fulfilled and led on by the Spirit that an anthropology of the spiritual body has a built-in tendency toward apophaticism. The Spirit draws us into the unknowable reality of God, into the mystery in which each unique human life finds its fulfillment. Thus the question of human nature and the definition of human dignity must always be left open. By contrast a cataphatic anthropology will always try to define, describe, and delimit human nature. And in telling us who we are, it often becomes self-fulfilling, fixing in us the nature it claims to describe. This is most pronounced, perhaps, when human nature is defined in terms of given bodily characteristics, for to a greater extent than soul or spirit, body can be identified, isolated, studied, classified, measured, contained, and pinned down.

Over the course of its long and complex history, Christianity has both endorsed and undermined cataphatic anthropologies of heavy corporeality — particularly in relation to women. We can see the process of endorsement getting underway as early as some of the New Testament documents, as when we read that woman is to keep silent and not to teach or "have authority over men," but "will be saved through bearing children" (1 Tim. 2:12, 15). Whereas a woman's reproductive function disqualifies her from leadership in the church, a man's qualifies him, for a bishop "must manage his own household well, keeping his children submissive and respectful in every way" (1 Tim. 3:4). But fatherhood was quickly spiritualized in a way motherhood never was. It was accepted, in other words, that fatherhood was a spiritual calling more than a biological determination, so that the most important fathers of all — pope *(papa),* abbot *(abba),* clergy (reverend father) — were actually prevented from having biological children in order to tend to their spiritual children. But for many women, biology remained destiny and nature; though even then Christianity left open some escape routes — most notably the path of monastic purification.

For a number of reasons which need not trouble us here, contemporary theology and ethics displays a strong tendency to overturn the traditional hierarchy of body and spirit in favor of the body. Humans are presented as bodily creatures rather than spiritual bodies, and there is a notable tendency to exalt and value the body and stress its centrality in making us who we are. Nowhere is this clearer than in relation to the important debates surrounding the use of new medical technologies (see the chapter by Soulen in this vol-

13. For such a reading see John Dominic Crossan, *Jesus: A Revolutionary Biography* (San Francisco: HarperSanFrancisco, 1995).

ume). Some Christian witness in this area is a natural outgrowth of concern about maintaining a traditional family unit and gender roles, particularly when the subject of debate is new reproductive technologies. But there is a deeper concern about any moves that threaten to interfere with the genetic makeup of the human being. The language itself reflects the basic commitments of a Christian anthropology whose starting point is so often the belief that our biological — and genetic — makeup is given by God and consequently must not be altered in any way (to do so would be to "play God").

Even so moderate a textbook as Gilbert Meilaender's *Bioethics: A Primer for Christians* opens by stating — almost as if this were the only possible Christian viewpoint — that we are created by God as the embodied beings we are, that we are made female and male, that we are called to cleave to one another and have children by natural means, and that *anything* that interferes with this natural order of things should not be condoned.[14] The implication, he argues in the rest of the book, is that the whole range of medical technologies he reviews — from IVF to genetic modification — must be resisted by Christians. His position, wholly consistent, rests on two major assumptions: first, that the way our bodies are is the way *they* must stay, and, second, that the way our bodies are is the way *we* must stay. If my ovaries are not producing eggs, then I am an infertile woman and that is the way I must stay. My bodily condition determines who I am.

By contrast, an anthropology of the spiritual body is less willing to admit that my body plays the controlling role in determining who I am, since this downgrades or ignores the supervening role of the Spirit. If a couple have opened themselves to God in prayer, have explored other possibilities with genuinely open hearts, and still feel called to love and nurture children and help them grow into the image of and likeness of God, then it may be appropriate for them to override the capacities or incapacities of their reproductive organs (if this can be done in a way that does not bring harm to others). It is human beings in relation to God who make the decision, not their bodily condition alone. If they feel they are growing into their real lives more fully through this course of action, and will be helping others to do so as well, then that may be more important than what their unassisted bodies can or cannot do.

The irony is that an anthropology of heavy corporeality may actually have much in common with the modern medical discourse and practice it claims to resist. As holistic medicine has been pointing out for over a century,

14. Gilbert Meilaender, *Bioethics: A Primer for Christians* (Grand Rapids: Eerdmans, 1996).

mainstream medicine tends to treat humans as bodies and nothing more. And despite sophisticated analysis and critique on the part of medical sociologists (among others), the medical profession still relies on handbooks of physical and mental disorders by which to diagnose and pigeonhole patients in an often grossly cataphatic fashion. Almost every human condition can now erect itself on a biological basis and possibly generate a pharmaceutical cure. Our desire to "sort out" even those "conditions" that cause no risk to the lives of those who "suffer" them leads to the most terrible interventions in order to normalize the "abnormal" (as in the relatively common case of intersex babies who are forced to endure surgical procedures and psychological manipulation in order to make them clearly male or female). Similarly, as the chapters in this volume by Soulen and Reinders remind us, our society has difficulty in accepting those whose bodies, behaviors, and mental capacities make them not only different but "handicapped." Rather than accepting that such individuals may be able to reveal to us aspects of the human condition we might not otherwise glimpse, our fixed ideas of what that condition can and cannot include tempts us to screen them out or shut them away.

Rather than simply condemn such foreclosure on human possibilities, we can admit the similar tendencies that lurk within the Christian tradition and our own hearts. We are anxious about many things, not least the dangerous and difficult task of living decent, worthwhile, generous, and courageous lives — or simply of living. The anthropological enterprise easily becomes handmaid to such anxiety, helping us deal with it by reassuring us that a normal, natural, faithful, holy life should be defined like this — but not like that. As Bonhoeffer reminded us, we all have a tendency to become the Pharisee who sorts out good and evil — rather than living in the place of genuine openness to God which is "beyond good and evil."[15]

The problem is that the way we should live is *not* laid out for us in a clear way — not inscribed into my flesh, not written in an instruction manual delivered at birth, and not laid down in the Bible or Jesus' teaching as clearly as we might want (why *couldn't* he have been a better moralist!). But the problem is also the gift and opportunity that life presents to us. We inherit a whole heap of bodily, social, and familial conditions, contexts, experiences, and "issues" — along with a frightening sense of under-determination, openness, and possibility. It is this mix that the idea of a "spiritual body" helps us to appreciate, as well as the faith and the hope that in entering more deeply into life we are assisted by the grace of a God who assists us to grow into the divine image.

15. Dietrich Bonhoeffer, *Ethics* (London: SCM, 1982), pp. 1-44.

It is not that "anything goes." The Spirit does not draw us toward "anything," but toward the God of Jesus Christ. What we are called to become is not "anything," but members of the body of Christ. As Paul puts it, we are called to die with Christ and to live the resurrection life. This excludes and rules out many things. Above all, it rules out lives of domination and control, lives that would secure their own positions by taking away the life, freedom, and dignity of others. It excludes "playing God" where our model of God is an all-powerful, dominating being who controls and disposes all things. In this sense, the stricture on "playing God" is correct. But to the extent that a life in the Spirit is a life of divinization, of living Christ's risen life, it is profoundly wrong. We *are* called to be divine, though the God who calls us is the one whom Jesus recognized and first called *abba* at the moment of his most profound helplessness and vulnerability. As Rowan Williams puts it, "Spirit is the pressure upon us towards Christ's relation with the Father, towards the self secure enough . . . to decide for the cross of powerlessness."[16] An apophatic anthropology requires that we open ourselves to the unknown in order to become more than we can possibly know. It is much safer and easier to choose a route that has already been clearly mapped out — but that is not the same as entering into Life.

---

16. Rowan Williams, *On Christian Theology* (Oxford: Blackwell, 2000), p. 124.

Human Dignity: Concepts and Experiences

FRASER WATTS

The idea of dignity has long been integral to how Christian thinkers have formulated the view that humanity reflects the image of God. In recent centuries, however — as suggested in the introduction — "dignity" has had a somewhat checkered history. First it was adopted as a secular concept by the Enlightenment and seen as an absolute and universal human quality. More recently, it has been re-imported back into Christian discourse. The use of secular concepts such as human dignity may seem capable of bringing a certain freshness and clarity to theological anthropology, which has not been one of the most lively areas of theology. Nevertheless, there remains a real question about whether this is the best term for theologians to use to make their points about human nature, or whether there is perhaps a certain cost associated with the adoption of a term such as "dignity," which now has so many secular connotations.

In this chapter I will contrast the Enlightenment concept of dignity with Christian approaches. Another distinctive feature of the chapter, and one that runs through most of my theological work, is that I do theology in dialogue with psychology. So I will be concerned here not only with ideas about dignity, but with how dignity is experienced; hence my subtitle. I will try to place the experience of dignity in the context of recent changes in human consciousness. I will also assume that dignity is something to be worked for, not something that can simply be assumed or something that can be demanded as a right.

The Grammar of Dignity

It will be helpful at the outset to attend to the grammar of how the concept of dignity is actually used. This immediately shows that there is a certain moral ambivalence about dignity; dignity is not from every point of view an unmitigated human good. It is clearly wrong to inflict indignities on other people, or to behave in an undignified way. On the other hand, it is clearly not good to "stand on your dignity." No one would welcome having to suffer indignities, but if they bore them with dignity they might become a good. This moral ambivalence about dignity, which is apparent in its grammar, can be developed in a more explicitly theological way. For example, a strong emphasis on human dignity sits uneasily with the principle of kenosis, with how Christ "emptied" himself (Phil. 2:7). If Christ emptied himself, there is surely a sense in which Christians should follow his example and do the same; and kenosis seems to involve setting dignity aside.

There is also a great difference between how one treats one's own dignity and how one treats the dignity of others. It may be right to set one's own dignity aside and "take the form of a servant." It would be quite another matter to act in a way that robbed others of their dignity, and there is no encouragement to do that in the Christian tradition. Respecting the dignity of others can perhaps be regarded as a virtue in all circumstances. Asserting one's own dignity is, morally, a much more doubtful matter.

Another problem with how dignity is viewed in the secular Enlightenment is that it leaves no place for vulnerability. It seems to assume that people are respected entirely for their positive capacities, especially their rationality. It seems doubtful, however, whether in reality this is so. There are probably cultural changes underway in the sorts of things for which people are respected. At least today, if not in previous generations, people are respected for their vulnerability, for example for their capacity to show grief and sadness. Not to show such vulnerability reveals a lack of sensitivity. From one point of view such insensitivity can perhaps be regarded as "dignified," though it is a quality that has ceased to win universal respect.

The Enlightenment idea of dignity as a universal and equal property of all human beings has probably not taken root in how we think and speak about dignity in everyday life as much as exclusive attention to the philosophical literature might suggest. If "ordinary language" philosophers of the Oxford school are right in proposing that we find the meaning of a word by attending to its usage, close attention to the way in which "dignity" is used suggests something more subtle and complicated than is set out in Enlightenment philosophy.

Creation, Eschatology, and Dignity

The Enlightenment idea that every human being has dignity, and that the dignity of each human being is equal, is unsatisfactory theologically because it is too static. It leaves no room for eschatology, no scope for a dynamic unfolding of God's purposes in relation to human dignity.

The Enlightenment view of human dignity is the equivalent in secular philosophy of *imago Dei,* of humans beings created in the image of God. We are all made in the image of God; we all have human dignity. If it is not to be flat-footed, however, a theology of dignity needs to be balanced by an eschatological approach; creation is a continuing process and is inseparable from eschatology. G. C. Berkouwer[1] has argued that the concept of humans being made in the image of God needs to handled eschatologically, with a sense of what humans might become, and I would argue the same for human dignity.

This requires that we distinguish different senses of dignity. In one sense we have dignity already, but in another sense we do not yet have dignity in all its fullness. There is both a present actuality and a future potentiality about human dignity. Both are essential to an adequate theology of dignity. The distinction we need is between an absolute or universal concept of human dignity and a relative or qualitative one.

In pre-Enlightenment thinking, dignity was relative; some people had positions of greater dignity than others. For Kant, dignity was absolute; everyone had the same absolute dignity that defied calibration. I suggest that we actually have both concepts jostling together in our current discourse, and that it inevitably causes confusion to endorse one and to ignore the other. Moreover, I claim that theologically we need both concepts, and that holding the doctrines of creation and eschatology together shows us how to use them alongside one another.

A theology of creation gives us an absolute concept of dignity. We are all made in the image of God. That bestows the same dignity on us all, and there is no light or shade about it. I suggest that we also need a qualitative concept of dignity that reflects the extent to which the potential that comes from being made in the image of God has been realized. The distinction between being made in the "image" of God, and growing into his "likeness," has sometimes been used in this way. Though terminology has not been consistent, "image" has often been an absolute concept, while "likeness" has been a qualitative one.

People differ in the extent to which they have realized the potential that comes from being created in the image of God. At the present time that fuller

---

1. G. C. Berkouwer, *Man: The Image of God* (Grand Rapids: Eerdmans, 1962).

dignity to which all are called, and for which we can hope, is more completely realized in some people than in others. All, however, are called to a fuller realization of the dignity that is part of God's purposes. In this eschatological between-time, we need a qualitative or relative sense of dignity. When that dignity is completely realized in everyone, we will return to an absolute, universal concept of dignity that is manifest equally in all people.

There is an analogy here with discourse about the soul. "Soul" has classically been used in a substantive sense. On this view, people have a soul; everyone has one; it is an absolute concept that underpins the moral equality of human beings. The analogy is a close one because the dignity tradition of the Enlightenment is doing much the same job as the soul tradition did in Christian theology. Alongside this, however, there has recently been a tendency to introduce a qualitative use of "soul."[2] The soul qualities of some people may be stronger than others; soul-making may have gone further in some people than in others.

I want to resist a debate about whether "soul" should be used in one way or the other, but rather to argue that we need both senses of soul, and that they are complementary. There is real value, especially from a moral point of view, in asserting that there is a basic sense in which everyone has a soul. However limited the capacities of some people might be in practice, they share, in some important sense, the core of soul with all other humans. There is also real value in the tradition of soul-making, however. It holds out the possibility that people's potential soul qualities can be strengthened and developed so that they become more of an actuality. Inevitably, some people go further along that path than others. In a parallel way, there is value in retaining both the basic concept of human dignity with which all humans are endowed in equal measure, and also the development and realization of that dignity which will go further in some people than others.

People can thus live in the space created between the basic dignity that is given to them and the fuller dignity to which they are called. It makes a crucial difference how this is experienced. The relationship between the ego and the Self in Jungian thought provides a helpful analogy that elucidates the existential relationship between these two senses of dignity. The ego is the basic core of self-consciousness and individuality. The Self (a technical term, used in a sense that is rather different from the everyday one) is the complete person toward whom we can develop, when we integrate unconscious and shadow elements of personality to achieve a state of wholeness.

2. Keith Ward, *Defending the Soul* (Oxford: Oneworld, 1992); Fraser Watts, *Theology and Psychology* (London: Ashgate, 2002).

This ego-Self axis provides a helpful analogue for Christian eschatological thought.[3] There is an eschatological "now already but not yet" about it. The ego is already a reality, but the Self is still to come. Yet the Self already makes its impact now, both as a vision of what it is possible for us to become and as a power that can facilitate our journey toward it. This is closely parallel to how, for the Christian, the kingdom is already announced; it provides a vision for the future and helps to transform the present.

For the ego-Self axis to work effectively, the relationship between them must remain open. It can collapse in different ways, which again are parallel to the pathologies of eschatological thought. The ego can become inflated and grandiose, and imagine itself already to be the self. That is like Christians assuming that the kingdom is already fully here, and that there is nothing left to come. Alternatively, the ego can become crushed and diminished, so that it has no sense of connectedness to the Self, and no capacity to move toward it. That is like Christians allowing the promised kingdom to recede into such a "never-never" land that it no longer gives hope to the present.

In a similar way, the proper human experience of dignity depends on keeping open the axis between the dignity that we have already as gift, and the fuller dignity that we are promised and toward which we are called. Neglect of either one is like a collapse of the ego-Self axis. To see dignity solely as a necessary property of human beings, as secular Enlightenment thought tends to do, is to lose touch with the eschatological promise that the dignity of humanity can become more of a reality. It is a concept of dignity that remains two-dimensional, and so does little to facilitate the human endeavor. On the other hand, if dignity is seen entirely as something that might develop more fully in the future, with no sense that it is already in some basic sense present, there would be no constraints on current indignities.

If our only concept of dignity were a universal and ontological one, it might be felt that there was nothing to be done about it, that human dignity could be neither destroyed nor improved upon. It is important, however, for people to sense that there is scope for them to treat others with greater respect, and to be so treated themselves. Only if there is a sense that human dignity could become more of a reality than is presently the case will people be motivated to work to make it more of a reality. This sense of dignity as something that remains to be realized can be seen as invitation and promise, a possibility that is held out to people, and to which they are invited to respond.

---

3. Fraser Watts, *Theology and Psychology* (Aldershot: Ashgate, 2002).

Reductionism and Human Dignity

There has been a tendency for people to feel that new intellectual developments such as Darwinism and Freudianism present a threat to human dignity, though that sense has diminished over time as these ideas have become more familiar. My particular point here is that the initial sense of threat to human dignity came from a confusion between the absolute and qualitative senses of dignity that I have tried to distinguish. Qualitative forms of reductionism are acceptable, and need not lead on to the stronger, ontological forms of reductionism that are inconsistent with religious belief.

The Darwinian proposition that we are descended from other primates suggests that we were likely to have continuities with the primates, which in turn implies that not all our behavior is as dignified as we might like to think. That is a point about qualitative dignity; an example would be that the tendency to fight under threat is something toward which there is a genetic disposition. This point, however, was often misheard as being a more absolute and ontological point about human dignity, that because we were descended from other animals we *are* just animals. Heard in that way, it is felt to be an attack on the proposition that we all have a basic dignity as members of the human race. I suggest that a clearer sense of the distinction between absolute and qualitative senses of the concept of dignity would have reduced the sense of threat presented by Darwinism.

The same is true of Freudianism. The Freudian proposition that much of our apparently higher behavior arises from an adjustment to the primitive instincts of the id suggests that our higher behaviors, on close examination, may turn out to be more morally ambivalent than we would like to think. Correctly understood, however, that does not lead to the conclusion that we are nothing but the products of our primitive instincts, or undermine the proposition that we have a basic, core dignity as human beings. It is a qualitative point about human beings, not an ontological one.

More generally, the distinction that has been made here between absolute and qualitative senses of dignity sheds light on the basic logical maneuver that underlies reductionist ideologies about human nature. "Nothing but" reductionism is always seeking to assert a proposition about the basic nature of humanity, that we are basically just this or that (the products of our genes, of our neurons, of our primitive instincts, and so on). Such reductionisms appear to be denying the basic ontological dignity of human beings. This, however, is a fallacious conclusion.

The conclusions that can properly be drawn about human beings from such premises are qualitative ones, not absolute ones. Our genes, our neurons, our basic instincts, and so on affect how we *function* qualitatively as human beings, but they do not yield absolute, ontological conclusions about what we *are*. It is the absolute forms of reductionism that are pernicious, incompatible with religious views, and to be resisted. There is no reason, however, why such absolute reductionist conclusions need be drawn from more subtle and relatively harmless forms of reductionism that are only qualitative in their claims.

It is noticeable that reductionism is not equally attractive to everyone. Some people are attracted to mystery, others are not. Stripping away the mystery has been one of the key driving forces of modern science from the beginning, as Mary Midgley has pointed out.[4] One of the very strange things about this program is that demystification was originally seen as an ally of religious orthodoxy in the battle against paganism. The instinctive alliances have shifted, however, and now people feel that preserving the sense of mystery is an ally of religious belief in the battle against atheism.

Another strand in the appeal of reductionism is probably its moral tone. Some people are attracted by a pious attitude and a high moral tone; others are irritated and offended by it. A key element in the appeal of reductionism is probably that people feel that it liberates them from moral cant and cloying piety. It comes like a breath of fresh air, ushering in a new moral climate that is less pretentious and restrictive. If so, the implications of reductionist positions for human dignity will be complex. What seems a clear implication to one person may not seem so to another. Mere assertions that reductionist approaches to human nature are a betrayal of human dignity will not convince. Others may find them attractive precisely because they seem to usher in a new and more satisfactory approach to human dignity.

A crucial issue for those concerned with the betrayal of human dignity is how much moral difference it makes if we have limited concepts of human nature. Certainly, ways of thinking can have implications for moral behavior. In the early modern period, the adoption of a view of animals as mere mechanisms sometimes led to their being badly treated. It is arguable that recent views of the natural environment have facilitated its exploitation. To think of nature as God's creation, or even as "Gaia," might restrain us.

More generally, there are indications that the distancing, "spectorial" stance that has been so prominent in the consciousness of modernity has had unwelcome consequence. For example, it seems that medicine gets better results when it adopts a "whole-person" approach, rather than treating human bodies as pieces of machinery to be repaired. Even industrial production is

---

4. Mary Midgley, *Evolution As Religion* (London: Methuen, 1992).

better for treating workers as people with dignity. The bracketing out of aspects of human nature in modern science, though it has brought benefits, is probably something for which we have paid quite a high price, though it is perhaps not a necessary feature of science.

Dignity As Gift or Right

Though both theology and secular thinking have a sense of human dignity as universal, they handle this in very different ways. It is of great theological importance that human dignity should be seen as a gift; there is no counterpart to that in the approach to dignity in the secular philosophy of the Enlightenment.

There are different ways in which something can be experienced as gift. It is possible for people to feel demeaned or patronized by being told that something is a gift when they feel it is a basic part of their nature or constitution, or something to which they are entitled. Alternatively, for people to be given a gift can be experienced as highly affirming and something very much to be welcomed. When the Christian tradition speaks of something being a gift of God, though the latter is intended, sometimes, in the context of post-Enlightenment thought, it is heard as being patronizing. How talk of "gift" is heard probably depends on people's sense of self-worth. For something to be called a gift is more likely to be experienced positively by people who are basically self-confident than by those who feel inadequate. From one point of view this is, of course, a paradoxical state of affairs, as it might be imagined that it would be those who felt least adequately endowed who would most appreciate a gift.

The human significance of being the recipient of a gift can be unpacked in various ways. For example, in the context of anthropology, it could be approached in the context of work on the significance of the gift in archaic societies. Using my own discipline of psychology, I will approach it in terms of attribution theory. The causal attributions with which people instinctively operate make a great deal of difference to how events are experienced. For example, if you experience successes as reflecting your own achievements and strengths, and experience failures as bad luck, your self-esteem will be much higher than if the pattern switches round and you experience failures as reflecting your own inadequacy and successes as mere good luck.

Attributions to God are an important aspect of religious thinking, and part of the human value of prayers of thanksgiving may lie in reshaping attributions so that they include God.[5] There are several unusual things in how attributions to God operate. As D. Z. Phillips has emphasized, there is a sense in which religious people learn to give thanks to God for everything, not just for what they regard as good experiences.[6] Also, attributions to God seem not to fall neatly into the division between internal and external attributions that is so important in all other attributions. Because God is both transcendent and immanent, attributions to God are both external and internal; he is both far beyond us and deep within us.

In human terms, such attributions can be very helpful. If people feel that they are entitled to have their dignity respected, they are more likely to "stand on their dignity." That leads to an arrogance and abrasiveness that is unconstructive from both a social and a psychological point of view. On the other hand, for people to feel that they have no dignity is unhelpful in a different way. It leaves them feeling vulnerable and inadequate, and people who feel that are always likely to react badly to events. For people to feel that they have dignity, but that the dignity is a gift of God, seems to offer a path between these unfortunate extremes. To have a sense of dignity at all protects against a sense of inadequacy. To see that dignity as gift is a safeguard against arrogance.

In secular thought, dignity and rights are closely intertwined. Either it is because people have dignity that they have various rights, or natural rights are taken as the basis of dignity. Christian theology must surely be cautious about the contemporary discourse of "rights." It is not that the Christian tradition regards the many things that people claim today "as of right" as being unimportant; quite the contrary. For example, people may claim the right to work. There is no problem in recognizing that the opportunity for work is appropriate for people, given our God-given human nature. The Christian tradition provides the resources to understand the value of work and why it is a human good. The question is whether the concept of rights is the one that Christians should choose in formulating these things.

To think theologically about dignity as gift represents a very different approach from the discourse about rights to which dignity is often tied in contemporary thought, and which theologians such as Moltmann often follow.[7] Seeing dignity as a gift carries tasks and obligations appropriate to good stewardship of the gift, whereas rights thinking carries no such obligation.

---

5. Fraser Watts, "Prayer and Psychology," in *Perspectives on Prayer,* ed. Fraser Watts (London: SPCK, 2001).

6. D. Z. Phillips, *The Concept of Prayer* (Oxford: Blackwell, 1965).

7. Jürgen Moltmann, *On Human Dignity: Political Theology and Ethics* (London: SCM, 1984).

Also, the language of rights is typically associated with assumptions about human autonomy, whereas the concept of gift implies a giver. For a Christian, everything that is appropriate for human beings must surely flow from God, and there is something unsatisfactory about conceptualizing what flows from God in terms of human "rights."

Interestingly, there is increasing unease about rights in the secular community. The range of rights that is asserted increases all the time. It has become the universal "off the shelf" language of moral argument, and Lenn Goodman has commented that the language of rights has been cheapened to the point of worthlessness.[8] Though the language of rights has been quite widely adopted by the churches (with the Catholic Church speaking, for example, of the right to life of the fetus), the wisdom of adopting this terminology is very debatable.

Rights are more widely asserted than they are accorded or recognized. In the Enlightenment tradition, dignity and rights were intended to be universal, but they have actually been applied in a selective way. Campaigning for rights comes almost entirely from minorities in the community who are asserting their own rights; there is less campaigning for the rights of others. People worry more about their own dignity and rights than about those of others. Of course, this may be just an unfortunate fact about the way in which an otherwise admirable concept is used and applied. It is more plausible, however, that there is something inherent in secular discourse about dignity and rights that lends itself to the assertiveness and self-preoccupation with which it is often associated.

There is a complex relationship between the concept of human rights and the place of religion in society. It has been suggested that the decline in the moral influence of the Christian church was a key reason why rights language was needed, to provide an alternative secular framework.[9] On the other hand, some have felt that the religious origins of rights language continues to be apparent, and that rights language is "irredeemably religious."[10] Talk of human dignity shows a similar, rather complex relationship with both secular and religious thought.

---

8. Lenn E. Goodman, *Judaism, Human Rights, and Human Values* (New York: Oxford University Press, 1998), p. vii.

9. S. Bailey, ed., *Human Rights and Responsibilities in Britain and Ireland: A Christian Perspective* (London: MacMillan, 1988).

10. Michael J. Perry, *The Idea of Human Rights: Four Inquiries* (Oxford: Oxford University Press, 1998).

Dignity and Changing Consciousness

It seems likely that the way in which the concept of human dignity has moved into secular thought and back into theological thought, evolving as it goes, reflects something more important than a mere change in how the word has been used. As Owen Barfield has argued, changes in the meaning of words often reflect more basic changes in consciousness.[11] Consistent with this, Charles Taylor has provided a masterly overview of how thinking about self has evolved, and again it seems likely that such changes in thinking about the self are intertwined with changes in how selfhood has actually been experienced.[12] It seems worthwhile to try to get some historical perspective on the current threats and opportunities concerning human dignity in the light of our changing consciousness.

In doing so, it is important to emphasize that the developments in human consciousness that in some ways seem to endanger dignity may also carry hopeful features. That seems to be the case for most shifts in collective consciousness. Every turn in the development of collective consciousness seems to be morally ambivalent, both bringing new moral dangers and also creating new moral opportunities. Changes in moral consciousness are generally too ambivalent to be regarded as either progress or decline. The language of progress that seemed obvious a century ago has now largely been abandoned. We need to understand how the moral consciousness of our own time both poses threats to human dignity and brings the promise of an enhancement of human dignity.

There has been a general tendency over the last few centuries for concepts to come to refer less exclusively to social position, and increasingly to more interior matters. This kind of shift toward inwardness is set out in general terms by both Owen Barfield and Charles Taylor. Lionel Trilling gives a specific example in his *Sincerity and Authenticity*, describing how "sincerity" used to be used in a way that was closely tied to public appearances.[13] A "sincere" wine was one that was in fact what it purported to be, and wines could be sincere in this sense as much as people. With the interior turn in human thought, "sincerity" has come to be used only of people, and to refer more to personal attitudes than to public appearances. The danger in this shift is the lack of concern with the external, social context of human life. But the aspira-

---

11. Owen Barfield, *History in English Words* (London: Faber and Faber, 1953).

12. Charles Taylor, *Sources of the Self: The Making of Modern Identity* (Cambridge: Cambridge University Press, 1989).

13. Lionel Trilling, *Sincerity and Authenticity* (London: Oxford University Press, 1974).

tion to integrity, which is such a marked feature of contemporary consciousness, carries a welcome concern that people should have the conditions necessary for their self-fulfillment.

There has probably been a somewhat similar shift in thinking about dignity. Attitudes to dignity, and feelings about it, have become much more important than they were back in the sixteenth century. Dignity is increasingly concerned not just with the externals of social position and behavior but with social experience and feelings. Respecting people's dignity now not only involves showing appropriate respect in social behavior, but increasingly also means ensuring that people have appropriate opportunities for self-expression. To put it another way, we increasingly need a psychology, not just a sociology, of human dignity to capture what the concept now means to us. Such a psychology of dignity will be an important dialogue partner for theology in reflecting on dignity, as it is in many other contexts.[14]

This contrast between external and interior human realities has also been addressed in the distinction anthropologists have made between shame cultures and guilt cultures. In the anthropological tradition, shame arises from public observation and perception of behavior, whereas guilt is a matter of private feelings about one's behavior. As I have pointed out elsewhere,[15] psychologists make the distinction differently, treating guilt as arising from specific behaviors and shame as being about one's whole being — and that seems to accord more closely to ordinary usage. It is the anthropological way of distinguishing shame and guilt that is relevant here, however. It is not so much that private feelings have supplanted issues of public standing as that they have provided an additional qualifying perspective. Violations of dignity arise now not just where there is some public humiliation, but where there are subjective feelings that dignity has been affronted.

With this new focus on interiority, differences between people in their mind-set have become much more significant. One person may feel that their dignity has been challenged where another would not. Hypersensitivity to affronts to dignity may be linked to the narcissism that Christopher Lasch has described as being widespread in our society.[16] This increasing sensitivity to possible indignities has rather mixed implications. On the one hand, such sensitizing may be desirable if it increases the respect with which people are

14. Watts, *Theology and Psychology.*

15. Fraser Watts, "Shame, Sin and Guilt," in *Forgiveness and Truth,* ed. A. McFadyen and M. Sarot (Edinburgh: T&T Clark, 2001), pp. 53-69.

16. Christopher Lasch, *The Culture of Narcissism: American Life in an Age of Diminishing Expectations* (New York: Norton, 1978).

treated. On the other hand, it may breed an excessive self-concern that sits uneasily with the Christian ideal of kenotic love.

Self-expression has become one of the central features of modern consciousness, as Taylor has described.[17] Just as the concern for universal dignity is a legacy of the Enlightenment, so the concern that everyone should have opportunities for self-expression is a legacy of Romanticism. These two movements have been so closely intertwined that in some ways they can perhaps be seen as two sides of the same coin, even though in other ways they point in opposite directions. Both dignity and self-expression have an ambivalent relationship with Christian thinking. They are both partly the heir to Christian themes, but they both develop them in explicitly secular directions.

Ideas about self-fulfillment that are central to the personal growth movement have been much criticized for being self-centered rather than God-centered.[18] Things are not as straightforward as this criticism suggests, however. The idea of self-fulfillment has Christian parallels, and is a secular counterpart to the concept of vocation. For someone to seek to fulfill his potential is in some ways parallel to a Christian responding to the call to make proper use of her God-given talents and capacities. This linkage between the two becomes quite explicit in some twentieth-century Christian thinkers such as Thomas Merton.[19]

Dignity and Imagination

In this final section, the key proposition that will be advanced is that enhanced respect for human dignity requires imagination. Such imagination can become impoverished or distorted in various ways, and we must locate current threats to human dignity more precisely to understand better exactly how failures of imagination bear on them. Such an approach to human dignity reflects some of the characteristic preoccupations and emphases of the last century, with the benefits and limitations that are associated with culturally specific theorizing.

As Taylor has described, this concern with how we see things, and with the possibility of seeing things differently, has become something of a modern obsession. The hope is held out that by imagining things appropriately we

17. Taylor, *Sources of the Self.*

18. Paul C. Vitz, *Psychology As Religion: The Cult of Self-Worship* (Grand Rapids: Eerdmans, 1977).

19. P. Morea, *In Search of Personality: Christianity and Modern Psychology* (London: SCM, 1997).

can escape the pitfalls of a mechanistic approach to life and re-experience what Gerard Manley Hopkins memorably called "freshness deep down things." As Taylor says, it "is felt as a liberation, because the experience can become more vivid and the activity more unhampered through being recognized, and alternatives open up in our stance towards the world which were quite hidden before."[20]

Though this preoccupation is very clear in modern thinking, it is not clear how it relates to what happens in practice. Our ideological obsession with the importance of seeing things straight has not obviously been accompanied by people making much headway in actually so seeing them. Indeed, the preoccupation may have arisen from a growing sense of alienation, and been some sort of attempt to repair that alienation.

The mechanistic strain in Enlightenment thinking that has culminated in the kind of reductionist moves in science that have already been considered in this chapter can be seen as a reflection of alienated experience. Indeed, reductionist science has probably exacerbated the problem of alienation, as well as being a reflection of it. Such alienated experience of life seems to arise from a failure of imagination, and from an impoverishment of our capacity properly to envisage the potential richness of our experience. In human relationships such a failure of imagination might be called a lack of empathy. There is something comparable that eats into our experience of the material world too, leaving it cold and impersonal.

Such failures of imagination are only half the problem. Alongside the poverty or failure of the imagination there are also distortions or pollutions of the imagination. Failures of imagination bring a sense of disenchantment. Meaning drains away, and reductionist "nothing but" ideas about human nature seem increasingly attractive. In contrast, where the imagination becomes distorted, excessive appetites arise in the form of addictions or sexual preoccupations. Particular situations, far from feeling meaningless, create powerful anxieties or worries.

Though failures and distortions of imagination are in some sense opposite, they can also coexist in an insidious way. Both can undermine the capacity for people to treat one another with respect. Failures of imagination can result in people being treated as mere objects, with no concern for what they might be thinking or feeling. Distortions of imagination, in contrast, can lead to people being treated as players in a perverted game. Rather than being treated with indifference, people are endowed with "projections" that result in our seeing in one another simply what we wish to see. In one case people

20. Taylor, *Sources of the Self,* p. 460.

are accorded no real identity at all; in the other case they are seen as mere extensions of our own needs and personality. In neither case is there any attentiveness to what people are actually like, nor any proper respect for their separate and distinct identity. That requires an imagination that is prepared to reach out to the other person and try to understand what it is like to be him or her.

The twin dangers being described here are similar in some ways to those described by Taylor in the final chapter of his *Sources of the Self*. He first describes the sense of impoverishment and detachment that accompanies what he calls the "instrumentalist" society, though he rejects many current criticisms of the instrumentalist society as being too extreme. Rather than rejecting it, he looks for what might be called its healing. He then goes on to describe the preoccupation with self-fulfillment that coexists with instrumentalism in a strange alliance, though again he is not against self-fulfillment; rather, he is arguing that it "needs to be sought within a life which is also aimed at other goods."[21]

There has been surprisingly little attempt to develop a theological appropriation of this modern line of thought about the importance of the imagination, though it is not difficult to see how that can be done. One key concept would be the gift of the Spirit that follows from the work of Christ, and which is the focus of the farewell discourses of St. John's Gospel (chapters 14–16). It may also be helpful to place this gift in the context of the evolution of human consciousness, as Rudolf Steiner and those influenced by him have done.[22] Very briefly, there seems to have been a loss of an old animistic consciousness that saw the spirit as speaking to humanity through the external world, and the development of a new kind of consciousness, made possible by Christ's gift of the Spirit, that can look at the external world with spirit-imbued eyes.

If we develop this line of thought, it is Christ's gift of the Spirit that makes possible the imaginative response to other people that is required if they are to be treated with proper dignity as creatures of God. Without the Spirit, imagination either remains impoverished or becomes distorted. It is the work of Christ to enrich and strengthen the imagination in the way that is necessary if human relationships of proper respect are to be established. The failure of imagination, and its pollution, represent twin dangers through which Christ can navigate humanity. This is graphically depicted in Rudolf Steiner's massive sculpture, the "group," which depicts Christ as representa-

21. Taylor, *Sources of the Self*, p. 511.
22. Watts, *Theology and Psychology*, pp. 137-39.

tive of the new humanity "bringing order and balance into the world of the two adversaries by directing them to those realms where their respective gifts can flourish without endangering man."[23]

This is not to claim that only those who acknowledge Christ can treat one another with proper respect; that would be manifestly false. It is, however, to suggest that the work of Christ, and the Spirit that flows from him, stands behind the hope that human beings will develop proper respect for one another.

---

23. Rudi Lissau, *Rudolf Steiner: Life, Work, Inner Path and Social Initiatives* (Stroud: Hawthorn, 1987), p. 83.

The "End" of the Human or the End of the "Human"? Human Dignity in Technological Perspective

ELAINE L. GRAHAM

Introduction

> *[T]he question can never be first of all "what are we doing with our technology?" but it must be "what are we becoming with our technology?"*[1]

In this essay, I want to consider some of the debate surrounding the advent of the so-called "posthuman condition,"[2] and in particular how themes of human dignity, its endangerment or rejuvenation, feature in relation to the impact of digital, biomedical, and cybernetic technologies.

Thinking about the impact of new technologies on what it means to be human brings sharply into focus the question of relationship between technological activity and "human becoming."[3] What's at stake in seeking to evaluate the significance of human engagement with its tools and technologies? Is technology a neutral instrument, an epiphenomenon to human nature; or is it an integral part not only of the formation of human material culture, but of our very ontology? This essay will argue that technologies and the work of material fabrication are indeed a substantive and not simply an incidental part of being human, and that this is evident in the ways in which in contemporary debates, advanced technologies are both heralded as the means by

---

1. Philip Hefner, *Technology and Human Becoming* (Minneapolis: Fortress, 2003), p. 9.

2. Judith Halberstam and Ira Livingston, eds., *Posthuman Bodies* (Indianapolis: Indiana University Press, 1995), p. vii.

3. Halberstam and Livingston, *Posthuman Bodies*, p. vii.

which humanity might attain its most fundamental aspirations — the *"end"* of the human — and perceived as constituting an urgent threat to human dignity: the end of the *"human."*

But this also implies that technological endeavor, if part of our humanity, needs to form part of our theological anthropology. What are the resources by which theology might enhance our understandings of what it means to be human in a technological age, both in critical and in reconstructive terms, by engaging with some of the dominant representations of the posthuman as they permeate not only scientific discourse but Western culture as a whole?

The challenge of the posthuman condition for theological anthropology has attracted the attention of a number of contemporary commentators.[4] In all cases, the prospects offered by digital, genetic, and cybernetic technologies — and particularly whether or not they represent threat or promise to human dignity — may be seen as a kind of thought experiment. Regardless of whether many of the more expansive technological developments ever materialize, the anticipated emergence of "techno sapiens"[5] is already shaping the Western cultural and scientific imagination, not to mention research and policy priorities. It would therefore seem important to trace some of the underlying values informing such visions of the technological future, what kinds of exemplary and normative understandings of the "posthuman" are circulating in Western culture, and what happens when these are subjected to critique. In particular, I shall consider whether strands of theological anthropology — particularly traditions which speak of humanity as *imago Dei*, or made in the image and likeness of God — might offer a normative framework for articulating a system of values, priorities, and criteria by which the proper *ends of humanity* might be adjudicated. This is particularly appropriate given, as I shall argue, that many of the visions of the posthuman future draw on religious values and theological terminology, albeit frequently implicit or occluded.

4. See, for example, E. Cruz, "The Nature of Being Human," in *Bridging Science and Religion*, ed. T. Peters and G. Bennett (London: SCM, 2002), pp. 173-84; Noreen L. Herzfeld, *In Our Image: Artificial Intelligence and the Human Spirit* (Minneapolis: Fortress, 2002); Antje Jackelen, "The Image of God As *Techno Sapiens*," *Zygon* 37, no. 2 (2002): 289-302; S. B. Murray, "Reimagining Humanity: The Transforming Influence of Augmenting Technologies upon Doctrines of Humanity," in *Technology and Transcendence*, ed. M. Breen, E. Conway, and B. McMillan (Dublin: Columba, 2003), pp. 195-216.

5. Jackelen, "The Image of God As *Techno Sapiens*."

Technologies and the "Posthuman Condition"

To what extent is technology reshaping our experiences and understandings of what it means to be human? Although my chief emphasis is on the contemporary challenge of the posthuman, it is important to identify strands of continuity and change in terms of the role of technology in human culture more generally. There is a tendency to regard "technology" as merely synonymous with advances in computing, genetic engineering, and the industrial age. But the root of the word — the Greek *techne,* or "craft" or "skill" — reminds us that technologies are both more basic and more ubiquitous within human culture. Indeed, they may be the very facility that distinguishes human beings from other nonhuman animals, insofar as they make possible sophisticated cultures, enable human beings to sustain long-term inhabitation of difficult environments, and, in addition, are the very medium through which cultural achievements — such as language, visual arts, material culture, economic production, exchange and consumption, and religion — are embodied. Technology is thus both a body of knowledge, in terms of accumulated know-how, and the material instruments and machines through which such knowledge is practiced.

All human societies may be said to be "technological," therefore, insofar as they deploy tools, devices, and procedures to assist human living. Such technologies also actually fuel human evolution, as we adapt to changing conditions by inventing technologies that enable us to maximize our chances of survival and development in previously hostile or problematic contexts. Yet those technologies, arguably, are more than mere appendages to autonomous human reason. They actually affect our experiences and apprehensions of what it means to be human so that we cannot conceive of ourselves independent of our tools and technologies.

Although philosophical speculation about the relationship between humanity and technologies has a long history, therefore, and current thinking can be placed in a long legacy of debate,[6] certain advances over the past half-century — most particularly the construction of the world's first stored-memory computer in 1948 and the identification of DNA in 1953 — do seem to represent an unprecedented intensification of technoscientific[7] potential.

---

6. See Robert C. Scharff and Val Dusek, eds., *Philosophy of Technology: An Anthology* (Oxford: Blackwell, 2003).

7. Use of the term "technoscience" is frequently attributed to Bruno Latour, whose work on the social contexts of scientific research implicitly refutes any notion of the separation of science and technology into "pure" and "applied" forms of knowledge. The priorities of practicing scientists are shaped by wider cultural factors, not least the availability of funding; and

The shift into a posthuman sensibility thus signals a recognition that technology as "other" to human existence is now assimilated into everyday human functioning — in a literal sense, in terms of the possibilities of devices such as cochlear implants, intraocular lenses, heart pacemakers, and other artificial organs or prostheses becoming a permanent part of human physiology, and in a more existential sense, insofar as most of the population of the "First World" is completely dependent on technologies such as computer-mediated communications, broadcasting media, transport infrastructure, and generation of power. Talk of the posthuman in this respect thus evokes a world in which, thanks to cybernetics, artificial intelligence, virtual reality, plastic surgery, gene therapies, and assisted reproduction, biological humans are everywhere surrounded — and transformed — into mixtures of machine and organism, where what we call "nature" has been significantly reshaped by technology, and technology, in turn, has become assimilated into "nature" as a fully functioning component of organic life itself.

The posthuman has thus become a shorthand metaphor for talking about a number of interrelated issues. First, there are the scientific and medical prospects for *enhancement of human physical and intellectual powers* by means of cybernetic implants or genetic modification, including increased longevity, resistance to congenital or other illnesses, and improved cognitive skills. Second, as a corollary to this, the posthuman has come to be identified for many with the emergence of a *new phase of human evolution,* albeit one technologically driven (and the result of human choices) rather than driven by the forces of natural selection.

As Bart Simon in a recent survey article on the posthuman points out, however, it is helpful to differentiate between these first two, which he terms "popular posthumanism," and a third strand, which he terms "critical posthumanism."[8] The latter is concerned not only to evaluate the material impact of technologies on economics, communications, sexuality and reproduction, embodiment, and so on, but to raise the question of the kind of models of human nature at work in the various discourses of "fear" and "hope" in the face of new technologies. The prevailing view within critical posthumanism would be that the social and ethical ramifications of the posthuman rest in its displacement of conventional benchmarks of human nature, the recognition of the malleability (and the commodification) of "na-

---

the logic of technological developments often exerts defining influences over cultural institutions and behavior, not least in the harnessing of scientific endeavors to corporate commercial interests.

8. Bart Simon, "Toward a Critique of Posthuman Futures," *Cultural Critique* 53 (2003): 1-9.

ture," and the realization that an era of "human self-design"[9] has dawned. The assumptions underlying two hundred years of post-Enlightenment thinking about human nature, based on liberal individualism, the ascendancy of reason, autonomous subjectivity, and a clear "ontological hygiene"[10] dividing humans from animals and machines, are coming under pressure. Writers within cultural studies, the philosophy of technology, and critical theory have therefore approached the idea of the posthuman as an opportunity to think anew about enduring issues having to do with the relationship between humans and their environments, artifacts, and tools. As I have argued elsewhere, this enables us to think of the posthuman as more than simply a *description* of a future species — as, rather, an *interrogation* into the terms by which Western culture has defined what it means to be human, and into how the many visions of the posthuman, positive and negative, rest on unexamined moral and teleological assumptions.[11]

Post/Human Dignity: Threat or Promise?

The impact of new technologies, represented by talk of the posthuman, has a number of dimensions. The first is the possibilities for achieving a "postbiological" existence, as in the incorporation of artificial organs or prosthetic limbs or our transformation into "post-bodied" individuals as we go online or experience virtual reality. Such processes are often signaled as the emergence of "cyborgs," or "cybernetic organisms," as hybrids of biological and technological components, but they raise wider questions about the integrity of embodiment as a distinctive marker of personal identity, and of whether computer-mediated media (such as the Internet and virtual reality) represent a valuable extension to the limits of human community, or a pale imitation of face-to-face interaction.

A second dimension is the sense that technological imperatives are autonomous of human design and have an independent status in determining economic, personal, cultural, and moral priorities. Technology has moved from being an instrument or tool in the hands of human agents, or even a means to transform the natural environment, and become a series of processes or interventions capable of reshaping human ontology. It also raises

9. Gregory Stock, *Redesigning Humans: Choosing Our Children's Genes* (London: Profile, 2002), p. 3.

10. Elaine L. Graham, *Representations of the Post/Human* (New Brunswick, NJ: Rutgers University Press, 2002), p. 11.

11. Graham, *Representations of the Post/Human*, p. 37.

the question of whether as cybernetic systems such as artificial intelligence become more sophisticated, technologies might acquire the facility to become self-programming.

Third, there is the ethical (or anthropological) basis on which judgments about the appropriate use and direction of new technologies might be made. If "critical posthumanism" is asking the question, "What does it mean to be human in an age of technologies?" where is it to look for an answer? If Homo sapiens is to be succeeded by "techno sapiens," what happens to our accounts of human subjectivity, and in particular the basis on which we might ascribe it a moral status? In the face of the alleged dissolution of any normative concept of human nature, how are criteria for differentiating between legitimate and illegitimate technological trajectories to be articulated?

Post-Biological: Transcendence of the Body

For some commentators, the advent of new technologies will protect us against physical disease and vulnerability. Technologies, long the means of enabling humanity to compensate for physical limitations by providing instruments of comfort and utility, now offer the opportunities to overcome the limitations of the flesh entirely.

In describing his own (temporary) transformation from organic human to cyborg via the implantation of a silicon chip transmitter in his forearm, Kevin Warwick is expansive in his speculations about the potential of such technological enhancement. "Might it be possible for humans to have extra capabilities, particularly mental attributes, and become super humans or, as some regard it, post humans [sic]?"[12] His enthusiasm encapsulates perfectly the vision of those who see the promise of cybernetic technologies as going beyond mere clinical benefits to embrace nothing less than an ontological transformation. Warwick sees no limit to the transcendence of normal physical and cognitive limitations, an achievement that for him signals nothing less than a new phase in human evolution.[13]

Similarly, the impact of computer-mediated communications can be traced in the way they change taken-for-granted categories of space, place, and time, the boundaries of the body and the interface of machine and human. In the case of the Internet, it collapses physical distance, transcends national boundaries, reinvents conventions of text and reading, transforms hu-

12. Kevin Warwick, *I, Cyborg* (London: Century, 2002), p. 175.
13. Warwick, *I, Cyborg*, pp. 295-96.

man interactions into the flow of information, and creates new artificial environments and machinic intelligences. For some, this offers unprecedented opportunities of freedom of information and communication, the creation of a global forum of exchange and interchange. For others, the very disembodied nature of virtual technologies such as the Internet represents a fundamental loss of moral grounding. Despite the many benefits of computer-assisted communication, it is feared that the lack of face-to-face contact will lead to the dissolution of human community, as individuals descend into what Andrew Feenberg characterizes as a "new narcissism":

> The collapse of public life and the decline of the family seem to cut individuality loose from its institutional moorings and sources of meaning. No longer concretized through real bonds and obligations, the person becomes a discontented spectator on his or her own life, engaged in strategies of manipulation and control directed towards the self and others alike.[14]

In some ways, the two discourses of enhancement and diminishment of human dignity may be intertwined. As Gerhold Becker argues, emerging biotechnological procedures appear to offer humanity the god-like powers to manipulate and redirect nature, but with the result that humanity potentially becomes the object as well as the agent of such processes. In striving for mastery over creation we reduce ourselves to components to be manipulated — with the danger that human nature is no longer seen as immutable, inviolable, and sacrosanct, and our notions of human distinctiveness begin to dissolve. Paradoxically, such developments threaten to undermine the very human dignity they were designed to promote, as Gerhold Becker notes:

> Has biotech just opened a new chapter in the long history of the scientific conquest of nature, or has it effectively closed the old volume and begun to write the first lines of an entirely different story? . . . Can we utilize its potential and carry on with our familiar worldviews and religious interpretations of the world, or is biotechnology in itself some sort of new ideology which challenges our traditional place in nature? Is it endowing us with the creative powers of God, or rather reducing us and the mystery of life to mere genetic components at the molecular level?[15]

14. Andrew Feenberg, *Critical Theory of Technology* (Oxford: Oxford University Press, 1991), p. 98.

15. Gerhold K. Becker, "Biotechnology — The New Ethical Frontier," in *Changing Nature's Course: The Ethical Challenge of Biotechnology,* ed. Gerhold K. Becker (Hong Kong: Hong Kong University Press, 1996), pp. 1-14, at p. 5.

One of the issues about the impact of technologies is thus their impact on personal identity, and in particular whether new technologies can facilitate a better quality of life or unleash Promethean powers which threaten our very humanity. Much of that attention and anxiety has come to be focused around the integrity of the body, and whether it is appropriate to dream of transcending the frailties of the flesh to embrace new physical forms, or whether the end of our embodiment would fatally compromise our essential humanity.

Trajectory of Technologies

There is a strong and influential strand in the philosophy of technology which argues that technology has assumed a deterministic character, insofar as the imperatives of efficiency, rationalization, and mass production have engulfed the priorities of human welfare. Jacques Ellul speaks of the degradation of creative production to the routinization of mere "technique";[16] Martin Heidegger argues that technology has a particular way of "revealing" the world to its users which obscures all other possibilities than that of "standing-reserve" — essentially, an objectification of nature which reduces everything to a commodity.[17]

Similarly, Arthur and Marilouise Kroker argue that despite the democratic pretensions of the Internet, it exists primarily as a commercial space, reflecting the stranglehold of global capitalism. The virtualization of human communication is rendering immaterial — literally — networks of solidarity and resistance, cloaking the increasing commodification of the world, continuing the polarization between "a global 'virtual class'"[18] whose interests masquerade as universal self-interest, and the majority of the world's population, who are dependent on an economy in which information itself has become the focus of production. Indeed, globalization itself would not have been possible were it not for developments in information technology.

The virtual elite is a mixture of predatory capitalists and visionary computer specialists for whom virtualization is about our disappearance into

16. Jacques Ellul, *The Technological Society,* trans. J. Wilkinson, intro. by R. Merton (London: Jonathan Cape, 1965).

17. Martin Heidegger, "The Question of Technology," in *Basic Writings,* ed. D. F. Krell (London: Routledge, 1993 [1954]), pp. 307-42.

18. Arthur Kroker and Marilouise Kroker, "Code Warriors," in *The Cybercultures Reader,* ed. D. Bell and B. M. Kennedy (London: Routledge, 2001), p. 99.

nothingness. We are talking about a systematic assault against the human species, a virtual war strategy where knowledge is reduced to data storage dumps, friendship is dissolved into floating cyber-interactions, and communication means the end of meaning. Virtualization in the cyber-hands of the new technological class is all about *our* being dumbed down.[19]

We might regard their analysis as a variation on Feuerbach's and Marx's concept of "alienation": technology, as the product of human labor, has itself become reified and now assumes a deterministic quality in which humans regard themselves as the objects of technological imperatives, rather than its agents. The impact of global capitalism on the bodies of the workforce becomes more acute and invasive; but the corresponding virtualization of communications serves as an opiate to dull our moral and political sensibilities.

There are also, however, far more optimistic accounts of the future of technologically assisted human development. This mood is particularly evident in what might broadly be termed a *technocratic* vision, in which technologies are understood as the benign tools of human self-actualization. Rather than envisaging the effacement of human agency, such an analysis is single-mindedly positive about the ability of technologies to facilitate problem-solving and advance human interests. Humans will continue to be the masters of their technological inventions, and this will enable them to "master" nonhuman nature as well. Underlying this vision is a version of Enlightenment humanism in which the rational subject, uninhibited by the external constraints of superstition, fear, or conservatism, is enabled to scale new heights of intellectual and technological achievement. Technologies are regarded as quintessentially neutral, neither good nor bad, merely instruments for achieving purposes and values enshrined elsewhere. They do not threaten or render human activities obsolete, but simply free human creativity to achieve new limits: "Buried in the murk of the human self lies an unformed golden core, and with technology . . . we can tap and transform this potential."[20]

The epitome of such an optimistic view of the posthuman future is the philosophy of "transhumanism." Described as "a radical new approach to future-oriented thinking,"[21] transhumanism is the high-tech heir to Enlight-

---

19. Kroker and Kroker, "Code Warriors," p. 101.

20. Erik Davis, *Techgnosis: Myth, Magic and Mysticism in the Age of Information* (London: Serpent's Tail, 1998), p. 128.

21. Nick Bostrom, "The Transhumanist FAQ" (online), 1999, 62 pp., accessed August 20, 2000, at http://www.transhumanist.org, section 4. A modified version of Bostrom's FAQ is currently available at http://www.transhumanism.org/resources/faq.html.

enment humanism in its emphasis on personal liberty, free enquiry, and self-determination. Transhumanists seek to harness advanced technologies in their pursuit of human perfection: the construction of artificial intelligence to augment intellectual functions, and the use of biomedical transplants, prostheses, genetic modification, and cryonic preservation to stave off the effects of disease and aging.[22] "The quest for immortality is one of the most ancient and deep-rooted of human aspirations," writes Nick Bostrom. "The human desire to acquire god-like attributes is presumably as ancient as the human species itself."[23] This vision of human transformation — the posthuman as *superhuman,* our evolving into "benevolent demi-gods"[24] — reveals a Promethean tenor as the dream of enhancing human potential extends to that of seizing the elemental energies of life itself.

In keeping with its humanist influences, however, this is a firmly secular philosophy, in which rational thinking, open enquiry, and constant growth keep the impediments of tradition, superstition, and entropy at bay: "No mysteries are sacrosanct, no limits unquestionable; the unknown will yield to the ingenious mind. We seek to understand the universe, not to tremble before mystery, as we continue to learn and grow and enjoy our lives ever more," says Max More.[25]

As well as reflecting the debates about the human impact of technologies to enhance or dehumanize, therefore, these various perspectives reflect alternative understandings of the nature of technologies themselves, and whether they bring "enslavement or liberation" to their human creators.[26] Arguably, however, neither the model which envisages humans as helpless puppets in the face of technological determinism, nor that which regards technologies as mere instruments at the disposal of the liberal humanist ego, are adequate to describe the relationship. We cannot essentialize technologies as if they had been created outside social contexts or political and economic choices, or even as if they were independent of human agency, either in order to *reify* technology as possessing powers beyond our control, or in order to *deify* it as the sure means to our future salvation. Instead, with Andrew

22. Brian Alexander, "Don't Die, Stay Pretty," *Wired* (online), issue 8.01, Jan. 2000 (http://www.wired.com/wired/archive/8.01/forever_pr.html).

23. Bostrom, "The Transhumanist FAQ," pp. 38-41.

24. Bostrom, "The Transhumanist FAQ," p. 33.

25. Max More, "The Extropian Principles: A Transhumanist Declaration, Version 3.0," (online), accessed March 19, 1999, at http://extropy.org.extprn.html, 13 pp., section 3. More's piece is currently available at http://www.maxmore.com/extprn3.htm.

26. David E. Cooper, "Technology: Liberation or Enslavement?" in *Philosophy and Technology,* ed. R. Fellows (Cambridge: Cambridge University Press, 1995), pp. 7-18.

Feenburg, I would argue for a rather more *reflexive* understanding of technologies,[27] in that they emerge from, and reflect, social, political, and economic priorities in terms of design and deployment, and are therefore never culturally, morally, or politically neutral. We return instead to the fundamental issue at the heart of critical posthumanism, that technologies shape our very engagement with the world, and potentially our very ontology.

Ethical Groundings of Human Dignity

A fundamental fault-line exists at the heart of all these perspectives on technology. Does the "posthuman condition" represent promise or endangerment, mastery or extinction? This is a question regarding the future trajectory of human engagement with technologies, and whether the transition from Homo sapiens to *Homo cyberneticus* will propel humanity toward greater knowledge and prosperity or diminish human uniqueness to the point of obsolescence.

Inevitably, these are questions about identity, about the future, about community, about technologies themselves; yet they also contain an invitation to reintroduce a level of discourse about human nature often ignored by secular humanism, and talk about normative and exemplary human nature in relation to an explicitly *theological* horizon. In some discussions of the posthuman there are strong religious resonances and ideologies at work, especially in some writers' expansive pronouncements on the mystical and metaphysical dimensions of cyberspace, their equation of new technologies with a kind of demiurgical power, and their expectations of technologies effecting the liberation of the human race from the limits of embodiment, finitude, and mortality; it is to a further exploration of these theological nuances to which we shall now turn.

In Whose Image?

I have identified some of the values about what it means to be human that are fueling the anxieties and hopes surrounding the emergence of cybernetic, genetic, and digital technologies. Despite the origins of these technologies in modern science, it is intriguing to identify a number of ways in which religious discourses still imbue many of the considerations of what should con-

---

27. Feenberg, *Critical Theory of Technology,* especially chap. 8.

stitute our posthuman future. Although appeals to spiritual values are made by many of those who regard technologies as responsible for the *disenchantment* of the world,[28] it is more intriguing to draw attention to the work of those who maintain the compatibility of religion and technologically driven human evolution. Yet the ways in which religion is evoked to support this project are also problematic, as critical dialogue between some of these tendencies and Christian theological anthropology will indicate.

For example, in advocating a form of "post-bodied" artificial intelligence as an exemplary model of the posthuman, Hans Moravec speaks of the "transmigration" of consciousness from the "meat" of living bodies into computer programs. David Noble argues that scientists have long regarded technology as akin to a religious vocation;[29] and Erik Davis characterizes emergent virtual communities as "techno-pagans," regarding technologies rather than nature as redolent with sacred power.[30]

This contradicts interpretations that regard science and religion as antipathetic, for here are new technologies as — to use David Noble's words — *instruments of deliverance,* vehicles of ascent to higher planes, means of harnessing elemental powers, and possessors of the power to transport their users into a sacred realm of "transcendence," free of the encumbrances of the flesh. Cyberspace is envisaged as a "mythic community,"[31] the apotheosis of an ancient project to transcend the physical world in search of perfection and immortality: "the subject," Scott Bukatman writes, "is dissolved in the swirls of cybernetic information, but is at the same time further empowered through an extension of motility and spatial possession. Here, then, are the paradoxically simultaneous experiences of death and immortality that are fundamental to religious practice."[32]

Erik Davis has perhaps done the most work in connecting contemporary advocates with a longer history of spirituality. He claims that such "techno-pagans," those who equate the sacred not with the natural but with the technological order, are latter-day incarnations of Hermetism. In regarding the tangible, material world as an elaborate cipher for divine power, in which the codes and bytes of digital information serve as the vehicles of

---

28. See, for example, Albert Borgmann, *Power Failure: Christianity in the Culture of Technology* (Grand Rapids: Brazos, 2003).

29. David F. Noble, *The Religion of Technology: The Divinity of Man and the Spirit of Invention,* second ed. (New York: Penguin, 1999).

30. Graham, *Representations of the Post/Human,* pp. 165-75.

31. Scott Bukatman, *Terminal Identity: The Virtual Subject in Post-Modern Science Fiction* (Durham, N.C.: Duke University Press, 1993), p. 151.

32. Bukatman, *Terminal Identity,* pp. 295-96.

transport into a higher reality, such contemporaries do indeed continue the arts and practices of earlier magi and demiurges. This may also be seen as a continuation of Platonic, even gnostic, tendencies, in which the fallen, prosaic, material world must be abandoned in favor of the secret, radiant realm of perfect order and information.[33]

The implications of this, however, are disturbing, not least because such a representation of humanity's religious quest through technoscientific endeavor rests on a distorted appropriation of the notion of "transcendence." What all these visions seem to share is a common appeal to a neo-Platonic ideal of "transcendence," or the drive to use human creative energies to abandon the physical world (as in the quest for outer space), or the wish to transform embodied experience into pure information (as in the human genome project), or characterization of cyberspace as the "heavenly city" free of the encumbrances of the flesh. The pursuit of this particular understanding of spirituality, motivated by "fear of death, loathing of the body, desire to be moral and free of error,"[34] is thus assumed to be normative. Narratives of transcendence, disembodiment, and mastery, masquerading as eternal, enduring, universal "religious" instincts, are elevated as exemplary ideals. In assuming that the end of humanity (as in its ultimate destiny) is to become like God, or the gods, therefore, an apparently secular doctrine of humanity continues to draw on a traditional theological motif: that of the *imago Dei*. Humans must seek to overcome those elements of their nature that are not divine (mortality, embodiment, contingency) in order to aspire to the true marks of divinity. Yet in fact this implicit religious vision bears little relation to the more materialist conceptions of the *imago Dei* that Christian theology has traditionally developed in the context of the doctrines of creation, incarnation, and salvation.

While there are many strands to the Christian notion of humanity made in the image or likeness of God,[35] it is perhaps in relation to God as Creator that alternative themes in relation to human *techne* and technological endeavor might be made; such themes would focus on values that do not deny the significance of human inventiveness, but that locate the *telos* of any such activity in a very different set of divine — and therefore human — attributes.

---

33. Davis, *Techgnosis.*

34. Bruce Mazlish, *The Fourth Discontinuity: The Co-Evolution of Humans and Machines* (New Haven: Yale University Press, 1993), p. 218.

35. Such as thinking of humanity as, for example, possessing certain qualities or capabilities (such as creativity or rationality), as essentially relational beings (after Trinitarian understandings), or as called to particular responsibilities and activities (such as stewardship), all of which are human expressions of divine nature. See Herzfeld, *In Our Image.*

It is certainly important to see *techne* as spiritually and theologically worthwhile, and to affirm that a quintessential aspect of our very humanity is realized in and through our relationships with our tools and technologies. Technologies may be regarded as tools by which our capacity to create is brought to fruition, as a way of resolving problems, of extending human capabilities and meeting needs.[36] Yet technologies are not merely means to the ends of faster communication, greater crop yields, or secure dwellings: they are objects of beauty as well as utility, artifacts and creations in their own right. They are thus both the vehicles and the expressions of human creativity, an integral part of our very human nature — or in the words of Philip Hefner, a necessary means of "human becoming."[37]

It is thus important to see technologies not simply as mere instruments of doing and making, but as vehicles of human development and self-realization. At the same time, however, the posthuman debate raises questions over what happens when human beings themselves become the objects of their own self-design, or when biological life can be modified and engineered in ways which "transcend" or surpass the workings of unassisted nature. Some further qualifications may therefore be necessary in relation to the potential and limits of human creativity.

First of all, the Christian understanding would be that although human inventiveness is affirmed, it is akin to divine creativity only by analogy and not by imitation. Humans are not capable of creating the universe *ex nihilo*, even though they may be capable of creating life by biological and technological means. The image of humanity as "created co-creators"[38] expresses this well, not least because it encapsulates a theological anthropology of likeness and affinity to the divine, yet limits any notion of humanity's complete or literal equivalence to God. Humanity is both creator and creature, affirming yet also conditioning claims to the autonomy of human self-design, and suggesting that the final ends of creation cannot be subsumed to either technological imperatives or contingent human ambitions.[39]

Thus, *imago Dei* cannot be used to justify narratives of the ascent of superhuman beings to become omniscient, omnipotent immortal demi-gods. This kind of rhetoric actually rests upon an unexamined identification of "religion" with a flight from contingency and materiality, and with a spirituality that seeks fulfillment in union with a "transcendent" deity entirely removed

36. Hefner, *Technology and Human Becoming*, p. 43.
37. Hefner, *Technology and Human Becoming*, p. 43.
38. Philip Hefner, *The Human Factor* (Minneapolis: Fortress, 1993), p. 260.
39. Peter Scott, *A Political Theology of Nature* (Cambridge: Cambridge University Press, 2003).

from the immanence of this mortal world. This is a misrepresentation of what "image" and "likeness" indicate, as well as a distortion of the very concept of "transcendence" in relation to the nature of God — a distortion that equates aspirations toward "becoming divine" with attainment of absolute power. A Christian theological anthropology, by contrast, sees things differently, not least in its eschewal of a symbolic of transcendence premised on omnipotence, individualism, and immortality. Rather than regarding the immanent, embodied, material world as an impediment to genuine spirituality, or — reminiscent of gnostic worldviews — as the profane, flawed, pale reflection of the authentic divine world, this vision sees it as the very realm of divine-human encounter. "Whatever it is, salvation will be an affirmation of the essential finitude of human nature, not an escape from it."[40]

Thus, the *imago Dei* in theological anthropology is an expression of the potential of human beings to grow into the likeness of God in Christ, and of Christ as the model for the perfection of humanity. Yet to aspire to *imago Dei*, to see human fulfillment in the image of God as revealed in Christ, properly leads to humility rather than self-aggrandizement. To "become divine" in Christian terms is to follow a pattern of divine *kenosis* in Christ; it is an acknowledgement of the unconditional, parental love of the Creator, and a commitment to absolute trust in the values of the kingdom rather than those of earthly powers. Again, this is not to argue for a rejection of technologies per se, but to recognize that if they are to be fully a part of human ends then they are necessarily complicit in activities which build worlds of moral value as well as those of material objects — worlds which take account of human existence in wider contexts of responsibility and mutuality with one another, with animals, with the environment and other living organisms. This is in part because if humans are *created* beings, then they share that status with the rest of nonhuman nature; but an acknowledgement of such a common affinity grounded in creatureliness is inconsistent with human engagement with nature, nonhuman animals, and technologies based on principles of mastery, control, and appropriation.

Another respect in which humanity in the image of God might offer normative criteria in the area of human dignity is this. If human identity is rooted in divine likeness, then in some respects it evades absolute categorization. Just as God is mystery, so too an element of the ineffable remains about human nature. Such an understanding could serve as a regulative ideal against some tendencies to adopt reductionist accounts of what it means to be human.

40. David H. Kelsey, "Human Being," in *Christian Theology: An Introduction to Its Traditions and Tasks*, ed. P. Hodgson and Robert King (London: SPCK, 1998), p. 144.

For example, many critics of posthuman technologies have argued that developments in biotechnology have opened the way to a range of therapeutic techniques which radically threaten the autonomy or self-determination of the individual. For example, this lies behind much of the opposition to the genetic diagnosis and selection of human embryos prior to implantation in cases where parents could adjudicate the fate of a pre-implanted embryo conceived by IVF on the basis of its providing a match for a terminally ill sibling. The concern is whether such a child has been brought into the world for its own sake, or as a means to an end. At the root of this lies the dignity of being permitted to be the author of one's own destiny in fellowship with God. However benign the motive, it is an abuse of another's inherent autonomy to choose his or her constitution, as might parents seeking genetic enhancement or selection for their offspring. To be the product of such interventions would be to be treated as less than human, as an object of another's ambition and design rather than the subject of one's own life-story. The manipulation of another's genome effectively renders her an object, displacing her into "the realm of artifacts and their production"[41] rather than ascribing her value simply by virtue of her status as a human being.

In sum, concerns about the eugenic implications of genetic screening or genetic modification are founded on the risks of the commodification or instrumentalization of human life, a loss of choice and autonomy for an individual which represents a fundamental dehumanization. In other ways, too, critics of much of the rhetoric of the Human Genome Project have argued that it fuels fantasies of capturing the essence of humanity in a bio-informatic database: a kind of genetic reductionism. Similarly, critics speak of the "geneticization" of human nature, in which all aspects of human experience are seen to be governed by genetic factors, to the exclusion of social, environmental, or behavioral influences: a kind of genetic determinism.[42] To speak of humanity created by God, in the image of God, thus provides an alternative horizon by which human value is located as transcending human utility or objectification and restored to a deeper irreducibility.

If we engage in such talk of humanity as in some degree self-constituting via its own technologies, as being capable of influencing the course of its own development, we fall prey to what we might term "hyper-humanism": a distortion of modernity's faith in the benevolence of human reason, producing the hubristic belief that humanity alone is in control of history. According to this model of technology and human becoming, hu-

41. Jürgen Habermas, *The Future of Human Nature* (Cambridge: Polity, 2003), p. 12.
42. Ruth Hubbard and Elijah Wald, *Exploding the Gene Myth* (Boston: Beacon, 1997).

manity comes to consider itself the supreme source of value, without reference to either its common origins in nature or its relationship to a horizon of otherness, such as a divine Creator. The notion that humanity can seek redemption via technocratic means alone — whether this be via genetic modification, cybernetic or prosthetic enhancement, or even social engineering — represents the ultimate in the elevation of human perfection as the apotheosis of our technological, moral, or political endeavors. Hyper-humanism may even be regarded, in theological perspective, as a form of *idolatry:* the elevation of human, finite creation as ultimate reality, and a confusion of the fabricated with the ineffable.

Amidst the discussion of technological endeavor as a legitimate sphere of human creative activity, therefore, it is also necessary to recognize the limits of such discourse. Theological anthropology can perform this task by affirming humanity as simultaneously creative *and* creaturely, as a counterweight to the self-interest of technocratic humanism seen, for example, in the tendency of the global elite to manufacture the posthuman in its own image to the neglect of wider questions of equity and distribution.[43] Yet to place human creativity — including new technologies — within the context of its divine giftedness fosters a different sensibility in which such activity is afforded an alternative horizon other than expediency. It argues that human will is, ultimately, bounded by the integrity of others; that natural resources, nonhuman animals, and subordinated human groups are not to be reduced to "standing reserves" for our disposal. Rather, everything retains its own purpose, to be routed back into the life of God; and human self-sufficiency — secular or merely self-regarding — is fatally fragile.

Conclusion

Should we play God? No, we should not play God in the Promethean sense. But we should play human in the *imago Dei* sense — that is, we should understand ourselves as created co-creators and press our scientific and technological creativity into the service of neighbor love, of beneficence.[44]

If "the posthuman condition is upon us,"[45] then the significance of this goes beyond the impact of specific technologies to embrace deeper questions

---

43. Elaine L. Graham, "Frankensteins and Cyborgs: Visions of the Global Future in an Age of Technology," *Studies in Christian Ethics* 16, no. 1 (2003): 29-43.

44. Ted Peters, *Playing God? Genetic Determinism and Human Freedom* (London: Routledge, 1997), p. 161.

45. Halberstam and Livingston, *Posthuman Bodies*, p. vii.

about the future of humanity itself. In surveying the range of responses to the posthuman, we have seen how the cybernetic, biotechnological, and digital age is regarded as simultaneously "endangerment" and "promise" to human integrity. Yet crucially, this only serves to illuminate implicit philosophies of the relationship between human agency and creativity, and its products: our tools, artifacts, and technologies.

I have argued that the notion of humanity as created in the image of God provides a useful benchmark for thinking about the future of human nature in a technological world. An understanding of *human* creativity as participation in *divine* creativity affirms the goodness of our inventive abilities; and I would wish to celebrate our capacity to be "builders of worlds," tool-makers and tool-users, and to see this as part of what makes us distinctive as a species. Yet to conceive of the transcendence of God as God's radical otherness does not necessarily imply a flight from the material. It may simply indicate the irreducibility of the divine to human self-interest. As such, it would serve as an important antidote to the narratives of hyper-humanism in which the "will to power" is used as the rationalization for aggrandizing versions of corporate interest and transhumanist superiority. Transcendence needs therefore to be linked with materialist and incarnational, rather than quasi-gnostic, doctrines of creation, signaling an understanding of humanity made in the image of God which, far from being granted license to conquer and subdue, recognizes that human *creativity* is always already framed by human *creatureliness* and interdependence. In turn, this offers a necessary reminder that our technologies are ultimately not our own, that our inventions, like the whole of creation, make sense only when offered up as part of a larger, divine purpose.[46]

Although the prospect of humans being mixed up with nature, machines, and nonhuman animals may seem disturbing, it is, I believe, simply a reflection of the fact that human beings have always, as it were, "co-evolved" with their environment, tools, and technologies. By that I mean that to be human is already to be in a web of relationships, where our humanity can be articulated only in and through our environment, our tools, our artifacts, and the networks of human and nonhuman life around us. Human nature is not "a template untouched by social contingencies and historical becoming";[47] indeed, theological anthropology calls for an incarnational, relational

46. See Scott, *A Political Theology of Nature,* for a discussion of how an eschatological understanding of creation also redirects discussion of human *telos* in a technological age, in that creation cannot be brought to fruition by human effort alone, but awaits divine completion.

47. Peter Scott, "Imaging God: Creatureliness and Technology," *New Blackfriars* 75, no. 928 (1998): 260-74, at p. 261.

model of human personhood that regards the material world and history as the proper sphere of creation and redemption, and humans as "created co-creators." It also means, I think, that we do not need to be afraid of our complicity with technologies, or fear our hybridity, or assume that proper knowledge of and access to God can come only through a withdrawal from these activities of world-building. What it means to be human, and what is happening to the material world, are not matters that divert us from the true task of spiritual reflection and Christian living, but their very preconditions.

Dying with Dignity?

GERHARD SAUTER

Our life relies on Christ's promise that human self-enclosure will be conquered. Nevertheless, we cannot avoid a certain inevitable aloneness in dying. Therefore, we are called honestly to recognize this aloneness in others' dying as well. We should not try to diminish its significance or to protect them from it by clinging to the networks of social relations for as long and as intensively as possible. Rather, at the moment of their ultimate isolation, we are called to impart God's blessing to them, a sign of "hoping against hope" (Rom. 4:18) that combats the loneliness caused by our self-enclosure; the blessing is meant to be a pointer toward the action of God, who dignifies us as he lets us both live and die in order to reveal God's justification of the life that God imparted to us.

The Reverend Joe Wahlin, a retired minister, said at a meeting of the Pastor-Theologian Program of the Center of Theological Inquiry in Princeton some years ago, "My task was to proclaim the gospel and to help people die." He did not mean carrying out euthanasia. He wanted to help people die an authentic, humane death, to prepare them for their dying as an immensely positive event. This preparation for dying cannot be embarked on early enough, and that is what the minister meant. He did not regard his pastoral work with children, adolescents, and adults as low-ranking at all, nor did he dedicate himself merely to the seriously ill. Helping people to die means, at the same time, helping them to live united with Jesus Christ. This counseling prevents the suffering from submerging into isolation, by pronouncing God's blessing. It strengthens our perception of death and life in light of the crucifixion and resurrection of Jesus Christ as the work of the triune God.[1] The dying of Jesus, his passion and suffering, are no mere passivity. He is subjected to the action of those who torture him in a different way than he is subjected to the action of God, to which he concedes and surrenders himself. The dying of Jesus crosses out our concepts of activity and passivity.

Being Alone — But Not Deserted

Some theological aid consists in heightening our awareness that every one of us will *be alone* as we die — that is, "alone" in a specific meaning: no other person can relieve us of our dying, of our own death. That was the message of one of Martin Luther's most famous sermons:

> The summons of death comes to us all, and no one can die for another. Every one must fight his own battle with death by himself, alone. We can shout into another's ears, but every one must himself be prepared for the time of death, for I will not be with you then, nor you with me. Therefore every one must himself know and be armed with the chief things which concern a Christian.[2]

Thus Luther began his *Invocavit* sermon on March 9, 1522. Exposed to mortal danger, he had come from the comparative safety of his retreat in the Wartburg castle to the maelstrom of Wittenberg, because there the reformation of the church had gone off course.

To those who were appealing to a radicalized Christian liberty in order to enforce amendments in the liturgy, he calls (as I paraphrase it): Have you forgotten your responsibility for your weaker brothers and sisters? Have you not been confusing Christian freedom with careless and reckless self-determination? This self-determination can all too easily become irresponsible! In the hour of death you are alone, alone to an extent that you cannot even think of now! Then you must account for faith, hope, and love. Are you prepared for that, do you know what is vital, are you fit as possible for that, as I need to be today as the preacher of the word of God? Because I could not preach in any other way, as life and death are always at stake!

Luther points to two different meanings of "being alone": the loneliness

---

1. This context has been forcefully explained by Robert W. Jenson, "Thinking Death," in *On Thinking the Human: Resolutions of Difficult Notions* (Grand Rapids: Eerdmans, 2003), pp. 1-15.

2. Martin Luther, *Sermons I*, vol. 51 of *Luther's Works*, ed. Jaroslav Pelikan and Helmut Lehmann, trans. John W. Doberstein (Philadelphia: Muhlenberg, 1959), p. 70.

of sheer autonomy that ends in desperate self-isolation versus the solitude of complete dedication to God of that "self" that ultimately will not be left alone because the triune God embraces it. By thus indicating the scale of individual responsibility, Luther does not aim to instill fear. Rather, he wants to call attention to the question of *what it means for a Christian to be a person.*

Part of the answer is that each of us, in our naked existence, is ultimately confronted with our own death. No one can stand in for, or take the place of, a dying person. Luther does not overlook the fact that people sometimes give their lives in order to spare the lives of others — but this only delays, not eliminates, the other's ultimate confrontation with death. And, of course, Luther does not forget that Jesus Christ has died for us, and that this sacrifice radically transforms our living and our dying. But everyone, in the end, must die his or her own death — nobody finally can substitute for another. For that, then, we must prepare ourselves, and, if we have this vocation, we must prepare others, in light of the Christian conviction that all people will come to stand before God and will have to account authentically for themselves alone, in front of God alone. Because we anticipate this accounting for ourselves alone, in the moment and momentum of death, the urgent need for justification of one's life may arise. This responsibility forbids us from living in such a way that we withdraw into ourselves, behaving in an isolated, self-enclosed manner. Death, therefore, is not only the final emergency of life but, even more, the decay of every attempt to justify our self-enclosure or to rely merely on the appraisal or rejection of others.

Death is not to be confused with becoming physically deceased — not even with death as the definitive result of dying. Nor is the battle of death equivalent with the death-struggle itself, which inevitably will be lost — that is a "dead certainty." Some people are spared that agony; their life seems to fade away. They "breathe it out," so to speak. Is there no battle of death for them? This battle cannot be evaluated by others and by their measuring instruments. The battle of death is distinct from the manner and timing of dying. In this respect, there is no difference between a so-called humane "dying in dignity" and a cruel death imposed by human force or natural disaster, a so-called unnatural death. We are shocked by a sudden death, especially of children. If their life is abruptly taken away, its promise seems unfulfilled. The living, therefore, are tempted to make sense of it by their commemorative endeavors — for example, taking actions in order to prevent dangers that may threaten other lives. This response may bear fruit, but its underlying presuppositions reveal all-too-human inventions for escaping the reality of death.

Of course, there are enormous differences in deaths that we should not overlook, and nobody knows what kind of a death he or she will face. But beyond all these differences, death is the battle with the "last enemy" (1 Cor. 15:26), a power to which we seem powerlessly exposed. We should not remain ignorant during our lifetime of what this hostility is about. "The wages of sin is death" (Rom. 6:23). This is *categorically* different from the idea that any life inevitably leads to death, and it is very different from a sentence of the French existentialist philosopher Jean Paul Sartre: "Death is the ultimate sarcasm of life."

By this meditation on one's own dying the sensitivity for irreducible individuality seems to be sharpened to the utmost extent. Awareness of one's own dying — not the perishing itself — is most tightly related to the dignity of human beings. Blaise Pascal argues along the same lines:

> A human being is only a reed [Isa. 42:3], the weakest in nature, but he is a thinking reed. To crush him, the whole universe does not have to arm itself. A mist, a drop of water, is enough to kill him. But if the universe were to crush the reed, the man would be nobler than his killer, since he knows that he is dying, and that the universe has the advantage over him. The universe knows nothing about this. — All our dignity consists therefore of thought.[3]

> Man's greatness lies in his capacity to recognize his wretchedness. A tree does not recognize its wretchedness. So it is wretched to know one is wretched, but there is greatness in the knowledge of one's wretchedness.[4]

The grandeur and misery of the human being originate from one's anticipation of one's own dying — and simultaneously being unable to know what one's very own dying will be. This anticipation is related to human self-consciousness: we don't merely perish, but also foreknow that we must perish. "So the grandeur and misery of man are fused together in the human reality and experience of death. To deny the indignity of death requires that the dignity of man be refused also."[5]

Therefore, how can we die humanely at all? If grandeur and misery, awareness and nescience coincide when we die — doesn't this also render any kind of dignity obsolete?

---

3. Blaise Pascal, *Pensées and Other Writings*, trans. Honor Levi (Oxford: Oxford University Press, 1995), pp. 72f. (fragment nos. 231-32).

4. Pascal, *Pensées*, pp. 36-37 (fragment no. 146).

5. Paul Ramsey, "The Indignity of 'Death with Dignity,'" in *On Moral Medicine: Theological Perspectives in Medical Ethics,* second ed., ed. Stephen E. Lammers and Allen Verhey (Grand Rapids: Eerdmans, 1998), p. 216. On Ramsey's concept of human dignity and on other contemporary concepts cf. Göran Collste, *Is Human Life Special? Religious and Philosophical Perspectives on the Principle of Human Dignity* (Bern: Peter Lang, 2002).

The dignity of dying seems to be restricted to the possibility that we human beings are powerful in the face of death by yet another means, that is, that anyone of us can say "I shall die," and that this "I" holds intentions even in dying. "Humane dying" then demands respect for this being-an-agent.

How many people nowadays are still allowed to die humanely *in this way?* Millions of human beings have been "destroyed"; even today many are being "extinguished" and "liquidated," to use the inhumane expression. The German National Socialists kept accurate records of all their victims, yet they wanted to destroy their names and thus take away even the last vestige of their dignity. Nowadays, weapons of "mass destruction" exterminate their victims, who die anonymously, deprived of any individuality and dignity.

Because we are deeply terrified in the face of such degradation, we tend to regard death as humane when the dying person is *not* merely the object of other people's action, not a mere "victim." This leads to the supposition that the dignity of human beings is not to be taken away. In the perspective of ethics, this is conclusive. Yet does it conversely mean that people whose lives are not taken by others through force (or by natural disasters) die "humanely"? If they die like Abraham, who "breathed his last and died in a good old age, an old man and full of years" (Gen. 25:8), are they dying a "natural" death?

In spite of all understandable and respectable efforts to guard against an "unnatural" dying, we are not permitted to equate any sort of "natural" dying with the dignity in dying. Rather, we must notice how little dying persons are in power of their statements anymore, regardless of how much they are cared for and how diligently their dignity as human beings is respected!

The concept of a "natural dying befitting a human being," a concept governed by ethics, directs our attention away from the theological perception of death. This perception, though, should be decisive for a theological anthropology, and in turn casts light on our whole concept of human dignity.

Against Isolation

"There is nobility and dignity in caring for the dying, but not in dying itself": thus Paul Ramsey[6] accurately portrays the gap in the attitude toward the dying that is predominant today. He ascertains that the reason for this is that death is regarded as a natural phenomenon, as an inevitable part of life, not as an enemy in the biblical sense. Therefore, it has become a custom to speak of "being deceased" or, philosophically more high-sounding, of "finitude." On

6. Ramsey, "Indignity of 'Death with Dignity,'" p. 210.

the contrary, the New Testament speaks in metaphors like the "battle with death," with the enemy who has been conquered by Christ and is yet our enemy nonetheless because he is allied with sin. Death befalls us, occurs to us. From the very start we are inferior to it; we are defeated. That is so even if everything in us revolts against this submission, because this submission alters us thoroughly and more lastingly than anything else does.

Thus, the attention is shifted away from death and toward the dying, away from being alone in dying and toward the loneliness of the dying.

"Humane dying" is a task that has become crucial because of the isolation which overcomes many who are fatally ill, and because of their submission to the action of others, like physicians, a situation which again leads to a rapid loss of self-determination. The dying person is being acted upon, yet not in such a way that he or she would any longer be able to be "himself" or "herself."

If human dignity is solely grounded in self-determination, then "death with dignity" might be equated with "ending life through the voluntary self-administration of lethal medication" — to be distinguished from euthanasia, which was defined by the "Oregon's Death with Dignity Act" (1994) as "when a physician or other person directly administers a medication to end another's life."[7] Then there is only one step further to physician-assisted suicide as a "virtue" of mercy.[8] And the most radical conclusion might be to view the self-administration of death as an act not merely of personal dignity but of social appropriateness. The question, then, is how much one can burden another, and not how much one can bear oneself. That seems to be a last act of control — but it is really a desperate effort to evade the finality of death as the end of agency: the sign of a death-denying culture, a nihilistic "art of dying."

The capacity of modern medicine to extend life, at times to extend life in an unbearable way, creates an ethical dilemma for us: a life that is being extended at all costs can become unbearable and indeed inhumane. An increasing isolation intensifies this dilemma. This isolation arises because the dying are abandoned. There are many reasons for this: the institution of the family decays, and it becomes more and more difficult to take care of the elderly and the ill; in addition, as life expectancy has increased, far too much is being asked of the relatives.

---

7. http://www.deathwithdignity.org/resources/acthistory.htm.

8. E.g., Peter Rogatz, "The Virtues of Physician-Assisted Suicide," *The Humanist* 61 (November/December 2001) (http://www.thehumanist.org./humanist/articles/rogatz.htm). Rogatz is a member of the Ethics Committee on Bioethical Issues of Hospice Care Network (Long Island and Queens) and a member of the Committee on Bioethical Issues of the State of New York.

The answer consists in personal companionship or accompaniment in dying. In particular, the hospice movement has made this accompaniment its task. The movement originated when dying became increasingly undignified, because dying persons were submitted to the determination of their lives by the action or inaction of others, especially of physicians and nurses in hospital intensive-care units. The obligation of personal accompaniment resulted in some very helpful practices: for example, the terminally ill may remain in their familiar environment as long as possible, but they can call for professional help at any time. The aim of personal accompaniment in dying is to cushion the inevitable isolation of dying persons as far as possible, not to leave dying persons alone. By medical means this aim is supported by pain management, though this can move indistinguishably close to euthanasia.

Some time ago, a young minister telephoned me — a former student of mine. She had been very active in the hospice movement, but had discovered that this engagement kept her from fulfilling her vocation for pastoral counseling. Why? She was rarely allowed to prepare the dying for encountering their own death. Instead, all energies were concentrated on the efforts to help the dying have a self-determined and a social life, even if a more and more restricted one. Pastoral care needs to be integrated into an interdisciplinary endeavor to maintain a multifaceted view of death, but one based on the desire to die in a dignified way — a modern variation of the *ars moriendi* of the Middle Ages.

To respect the dying as persons and to attend to them deserves great approval. I do not by any means want to question this. Yet it strikes me that this personal accompaniment in dying attempts to ward off the isolation — as many think — of the dying by keeping them embedded in the social network as long and as intensely as possible. Here, dying is viewed simply as the final removal of the normal social fabric that destroys individual moral choice and interaction with other human beings.

This casts a spotlight on an anthropologically profoundly altered concept of what it means to be a human being, that is, being constituted by relations. On the one hand, we have become accustomed to undergird created, yet finite, humanity with a network of social relations, which we are constantly weaving into a network meant for our support. Yet, on the other hand, anyone who can no longer contribute to the work of this network depends on others to include them, lest they should fall out of a shared human world. This is why the suffering, the elderly, and the dying in particular lapse into a desperate loneliness. They neither participate in the work of the social fabric nor are looked upon by others as if they do belong within it. Because of our rising need for human kindness, our neighbors wish they could draw closer to us, and yet, because of our feeling of isolation, we exclude more and more people from our social interactions. Thus, so many become more and more isolated today. Isolation is a growing epidemic that must be understood as a contemporary social disease.

Personal accompaniment in dying aims to cope with this isolation by relieving a symptom of this disease — the specific isolation and consequent dehumanization of the dying. But can the roots of this disease be tackled in this way? Or, on the contrary, are they merely retained, growing new weeds of isolation in other social venues?

In church and theology, providing a sufficient personal accompaniment to the dying was adopted by leading trends of pastoral counseling, resulting in some compassionate advice, but avoiding any pronouncement about God's blessing in the darkness of death, let alone any commitment to prepare for the last battle with death. The aim of this pastoral counseling is to attend to the dying on their way, as far as possible, and to back up other supports: it is an "assistance in dying" that, on closer examination, turns out to be aiming at a concluding and integrating assistance in living. It assumes that the social relationships that carry all human individuality should be preserved for as long as possible, even if the dying person is gradually taking leave of them. Therefore, while pastoral counselors help people who are dying to prepare for *dying,* often they do not help them to prepare for their *death,* as they are encouraging them to look back on their lives and bring them into order as much as possible. The anticipation of the end creates opportunities of decision and challenges to action in the present and thus helps us to cope better with our daily lives. Anticipating death should help us find the way back to enhanced individual lives. Once the image of death passes and the image of unrestricted time resumes, we return, changed, to our daily lives. The leading understanding is, therefore, that this catharsis must not be destroyed by false hope. For this reason, every hope is said to be dangerous if it does not introduce within the context of life and action something that outlives the person's death.

A further symptom: in many areas, intercessions in Protestant church services no longer remember the dead. Prayer for the fate of the dead has not been offered for a long time, for doctrinal reasons that merit closer examination.[9] Yet, there is a decisive contrast between, on the one hand, a pastor remembering dead members of a parish before God and commending them to God as to the one who has called them, and, on the other, a pastor merely in-

---

9. Gerhard Sauter, *What Dare We Hope? Reconsidering Eschatology* (Harrisburg: Trinity Press International, 1999), pp. 188-97.

forming the congregation that a member died and that the intercession will include those close to the dead. The conviction behind the latter sounds something like this: "The dead is dead: let us concern ourselves with the living, their mourning and their future." Many funeral services treat the matter so; they are essentially there for the sake of those left behind. The gaps in the net of social reality, caused once again by death and brought to consciousness by the death of a person, should be closed up again as quickly as possible.

The concept according to which our world is one giant network has fatal consequences for the dead. For they have fallen out of the network of social relations for all time. They cannot be acted on anymore — one cannot, *sit venia verbo,* "do" anything with them.

Preparing to Die

Any conceivable effort not to leave the dying alone in their loneliness, into which they inevitably fall, merits respect, gratitude, and support. This applies in the fullest degree to pastoral care as well. Still the question must be raised whether it can carry out its decisive task that way. I want to pinpoint this claim: *the dignity of the dying can also be violated if they are not prepared for death.* To be prepared for death is based on the promise of everlasting life. Therefore, preparing another for death means to communicate this promise — and, by any possible means, to make more of an effort than merely "addressing the issue."

In a comprehensive American publication on *Dignity and Dying,* there can be found only one distinctly theological contribution.[10] The author sees his pastoral task in making the presence of the merciful God accessible by means of his, the minister's, presence at the deathbed, that is, in representing God's presence. There is no real communication in this book of "hoping against hope," as Paul marks the decisive character of the Christian faithful hope that trusts in God who "gives life to the dead and calls into existence the things that do not exist" (Rom. 4:17-18). And absolutely nothing is said about the preparation needed when a dying person is encountering his or her own death.

Modern Protestant theology has shown a typical radicalism in sharpening the notion of death as annihilation of all kinds of relations — relations of the individual's body and soul and relations of the dead and the living. This

---

10. Dennis P. Hollinger, "Congregational Ministry," in *Dignity and Dying: A Christian Appraisal,* ed. John F. Kilner et al. (Grand Rapids: Eerdmans, 1996), pp. 232-42.

radicalism has sometimes been supported by pointing to "God as my hereaf-ter" (Karl Barth and Eberhard Jüngel) or to "resurrection in contradiction to immortality" (Oscar Cullmann).[11] The psychiatrist Joachim Ernst Meyer has observed that many Protestant patients have an exaggerated fear of death: they fear their self will, so to speak, be erased. He attributes this to a doctrinal deficit in theology: It gives rise to the impression that death extinguishes all that has ever been experienced.[12] It might be that "eschatologenic"[13] neuroses have been generated by those radicalisms. In Roman Catholic eschatology, hope that extends beyond death is based on the belief that God does not abandon his creatures. Protestant theology, in contrast, sometimes avoids speaking of any continuous relation of the self. Instead, Protestants talk of "new creation." Are these really inconsistent alternatives? What is lacking in each of the answers if it is detached from the other?

Our hope depends on God choosing us and calling us by name. Human dignity is *imparted* to the human being by God and thus is beyond the possi-bility of any revocation by merely human means. *Dignity consists in the con-tingency of every person. That I am created the way I am* and in no other is hard to believe, and even harder to conceive. For Philipp Melanchthon, this was one of the two theological questions that he could not answer during his life-time and for which he hoped that God would provide him an answer after his death. If the contingency of humanity can no longer be believed, then human dignity can be questioned and violated, particularly if one wants to be other than one is, or if one is determined to be different.

Therefore, I have to sharpen the question: "How can we prepare other people to encounter their own deaths? *What* ought we to say here, what are we obliged to say, what are we committed to communicate under all circum-stances?" Of course, we must also consider as diligently as possible *how* we can communicate this under the most difficult circumstances, sensitively, with empathy, and as cautiously as is needed under specific conditions. But these modes of communication are not the task here. We have to question our theological perception of encountering death.

Ludwig Wittgenstein has noticed that only the "demeanor of pain" is

---

11. Oscar Cullmann, *Immortality of the Soul; or, Resurrection of the Dead? The Witness of the New Testament* (New York: Macmillan, 1958).

12. Joachim Ernst Meyer, *Todesangst und das Todesbewußtsein der Gegenwart* (Berlin: Springer, 1979), pp. 18-23. See also Meyer, "Psychotherapeutische Fragen an die Theologie," *Evangelische Theologie* 41 (1981): 57-65; here Meyer questions Eberhard Jüngel's *Death: The Rid-dle and the Mystery*, trans. Ian and Ute Nicol (Philadelphia: Westminster, 1975).

13. "Eschatologenic" in the sense of caused by a confusing eschatology that destroys the character of living hope as a token of our life imparted by God.

communicable.[14] This is a biblical insight as well: "The heart knows its own bitterness, and no stranger shares its joy" (Prov. 14:10). This inner loneliness is to be distinguished from introversion. It does not indicate the limits of our desire to communicate ourselves. Certain experiences cannot be shared any longer — this is aggravated in severe illness and in dying.

The loneliness of the piercing pain, the isolation in suffering, the cutting off of "disabled" and older persons who can no longer communicate seems to refuse pastoral care. It is the limit of acting as such, that is, of what we usually think offered action would be like. Are the sufferings an exception to normal "human being"? On the contrary, we need to conceptualize being human as a limited redemption from the loneliness of suffering, a redemption that is not granted to all.

We must be sensitive to our ordinary use of language. "*I* have to die, *I* am going to die": such first-person declarations are distinct from the external, third-person views of a spectator: "They are going to die, they are dying, they are dead." "I die" questions radically the pretence of infinity in the widespread use of the phrase "I am." But does this notion make any difference? Often people even try to neglect it. They avoid saying, "he or she died." They prefer to speak more euphemistically of "departing" or "passing away." Physicians think they have sufficient instruments to measure and to determine brain death, even though some of them are rather reluctant to make such a definitive statement. But if one is confronted with his or her own death and utters, "I die" — maybe without words — that is an openness to something beyond all experiences, even external to all experiences. It is not even a reflection about the finitude of all beings and the finiteness of my own being. There are mysteries in the process of dying, ways of spiritual communication that exceed language, which reach beyond other bodily signals, even beyond a silent empathy.

In the New Testament, death is often viewed as an inconceivable, annihilating power. It is called the last enemy that is able and is ready to alienate us from God, to estrange us from all other creatures, and to destroy us definitively. That is said only in the light of Jesus Christ's victory over the power of death, the power that consists in the judgment, "there is nothing more left." But this is not the last word. Indeed, it is no judgment at all, if Jesus Christ is expected and trusted as the now-ruling and coming judge.

This hope is vividly expressed in the first question of the Reformed *Heidelberg Catechism* (1563) and its answer: "What is your only consolation in life

14. Ludwig Wittgenstein, *Philosophical Investigations*, fourth ed. (Oxford: Blackwell, 1967), p. 89 (nos. 244-46).

and in death? That I, with body and soul, do not belong to myself, but to my faithful savior Jesus Christ." In Jesus' victory over death, God appears solely as he is present in Jesus Christ, with the promise of everlasting life: *The presence of Christ, his suffering action upon us and with us — that, and all the effects of that, and nothing else, will remain.* That means that we are integrated into the ongoing story of Jesus Christ: we are ever embraced by him, the coming one.

Preparing for death means communicating the promise of the gospel — and doing so by every possible means, making more than merely a token effort. Life with Christ entails a certain kind of dying, the death of my alienation from God, of my self-enclosure (*incurvatio in seipsum,* Luther's paraphrase of "sin").[15] *I died to the endeavor to choose and to justify my own existence by my achievements because God has chosen me in Jesus Christ. That* death I already died (Gal. 2:19), even if it is a dying day by day. This dying shapes all my life, my acting and my suffering. We are used to thinking of death as the conclusion of my life; therefore we say, "death follows life." But Paul speaks about baptism as dying: "All of us who have been baptized into Christ Jesus were baptized into his death" (Rom. 6:3; cf. Col. 3:3). For Paul, baptism creates another sequence: *Life, that is, living with Christ, follows death.* You may say that here the term "death" is just a metaphor. But this metaphor transfers and transforms us into the death and life of Jesus Christ. This metaphor captures the essence of a Christian's "new life" in Christ. Christians ought to learn to live, to think, and to act according to the sequence *life follows death.*

If, when I perish, all that remains is my "having-been-for-myself," then nothing remains. Therefore, preparing for death is also preparing for what in the face of death marks "my life" — though this is concealed from me and others most of the time. Fear of being alone lies at the heart of fear of death. Loneliness is unmasked as self-enclosure, as *incurvatio in seipsum.*

If that is true, there might be other notions of dying and death. If I do not belong to myself, then death does not end with self-confrontation.

How can we move forward toward such a perception? It cannot be a strictly systematized reflection, certainly not a self-reflection, because of the nature of encountering our death. Even if you start with a christological premise, you must be aware that this leads to the expectation of Jesus Christ as the coming one. Theological argumentation has to insist on this expectation. It implies "an accounting for the hope that is in you" (1 Peter 3:15). I ought to interrupt myself when I have to point to God's acting in Jesus Christ and the promise of life imparted by him, as Paul argues: I live, but "it is no

---

15. Martin Luther, *Lectures on Romans* (1515/16), vol. 25 of *Luther's Works,* trans. Hilton C. Oswald (Saint Louis: Concordia, 1972), pp. 291, 313, 345, 513.

longer I who live, but it is Christ who lives in me" (Gal. 2:20). Sometimes I have to pause in order to get a clearer view of the complexity of perceptions, which are needed here. I may listen to the witness of other people without overstating their experiences because death is beyond all experiences you can talk about — death is external to them. Therefore, to talk about encountering your own death might be generally a test case of the theological *modus loquendi.*

People who accompany and assist dying persons tell us that the dying are active as they die. If a Christian says, "I die," this means that he or she carries his or her special, contingent vocation in a distinctively Christian manner. The theologian Heiko A. Oberman, who died in 2001, said in the face of his dying that he was about to pass from one hand of God into the other.

Death is not only a corporeal occurrence. In many ways death shapes all who have had to do with the corporality of the one who has died. One who really accompanies a dying person will be affected by that and will not remain as he or she was. Death is such a powerful occurrence that it alters all who come near it. It becomes more powerful the more it is experienced in the sign of its being conquered by Jesus Christ. The mercy, which is conveyed through this occurrence, will touch and mature all who are present.

The death of Jesus has changed the world. Our death, too, will change many things: the life of our family, our relatives, all those who are somehow affected by it. By virtue of the gospel, death will not have a destructive, but rather a fruitful, effect.

For many pastors, blessing the dying has gained an inestimable significance as passing on what God has promised and appointed us to do. We cannot say last rites to ourselves, we only can receive them as affirmation of God's presence, and we cannot keep it to ourselves. Blessing proclaims the truth of reality against anything that separates truth from reality. With God's blessing we can die, because our future is the rising of our hidden life with God: we advance from the narrowness of temptation into the vastness of God.

A further act, by means of signs, is the *communio* of the church in the Lord's Supper. In the Apostles' Creed and in the Creed of Nicaea-Constantinople (381), forgiveness of sins, resurrection of the dead, and eternal life (or "the life of the world to come") are being named in one breath. Is this merely a list of "last things"? Or is it a meager yet expressive hint that this forgiveness of sins is the foretaste of eternal life? How often has this forgiveness been announced to us, imparted to us in the Lord's Supper! Will we gather to receive forgiveness in the face of death, or will we be plagued by that elephant's memory of all our neglects and our unfulfilled desires? With baptism and Eucharist, we are being incorporated into the body of Christ. The whole church is present here, even at the bed of the dying person. The perception that the dying are surrounded by their ancestors is very vivid among Africans and African-Americans.[16] Yet this notion can be a burdensome one, as is often the case in Korea, for example. The communion of the church connects us with all living and dead who glorify God.

It makes a substantial, even decisive, difference if we think of our living and dying as "completed" at a time and in a way we cannot determine. As Charles Wesley wrote in 1762,

> Ready for all Thy perfect will,
> My acts of faith and love repeat,
> Till death Thy endless mercies seal,
> And make the sacrifice complete.[17]

Death is the end of agency but not the ultimate destiny of humans as persons, because there is a sense of incompleteness in the face of being alone for God.

Now, facing my own death, "I" will be alone because no one can die for another. But I am not deserted. My consolation and hope of not being alone are based on a manifold promise:

First, God speaks the last word on my life; therefore, I am not left hopelessly alone with the judgment that I pass on.

Second, when we are radically confronted only with ourselves, Jesus Christ will step in between the "I" and its conceptualization of the power of death (merciless destruction), of sin (irreparable failure), and of hell (complete, irrecoverable, terminal forlornness). Death, sin, and hell are pictures from which God's word turns us away. It says to us "that Christ's life overcame my death in his death, that his obedience blotted out my sin in his suffering, that his love destroyed my hell in his forsakenness."[18] Only the gaze at the Christ who is exalted on the cross grants eternal life (John 3:14-15). We may look away from ourselves — from our picture of death, of sin, and of hell — not because they are mere illusions, but because they seduce us to overlook the commanding presence of Jesus Christ.

Third, God surveys my life in a different way than I can perceive and understand myself. By means of God's judgment on me God's concealed acting in my existence is revealed. Likewise, all the inconceivable networks, pre-

---

16. Karla F. C. Holloway, *Passed On: African American Mourning Stories: A Memorial* (Durham, N.C.: Duke University Press, 2002).

17. "O Thou Who Camest from Above," fourth stanza, *Wesley Hymn Book*, second ed., ed. Franz Hildebrandt (London: Weekes, 1960), no. 100.

18. Martin Luther, "A Sermon on Preparing to Die" (1519), in *Devotional Writings I*, vol. 42 of *Luther's Works*, trans. Martin H. Bertram (Philadelphia: Fortress, 1960), p. 109.

suppositions, and effects by which my responsibility has been established are revealed, such that I recognize — not merely believe — that I am created as I am and no different.

Fourth, I will recognize how I am being recognized by God (1 Cor. 13:12).

Finally, the life I have lived forms an unexpected unity, because it is being carried by the context of the action of God and is interwoven with it. God's justice emanates from it, and all injustice falls from it. By the relation of my suffering to my action, it will become translucent that "it is no longer I who live, but it is Christ who lives in me" (Gal. 2:20).

THE MULTIDIMENSIONALITY
OF HUMAN DIGNITY

Human Dignity, Human Complexity, and Human Goods

DON S. BROWNING

Contemporary endangerments to human dignity have many sources. The rise of tyrannies deprives humans of their political rights. Natural disasters rob humans of the necessities of life. Spreading technologies render humans as means to ends over which they have no control. What is common to these diverse assaults on human dignity? They all fail to *respect* the multidimensional character of the human being.

Several chapters in this collection also address the multidimensionality of the human, especially those by Polkinghorne, Schwöbel, and Welker.[1] In coupling the word "respect" with the word "multidimensionality," I propose broadening the dimensions of the human commonly thought to be objects of respect. In contrast to the followers of Kant, I contend that the object of respect includes but goes beyond the rational capacities of humans.[2] Because there are several dimensions to the human that deserve respect, the word "respect" should have different meanings depending on the dimension under consideration.

---

1. John Polkinghorne in "Anthropology in an Evolutionary Context" addresses the issue from the perspective of reality; reality too, as well as human nature, is multidimensional and contains mathematical and metaphysical dimensions which contemporary evolutionary theory, in spite of its important insights, does not capture. Michael Welker in "Theological Anthropology versus Anthropological Reductionism" is concerned to overcome the modern reduction of the human to subjectivity by capturing the human both in front of and behind the classical idea of person as mask. And Christoph Schwöbel in "Recovering Human Dignity" develops a multidimensional analysis of the ontological significance of the human being as defined in relation to God.

2. Immanuel Kant, *Foundations of the Metaphysics of Morals* (Indianapolis: Bobbs-Merrill, 1959).

The various endangerments to dignity mentioned above all reduce humans to a limited portion of their full multidimensionality. Human dignity is a many-splendored thing and can be realized only through the *full* recognition of its complexity. Some academic disciplines attempt to overcome fragmentation by reducing the human to one of a variety of perspectives. Behaviorism, rational-choice theory, sociobiology, psychoanalysis, Marxism, and social constructivism are all current aggressive attempts to achieve a unified view of the human dictated by a single narrow perspective. Even theological reductionism is possible; this happens when the spiritual perspective fails also to include the material, economic, psychological, and moral dimensions of humans.

Multidimensionality within Theological Anthropology

Most great theological anthropologies implicitly acknowledge the multidimensional character of the human, but only a few make this explicit. Paul Tillich introduced multidimensionality directly into his thought. Using the insights of phenomenological description, he listed the inorganic, the organic, the psychic, and the spiritual as the fundamental dimensions of the human.[3] William Schweiker, in an effort to develop a responsibility ethic for a new Christian humanism, lists three dimensions of basic human goods — premoral, social, and reflective goods.[4]

Schweiker's formulation has importance for my primary thesis, namely, that responding to the endangerment of the human requires a religious and cultural program that *not only respects the full multidimensional character of the human but also protects the frequently ignored dimension of premoral goods or values.*

By the phrase "premoral good," I refer to the numerous ways we use the words "good" and "value" to refer to experiences and objects that are considered pleasant, fulfilling, agreeable, healthy, or in some way enhancing to human life. Premoral goods, however, should not be considered as directly or fully moral goods.[5] Here are some examples. Education is a pre-

---

3. Paul Tillich, *Systematic Theology*, vol. 3 (Chicago: University of Chicago Press, 1963), pp. 22-23.

4. William Schweiker, *Responsibility and Christian Ethics* (Cambridge: Cambridge University Press, 1995), pp. 120-21.

5. William Frankena makes a distinction between nonmoral and moral good. See William Frankena, *Ethics* (Englewood Cliffs, N.J.: Prentice Hall, 1973). Janssens makes what I think is the more helpful distinction between moral and premoral good. It communicates that

moral good; it extends our cognitive powers and often leads to higher earnings. But it is not a fully moral good unless it is guided by just purposes and considers the needs of others. Health is a good, but not necessarily a moral good. Some people are physically and mentally healthy but quite immoral. Safe transportation, good roads, and clean air and water are premoral goods, but not necessarily moral goods. They all can be used justly or unjustly. They are, however, important goods, and it would be immoral for us not to justly pursue them.

Premoral goods can conflict with one another. Good things often compete with and stamp out other good things; good food can damage the good of health if we eat too much. *Reconciling conflicting goods when they are in tension is generally viewed as a distinctively moral task.* Premoral goods may be relevant to judgments about the moral good, but they are not in-and-of-themselves moral goods.

The premoral level of experience is part of the multidimensional nature of the human that contemporary theology has had difficulties conceptualizing. Increasingly, it is this dimension of life that social sciences such as economics, evolutionary psychology, and the health fields have tried to clarify. This turn to the social sciences has led to the exclusion of theology as a resource for clarifying public issues. Theology is thought to have little to contribute to the clarification of these goods.

I will illustrate the nature of premoral goods by locating them within a larger view of the multidimensional nature of the human. In a series of essays and books stretching from the early 1980s, I have identified five levels or dimensions of the human.[6] I argue that these dimensions are implicit in all acts of moral thinking or practical reason. All examples of such thinking reveal, I believe, the following: (1) a visional dimension of reflection generally conveyed by narratives and metaphors about the ultimate context of experience

---

premoral goods are morally relevant but not morally definitive. See Louis Janssens, "Norms and Priorities of a Love Ethics," *Louvain Studies* (1977): 207-38.

6. For the latest statement of these five dimensions, see my *A Fundamental Practical Theology* (Minneapolis: Fortress, 1991), pp. 94-109, 139-70. I have recently decided that, when viewed from the perspective of the actual concrete functioning of practical reason rather than from the angle of its hierarchical patterns, these five dimensions should be ordered in the following manner. (This order represents the patterns of phronêsis implied by Paul Ricoeur in his *Oneself As Another* [1992] and other writings). Here is the order stated as a formula: (1) Humans are desiring creatures, (2) who pursue their wants through practices and habits, (3) assign meaning to these practices through narratives about life's purpose, (4) test resolutions of conflicting wants and practices through general principles (in Ricoeur's case, a slight amendment to Kant's categorical imperative), and (5) refine these ideal solutions with attention to the social and natural constraints of concrete situations.

or, as Christoph Schwöbel says, the nature "of *being*";[7] (2) an obligational dimension guided by an implicit or explicit general moral principle, for example, the Golden Rule or the utilitarian principle of the greatest good for the greatest number; (3) a dimension containing assumptions about the premoral tendencies and related goods necessary for basic human survival and well-being; (4) a dimension holding assumptions about regnant social and ecological patterns (feudalism, modern urbanism, gravity, cold weather) that channel and constrain our various needs; and, finally, (5) a level of concrete practices and rules that are shaped by all the foregoing dimensions — for example, farming, playing the piano, driving a car, training to be a lawyer. These practices and rules are thick and can be analyzed in terms of how the other four dimensions shape them. In fact, it is good to think about the thickness of moral thinking in reverse of how I presented it here, starting with practices first.

Reinhold Niebuhr and Multidimensionality of the Human

Let's examine the theological anthropology of Reinhold Niebuhr from the perspective of these five dimensions of practical reflection. Niebuhr is generally not perceived to have elaborated a multidimensional anthropology in the manner of Tillich. And indeed, he did not explicitly do so. But the dimensions are there nonetheless, as they are in all manifestations of the human.

First, Niebuhr begins with humans as desiring creatures. In volume 1 of *The Nature and Destiny of Man,* he depicts a human being as "a child of nature, subject to its vicissitudes, compelled by its necessities, driven by its impulses and confined within the brevity . . . which nature permits."[8] From one perspective, such words suggest the finitude of human existence. From another, they show the creaturely, desiring, and teleological aspects of humans — vitalities that were also for him a source of both form and creativity.[9] In the language of my five dimensions, they demonstrate how Niebuhr understood the human search for premoral goods. Indeed, he mentioned a few that were firmly anchored in our creaturely nature and gleaned from reading the Bible, Darwin, and Freud. He thought humans have survival instincts, primal needs for attachment, needs for material acquisition, needs for group related-

---

7. Schwöbel, "Recovering Human Dignity," p. 46 in this volume.

8. Reinhold Niebuhr, *The Nature and Destiny of Man,* vol. 1 (New York: Charles Scribner's Sons, 1941), p. 3.

9. Niebuhr, *Nature and Destiny of Man,* vol. 1, pp. 26-27.

ness, and sexual urges that express themselves through the differentiation of male and female.[10]

Niebuhr believed that all of these tendencies were premorally good when viewed from the perspective of the ontology, that is, the view of being, implicit in the Christian doctrine of creation. But Niebuhr also viewed desiring and finite humans as being in dialectical tension with their capacity for freedom and self-transcendence.[11] It is from the anxiety of this freedom that sin emerges — the prideful and sensual drive to protect oneself from the anxiety of freedom rather than trust in God.[12] Sin distorts our pursuit of the goods of life.

Surrounding his view of humans as desiring creatures is the second dimension of Niebuhr's anthropology. This is a *narrative* — cosmological in scope — about the nature and action of God in relation to the world. Niebuhr unfolds this narrative around deep metaphors gained from Scriptures. God is Creator, Governor, and Redeemer.[13] These features of God are dimly revealed in general experience and explicitly manifest in the revelation of Jesus Christ. These metaphors reveal God's relation to the world and define the ultimate context of Christian anthropology. God as Creator means that the material world and basic human desires are good in the premoral sense of goodness. These include our sexual and acquisitive desires, our defensive needs, and even our aggressive tendencies; all of these have their proper place in human life. Furthermore, humans are dependent for all these goods on their *relation to God*. This relationality, in fact, is the nature of the image of God in humans, a point Schwöbel and Welker also bring out in this volume.[14]

Good too, in the premoral sense, is the human condition of finitude, freedom, and anxiety. Sin and moral evil enter the world not through our basic desires and needs but through the way we handle them in relation to the anxiety of freedom and finitude. In response to the distortions of sin, God emerges as Governor to judge injustice and maintain the moral framework of the world. God the Redeemer works through all history but acts decisively in Jesus the Christ. This salvatory initiative by God provides the grace and forgiveness to overcome in principle the distortions of sin's prideful and idolatrous response to anxiety and freedom.

This narrative is the *envelope* that surrounds and largely, although not totally, shapes Niebuhr's theological anthropology. The metaphor of the en-

10. For a review of the various natural needs and tendencies that humans have in Niebuhr's thought, see *Nature and Destiny of Man*, vol. 1, pp. 28-53.

11. Niebuhr, *Nature and Destiny of Man*, vol. 1, pp. 3-4.

12. Niebuhr, *Nature and Destiny of Man*, vol. 1, pp. 186-207, 228-40.

13. Niebuhr, *Nature and Destiny of Man*, vol. 1, p. 132.

14. See pp. 47-49 of Schwöbel's essay and pp. 320-25 of Welker's.

velope communicates the way his narrative frames his moral thinking. It is not meant to suggest something that either he or we should throw in the trash, as we do with envelopes when we open letters. But the full content of his theological view of the human is not derived entirely from this narrative. Niebuhr's view of humans as a dialectic between nature and spirit was also derived from a phenomenological analysis of the situation of being human. More specifically, it was a product of radical empiricism in the specifically Jamesian sense of that term. An understanding of the human could be derived, Niebuhr believed, from the general testimony of experience.[15] Niebuhr held that the reality of sin itself is evident from experience even though its deeper meaning is also revealed by God in the dramas of judgment and redemption. This observation is important; it shows that Niebuhr held that the multiple dimensions of the human *cannot* be fully derived from any one of them, even the narrative dimension.

The third dimension is more distinctively moral. It is also problematic. Niebuhr believed that self-sacrificial love, exemplified by Christ's death on a cross, is the highest principle of Christian morality. We are called by God to lay down our lives for our neighbor; this is the perfect love that Christians should live by.[16] Because of finitude and sin, however, this is a perfection that "is not attainable in history."[17] At best, it is an ideal by which life is measured but which can be attained in only fragmentary ways. At the level of actual historical existence, Niebuhr believed that justice in the form of reciprocity was the highest that humans realistically could attain.[18]

My goal here is to illustrate Niebuhr's multidimensionality and not to give a full evaluation of the moral implications of his view of love. Nevertheless, mentioning now some important feminist critiques will be useful for my later arguments.[19] From the feminist perspective, Niebuhr makes two mis-

15. Reinhold Niebuhr, *The Self and the Dramas of History* (New York: Charles Scribner's Sons, 1955), pp. 129-30. It is often overlooked that Niebuhr had a healthy respect for experience when it is conceived in its broadest dimensions. He was critical of narrowly scientific approaches to experience that measure it in terms of discrete data, but believed that experience in the larger sense (as William James used the term) testified to the ubiquitous reality of anxiety and sin. Jamesian radical empiricism provided for Niebuhr some of the values that European phenomenology would provide for a slightly later generation. We should be reminded, however, that Husserl himself got many of his first insights into phenomenology from William James.

16. Niebuhr, *The Nature and Destiny of Man*, vol. 2 (New York: Charles Scribner's Sons, 1943), p. 74.

17. Niebuhr, *Nature and Destiny of Man*, vol. 2, p. 151.

18. Niebuhr, *Nature and Destiny of Man*, vol. 2, p. 69.

19. For one of the more articulate critiques, see Barbara Andolsen, "Agape in Feminist Ethics," *Journal of Religious Ethics* (Spring 1984): 69-81.

takes. First, he debases a full theory of mutuality by reducing it to a conditional reciprocal exchange. There are forms of mutuality in which one takes the other as an end just as one expects the other to take oneself as an end. Second, he identifies *agape* too completely with self-sacrificial love. A more balanced view of Christian love (the central moral principle for Christians) is to understand it as mutuality or equal regard for both other and self. Furthermore, if love defined as equal regard is more central biblically, it follows that we should think of self-sacrificial love not as the Christian ideal but as a moment in the fullness of love required to renew mutuality in the midst of sin and brokenness.[20] This is a view I will later expand.

The fourth dimension has to do with Niebuhr's awareness of the social and natural systems shaping the human. Niebuhr was both weak and strong at this level of his theological anthropology. He had nothing to say directly about environmental or ecological factors that constrain human action; these concerns had not yet emerged in academic theology. On the social side, he was aware of the challenges of industrialization, especially how the demands of efficiency and profit affect the wages, health, and freedom of the working classes and support the privileges of the managerial classes. But even though Niebuhr did not work out fully the influence of social systems on the human, the attention he did give provides us with the space to apply and further develop what he began.

Fifth, although Niebuhr had little to say theoretically about the dimension of practices and the rules that govern them, and was not a theoretician of practices in the sense of Alasdair MacIntyre or Pierre Bourdieu,[21] his respect for insights found in Marxism and philosophical pragmatism demonstrates his appreciation for the power of concrete practices as well as the perpetual need to critique them. A concern with humans as creatures embedded in shared practices was a pervasive component of his multidimensional theological anthropology.

Distortions of the Human in Contemporary Discourse

Most of the powerful contemporary secular anthropologies concentrate on one of these five dimensions at the neglect of others. Many reductive

---

20. Janssens, "Norms and Priorities of a Love Ethics," pp. 207-38.

21. Alasdair MacIntyre, *After Virtue* (Notre Dame, Ind.: University of Notre Dame Press, 1988); Pierre Bourdieu, *The Logic of Practice* (Stanford, Calif.: Stanford University Press, 1990), pp. 53-54.

anthropologies do not explicitly make judgments at each of the levels of practical reason but do so implicitly and unwittingly.

Modern Psychologies

Many modern psychologies aspire to advance scientific understandings of motivation and health, but they also often unknowingly inject moral principles as well as implicit visions and metaphors. Take the humanistic psychologies of Rogers and Maslow. Health for them had to do with self-actualization. They were unaware, however, that without further qualification, health defined as the actualization of one's potentialities is actually an ethical-egoist theory of moral obligation.[22] The logic went like this: to be healthy is to self-actualize; therefore, you have an implicit moral obligation to actualize your potentials.

Ethical egoism, however, is generally thought by moral philosophers to be an inferior theory of obligation; it cannot solve conflicts without assuming that my antagonist eventually will give up and yield to my self-actualization. Even worse, the ethical egoism of humanistic psychology avoided recognizing conflict by unconsciously resorting to a metaphysical judgment that at the depths of things, all genuine self-actualizations are harmonious and cannot legitimately conflict.[23] Hence, in two ways, humanistic psychology implicitly goes beyond its alleged scientific theory of motivation and health by making both moral judgments of an ethical egoist kind and metaphysical assumptions about the ultimate harmony of the world.

Freud also went beyond psychology's proper concern to describe our basic tendencies and delved into the other dimensions of practical reason. His mature theory of motivation was built around the dual instinct theory of *eros* and *thanatos*. In contrast to Rogers and Maslow, Freud recognized the conflictual nature of our fundamental motivations. But, in the end, his theory of health was also an implicit ethical egoism — one based not on actualizing our potentials but on directing our instincts toward pleasurable satisfactions, as Philip Rieff points out, in safe and realistic ways.[24] Freud too, in his later theory, drifted into the area of metaphysical narratives by speculating that his dual instinct theory of life against death might reveal the fundamental dy-

22. See Don Browning, *Religious Thought and the Modern Psychologies* (Minneapolis: Fortress, 1987). A second edition co-authored with Terry Cooper was published in 2004.

23. For William Frankena's critique of ethical egoism, see his *Ethics*, p. 19.

24. Philip Rieff, *Freud: The Mind of a Moralist* (New York: Viking, 1959), and his *The Triumph of the Therapeutic* (New York: Harper and Row, 1966).

namics of the cosmos — *eros* versus *thanatos*.[25] If space permitted, I could extend these brief illustrations about the moral and visional horizons of the modern psychologies with references to Skinner, Jung, Erikson, and Kohut, as I have done in *Religious Thought and the Modern Psychologies*.

Rational-Choice Economics and Evolutionary Psychology

The fields of economics and evolutionary psychology are also reductionistic, yet they casually wander into morality and metaphysics. Rational-choice theory is the dominant model of economics. It is built on a parsimonious theory of human motivation and a minimalist theory of rationality. It contains, as Douglas Meeks points out, its own market anthropological theory.[26] Human beings, according to this view, are motivated by a limited number of hardwired bio-psychological wants and needs. These include inclinations toward "health, prestige, sensual pleasure, benevolence, or envy." Benevolence refers to parents' concern for their own blood-related kin, who are both sources of emotional satisfaction and carriers of our genes.[27] Rationality in economic activity, and other forms of action, entails choosing the most efficient means to the satisfaction of these inclinations. Furthermore, all objects that satisfy these inclinations are commensurate; whether we decide to buy a car, invest in art, get married, or have a child is based on rational calculations about which of these choices will yield overall the greatest amount of satisfaction. If the costs of having a child have gone up and the satisfactions gone down, we might instead choose a Mercedes or a European vacation.[28]

Rational-choice theory, like humanistic psychology and psychoanalysis, elevates an ethical-egoist theory of motivation into a normative theory of ethical obligation. The message goes like this: "We *are* by nature ethical egoists, therefore we *should* conform to this theory of moral obligation in all of our actions."

One is struck, however, by how rational-choice theorists elevate the virtues of industry and efficiency. This leads economist and social philosopher Donald McCloskey to render a very interesting judgment about the as-

25. Browning, *Religious Thought and the Modern Psychologies*, pp. 41-43.

26. Douglas Meeks, "The Economy of Grace: Human Dignity in the Market System," pp. 196-200.

27. Gary Becker, *The Economic Approach to Human Behavior* (Chicago: University of Chicago Press, 1991), p. 5.

28. Gary Becker, *A Treatise on the Family* (Cambridge, Mass: Harvard University Press, 1991), p. 138.

sumed narrative background to this perspective in economics. McCloskey says rational-choice theories assume a moral and narrative horizon not unlike the Protestant ethic that has shaped so much of Western cultural life; rational-choice theory does not emphasize a passive economic consumptionism but rather an energetic economic productivity.[29] Rational-choice theory unwittingly exhibits that human nature is a multidimensional reality; it tries to deny this, but the omitted dimensions unknowingly creep back.

Evolutionary psychology can be similarly critiqued. In fact, increasingly, there is a marriage between rational-choice theory and evolutionary psychology in a *general bio-economic view of the human.* This synthesis, along with other forces, feeds the new eugenics discussed by Kendall Soulen in this volume.[30] Analogies are drawn in this synthesis between the demands of markets in economic theory and natural selection in biology.[31] Furthermore, evolutionary psychology, like rational-choice theory, assumes that humans have hardwired inclinations, the most important of which are captured by the twin concepts of kin altruism and inclusive fitness. These concepts argue that human altruism is derived from our preferential feelings for those who share and pass on our genes, a theory we saw in the bio-economic theories of rational-choice.[32]

Evolutionary psychology lapses into the ethical dimension of the human, but it does so intentionally. E. O. Wilson, Richard Alexander, Robert Reich, and Frans de Waal are just a few of the sociobiologists and evolutionary psychologists who believe that these disciplines hold the key to a viable theory of ethics for our time. Nonetheless, evolutionary psychology is similar to the modern psychologies and to rational-choice theory in proffering an essentially ethical-egoist theory of moral obligation. Evolutionary psychologists believe that humans are basically motivated to enhance the present and future viability (indeed, immortality) of their own genes, although they extend this ethical egoism into complicated theories of kin altruism and reciprocal altruism. Kin altruism, so the theory goes, gives birth to empathy; in loving our children as parts of ourselves, we also feel their pains and joys as

29. Don McCloskey, *If You're So Smart: The Narrative of Economic Expertise* (Chicago: University of Chicago Press, 1990), pp. 135-40.

30. Kendall Soulen, "Cruising Toward Bethlehem: Human Dignity and the New Eugenics," pp. 104-20 in this volume.

31. See Richard Posner, *Sex and Reason* (Cambridge: Harvard University Press, 1992).

32. For introductions to evolutionary psychology, see Donald Symons, *The Evolution of Human Sexuality* (Oxford: Oxford University Press, 1979), and Martin Daly and Margo Wilson, *Sex, Evolution and Behavior* (Belmont, Calif.: Wadsworth, 1978).

we would our own.[33] Nonetheless, kin altruism is still a form of ethical egoism; we advance the life of others as a way of advancing our own lives. Elaborate forms of reciprocal altruism are also basically complicated forms of ethical egoism. We learn to help others, evolutionist Richard Alexander claims, because this stores up capital for the day we need help in return.[34]

Evolutionary psychology is less explicit about its general vision of life. Nonetheless, an analysis of the horizons of evolutionary psychology suggests that it assumes an *agonistic vision — a metaphysical narrative that assumes that strife and violence are the fundamental qualities of being.* John Milbank in his provocative *Theology and Social Theory* has argued that much of modern economic theory, influenced primarily by Nietzsche and Darwin, assumes such an agonistic ontology.[35] I think his critique applies to evolutionary psychology as well. Although some forms of evolutionary psychology use kin altruism to show the origins of our capacity to empathize with offspring and other kin and then analogically with those beyond the family circle, these theories never deliver empathy from the logic of self-interest. Hence, it is easy to see why rational-choice economics and evolutionary psychology are joining forces to create a powerful new form of reductionism with an ethical-egoist morality and an agonistic ontology.

When the full reality of the so-called secular disciplines is uncovered, they often look more like theology than is generally recognized. *The basic difference between theological anthropology and the anthropologies of other disciplines, thus, is not that theology is morally and metaphysically freighted and the others are not. It is rather that theological anthropology takes responsibility for its moral and metaphysical judgments while many other contemporary anthropologies do not.* If this observation holds, then theology and the secular disciplines are on far more equal grounds than is generally recognized.

The Premoral Good and Moral Obligation

So far I have argued for the multidimensional richness of theological anthropology, at least the theological anthropology of Reinhold Niebuhr. I have not argued for the correctness of his view of these dimensions. That is another task. I have observed, with favorable comment, that these dimensions in

---

33. Frans de Waal, *Good Natured* (Cambridge, Mass.: Harvard University Press, 1996).

34. Richard Alexander, *The Biology of Moral Systems* (New York: Aldine de Gruyter, 1987), p. 68.

35. John Milbank, *Theology and Social Theory* (Oxford: Basil Blackwell, 1990), pp. 5, 27-45.

Niebuhr reciprocally qualify each other; the moral, premoral, social, and natural are not derived deductively from the visional and narrative dimension even though they are all qualified and informed by that dimension. This gives Niebuhr a flexibility and power in interdisciplinary conversations that many theologians have difficulty achieving.

Theological anthropology has the potential of being more explicitly multidimensional than the anthropologies of other disciplines. Nonetheless, it *must do more to strengthen and differentiate its theories of premoral goods and demonstrate more convincingly how these goods are related to its theory of narrative and moral obligation.*

For the most part, Protestant theological anthropologies have been weak in contributing to public discourse about premoral goods. Roman Catholic moral theology, because of its tradition of natural law, has been better at addressing issues pertaining to premoral values, but often in ways thought to be incomplete. As I pointed out above, rational-choice theory, for the most part, assumes a relatively short list of hardwired desires that propel humans toward a range of satisfying goods. This approach holds not only an ethical-egoist ethic, but a concept of the commensurability of premoral goods. It teaches that these goods are fungible; it is the overall satisfaction that is aimed for. Health may be sacrificed for prestige. Having children may be sacrificed for more nights at fine restaurants.

John Finnis and the Catholic Natural Law Theorists

The legal scholar John Finnis has formulated a theory of basic premoral goods, made it fundamental to his ethics, but tried to avoid the pitfalls of seeing goods as commensurate, exchangeable, and calculable. It is offensive to him to think that having a child might rank on the same scale of satisfactions as a new car or a trip to the Bahamas and that one might intentionally abort it if the costs of having the child were too high. Basic premoral goods for him are incommensurate, and it is immoral to intentionally sacrifice any of them. Finnis lists, for example, "life, knowledge, play, aesthetic experience, sociability (friendship), practical reasonableness and religion" as fundamental aspects of human flourishing.[36] These goods are not derived from an analysis of human potentialities; they are self-evident "insights" into the overall experience of our inclinations in relation to truly satisfying objects.[37] Although

---

36. John Finnis, *Fundamentals of Ethics* (Washington, D.C.: Georgetown University Press, 1983), p. 51.

these goods are fundamental to fully formed ethical judgments, they require a theory of obligation in order to morally take into account the basic goods of others. Hence, Finnis expands Kant's second formulation of the categorical imperative. Kant's principle of treating the "humanity" of other and self as an end now contains in Finnis's reformulation an enlarged view of humanity. Humanity is more than rationality; it now includes all the other basic premoral goods necessary for human flourishing.[38]

Since no one of these basic goods should ever be sacrificed intentionally on behalf of another, Finnis rejects all ethical-egoist, utilitarian, or proportionalist perspectives that entertain the possibility of doing that. Of course, natural law theorists such as Finnis, proportionalists, and utilitarians are all kinds of teleologists; they share the belief that rational discourse about the basic premoral goods is possible and morally relevant. They are different from strict Kantians, strict divine command theorists, and even intersubjective Kantians such as Habermas, all of whom play down discussions of the good.[39] Since much of public policy is about choices in the realm of premoral goods, natural law theorists at least have resources to join this conversation and often compete with some success with utilitarians in shaping public life. But natural law scholars also are perceived by many as too rigid. Neither their list of basic goods nor the idea of the incommensurability of goods has found wide acceptance in larger public debates. Finnis may be right that we should not intentionally sacrifice any basic good, but circumstances may nonetheless force us rightly to assign them different priorities.

Martha Nussbaum and Capabilities As Goods

Another more successful view can be seen in the moral philosophy of Martha Nussbaum. Nussbaum, like Finnis, is a neo-Aristotelian. She is a kind of teleologist in that she believes the task of ethics is to actualize within a moral framework the premoral goods of life. But her list is both similar to and different from that of Finnis. Nussbaum talks more about capabilities than goods, but capabilities *are* basic goods. Her list includes life; health; bodily in-

---

37. Finnis, *Fundamentals of Ethics,* p. 51.

38. Finnis, *Fundamentals of Ethics,* pp. 120-23.

39. For an intersubjective reformulation of the Kantian categorical imperative, see Jürgen Habermas, *Moral Consciousness and Communication* (Cambridge, Mass.: MIT Press, 1990).

tegrity; senses, imagination, thought; emotions; practical reason; affiliation; other species; play; and control over one's environment.[40]

I will not give a detailed discussion of either the rational-choice list, Finnis's list, or the list of Nussbaum. They all affirm, however, the goods of life and health. Finnis and Nussbaum also mention practical reason, a good conspicuously absent from the rational-choice list. Finnis lists aesthetic experience and Nussbaum lists an analogous good which she calls play. Finnis lists friendship and Nussbaum affiliation; the rational-choice model ignores both friendship and aesthetic experience.

Nussbaum derives her list of capability goods from a combination of sources but mainly from the history of philosophy and recent trends in modern psychology. She claims that these goods should be pursued under the guidance of the Kantian categorical imperative.[41] In bringing together a thick theory of premoral goods guided by Kantian universalized respect for others, she is close to Finnis. Kant has been accepted but thickened to include judgments about premoral goods. According to Nussbaum, societies throughout the world should be judged from the perspective of how they facilitate the pursuit of these capability goods by all citizens.[42]

But her theories are not without criticism. Roman Catholic moral theologian Lisa Sowle Cahill appreciates Nussbaum's thought yet is critical of it, especially with regard to its implications for women. Cahill's critique illuminates the interaction of tradition and the human sciences in analyzing and ranking premoral goods. She affirms Nussbaum's list of capabilities and their relevance to women but complains that they exclude the capability of kin altruism, which for women takes the form of motherhood. (It is not clear why Cahill does not criticize Nussbaum for neglecting the kin-altruistic capability of fatherhood.) Motherhood is a capability, says Cahill, and one that women throughout the world want to actualize. Both tradition (especially the works of Aristotle and Thomas Aquinas) and the modern evolutionary disciplines, with their insights into the centrality of kin altruism, are together sources of Cahill's emphasis on the capability of parenthood. She asks, should not a society be judged in light of its support for this capability also, as well as the other capabilities promoted by Nussbaum?[43]

40. Martha Nussbaum, *Sex and Social Justice* (New York: Oxford University Press, 1999), p. 42.

41. Martha Nussbaum, *Women and Human Development: A Capabilities Approach* (Cambridge: Cambridge University Press, 2000), pp. 73, 159.

42. Nussbaum, *Sex and Social Justice*, p. 43.

43. Lisa Sowle Cahill, *Sex, Gender, and Christian Ethics* (Cambridge: Cambridge University Press, 1995).

And finally, neither Nussbaum nor Finnis has an explicit narrative envelope for their list of basic goods and capabilities. This is a loss because our religious narratives do a variety of things for our pursuit of the premoral goods of life. I turn to illustrating that point in the next and final section of this essay — with special reference to one particular version of the Christian narrative.

Niebuhr, Premoral Goods, and the Christian Narrative

Reinhold Niebuhr needs to be brought back into this discussion. As I pointed out above, Niebuhr had his indices of goods, but they were not well developed. He recognized the premoral goods of survival (life), attachment (similar to affiliation in Nussbaum and friendship in Finnis), material acquisition, group relations such as kinship and ethnicity, and sexual urges (which included both pleasure and the desire to have offspring). This is a good but rather thin list. The absence of a rich theory of premoral goods and his neglect of the question of commensurability of goods explains why Niebuhr, in spite of the richness of his theological anthropology, is not used by today's theological ethicists in the difficult issues of medical ethics, biomedical research, ecology, business ethics, or public policy. Theology needs a more adequate view of these goods.

I will not settle in this essay the question of an adequate model of premoral goods. I have said that the good of kin altruism should be introduced in Nussbaum and clarified in Finnis. I will say this: developing such a model should begin with the interpretive task of identifying how the normative texts of a tradition — in our case, Christianity — have defined and ranked these goods. Christian theology should then encourage other traditions to do the same. Then each tradition should enter a correlational dialogue with other traditions and with the human sciences to develop heuristic models of what human beings require to live well and to flourish. They also should develop views about how these goods can be weighed and justly prioritized within various social and natural constraints.

But what is the role of the Christian story in discovering and ordering the premoral goods of life? The Christian narrative provides implicit hierarchies of these goods. It offers needed ontological groundings, energizing motivations, and motifs of recovery that help realize the premoral and moral norms of life. The moral life is more than a matter of actualizing premoral values in ways that show justice and respect to one's neighbor. It entails believing the moral life is worthwhile to begin with, that one's neighbor is worth respecting, that one should persist when one is failing, and that one should have hope in the face of discouragement.

In various writings, I have discussed several ways the Christian narrative influences what I call "the inner core" of Christian ethics. This inner core has formal similarities to the mixed deontological theory of obligation that we have found in Finnis and Nussbaum. It contains indices of premoral values surrounded by a Kantian-like principle of justice. It is Kantian-like because it need not be derived and formulated explicitly as Kant did his categorical imperative. It can also, and more profoundly, be based on the New Testament love command or the biblical golden rule. I have used Paul Ricoeur and Louis Janssens to formulate the inner core of Christian ethics. Loving your neighbor as yourself means, according to them, doing *good* to your neighbor as you would have them to do *good* unto you.[44] In this formulation of Christian neighbor love, mutual respect and justice guide the subordinate concern with actualizing premoral goods. Janssens calls this a love ethic of "equal regard."

Here are some ways that the Christian narrative enriches the double interest of Christian love to both exhibit equal regard *and* actualize the premoral goods of life. Once again, I will follow the narrative formulation of Niebuhr.[45] First and foremost, the metaphor of God the Creator bestows the ontological status of goodness on all the created world. This is a testimony about the nature of *being* in relation to the finite givens of life. The implication of this is radical; it suggests that all fundamental human tendencies and basic patterns of the created natural world are good in the premoral sense of that word. "God saw everything he had made, and indeed, it was very good" (Gen. 1:31). The premoral goods listed in the systems above, insofar as they are truly basic, are endowed with a sacred valence from the standpoint of the Christian narrative. They are blessed by God and should be respected by humans. They should be taken seriously as they received further moral refinement, prioritization, and organization.

Second, the metaphor of God the Creator assigns a special status to humans as made in God's image. The core of moral reason requires respect for both other and self as ends who must never be reduced to means and never commodified. The Jewish and Christian doctrine of the *imago Dei* gives ultimate seriousness to the status of humans as ends. Kant grounded respect for

44. Janssens, "Norms and Priorities of a Love Ethics," pp. 207-38; Paul Ricoeur, "The Teleological and Deontological Structures of Action: Aristotle and/or Kant?" in *Contemporary French Philosophy*, ed. Phillips Griffiths (Cambridge: Cambridge University Press, 1987), p. 109.

45. I develop the following points in Browning, *A Fundamental Practical Theology*, pp. 194-99.

other and self on the basis of human rationality. This does not necessarily contradict also grounding respect on the basis of the *imago Dei*. Furthermore, basing respect on the primordial relation all humans have with the divine requires that we show respect to the neighbor with all the more seriousness. It is one thing to be a rational animal; it is something even more profound to be a child of God.

Third, the metaphor of God the Creator informs love as equal regard about the limits of life. The narrative of creation tells us that humans are finite. This means that they can never actualize all of life's premoral goods. A central dilemma of life is that there are more goods to seek than can be actualized within the context of finitude. Furthermore, goods conflict, and in spite of Finnis's point that it is immoral to will intentionally the destruction of a basic good,[46] I argue that the contingencies of life force humans nonetheless to establish priorities among life's goods. It is, for example, partially because Nussbaum has no narrative that acknowledges life's finitude that she has no consolation about the tragedy of conflicting goods and capabilities. The story of creation tells us that we must have our theories of the goods of life, but none can be absolutized and all must be subservient to the principle (or kingdom) of love as equal regard among all humans.

Fourth, the metaphor of God the Governor is also a part of the Christian story. Humans become anxious, and they sin. The premoral goods of life naturally conflict, and this can produce, as Louis Janssens aptly says, premoral or ontic evil. But premoral evil, the natural conflict of finite goods in a finite world, is not itself sin and not itself moral evil. Sin and moral evil result from the misuse of our freedom and will. It is in view of sin and moral evil that God in the Christian narrative emerges as a moral Governor. I follow those who have spotted a congruence between God the Governor and the abstract character of practical reason. God is a God of impartial justice but also a God who works for our good in the premoral sense. In this way, God as Governor is a model of and a reinforcement for the inner core of Christian obligation, namely, an ethic of equal regard defined as justly respecting both self and other while also working for the good of both self and other.

Fifth, the doctrines of sin, grace, and forgiveness make it possible for the inner core of Christian obligation to become relatively free from the inordinate self-interest and self-justifying maneuvers that typically corrupt human efforts to be just and to do good. Knowledge about the reality of sin, however, gives the Christian a tool of self-criticism. Awareness of sin should make Christians suspicious that their claims to justice and love are not as pure as

46. Finnis, *Fundamentals of Ethics*, p. 126.

they might think. God's forgiveness and grace should liberate Christians to risk equal regard with the assurance that they are justified before God even if they fall short.[47]

Sixth, the Christian narrative of the cross adds an element of supererogation to the love ethic of equal regard. The narrative of Jesus' passion — his trial and crucifixion, and the mingling of these events with the motifs of the Suffering Servant from Isaiah 53 — adds an element of self-sacrificial love to Christian love as equal regard. Neither a flat love ethic of equal regard nor a mixed-deontological theory of the kind found in Finnis and Nussbaum can address the disruptions of sin and evil. The Christian story, as Louis Janssens interprets it, does not tell us to sacrifice ourselves aimlessly.[48] It does not even tell us that self-sacrificial love is the center of the Christian life. Instead, it tells a profound story showing that in order to live a love ethic of equal regard, one must be willing to go the second mile — to work hard, endure, and even sacrifice — not as an end in itself but as a means to restoring love as equal regard. The Christian story tells about the role of sacrifice in renewing the core ethic of mutuality and equal regard. Neither Finnis nor Nussbaum, devoid as they are of narratives of the cross and forgiveness, say anything about how just love for the good of other and self is sustained and renewed in light of sin and brokenness.

Conclusion

These are some of the ways that the Christian narrative informs and enriches the more directly ethical dimension of human existence. This narrative, however, if devoid of a principle of obligation and a view of premoral goods, can be vague about what we should do to address the ethical challenges of life. Indeed, it may be the contemporary drift toward a vague narrative ethics that accounts for the church's marginalization in public life. This also may explain the church's impotence to address moral issues such as homosexuality, abortion, assisted suicide, divorce, and marital disruption.

Christian anthropology is multidimensional, and so is the Christian story when properly told. I have described this multidimensionality. Most likely, readers will sense that my position represents a tentative step toward a new Christian humanism — a Christianity that includes within the themes of creation, judgment, and salvation a proximate concern for human flourishing. If this is what readers conclude, they will be right.

47. Browning, *A Fundamental Practical Theology*, p. 198.
48. Janssens, "Norms and Priorities of a Love Ethics," p. 228.

Theological Anthropology versus Anthropological Reductionism

MICHAEL WELKER

This final essay addresses the problem of anthropological reductionism. The dominant anthropological paradigm of modernity centers on self-conscious subjectivity. Today, along with its religious "grounding" and its moral challenges, this paradigm is increasingly questioned and criticized by new approaches toward human-being being made in the sciences and humanities. In this chapter I argue that theology should not go to war on the side of new reductionistic approaches against the old ones. It should first appreciate the integrating power of the standard modern paradigm of theological and philosophical anthropology based on self-conscious subjectivity. At the same time, however, it should work on an "Aufhebung" (a sublation), a relativization and development of this paradigm. More precisely, it should try to provide a genuinely theological framework that allows it to host and to relate several anthropological approaches, including the modern one, in order to do justice to the complexity of the human being and to respect the nobility of God's purposes with humankind.

In recent years, brain research, research on the genome, the exploration of individual and communal memory, a new focus on the bodiliness and physicality of human existence, new interests in the textures of emotion and feeling, and other innovations in the field of anthropological research have created great expectations and considerable enthusiasm. On the one hand, very old questions such as "What are the essential characteristics of the human being?" or "What does it mean to be human?" have been given the promise of new and inspiring answers. On the other hand, what seemed to turn into a new world or a golden age of deepened anthropological research and discourse soon appeared as an intimidating maze or even as a frightening minefield. The field of anthropological research and discourse has been over-shadowed by the pressing problem of reductionism or, rather, competing reductionisms. And some of the forms of reductionism seem to have most unpleasant or even dangerous repercussions not only on the way we think about human life but also on human life itself.

Reductionisms: Unavoidable Ones and Dangerous Ones

Reductionisms emerge when certain phenomena of an area of possible expe-rience, or certain theoretical or experimental tools and certain figures of thought that can help to disclose this area, are taken to be the *only* phenom-ena, the *one* guiding principle, or the *sole* key to disclose it. As soon as such an approach convinces a broader group of scholars or even a broader public, a reductionism becomes "live." A reductionism can become powerful as soon as research working with it comes up with astounding new insights which lead to all kinds of successes in theory and praxis. If the research promises new potentials not only to produce further insights but also to enhance polit-ical and military power, technological and economic success, or physical wel-fare and new possibilities of healing, the power of the reductionism increases considerably.

Seen in this perspective, a reductionism does not only have an impact on scholarly opinions, does not only make its way into encyclopedias and textbooks: it starts to have an impact on political and economic policies and their readiness to distribute trust and money. It leads to the institution-alization of new academic disciplines, laboratories, and research institutes. In anthropology it awakens public hopes for better, easier, less endangered, and longer lives; economic expectations of new sources of how to increase indus-trial income; and political calculations of maximized loyalty and power. By all this it awakes a potentially unlimited willingness to invest money; media at-tention; personal, public, and political trust; and academic and technological energy into its enterprise. It thus becomes a real power in many areas of social and cultural life.

The enormous success of a reductionistic academic enterprise is not necessarily a danger in itself. As a rule, a successful reductionism of the form sketched above remains a latent paradigm and can indeed be stimulating for a while. As soon as its potential to generate new insights ceases, it can be seen as having been a reductionism, or it even proves to be stale or boring. It then has to make room for corrected, broader, and more subtle views on the topic it is concerned with — or for other reductionisms. There is, however, the danger that a reductionism becomes so powerful that it systematically blocks and distorts other processes of research and potentials of insight. It is this danger that is feared in the current interdisciplinary discourse on issues in anthropology.

Although the humanities, philosophy, the law, theology, and religious studies are at present afraid of several "physicalist" anthropological reductionisms in particular — connected with the recent successes in research on the brain and the genome — sensitive scholars see the same danger on the "mentalist" side. Increased sensitivities in the dialogue between the natural sciences and the humanities (including religious studies and theology) to this danger of a powerful reductionism also in the humanities have led to a growing dissatisfaction with classical starting points of anthropological research and discourse within social, cultural, psychological, philosophical, and theological studies. Classical starting points in anthropology like "the human being" as a self-referential subject, as a reference-point in I-Thou-constellations,[1] or as the typical or the unique member and co-shaper of a moral community or of an environment of sociable interaction[2] have come into question. Deeper, more realistic and subtle forms of anthropology that would help to grasp the "koinonial" and embodied human being have been sought.[3] Anthropologies that only work within a (post-)Cartesian, a (post-) transcendental approach no longer seemed able to provide such forms and frameworks.

The same seems to hold true for what is probably the most widespread model in theology, namely, the model of a dialogical encounter between God and "the human." There are simply too many anthropological insights and burning questions in social and cultural studies and in the natural sciences that cannot be hosted by this model. The challenge to offer a more complex framework in anthropological theory and research has come not only from areas other than theology. Also *within* theology, the insistence on a multidimensionality in theological anthropology within the biblical traditions has led to the questioning of frameworks and guiding principles which for a long time focused anthropological thinking and discourse. In order to

---

1. Cf. the contribution of Alan J. Torrance, "What Is a Person?" in *From Cells to Souls — and Beyond: Changing Portraits of Human Nature,* ed. Malcolm Jeeves (Grand Rapids: Eerdmans, 2004), pp. 199-222.

2. Cf. Friedrich Schleiermacher, "Notes on Aristotle: Nichomachean Ethics 8-9," trans. John Hoffmeyer, *Theology Today* 56 (1999): 164-68; Michael Welker, "'We Live Deeper Than We Think': The Genius of Schleiermacher's Earliest Ethics," *Theology Today* 56 (1999): 169-79.

3. Cf. Torrance, "What Is a Person?" following John Zizioulas.

gain a clear perspective on the problem, it seems helpful to introduce a differentiation analogous to a basic differentiation used by economic theory and thinking: the difference between microeconomics and macroeconomics.[4]

Differentiating and Relating Micro-Anthropological and Macro-Anthropological Approaches

Microeconomics deals "primarily with the individual parts of an economy, such as individual households, firms and industries. Each of these units represents a separate market, and the behavior of these units involving specific goods and services needs to be analyzed and understood." "Macroeconomics, on the other hand, deals with the sum of these parts. . . ." "Macroeconomic models are simplified descriptions of the relationship between some collections of macroeconomic variables . . . used . . . to chart the likely course of the aggregate economy."[5] There should, of course, be no association of "macro and micro" with "more and less important." Both approaches are crucial for a circumspect analysis.

The canon, large-scale history, multi-loci dogmatics, and ecumenical and interdisciplinary tasks challenge theological thinking to deal with macro-anthropological constellations and contents. They offer multicontextual, multisystemic, multiform locations and descriptions of human beings and affairs. In order to gain topical concentration, however, micro-anthropological approaches have to be cultivated which are monocontextual and monosystemic in nature. Such approaches permit growth in certainty and consensus and progressive academic orientation and decision-making. This invites us to test *the ability of specific micro-anthropological approaches to host macro-anthropological constellations.* Once we start working on such a task, the strengths of the post-Cartesian and post-Kantian anthropologies that center on the self-conscious "subjectivity" appear impressive. Such anthropologies have often emphasized the self's inner certainty, its ability for autonomy, its immediate relation to "the Divine," and the grounding of human freedom, equality, and dignity in this basic God-relation.

Despite the sharp criticism of this reductionistic micro-anthropological

4. I am most grateful to my Princeton colleague Leong Seow for an inspiring conversation during a Pastor-Theologian Consultation in which the idea to differentiate between micro-anthropological and macro-anthropological approaches arose. The following passages pick up, unfold, and develop further some reflections from my contribution to Jeeves, *From Cells to Souls,* pp. 223-32.

5. Frank N. Magill, ed., *International Encyclopedia of Economics,* vol. 2 (London: Fitzroy Dearborn, 1997), pp. 973 and 895.

figure of thought by other anthropological starting points mentioned above, it has to be acknowledged that the integrating power of the modernist model is considerable. Philosophical, legal, political, and religious modes of conceiving the human being were combined in this approach. Despite the obviously distortive reductionism connected with this model — a reductionism heavily lamented on many sides — its capacity to host macro-anthropological perspectives is considerable. The model sets high standards and should not be dismissed, unless a sublation, an "Aufhebung," of its potentials — in the Hegelian sense — can be achieved in a more comprehensive framework.

The question is which theological anthropological framework could incorporate and host macro-anthropological constellations and offer structures to differentiate and to relate several micro-anthropologies in illuminating ways. My proposal is to start with a large-scale *cosmological* framework — all too easily ignored in anthropological studies — and with the general religious questions raised by it.

John Polkinghorne has sketched such a large-scale framework under the title "Windows onto Reality: Light and Darkness":

> The window of fundamental physical science discloses a universe whose rational transparency makes science possible and whose rational beauty rewards the scientific enquirer with a profound sense of wonder. In short, the cosmos is shot through with signs of mind and it is an attractive, though not inevitable, thought that it is indeed the mind of the creator that is partially disclosed in this way.[6]

Yet the stunning cosmic order, cosmic fruitfulness, the dawning of consciousness, and the emergence of religious awareness, which Polkinghorne names as illuminating "windows onto reality," are not the full picture. The cosmological framework also offers what he calls "moral and physical evil," thus *questioning* a divine mind behind it and involved in it. Finally, it also points to an *ultimate cosmic futility:*

> Science tells us, most reliably, that the universe is going to die, through either collapse or decay, over a timespan of tens of billions of years, just as surely as we are going to die over a timespan of tens of years. Both realizations question what could be the ultimate purpose of the creator of a world of such transience.[7]

---

6. John Polkinghorne and Michael Welker, *Faith in the Living God: A Dialogue* (Grand Rapids: Eerdmans, 2001), pp. 19-23.

7. Polkinghorne and Welker, *Faith in the Living God,* pp. 19 and 23.

Although the scientific discussion of most recent years has again put a question mark behind the firm conviction that the universe is going to die,[8] the position just sketched can easily lead to the impression that the universe is of an ultimate "pointlessness."[9]

This picture stimulates high expectations toward a being who is worthy of being named "divine" or "God." A bringing forth of the universe and its sustenance for a limited time alone are not sufficient to recognize, trust, and honor such a being. The sustaining power has to be complemented by a rescuing and saving power. The saving power, however, must not be regarded only as keeping or bringing back creation onto the level of sustenance. Only the ennobling and elevating creativity of God responds to the challenge of cosmic futility and pointlessness.

Focusing on this challenge, a theological anthropology in search of a broad framework for interdisciplinary work about anthropological issues should concentrate on the threefold "relation" of — or, rather, focus on the three dimensions of — the divine activity directed toward creation and human beings — namely, God's activities of *sustaining, rescuing/saving,* and *elevating/ennobling* the creatures.

Thus a micro-anthropological approach (focusing on God's complex creative "relation" to human creatures) can host rich macro-anthropological constellations (a multitude of anthropological phenomena connected with the dimensions of God's sustaining, rescuing, and ennobling creativity).

This differentiated perspective gained from a religiously reflected general cosmological perspective can be complemented by a specifically Christian theological approach. This approach is based on large-scale observations in the Old Testament and New Testament traditions, on reflections on the differentiated identity of God in general, and on a study of a growing consensus in the Christian ecumene on basic issues in Holy Communion in particular.[10] In the following I will first focus on the emerging ecumenical consensus.

The growing ecumenical consensus, reached in several decades of conversations of the churches on the world level, focuses on the three-dimensional working of the triune God in the Eucharist. The differentiation and connection of God's creative sustaining, rescuing and saving, and finally ennobling and elevating workings on the creatures can be observed in a careful meditation and reflection of the different steps taken in the celebration of the sacrament.

8. I owe this cautioning to my Heidelberg physicist colleague Jörg Hüfner.

9. Steven Weinberg, *The First Three Minutes: A Modern View of the Origins of the Universe* (New York: Basic, 1977), p. 149.

10. Cf. Michael Welker, *What Happens in Holy Communion?* trans. John Hoffmeyer (Grand Rapids: Eerdmans, 2000), esp. chapter 12.

The thanksgiving to the Creator *(eucharist),* the remembrance of Christ *(memorial, anamnesis),* and the invocation of the Holy Spirit *(epiklesis)* are emphasized in different ways in the different churches and communities of faith. But all three dimensions have to be present in a celebration of the symbolic meal that can be regarded as Holy Communion or Eucharist.

The thanksgiving to the Creator is in the most immediate dimension related to bread and wine, the gifts of creation. It opens the eyes for the loadedness of the term "creation," which is not to be confused with "nature." Both the course of nature and human culture have to cooperate fruitfully in order to bring forth bread and wine as "gifts of creation." The fact that these gifts are in the midst of the assembled community indicates a powerful precedence and presence of divine sustenance and care. It also opens the eyes for the depth of the dimension of "creation," such as the peaceful assembly of the community, the willingness to communicate, the readiness to share and to express symbolic table-fellowship, the ability to relate to a religious tradition and to a canonic memory. All these gifts of God give ample reason to thank God the creator for his creative work.

The more we stress this dimension and the power of symbolic table-fellowship, the expression of peace on earth and love among our fellow human beings, and the spiritual communication and its strength and radiation, the more we are put in awe by the second dimension of the sacrament: the remembrance of Christ, centered on the "night of betrayal" and death on the cross. This dimension reveals the good creation in jeopardy and under self-jeopardizing powers and dynamics. Jesus is put to death in the name of the Jewish religion, in the name of Roman politics, under the Jewish and the Roman laws, and with the support of public moral opinion. Jews and Gentiles, friends and foes work together. Even his disciples do not make a difference. Jesus celebrates the Last Supper with Peter, who betrays and denies him, and with the other disciples, who deny and flee him. Not even Judas, who hands him over to those who kill him, is excluded from the table. It is against these powers, which the Bible calls "sin," that God's rescuing and saving might stands. The remembrance of Christ reveals this situation, the abyss of the night of betrayal and the forsakenness on the cross. It also reveals God's will to engage and to overcome the agony of the world.

Recent theological and interdisciplinary research has carefully explored how this rescuing and saving work is accomplished in the resurrection.[11] It

11. Cf. Michael Welker, "Resurrection and the Reign of God," The 1993 Frederick Neumann Symposium on the Theological Interpretation of Scripture: Hope for the Kingdom and Responsibility for the World, *The Princeton Seminary Bulletin,* Supplementary Issue, no. 3,

MICHAEL WELKER

has problematized the idea that the merely resuscitated Jesus of the funda-
mentalists and the magnificently triumphant Jesus of the Isenheim altar are
compatible with the witnesses to the resurrection given by the biblical traditions. It has focused on the perplexing tensions between palpable encounters
and appearances, theophanies and doubt, in the biblical texts. The witnesses
of the New Testament "see" the risen Christ "not with the eyes only."

They "see" him in his speaking to them, in the breaking of the bread, in
the greeting of peace, in his opening the Scriptures to them, in his sending
them, and in other signs. They "see" him in actual and symbolic actions
which become ritual forms of the liturgy and the life of the early church and
the Christian church in general.[12] Not a resuscitated Jesus, but the *whole* Jesus
Christ and his life in its *fullness* become present in the resurrection "in the
Spirit and in faith."

This "spiritual body" is extremely hard to grasp for a naturalistic and
scientistic way of thinking. Although we long for a sense of this presence of
the whole fullness of a person and a life, as every story of love and every story
of loss can tell us, we have great difficulty in appreciating the message of the
resurrection. This explains the shallow and agonizing pro and contra of a
physical reanimation in so much discourse on the resurrection. The risen
Christ, however, becomes present in a way that retains the multidimensionality of his person and radiation as well as the multidimensionality of access
to his person and influence. The powers and the gifts of the Spirit come with
the resurrected: love; forgiveness; healing; the attention to children, to the
weak, to the rejected, to the sick, and to the suffering; the search for truth and
justice; and the ability to challenge political and religious "principalities and
powers" are communicated with the presence of the risen Christ.[13]

ed. Daniel Migliore (Princeton, 1994), pp. 3-16; S. T. Davis, D. Kendall, and G. O'Collins, eds.,
The Resurrection: An Interdisciplinary Symposium on the Resurrection of Jesus (Oxford: Oxford
University Press, 1997); Joachim Ringleben, *Wahrhaft auferstanden. Zur Begründung der
Theologie des lebendigen Gottes* (Tübingen: Mohr, 1998); H.-J. Eckstein and M. Welker, eds., *Die
Wirklichkeit der Auferstehung* (Neukirchen-Vluyn: Neukirchener, 2002; second ed. 2004); T. Pe-
ters, R. Russell, and M. Welker, eds., *Resurrection: Theological and Scientific Assessments* (Grand
Rapids: Eerdmans, 2002; second ed. 2005); N. T. Wright, *The Resurrection of the Son of God*
(London: SPCK, 2003).

12. Cf. Sarah Coakley, "The Resurrection and the 'Spiritual Senses': On Wittgenstein,
Epistemology and the Risen Christ," in her *Powers and Submissions: Spirituality, Philosophy and
Gender* (Oxford: Blackwell, 2002); Francis Schüssler Fiorenza, "The Resurrection of Jesus and
Roman Catholic Fundamental Theology," in *The Resurrection*, ed. Davis, Kendall, and O'Col-
lins, pp. 213-48.

13. Cf. Michael Welker, "Who Is Jesus Christ for Us Today?" *Harvard Theological Review*
95, no. 2 (2002): 129-46.

The focus on cross and resurrection, on the remembrance of Christ and the witness to his eschatological presence, is not the last and ultimate dimension of God's working on the creation and on human beings. The third dimension discloses that God mediates, by the power of the Holy Spirit, the witness and the radiance of Christ to his believers and that God draws Christ's witnesses into the divine and eternal life. The Holy Spirit thus ennobles and elevates the witnesses of Christ: they become a "new creation," they become "members of the body of Christ," they become a "temple of the living God." How does this complex creative and redemptive "relation" of God to human creatures illuminate and orient a nonreductive anthropology, which deserves interdisciplinary attention beyond the realm of theology proper?

God's Sustaining, Rescuing, and Ennobling Creativity As a Basis for a Nonreductionistic Anthropology

A refined understanding of divine sustenance does more than simply disclose multifarious relations between bodily existence; social, cultural, and historical environments; the "regularities which shape all created matter . . . [determining] both the natural and social world and their interconnection";[14] institutional and symbolic forms of providing common forms of memory; "analogical imaginations" (David Tracy); "security of expectation" and attuned action; and so on. Not a simple relation between points of reference, but an extremely complex localization in a body and in a mind has to be taken into account, within the smaller and the larger family, within a household, within a neighborhood, in an educational system and within medical evolution, under regional and national political conditions, within broader social and cultural settings — a location within national and global history, a location on the surface of the globe, a location in an urban or a rural environment, a location within natural and political climatic conditions, a location under a zeitgeist and within religious traditions and potentials.

A refined understanding of divine sustenance is also aware of the fact that the element of rescue is involved in every breath of creaturely existence. This is heavily blurred by the fact that many people in many parts of the world today have no immediate awareness of agricultural processes and their endangerment, that the improvements of health care and the struggles to prevent infant mortality are taken for granted, that such achievements as electric light and public security have weakened or even eradicated many sensitivities

14. Cf. Christoph Schwöbel's contribution to this volume, pp. 44-58.

for the improbability that life is a big routine. Such sensitivities, in which the biblical traditions abound, are lost.

More important, the awareness has to be cultivated again that God sustains creation for a great purpose, that human life is not just meant for a "bad infinity" (Hegel) of as many days as physically possible on this earth, that God elects the human beings as caretakers of creation and as witnesses to God's glory. The same human body that can be regarded as perishable "flesh" is destined to become the "temple of God." The same spirit that can be corrupted by the power of sin is destined to become freed and strengthened by God's creative Word and by God's Holy Spirit in order to witness to God's good intentions for creation in manifold ways.[15]

The Dimension of Sustenance

On this first level, the level of sustenance, the focus on human dignity, so central to the classical modern anthropological discourse, should not be given up too easily. It was an important political, legal, and moral achievement that human dignity was introduced as "Ur-Principle."[16] The theological questions and complexities connected with it[17] should not lead us to an underestimation of this modern interdisciplinary achievement.

Over several decades, the notion of human dignity seemed to serve well as an integrating topic of various forms of anthropological discourse. It has been a common topic of legal, political, philosophical, and theological research and conversation between the disciplines. Based on Reformation claims, modern philosophical thought, and international declarations of human rights, and loosely connected with a scriptural reference to Genesis 1, the (theologically grounded version of the) argument which tried to integrate perspectives of the different disciplines and at the same time appeal to common sense ran as follows: The personhood of the human is inseparably connected with his or her dignity. The dignity of the human is grounded in his or her being the *imago Dei*, the image of God. The image of God carries an immediate

---

15. Russel Botman's contribution to this volume (pp. 84-98) adopts a similar framework to coordinate distinct discourses of human dignity in contemporary South Africa.

16. This formulation was brought in by John Witte's contribution to the consultation.

17. My sensitivities were intensified by Wallace Alston's rightly skeptical comments in the beginning of our consultations and Clifton Black's contribution; cf. Michael Welker, "Menschenwürde und Gottebenbildlichkeit," in *Jahrbuch für Biblische Theologie*, vol. 15: *Würde des Menschen*, ed. B. Hamm and M. Welker (Neukirchen-Vluyn: Neukirchener, 2001), pp. 247-62.

relation of every human being to God. This is the basis of a fundamental equality of all human beings and the ground of universal human rights. Such statements, which for a long time were regarded as quite convincing, have elicited a whole series of critical reflections and questions in the recent past.

To begin with, it is not clear whether the concept of the *imago Dei*, the image of God, rooted in the Jewish and Christian religious traditions, can be expected to convince and to bind human beings of other religions or those of no religion at all. Moreover, it is not very clear what the image of God according to the biblical traditions really means. Does it mean that human beings are destined to live in a dialogical connection with God and with each other?[18] Does it mean that they are destined to live in compassionate sociality with all the other creatures?[19] Does it mean that they are destined to exercise the *dominium terrae*, that is, to rule over the creation?[20] Or does it mean that they are destined to be bearers of God's revelation in a much broader sense?[21]

A clarification is necessary of what the Old and the New Testament witnesses understand by the *imago Dei* before any attempt to answer these questions can be made. To complicate matters further, not only has the image of God become a problematic concept, but also the notion of "human dignity." As the introduction to this volume notes, this notion has been questioned in and beyond the academy. On the one hand, human dignity is a central concept in political and ethical documents of great importance.[22] The Charter of the United Nations, the General Declaration of Human Rights, or, for instance, the Inaugural Addresses of most American presidents, or the German Grundgesetz (Statute Law) reflect this fact. Most legal systems and most law scholars would confirm that human dignity is a fundamental anthropological

---

18. Cf. Karl Barth, *Church Dogmatics* III/1 (Edinburgh: T&T Clark, 1958), esp. pp. 206ff.; Ingolf Dalferth and Eberhard Jüngel, "Menschenwürde und Gottebenbildlichkeit," *Christlicher Glaube in moderner Gesellschaft*, vol. 24 (1981): 85f.; this "personalistic" and "dialogistic" interpretation of human dignity is also used by the influential German law-scholar Günter Düring in his interpretation of the Grundgesetz: *Gesammelte Schriften 1952-1983* (Berlin, 1984), pp. 27ff. and 127ff.

19. This interpretation became popular in response to increasing ecological worries: cf. Jürgen Moltmann, *Gott in der Schöpfung. Ökologische Schöpfungslehre* (München: Kaiser, 1985), pp. 222ff.

20. See my references to the recent Jewish and Christian exegetical discourse, in *Creation and Reality: Theological and Biblical Perspectives* (Philadelphia: Fortress, 1999), esp. chapter 5.

21. For a christological interpretation of the concept of dignity see Peter Saladin, *Verantwortung als Staatsprinzip* (Bern: P. Haupt, 1984), pp. 198ff.

22. Cf. the Habilitationsschrift of Wolfgang Vögele, *Menschenwürde zwischen Recht und Theologie. Begründungen von Menschenrechten in der Perspektive öffentlicher Theologie* (Gütersloh: Christian Kaiser/GVH, 2000), esp. pp. 201ff.

premise.[23] On the other hand, scholars have increasingly tended to regard human dignity as a mere cipher, as an "empty formula"[24] or even as an illusion.[25] They complain that the term "human dignity" is mostly addressed in religious or quasi-religious language.

The Dimension of Rescue and Saving

Although God's rescuing and saving power is already present within the realm of divine sustenance, the second dimension, in which God's creativity is fully devoted to the rescue of the creatures, is much more dramatic in scope. This becomes obvious when we juxtapose extremes of personal existence. Think of an obviously or seemingly blessed existence, localized within a complex world with good potential for choice and development: a healthy person in a loving family, in a well-organized and financially secure household, within a safe and supporting neighborhood, in a prospering educational and medical system, under law-abiding and peaceful political conditions, in an ideologically self-critical and upscale historical phase, in an area of the world not hit by climatic, ideological, and military distortions. Under these conditions a reductionism emphasizing divine sustenance easily sets in.

Then think of the other extreme: persons hit by bodily and/or mental illness and suffering, in nonsupportive families and dangerous neighborhoods, with poor educational conditions and lack of health care, under corrupted and violent political conditions, with a depressed and guilt-ridden historical and moral consciousness, even strangled by fatalism with respect to a climate that by continuous drought or flooding or earthquake endangers

23. Cf. the use of extremely weighty terms, such as (my translation) "anthropological premise": Peter Häberle, "Menschenwürde und Verfassung . . . ," *Rechtstheorie*, vol. 11 (1980): 389ff., 410; "fundamental norm": Werner Maihofer, *Rechtsstaat und menschliche Würde* (Frankfurt am Main: n.p., 1968), p. 9; even "eternal fundamental norm of the constitution": Wolfgang Graf Vitzthum, "Gentechnologie und Menschenwürdeargument," *Zeitschrift für Rechtspolitik*, vol. 20 (1987): 33ff., at 33; "key term of the constitution": Albert Bleckmann, *Staatsrecht*, vol. 2: *Die Grundrechte*, third ed. (Köln: Carl Heymanns, 1989), p. 446; "structuring norm" for state and society: Peter Häberle, "Die Menschenwürde als Grundlage der staatlichen Gemeinschaft," in *Handbuch des Staatsrechts der Bundesrepublik Deutschland*, vol. 1, ed. J. Isensee and P. Kirchhof (Heidelberg: C. I. Müller, 1987), pp. 815ff., 844.

24. Viktor Pöschl and Panajotis Kondylis, "Art.: Würde," in *Geschichtliche Grundbegriffe*, vol. 7 (Stuttgart: Klett-Cotta, 1992), pp. 637ff.

25. Franz Josef Wetz, "Die Würde des Menschen — eine Illusion," in Wetz's *Die Würde des Menschen ist antastbar. Eine Provokation* (Stuttgart: Klett-Cotta, 1998), pp. 94ff.

individual and communal existence, and, finally, brought up in a religion that fosters passivity and fatalism. Here the emphasis on the first dimension of mere sustenance would be cynical.

The moralizing of modern theologies, the inability of much of modern theology to deal with the notion of sin[26] and God's working against it, the strong concentration on the mere co-suffering of God with God's people and with Christ in recent theologies of the cross — and various other theological shortcomings — have darkened this aspect of God's saving passion. A theology determined to deal with the rescuing and saving power of God in a christological perspective would have to acknowledge and carefully study the web of social, cultural, political, and religious conflicts in which Jesus' proclamation of the coming reign of God becomes seminal. The revelation through the cross of the "principalities and powers" dominated by sin, the unspectacular countermeasures of God's guidance in the resurrection witnesses, and the emergent coming of the reign must be unfolded.[27] In general, the risk-laden transformation and revolution of normative constellations and powers is the topic in this field. It is central that sensitivities to human self-endangerment and self-jeopardizing are developed by attention to the divine word and its liberation from many forms of tyranny and chaos.

Again, a careful investigation of the issues involved discloses the perichoretical overlap with the first (sustenance) and the third (ennoblement) dimensions. The sustenance of religious, political, legal, and moral forms of life requires their gradual transformation. To achieve this aim without losing normative security of expectations is one of the indispensable tasks of religion in general.[28]

The Dimension of Ennoblement and Elevation

The third dimension is probably the most difficult to explore. With regard to the overlap with the dimensions of sustenance and rescue, one could point to the aesthetic, scientific, moral, and political capacities and ingenious achievements, from which so many profit and benefit, in which so many have a joyful

---

26. Cf. S. Brandt and M. Suchocki, eds., *Sünde. Ein unverständlich gewordenes Thema* (Neukirchen-Vluyn: Neukirchener, 1997).

27. Cf. Welker, "Who Is Jesus Christ for Us Today?" pp. 129-46.

28. Cf. Jan Assmann, Bernd Janowski, and Michael Welker, eds., *Gerechtigkeit. Richten und Retten in der abendländischen Tradition und ihren altorientalischen Ursprüngen* (München: Fink, 1998).

and relief-bringing share.[29] The main aspect of this dimension, however, is, of course, the involvement in the divine life itself, by way of being a witness, by becoming a mirror of God's purpose and glory. Here the liturgy, the power of the celebration of the sacraments, the common search for truth and justice, faith seeking understanding, the teaching, the proclamation, and the diaconal mission of the church become central, the life in discipleship and free and creative self-withdrawal in favor of co-creatures.[30]

In these three dimensions, God's life-furthering and life-enhancing creativity offers a rich framework for macro- and micro-anthropologies. There are anthropologies that focus primarily on the physical, social, and cultural stability and continuity of human existence and life; anthropologies that center above all on the endangerment and self-endangerment of human beings and the powers that prevent and work against human viciousness and frailty; and anthropologies that first want to explore the dimensions of spiritual communication and spiritual flourishing and growth.

Very different anthropologies have to be differentiated and related to one another. An explicitly Trinitarian approach might be the only adequate ultimate framework for such an anthropological endeavor. Such an approach, however, requires a careful discussion of theological reductionisms of the past which blocked the unfolding of "the relation" of God and humanity in creation, in Christ's saving work, and in the working of the Holy Spirit.[31] Outside of such a context, the classical modern discourse about the *imago Dei,* the model of a dialogical "encounter" of the human being with God, and the notion of human dignity based upon it, are reductionistic.

29. Cf. Polkinghorne and Welker, *Faith in the Living God;* John Polkinghorne, *Science and the Trinity: The Christian Encounter with Reality* (London: SPCK, 2004), esp. chapters 3 and 5; see also Polkinghorne's contribution to this volume (pp. 89-103).

30. The concept of "free and creative self-withdrawal" is elaborated in Michael Welker, "The Reign of God," *Theology Today* 49 (1992): 500-515.

31. One example would be the reduction of the working of the Holy Spirit to divine sustenance in some twentieth-century theologies. I am grateful to Don Browning for drawing my attention to this problem.

Index